BARRY BRIGGS

WEMBLEY AND BEYOND

MY INCREDIBLE JOURNEY

sphere

SPHERE

First published in Great Britain in 2009 by Circle Productions
This paperback edition published in 2012 by Sphere

A CIP catalogue record for this book
is available from the British Library.

ISBN 978-0-7515-4965-2

Printed and bound in Great Britain by
Clays Ltd, St Ives plc

Papers used by Sphere are from well-managed forests
and other responsible sources.

MIX
Paper from
responsible sources
FSC
www.fsc.org   FSC® C104740

Sphere
An imprint of
Little, Brown Book Group
100 Victoria Embankment
London EC4Y 0DY

An Hachette UK Company
www.hachette.co.uk

www.littlebrown.co.uk

Dedication

To the two ladies and loves of my life.

Junie

Jan

In memory of 'Uncle' Tom Wheatcroft,
a proper bloke

Readers' warning:
If you don't understand something or the language in
which it's written, then count to 10 and think again!
It's the Kiwi in me and my unusual sense of humour.

Barry B 2009

Introduction
by Philip Rising

THERE are a good many words in the English language that can be used to describe my mate Briggo but the one that I think possibly suits best will doubtless raise a few eyebrows.

In my view he is simply irresistible!

That certainly doesn't mean that I go dewy eyed and weak at the knees every time I see this motorcycling colossus.

But he does possess an amazing knack of being able to persuade me to join him in a whole variety of projects, just about all of which have in one way or another enriched my life.

My first contact with BB (as I like to call him) came when I was a very raw soccer journalist back in the early 1960s and was instructed to cover some speedway events at Wimbledon, not far from where I lived in Surbiton. It was a task I immediately enjoyed and one that was to shape my future career and journalistic destiny.

I had chased Briggo for a few quotes when Swindon visited Wimbledon but had little real dealings with him until around 1966. I was ghosting a few soccer columns for some people on the periphery of England's squad in soccer's World Cup being staged on home soil. One of those commissioning the work enquired whether I could also do some for Barry Briggs, at that stage World Champion for a fourth time and a genuine superstar.

Compared with some of the pampered and monotone soccer stars he was a giant. And money was never an issue.

A few years later, at an end-of-season Wimbledon dinner and dance, BB asked whether I would be interested in writing his autobiography. A little over-awed by the prospect, I solicited the help of Martin Rogers, who had mentored me at both Soccer Star and Speedway Star.

My friendship with Barry blossomed and I have been involved with him in speedway meetings in the USA – at the Houston Astrodome, in California, and the 1982 World Final at the Los Angeles Coliseum. I was chuffed to be closely involved in the production of the *This Is Your Life* programme that featured Briggo in 1974.

He has been a true mate in some difficult times and I owe him a great deal. Many years ago we occasionally played squash and I probably thought I was marginally the better player and could come out on top. But, flushed with such thoughts, on one occasion I foolishly challenged Briggo to a game for money, not a lot, but enough to add a little spice.

Unfortunately for me it turned on the tap to his competitive juices. The stake wasn't important but I had laid down a gauntlet that Barry could not resist picking up and I was well and truly thrashed.

BB is still a fierce competitor … just ask Kelvin Tatum when we get together for a round of golf. He was always a sporting hero to me, alongside people like Gareth Edwards, Steve Waugh, Bobby Charlton, Rod Laver and Seve Ballesteros. He is worthy of their company. Barry has been determined to tell the varied and many stories in this book for a long, long time. It took a while for me to come on board but, as I said at the start, he is irresistible. And I am delighted that I did.

Another mate of mine, respected journalist Richard Frost, has helped too but ultimately the words remain those of Barry Briggs, MBE. We just sorted them out a little and had a lot of fun doing so.

Foreword

By Bernie Ecclestone

I HAD just returned to my then office in Surbiton and tried to call Alex Whittaker, who also worked there. Alex ran the Formula One television operations but after several attempts there was still no reply from his extension.

I asked my secretary Judith why Alex wasn't taking calls and she said: "Oh, he's got a gentleman called Barry Briggs with him. I don't know who he is."

I recognised the name though we had never met. I raced on grasstracks around the Brands Hatch area when I was young, and having been in the motorcycle business for many years, knew many of the boys who raced bikes.

I was at Wembley, along with 85,000 others, when Barry Briggs won speedway's World Championship for a second time in 1958. I remember going to Wembley with a couple of mates, riding my Ariel Square Four that, at the time, was my pride and joy.

And now, some 16 years later, unbeknown to me Briggo was in our office block. I went along to Alex's office and spent an hour or so talking about speedway. And that was how my friendship with Barry began.

Barry is modest and self-effacing, ready for a laugh and doesn't appear to take himself too seriously. We get on very well.

Over the years he has tried to sell me shares in gold and diamond mines, plus other bits and pieces. It is obvious that speedway has always been his great love and I can see why.

I have always thought that top class speedway is tailor made for television. It is quick, colourful, action packed, everything takes place in full view and a race lasts about a minute and even a bad one is rapidly replaced by another.

We just about got into bed a couple of times to promote speedway and BB had visions of a Grand Prix-style series before the current one sprang into life. We both visualised it as a great indoor sport, especially as Barry had ridden in or promoted at some of the great stadiums in the world, including Wembley, Madison Square Gardens in New York, the Los Angeles Coliseum and the Houston Astrodome.

At one time I suggested to him that we could build speedway tracks at F1 venues and run the two over the same weekend. All the television facilities would already be on site, which would have cut the costs, but Barry was worried about spectator facilities, getting a crowd in, etc.

In the end it came to nothing but Barry was never slow in sensing an opportunity to work together. Once, on our way by helicopter to a practice session prior to a British Grand Prix at Silverstone, I mentioned that I wanted to run a F1 event in the USA.

Two weeks later we had lunch and Barry put forward a proposal for us to run a F1 race at the Las Vegas Motor Speedway. I had tried to do a deal there a year earlier and it came to nothing but Barry knew Ritchie Clyne who owned the track and tried to broker a new deal but, unfortunately, it still didn't quite add up.

And, sadly, we never managed to get a speedway deal into place either. Once, when we were very close with a World Indoor Series, I asked Barry to get the promoters from the different countries that we intended a joint venture with into my office at the end of the following week.

But we needed more time and it never happened. Full marks to Barry, I knew it meant a lot to him but we didn't want to end up looking silly.

At that time there was a real breakdown in our relationship and some red-hot faxes passed between us, extolling each other's virtues … or lack of them!

But it proved that close friendships can withstand problems and disagreements. From that impromptu meeting we had 35 years ago, I am still buying him lunch, though sometimes he does offer to pay! One day I will call his bluff and let him.

Recently Barry has sold me on another of his proposals that will be announced later and will feature in this book. I should have kept my big mouth shut but it is for a good cause and is typical Briggo.

Harry Oxley, Briggo and Ivan Mauger … co-promoters (with Jack Milne) of the 1982 World Final.

The Briggs clan

The break-up of my parents' marriage helped set the tone for my future life

THE break-up of the Briggs family home in Christchurch when my parents, Maurice and Eileen, split in 1946, was a big blow to my two younger brothers, Murray and Wayne, and me.

Memories of my childhood growing up in Rose Street are happy ones but my life took on a very different shape after dad left. I think I inherited some of his genes in that he was very dedicated to things that he did. I was told that he could brush paint a car as well as anyone else at the time could spray one and he was obviously good and inventive with his hands.

Dad was also a professional pushbike racer and won the prestigious Waimate to Christchurch road race. Apparently he should have made the New Zealand team for the Olympic games but didn't because of politics within the cycle game. The smell of liniment was strong in our washhouse where he used to rub down the top cyclists he trained. Unfortunately all that came to an end and I had to continue without a father's shoulder to lean on.

Mum became the breadwinner, she was strong and tough and

held down a couple of jobs in order to keep everything running. But I missed having a dad and was quite jealous when I saw other riders being helped by theirs.

But I suppose it made me stand on my own feet and to sort out my own problems. It still makes me sad when I see sons being disrespectful to their fathers who are only trying to do their best. The pressures that are heaped on to some offspring is tough but the shame is that many parents never get to appreciate what they are going through.

My mum could never fathom out why, on the day of a speedway meeting, I wasn't 'Mr. Jovial'. Before speedway captured my heart I was always busy playing sports in and around Christchurch. I played soccer, rugby (the league rather than union version) and hockey, boxed and wrestled as well, mostly with mixed fortunes.

My biggest success was scoring a goal in front of 20,000 people during a curtain-raiser for an international soccer match between New Zealand and South Africa at Lancaster Park. Not long after I represented the Canterbury rugby league team against the West Coast, also a curtain-raiser, this time for the Kiwis versus Great Britain with a crowd of around 12,000.

One thing I recall about this game is that about three-quarters of the way through I was really knackered. Maybe it was because that morning I had played a tough game for my Nomads soccer team in the local league.

To earn a bit of money I had a deal with the local newspaper to gather all the results from 20 games that took place at Hagley Park in the morning. At the finish of my game I would jump on my trusty steed pushbike and, still in my playing kit, race round to all the other games to get the results for the evening paper. So, I did have an excuse for being knackered!

Boxing was a sport that I quickly learned required more than just bravado. After a few fairly successful fights I met this 'giant' of a kid called Skinny McClintock. As his name implied, there was nothing of him but, boy, did he give me a pasting.

I tried to whack him but he was never there, he had skipped to somewhere else. I only really knew where he was when he hit me from his new position. It was like boxing a shadow but one that carried a big punch. After coming across Skinny McClintock I lost interest in boxing.

IT was 4pm on a Friday afternoon and school was finished for the week. Boy, what a weekend I had planned, the anticipation was killing me but, so too, was the pain in my right knee.

I had sustained a heavy knock playing hockey earlier in the week from our own god-given team captain, an idiot called Shawn Spencer. He really believed he was a hockey superstar but I figured that if he couldn't even distinguish between a hockey ball and the knee of one of his own team-mates his true status was anything but that. Or perhaps he didn't like me ...

Even at the age of 14 I was starting to realise that life is not all sweetness and light but is tough and demanding. I had already developed a mindset that enabled me to block out pain, something that would prove invaluable as I made my journey along life's bumpy road.

The break-up of my parents' marriage was another type of hurt that had to be controlled. Mum, Murray, Wayne and I went from a lovely house in a suburb of Christchurch to living in three converted army huts. Without a father the onus of taking a lead role in the welfare of our family fell on me.

We had no running water and each of us took turns in taking a bucket to Uncle Bob's farm over the road to collect water. We also had a rota system to determine who it was had to dig holes to bury the toilet waste.

None of this helped further brotherly love but I had to help mum with running our improvised household, through circumstances not of my own making, and this helped programme me for the rest of my life.

So, a painful knee sure as hell wasn't going to wreck my cherished weekend. It was time to get my arse into gear as my first 'biggy' was waiting for me just down the road.

It was actually a three-mile cycle ride from school into a strong headwind to out-of-town Henderson Road, which was a straight and wide gravel road. I made it on time but had to wait for my cousin George, which at least gave me the chance for a brief rest.

When George arrived we both shouted: "It's sliding time!" George is on his 350 Matchless, I got beside him on my pushbike, hold onto his left shoulder with my right hand as we start slowly down the road. The pace of the motorcycle now controls our speed and it rises slowly.

Glancing across at the speedo I can see that we are doing 25mph. The Matchy is starting to rev and my hand is now glued to George's shoulder. Over the roar of the engine I yell at him "30 will do" as my old, stripped down, aluminum-painted bike is starting to rattle and vibrate.

At 30mph I heave myself clear and immediately pitch my groaning bike sideways. My school uniform, cap on backwards, short pants, offers scant protection.

It certainly doesn't do a lot for my school shoes but I will clean them before mum sees them.

After five runs we stop and I turn to my cousin and say: "Thanks George, I think my best controlled slide was my fifth and last go." Just the thought of it made me smile and I flashed George a lopsided grin.

George stopped the engine of his motorcycle and instantly we were back to the tranquility of the South Island countryside again. "I think you are right, your last one was probably your best, Barry," answered George. "When you get home, I would definitely check the spokes on both wheels as I don't think they are made to slide at that speed."

I told George that I would and had, in fact, bought a special tool to do the job. As George was leaving he told me: "If you are going to ride the Matchless next week you had better bring your cleaning gear as I think you are getting behind on our trade-off."

George and I had a deal … I cleaned the bike in exchange for him letting me ride it.

My mind was racing. "I bet even Ronnie (Moore) couldn't do the slides better than my last one," I muttered to myself. The previous year Ronnie had been in the same cycle speedway team as me. He was the envy of all the boys in Christchurch. He was, like his father Les, a "Wall of Death" rider and had ridden a Triumph motorcycle to school and, best of all, the local girls chased after him.

Ronnie had just arrived back home after his first season of racing speedway in Great Britain. He drove around Christchurch in his recently imported classic Italian Lagonda sports car.

What a life he had, making a living out of something I would pay to do. My only thought was: how the hell am I going to be able to do the same? If someone had seen me smiling to myself they would have thought I was mad.

All this was going on while I was cycling back home, there was still two miles to go, the exhilaration of my sliding was over-whelming but my bloody knee was throbbing like hell.

My school friend Russell and I had managed to each scrape together seven pounds and ten shillings to buy an old Royal Enfield sloper. I learnt most about the mechanics of motorcycles from working on our old bitza, our new pet name for the much altered Royal Enfield, which frequently broke down!

Riding it through mud holes and on the sides of greasy hills taught me about the balance and throttle control required to be in unison with the bike as I negotiated through these tricky riding conditions. A hard-earned lesson was one bad move could result in a good deal of pain.

"Do it right or the motorcycle will thrash you into the ground," was one motto I taught myself at an early age. To ride well you must always respect your bike.

I would practice for as long as I had petrol in the tank. When it was empty, practice was over.

Then it was time to try and earn some more money to refuel the bike and get back on the treadmill of fun.

A small speedway track had been built on a vacant section of land at the back of the Uniweld factory in Stockburn where motorcycle exhaust pipes were manufactured.

It was a tough ride to get there from home on my pushbike. Part of the road was gravel, other parts were paved, which were heaven. But it still took a couple of hours of hard slog to get there. You could ride one or other of the two old speedway bikes that Uniweld

I'm about to do battle in a miniature TT race in Christchurch.

Me with Ronnie Moore.

owned, one had an old Rudge engine, the other was fitted with a Matchless engine.

Practice cost sixpence a lap but, unfortunately, I couldn't afford that. So, I was the roustabout that everybody got to yell at: "Hey kid, this bike needs fuel; this bike has a flat tyre." I didn't care; I could take all the abuse knowing that at the end of the day my time would come. My roustabout wage was 10 free laps, it was like winning the lottery.

A couple of riders, who could just barely slide their bikes, figured they were already champions. They could wind the throttle flat out for a very short distance along the straights but the corners had them knackered.

I figured you could teach a monkey to do that. I was young but already had my theories and my chance was coming. Before I even threw a leg over my bike, I had a plan and had thought it through thoroughly so I knew exactly what I was going to do on my allotted laps. But when I rode I had to withstand even more verbals as the other riders continually took the mickey as I went half throttle down the straights but as fast as possible around the corners.

I told myself to stand tall, get my weight off the rear wheel to allow it to spin and that really helped me to turn the corners. I wasn't afraid to lay the bike down low and I had learned much by riding our old Royal Enfield.

There was still loads of work to be done on the old bitza, and because I was working so much on it my mate didn't get much riding time, so I decided to buy my mate's half share. My mate was great and gave me plenty of time to pay, he could have a ride here and there, it was a bit like paying him interest on his seven plus quid.

I worked after school every day for the local grocer as a delivery boy, carrying the goods in a basket in the front of my bike, rather like Granville in the TV series *Open All Hours* starring Ronnie Barker and David Jason.

I was earning ten shillings a week and decided to buy a new pushbike. This finished up being the hardest lesson in my short life about the value of money or the lack of it. It was rammed home.

I went to the Saturday morning movies at our local cinema and left my new pushbike outside. Some bastard stole it after only four days of ownership. The crunch was that for two years I had to pay out virtually all of my wages for a bike that I never had. Out of the shed came my old ally painted bike, it was refreshed, after a four day rest, now it was restored to be number one again, and back into action on the Christchurch roads.

Aranui Speedway was really big in Christchurch and was drawing massive crowds. So I dreamed up a way to get involved. I am not sure whether I bought, borrowed or stole a pair of white overalls and they were to do the trick for me. One of our neighbours, Jack Lang, was a track official, so every Saturday night he would give me a ride to the speedway.

Putting on my overalls, I was ready to sell myself, which wasn't my best quality. Standing outside the back pit gate dressed in my white overalls, I felt like an orphan: "Please sir, could I help you to push your bike, carry your leathers, toolbox, whatever."

My roustabout job had obviously been good training as I always got jobs. The touring riders always needed help, I was their man, or boy! Of course the big bonus was that I was in the pits, right in the action. It was a start.

The biggest break as an oil-rag man came when I was able to help the Wembley Lion and New Zealand Champion Bruce Abernethy. He quickly became my hero, even letting me warm up his bike before the meeting. I felt ten feet tall, all my mates were dying with envy. Later I became great mates with Bruce.

My life changed when an older man, Charlie Roscoe, approached me in the pits at our local Aranui track in Christchurch. "Hey," he said, "I believe you ride a little?"

"A little," I answered, "but I have never raced." He then said: "How would you like to ride one of my bikes? We will split what you earn 50/50. Practice is in two weeks' time, bring your leathers."

It didn't matter whether he felt sorry for me or had heard that I had promise. I was going to get to ride!

There was, however, a problem. I didn't have any leathers and, yet, this man was going to change my life. Faced with the dilemma of acquiring some leathers I did what I have continued to do throughout my life … I improvised and made my own.

I found an old pair of jodhpurs and cut them up to use as a pattern. Mum was great, she managed to get some leather and let me use her treadle Singer sewing machine. After about 15 broken needles my leathers were finished. They didn't fit that well but speedway at that time wasn't very fashion-conscious.

I also needed boots. I made some tops and sewed them on to the top of my football boots. A sob story to local speedway star Trevor Redmond, who was later to become my guardian when I went to England, found me a lemon-coloured crash helmet, but I had to pad it out because it dropped over my eyes, not recommended when racing a speedway bike.

I was now on a mission but still had to ride to the track on my pushbike with my leathers and boots balancing on my handlebars.

An early photo of me trying to pass Harringay Racer Ron How, who later became my Wimbledon team-mate.

It was seven miles each way but I had so much enthusiasm it was like I had a motor powering it. Finally, I had my first speedway race. I certainly didn't set the world on fire and, to my embarrassment, crashed when the race was over. A trip to hospital followed to have fluid drained from my knee.

Mum wasn't too thrilled that I was racing but came along to the hospital with sweets and a couple of motorcycle magazines so couldn't have been too upset. My leathers were seriously short of padding so before I rode again I got some carpet underlay to offer a bit more protection. I didn't fall on my knee again that season so didn't get to know whether there was a design fault or not.

Later in the year I managed to get into the local Canterbury team and was dazzled by that. It meant I got to ride at five or six different tracks in New Zealand but my ambition was to follow Ronnie Moore and go to England to race speedway there. It was all I wanted to do but it was a long way to swim and with a serious lack of finance that seemed like my only option!

I was earning less than two pounds a week at an advertising agency and this wasn't going to get me very far. A friend who worked at the Islington Abattoir got me a job there and the boss, realising what I needed it for, gave me the jobs that paid the most, like packing kidneys, and plenty of overtime. A couple of other workers thought I was getting preferential treatment and didn't like it. I was still a skinny kid and had to stand up for myself. It was a no-win situation for me and some fisticuffs ended the problem.

Eventually, of course, I did get to England and when I got home I went to see Charlie and told him that I wanted to continue with our deal even though I now had my own bike.

He simply laughed in my face then told me beautifully: "What, are you fucking mad, piss off, just get me a ticket when I want to come and watch you race." I wasn't surprised, he was a proper bloke. In fact Charlie, whose brother Steve was a star at the old local Monica Park speedway during the 1930s, never took a penny off me.

Me with my Wimbledon team-mates

Saving enough money for my fare to England but mum helped, too

2

AFTER paying for my fare of £85 to travel by ship to England with my kidney-packing money, I had very little left, so I had to sell my old bitza bike, then my push bike and anything else to gain a few more bob. Mum was the saviour and, unbeknown to me, had been saving for my trip as well. The money was hard earned but her £65 was a blessing, especially as I knew that she didn't really want me to go.

The few days on the small cargo boat to Aussie were a doddle. Along with me on their first trips to England to race were fellow riders Brian McKeown, from Christchurch, and Aston Quinn from Dunedin who was to become a great mate on the ship.

On arriving in Sydney we found that our ship to Britain, the SS *Ranchi*, had had a fire on board, so we had to find accommodation for an extra ten days while it was in port for repairs. My meagre finances were struggling and the local YMCA put a roof over our heads. But then my 17-year-old attitude clicked in, what the hell!

When we arrived at Southampton after a long, tedious trip from the other side of the world it was great to see the friendly face of Trevor Redmond there to meet me. By the time I arrived in England, Ronnie Moore, who left Christchurch after me, had broken his leg riding for Wimbledon but was back in the saddle.

I left New Zealand assuming that I would be riding for Aldershot in the third division and that fellow Kiwi Redmond would be my legal guardian. But, during the sea voyage, Wimbledon promoter Ronnie Greene tricked me with a series of half-truths in a number of telegrams into joining Ronnie at high-flying Wimbledon. I was being thrown in at the deep end.

During my initial season in the toughest league in the world I scored two paid maximums (unbeaten by an opponent) and both were due to the unselfish efforts of my mate and mentor Ronnie.

Our relationship dated back to when I was 14-years-old and raced in the same cycle speedway team. At that time I never thought I would ever race proper speedway, let alone that within three years I would be the partner of our local hero for the famous Wimbledon Dons. It was like a dream. Ronnie and another New Zealander, Geoff Mardon, were already established stars with the Dons. I knew that I was out of my depth so all I could do was keep my head down and do my best.

Soon after my debut, on May 17, I was confronted with the harsh realities of big-time speedway and the serious risks involved. The Dons were contesting a London Cup match at West Ham when our American favourite, Ernie Roccio, was killed. I was only a 17-year-old kid, thinking everything in England was great and then, suddenly, one of our team-mates gets fatally injured.

I was actually programmed to ride in that race but Greene pulled me out and chose Cyril Maidment to partner Ernie instead. Maido got some serious stick from people suggesting that he had caused the accident that resulted in Ernie's tragic death. My own interpretation of the incident was that Ernie lost speed when he took his throttle hand (right) off his handlebars to pull down his dirt-covered goggles.

The pits were at the other end of the track to where the accident happened, so we were a long way from the crash, but Ernie appeared to half-stop, as the bike would if you let go of the throttle, it automatically shuts itself off and, with the high compression of a speedway engine, it is just like slamming on brakes.

Maido had no warning and ran into the back of Ernie and cannoned him into the fence. It wasn't as if he had gone roaring under Ernie and skittled him. Track conditions were muddy and Maido's vision would have been impaired and it was also on the fastest part of the track.

In my opinion it was just a speedway accident, though a tragic one, something that I experienced from even closer quarters while riding for Southampton at Ipswich in April 1962.

I was looking on from the pits and it was a very tight first corner. Jack Unstead clipped his opponent's back wheel with his front wheel, which immediately straightened up his machine, and poor Jack was propelled straight into the solid wooden Ipswich fence.

The force of the impact was too much for a human body to withstand and Jack sadly died shortly afterwards.

I orchestrated a tribute to the 120 riders who have paid the ultimate sacrifice during speedway's 60-year history with a dedicated 'Lest we forget' memorial within the impressive Speedway Hall of Fame I masterminded and built at Donington Park in 1989.

My links with America began when I helped Ernie Roccio's family arrange for his body to be flown back to the States and his home town of Whittier in Southern California. His sister-in-law Jeanine came to England to help and I became great friends with their family. When I went to the USA for the first time I stayed with Ernie's brother Johnny and Jeanine. Johnny had just retired from racing out there.

Although I was seriously affected by Ernie's death I had no intention of making an early retirement from speedway to get a normal job. Ernie's funeral made me appreciate my own vulnerability. I was to stare death in the face several times during my own speedway career.

One of my most serious crashes occurred one night at Belle Vue in Manchester when Aussie John Langfield lost control when he reared up on one wheel in the middle of the corner and his bike wiped me out. I can still recall the nightmare as

Langfield's out-of-control bike headed straight for the fence, taking me with it. I still remember the superhuman effort I made. Your strength in this situation is amazing, but your life is on the line. I had to stop Langfield's raging, out-of-control bike from splattering me onto the Hyde Road fence.

Just before I lost consciousness I didn't know whether I had won the battle with Langy's bike or not. If I had died I wouldn't have known either! Langy was a tough bloke and wouldn't have taken me out deliberately. Later, at the hospital where I was taken, he was there, making a lot of noise and thought (as I was told later) it was my fault.

After regaining consciousness I just wanted to get out of there and to go home to Southampton.

Our local doctor, Doctor Kerr, was a tough old South African coot and he told me in no uncertain manner that I had to stay in bed until he saw me in five days' time. I was black and blue just about everywhere and was definitely feeling second hand, not even well enough to complain. On the second day I had a visitor – John Langfield who, by now, knew the real circumstances of our accident. He came into my bedroom and kneeled beside my bed. I couldn't believe my eyes – this tough Aussie had tears running down his face.

I lightened the mood, saying: "Langy, tell me that I am not in heaven because I cannot believe a fucking Aussie bastard can cry." We roared with laughter. Speedway is dangerous and accidents do happen. I still don't know how I managed to survive that one, my bike and I took out over 15 feet of fencing when I crashed.

Given my natural thirst for racing and youthful inclination to grab a handful of throttle I had more than my fair share of scrapes in my early days and it is a wonder that I am still in one piece to tell my story.

My most serious crash came in 1972 when I was riding in the World Final at Wembley hoping to equal Ove Fundin's record of five World titles. I have covered the events of that fateful night elsewhere in this book.

When I rode for Wimbledon as an 18-year-old and had a Sunday free I would ride scrambles (motocross) and would thrash around over jumps and through mud-covered tracks. My biggest problem was that I would try and maintain my speed even though my body was screaming that it had had enough.

I would just keep pushing the bar higher and then I'd get into trouble, losing complete control, bouncing off a few trees, and finally would crash. On one occasion I broke my right thumb, only two days before Wimbledon were due to race at West Ham. If my boss, Ronnie Greene, had known what I was up to he would have killed me himself! Ironically, I rode better with my broken thumb, it cooled me down a little and I actually went faster.

I almost gave up speedway at one stage to concentrate on motocross with a number of Aussie boys who were touring the continent. I just enjoyed it so much.

My younger brother Murray came to the UK and won the 350cc and 500cc English grasstrack championships. He had no transport so I would take him to the meetings and, as I was there anyway, it seemed crazy not to join in. The day after I won my first World Championship at Wembley in front of 70,000 fans in 1957 I rode in the South Eastern Centre Grasstrack championship at Rhodes Minis in Kent.

In less than 24 hours I had gone from the posh Wembley dressing rooms to dropping my trousers in front of all onlookers on the grass beside my car. I won £500 at Wembley and a further 30 quid for becoming South Eastern Centre Grasstrack Champion.

On another occasion I spent the day on my feet at the Earls Court Motorcycle Show before racing in the World Final at Wembley in the evening. Looking back now, it was madness.

Once I practiced at Swindon the same day as the World Final because I thought it would help me to warm up for the Wembley meeting. In fact I blew up my best engine, which was not what I had in mind. It turned something that I thought was a good idea into a disaster.

Things were going badly wrong that day and I had to rely on a police escort from Hanger Lane through the traffic jams to get to Wembley, and only just made my first race. I was certainly 'warmed up' but not in the manner I had envisaged. In fact, I was boiling over.

But that was me and many people have said many times that I should have won more World titles than the four I managed in 1957, 1958, 1964 and 1966. It has often been levelled against me that my bikes were not always the best to look at, with bits of wire hanging off here and there. I had learned the mechanical side of the sport the hard way.

My first speedway bike in England was one of the old ones that were being used by an American team of touring riders based at Shelbourne Park in Dublin, Ireland, where Ronnie Greene was also at the helm.

I was only a raw kid when I arrived at Wimbledon and was last in line to have my bike looked after at the track's workshops. I was lucky if it got cleaned let alone tuned. I was in and out of the team for a while and I could easily have been discarded because Greeney was bloody tough and he really didn't know if I was going to be any good. I didn't know myself, but I certainly didn't lack determination.

I believe that Greene gave me the bike because he thought I was another Ronnie Moore but I never had his talent. I think I have always been honest with myself. At times I would blame myself for riding crap but, a lot of the time it was down to my bike being rubbish.

Ronnie had an average (calculated on how many points you score in each race) of about 11.6. The highest a rider can attain is 12 so he was almost perfect. At one meeting Ronnie's bike quit and I lent him mine. He finished in a very poor third place and when he came back to the pits after the race, he went mad at the Wimbledon mechanics for giving me such a bad bike to ride.

Being eighth in line to have my bike tuned in the Wimbledon workshops wasn't doing me any favours so I started to look after it myself with the help of Trevor Redmond, who lived with Ronnie, Geoff Mardon and I in a rented house in Sutton, Surrey.

Trevor, like me, wasn't a great mechanic but was there to lend a hand. We had no workshop at the house and had to utilise the back yard, often in the rain. It wasn't exactly ideal as often I would work with an old overcoat thrown over me and my bike while we had the cylinder head off the engine. I wonder what the modern day tuners would make of that? I just had to learn as I went along. Once I put the carburettor slide in backwards and, when I went to push start my bike before the meeting that night, it wouldn't start and I didn't know what I had done wrong.

The Kiwi outpost in suburban Surrey was not always the most harmonious place to be. After my JAP powered bike broke down once too often Trevor and I had a few arguments over what was going wrong with my bike. Trevor was a funny guy although at the time he probably didn't realise how humorous he was being. He was also very stubborn (not like me of course!) and most times our disagreements resulted in stalemate.

To get things moving again Trevor would make me stand on a box in the middle of the road making a public apology after complaining that I would never ride the bike again if he was involved in preparing it. Sometimes I look back at many of the most successful riders during my racing days ... Ove Fundin, who never used a spanner in his life, Ronnie, whose bikes were lovingly looked after by the team of mechanics at Wimbledon, Ivan Mauger and Ole Olsen having their engines tuned by Guy Allott.

I always did my own bikes so everything I won was down to how I prepared my engines. Sometimes I would even change a motor between races and then, when I put on my helmet, couldn't see through my goggles because I was so hot and sweaty they had become fogged up. I always seemed to be racing against the clock as much as the opposition. It wasn't a question of not wanting to delegate responsibility for my engines, or not wishing to spend any money on people looking after them. It was just that I couldn't find the right person to do the job as and when I wanted.

I did start to take engines to Mike Erskine but then 20 other guys did the same and I found myself last on the list again, always battling to get my stuff done when I needed it.

Anyway, I always felt it was important to have some control over what I was riding and how my bikes were looked after.

I thought that my greatest success was when I married Junie Rashbrook in October 1956. The next day we were off on our honeymoon to South Africa. Junie always joked that I had to be married before I could become World Champion. Then when I got married, what happened? I managed to win four World Speedway Championships, the girl must have known something.

We were blessed in that we produced two great boys. Gary, was born in New Zealand, while it was England for Tony. Although I hated the English boarding school system, and so did Tony with a passion, I think in the long run it helped them to take better care of themselves, and they were a little more independent. After pre-school both boys went to our local Stroud school. Both were boarders and educated at Millfield School in Somerset.

While in South Africa, I learnt a lot about tuning my bikes. Johannesburg was 6,000 above sea level, and a 500cc engine performed just like a 250cc. Straight away I learnt how to never shut the throttle as the altitude was really detrimental to a racing engine. But when you raced down in Durban at sea level, it was like trying to ride a drug-crazed bull. The bike felt like a 1000cc, it was the difference between night and day. But most of the time I could still manage to hold it flat out, but I'm sure that the boys riding with me didn't quite know in what direction I was going to go. I wanted to take care of the engines myself, and I think my engines improved significantly.

My flat-out riding style was earning me some rave notices, and favourable comparisons with Ronnie Moore. But it also really took a toll on my machinery. There was another drawback to preparing your own engines, especially if you were like me. I would be the first to admit that I've always been a terrible one for experimenting and I'm sure it cost me world titles.

He looks like he is still at school ... but Peter Craven is World Champion in 1955.

Victory lost in the 1955 World Final and a tough push home for bronze **3**

UNLUCKILY for me I had a little spare time before the 1955 World Final and my form was good and my bike was running well. I took quite a bit of stick about my tuning skills and the World Final was one meeting you didn't want any engine failures.

I decided to change the big-end, the one in the bike was fine but for once I was determined to be ultra careful. For some reason I couldn't obtain an original JAP big-end so I fitted a copy one, which a few of the boys at the time were using without problems.

On reflection, making these modifications so close to the Final and not being able to test the engine before the big night was a bit stupid. At the start of the meeting my bike was going great, winning my first race, but then, on the last lap of my third race, it seemed to be struggling, the engine wouldn't rev out as it should.

Back in the pits I said to my mate, Aussie Jack Young, who was parked opposite me: "Youngie, look at all that bloody metal in the oil coming out the bottom of the engine. What do you think?"

"Briggo, your big-end is on the way out, how's it going?" he asked in reply. I told him: "It was going great, then in our race on the last lap it started to labour and wasn't revving out. I thought you might have got past me."

Youngie told me: "I'm sure the big-end is knackered, but it will finish the meeting okay. If you get stuck you can have a ride on my bike, I'm out of it, but my bike isn't going that great."

In those days we only had one bike each at a World Final but my Wimbledon team-mate, Cyril Brine, had brought along his, complete with its funny-shaped handlebars, as a back-up if I needed it. Had I ever ridden this bike? No, never!

I was having a bit of trouble on the track as well and incurred the wrath of the Wembley crowd with a stormy fourth ride in Heat 13. In the first corner Eric Williams charged into me from the inside and that knocked me into the path of the local Wembley hero, England's Brian Crutcher. Crutch had nowhere to go and fell and I couldn't believe that the referee excluded him.

The domino effect had been started by the 'Welsh Bunny' Williams and, as it turned out, it was not our last clash of the night. Ove Fundin out-gated and beat me in Heat 20 to finally deny me the chance of a run-off for the title against Peter Craven, who I had easily beaten when my engine was running sweetly.

A point behind Craven, I was left with a run-off against my great mate Ronnie Moore and Williams to determine the other rostrum placings. Ronnie led all the way to clinch silver and I was set for third when, in the middle of the last corner, Williams came charging again, causing a crash that left us both on the ground. It was another case of the aggressive Williams taking things over the accepted limit but, of course, the majority of the fans at Wembley were still blaming me for their hero Crutcher's earlier exclusion and I was the villain on whom they wished to vent their anger.

I can still vividly remember the conclusion to this, my second World Final. My bike was getting slower but I was on the right line when Williams ran into me when he could have gone around me. By now I had become a bit tired of being knocked over by Williams. Here we were, sitting in the middle of the track, with 70,000 pairs of eyes focused on us. I was feeling very sorry for myself, not sure that I would ever have another opportunity to win speedway's World Championship.

Then I saw Eric get up, grab his bike and attempt to push start his engine and get to the finish to secure third place behind Fundin and Moore. But, because he was so pent-up, he didn't pull the engine back on compression. Even pushing hard, the rear wheel refused to turn, so the engine wouldn't fire up.

The bronze medal was only just 50 yards away from where I was sitting on the track to the chequered flag.

Although I was pissed off by what had happened, I managed to keep a clear head and got my emotions back under control. I picked up my bike, pulled it back on compression, bounced my bum on the saddle to start the engine and rode side-saddle across the line to secure third place.

The unfancied Craven had won the first of his two World titles while I was left to rue the one that had got away. I had the meeting won before my bike started to get slower and I wasn't smart enough to make the decision to switch to Briney's bike.

American Jack Milne, a double World Champion before I even got to England, once told me that he rode virtually the same bike throughout his career and he never changed anything, not even a carburettor. He said he knew exactly how his bike would react in any given situation.

Sometimes I went out for a race and didn't know how my bike was going to respond, whether it would be a spinny engine or maybe too grippy, would it be fast or slow? Who knew, I certainly didn't. I was always very hard on my bikes and, later in our careers, Ivan (Mauger) said that he hated lending me his bike.

In terms of wear and tear on the engine, he reckoned that every race I did on his bike was the equivalent of five when he was riding it. It was how I learned to ride. I always thought that I couldn't go any faster than flat out!

One of the funniest situations I found myself in over a bike was at Coventry when racing in the 1954 Brandonapolis. This was one of the major individual events on the domestic speedway calendar and was held soon after the World Final at Wembley and always featured the newly crowned champion.

In my first race I ran my front wheel over the slippery concrete white line, I lost my front wheel and crashed heavily, wrecking my bike.

Speedway riders are usually very generous and Arthur Forrest kindly lent me his second bike for my remaining four rides. He came from a rich family, so he had two bikes at the meeting. I liked Arthur, and they nicknamed him the 'Black Prince' and he was always immaculate in his beautiful, shiny black leathers and long, white flowing scarf.

I won my next four races by a mile and ended up in a run-off for the title against two other riders on 12 points. Geoff Mardon and guess who? You got it … Arthur Forrest!

Arthur took his bike back, and I can't remember whose bike I borrowed for the run-off, which Geoff won, Arthur was second and I filled in the third position. Afterwards Youngie went nuts at Arthur for not allowing me to continue using his second bike in the run off against him and Geoff. However, I could understand why. He was good enough to lend it to me in the first place and, let's be honest, I was only in the run-off thanks to Arthur anyway, and so I couldn't complain.

I wasn't mechanically minded, and on leaving school I worked in an advertising agency. I only worked on my push bike and my old bitza motor bike for a couple of years and, as far as my speedway bike was concerned, it was always a case of 'suck it and see'.

After a while I got much better at setting up my bike but it was always a problem finding enough time to do everything that needed to be done. I think the American Bruce Penhall, who became a speedway superstar, twice winning the World Championship before quitting for a Hollywood career, was one of the cleverest.

He went outside of the speedway loop and found Eddie Bull, a normal mechanic from a local motorcycle shop in the West Midlands of England, to do his bikes for him. When I needed someone to help with my Jawa business in Southampton in the mid-1960s I employed David Waterhouse who was a car mechanic, and his speedway interest was that he used to take photos at the local cycle speedway track. Dave later helped to prepare my bikes.

Best day of my life, tying the knot with Junie, October, 1956.

The title is mine but still controversy with Ove Fundin lingers on and on

4

OVE Fundin and I had many, many on-track incidents but the one that is undoubtedly the most talked about took place during the 1957 World Final at Wembley. I was, and still am, adamant that I did nothing wrong when Ove went on his arse going into the pits corner of the third lap of our run-off for the title.

It still rates as the most satisfying of my four World Championship successes. Being the person still on his bike I have no doubt that I fully deserved to win my first World Championship.

Just before going out for the race, my fellow Kiwi, Ron Johnston, really wound me up and told me straight: "Briggo, Fundin won't care a fuck what he does to beat you, don't let him put one over on you."

Ove made the better start but it didn't matter as I was in great form and had no problem pulling him back within a couple of laps. At the start of lap three I made a perfect entry into the corner and my turn back was spot on to get a long drive out of the corner down the back straight which, if you do it right, can gain you several lengths on your opponent.

Halfway down the straight Ove was in shock as we were now elbow to elbow. He was aware that I had the advantage, being on the inside line as we approached the crucial pits bend, he started to lean on me, and then put his left arm over my throttle hand. Bloody hell, I thought, this could be a real disaster. I am faster into the corners than Ove and now he had to try and get into the corner faster than he wanted. He had two options: stay with me and try to remain on his bike, or shut off, which I knew he would never do.

I was all too aware that I had to stay tight on the inside white line. If I drifted even an inch off it I would risk being excluded had we touched. I had a big advantage in the way that I rode, I could lay my bike down really low because of the high speed that I carried into a corner.

When we finally reached the corner I just dug my bike in very low and stuck to the white line like glue. Ove couldn't cope with my entry speed and he unloaded. I am sure that he had fingers crossed that I would be excluded.

I was left to complete the final lap on my own, all the time worrying that my bike was going to suffer a mechanical failure. But, no, I was World Champion. I went round the track to offer Ove a lift back to the pits but he was still doing his dying swan act against the fence.

The boys rushed out of the pits, as is tradition, to toss me in the air. The first face that I saw was that of Johnno sporting the biggest smile and his wink said it all.

Ove said later that he would have done the same had our positions been reversed. If I had been where he was, on the outside, I would have tried to crowd him but would still have gone into the corner flat out. I certainly wouldn't have hooked my arm over his, in the way he did, as it put him horribly out of balance for a tough corner ahead.

The referee obviously shared my view but it isn't always satisfactory when a fair victory is tinged with controversy.

I clutched the *Sunday Dispatch* trophy and the winner's cheque for £500. Being crowned World Champion for the first time in four attempts, I felt happy with myself. It certainly eased the hurt I felt at losing the 1955 World Final through bad management and through no fault of my own riding. At that time I thought that I wouldn't have another chance of ever being World Champion again, but I had at last made it.

There were a few problems in the Wembley crowd amongst the hordes of Fundin fans from Norwich who didn't take too kindly to me taking away his crown. One angry idiotic supporter slapped the face of my wife Junie but they weren't going to get a second shot as she was sitting amongst a load of our friends.

That left a bit of a sour taste in my mouth, as does the fact that some people still seem to doubt whether Fundin was treated fairly. I was at Poole at the start of the 2008 speedway season for a meeting that carried a £60,000 first prize ... a far cry from what I received at Wembley, though I wouldn't swap any amount of money for a World title.

Dave Lanning, who was the announcer that day, interviewed me on the centre green and brought the subject up again. He said something about me being lucky not to have been excluded but it wasn't the time or place to argue my case so I let it pass. But, believe me, I am 100 per cent sure that it was a clean pass and nothing will convince me otherwise.

The New Zealand team give the South Africans a taste of the world famous Haka.

Me with my first mechanic, Eddie (Books) Toogood.

The newly-weds tour to South Africa with Brenda and Peter Craven.

I finally did it, my first world title

Back in Christchurch as World Champion for the first time

5

IT was wonderful to go back to New Zealand as World Champion for the first time at the end of the 1957 season. Life had been very hectic in England and I was really looking forward to the break.

When I got back to Christchurch I had a telephone call from Bruce Abernethy congratulating me on my Wembley success and saying that I should ensure I was well paid if I was going to race in New Zealand as the current World Champion. I told him that I didn't want to ride at all, it had been a really hard season in the UK and I just wanted a rest.

My cousin Keith was working at the big sheep stations in North Canterbury spraying gorse so I gave him a call and asked if he wanted some free labour.

It was an offer he couldn't refuse but he was leaving for a couple of weeks. That suited me as I wanted to spend some time with mum and my youngest brother Wayne.

There was speedway taking place in Christchurch but it was being staged by a new promoter who many people weren't too sure about. I had a really good time over the next few months just cruising around. For much of the time I was up in the mountains five days a week, getting up early in the morning, gulping down a huge farmer's breakfast with the shepherds and sheep-shearers and taking in the fresh air and unbelievable scenery.

Throughout this period the Christchurch promoter had been making discreet enquiries, trying to find out what I was up to and anxious to make some money for himself by getting me to ride. Eventually, we had a meeting and decided that we would run a meeting and split the proceeds 50/50.

I was quite excited getting ready for my first appearance in my home town as World Champion. I wanted to sort out all the expenses for the meeting before the tapes went up as I hate arguing about such things after the event. But, on the morning of the meeting, I was none the wiser and when we met he was dragging his feet. Eventually he came up with a list, but he must have thought I was wet behind the ears. There was a host of things that had no relevance to our meeting – weeding the track at the start of the season, a wreath for a rider killed earlier, painting the fence weeks before, the list went on and on.

I told him that I couldn't agree and as we argued more and more I trusted him less and less. He felt that he had me over a barrel but I got up to leave saying that a pain in my back was getting worse and could force me to miss the meeting. I gave him a piece of paper with a number on it and told him that was the fee I required to be given to a friend in cash at 5pm that evening otherwise I would be forced to go to hospital to have my 'bad back' x-rayed.

He took the paper, looked at it then went outside to gauge what he thought of the weather. Coming back inside, he said: "Right, we've got a deal." He offered his hand to shake on the deal, normally a sign of trust, but I wasn't interested. He had lost my trust.

What happened that night was unbelievable. I had my money as agreed but around 6.30pm, 90 minutes before the scheduled start, a sea mist rolled in and you could barely see from one end of the stadium to the other. The meeting went ahead, and was a success, but with fewer spectators than would have been the case had the weather not intervened. Do I thank the Lord for the fog, and for me changing my mind?

My time back home in New Zealand flew by and before long we were heading back to England for the 1958 season. I was seeded into the World Final and became only the second rider, after Jack Young, to successfully defend the title. After receiving the coveted *Sunday Dispatch* trophy from world land speed record holder Donald Campbell, I was allowed to keep it and it is now on show at Donington Park.

Winning my second World Final, again with a 15-point maximum, two more than my great rival Ove Fundin, made victory all the sweeter. I was on the top of my form and really feared nobody on a level playing field.

Back in New Zealand once more at the end of the year, Abbo (Bruce Abernethy's nickname) arranged a deal for me to ride in Auckland at Western Springs for the massive sum of £250. I sat by listening to Abbo's salesmanship as he negotiated the deal together with Auckland promoter Cocky McCormack.

I could hardly believe the words that were coming out of Abbo's mouth. "Cocky, I have got this kid who will fill your Western Springs stadium and you will end up making a ton of money. This Kiwi wonder boy is Barry Briggs, World Speedway Champion, and the third most famous New Zealander after Lord Rutherford, who split the atom, and Everest conqueror Edmund Hillary. He thrashed the cream of the world's best speedway riders at Wembley, the most famous stadium on this planet."

I couldn't listen to any more, I was so embarrassed, but then I saw the funny side of it and couldn't stop laughing. It seemed to me that I was worth more in New Zealand than England. Before leaving the UK I had failed to persuade Wimbledon promoter Ronnie Greene to cough up an extra £30 towards the cost of my boat fare between England and New Zealand.

He refused and I promptly retired. The Speedway Control Board rules at that time stated that the maximum a promoter could legally pay towards a boat ticket from either Australia or New Zealand was £250.

As double World Champion, I felt entitled to ask for the full £280, even though Junie and I intended to fly and pay for the difference (around £700) ourselves.

My emergence as an all-out racer and world-class performer at Plough Lane had led to a period of unprecedented success for the Dons but that obviously didn't impress Greene. Succeeding the great Wembley sides of the late 1940s and early 1950s, the boys from south-west London were crowned National League champions every year between 1954 and 1959 with the exception of 1957 when we were pipped by Swindon.

Under the counter deals were not uncommon at that time but Greene wouldn't break the rules to pay me a penny more than was on the table. We never had financial advisers in those days and were probably naïve and stupid. I remember advertising Astorias cigarettes and I didn't even smoke and also did a couple of drink adverts though I have never touched a drop of alcohol.

I felt convinced that drink played a part in the post-war break-up of my parents' marriage and have never gone near it.

I told Greene that I was retiring and left for New Zealand not knowing what the future had in store. A matter of principle and just 30 quid forced me out and perhaps that was stupid but I felt better about myself. There was, of course, nothing to stop me riding at Western Springs and Abbo's help and advice helped me a lot in future negotiations in my racing life.

It is easy for your brain to get set in a mode that says what you are doing for a living is sport. You are lucky to be getting paid for something you love, you should be thankful. But Abbo made me realise that if a promoter was making money out of me, through my name and reputation, then I should be given a fair deal. He also hammered into me that even if I didn't win all my races I must always give 100 per cent effort. If you don't let down the people that are paying to see you race they will ask you back again. Simple but true.

My entrepreneurial streak and a keen eye for a business deal showed itself when I opened both a record shop and a driving school in Garratt Lane, a stone's throw from Wimbledon Stadium, at the beginning of 1958.

Junie and I both loved music. I was a big fan of Elvis Presley and sold a tremendous amount of his records.

So, I was happily retired, we had our own home in Christchurch and had a beautiful son, Gary. Everything in the world was fine.

We had been working hard to get everything in place for our new life when I had an offer to go to Rockhampton in Queensland to ride for a couple of months. We thought it was a great idea, packed our bags and set off to Queensland for our holidays. I rode once a week, it was a large track and it was easy, you really didn't have to put yourself out too much to do well. The promoter there was Ted Price, a good, fair bloke and he sorted it out for us to stay with a friend, Horrie Harvey, which was great.

But Junie was to have a real black day. Gary was out in the sun a lot and looked really well. Horrie's wife, Edna, was going to the local Agricultural Show one Friday and talked Junie into putting Gary in the baby show, which she was really excited about. This excitement was to cease very quickly as both judges looked at Gary laying there in all his splendour and said in unison 'much too fat'. Junie was devastated and it took her a couple of days to get over it. Her description of the winner – 'a pale white scrawny half starved ugly baby' was a bit scathing. I think her emotions had a little to do with her description of the victorious winner.

After our spell in Queensland we went back to New Zealand and there was still no chance that I would return to England.

The Speedway Control Board made a vast amount of money from promoting the World Finals at Wembley but couldn't find an extra £30 to bring me back to defend my title.

They kept threatening me that I couldn't ride in the championship as I had retired but that was no big deal to me. I still have a letter from the SCB stating that if I wasn't back in the UK by a certain date I wouldn't be in the Final, and of course I must pay my own fare.

I chuckle about it now and then, especially when thinking that I have paid thousands in fares to have Bruce Penhall come from America, Nigel Boocock from Australia and others from around Europe to compete in the Golden Greats meetings that I staged in

England, Denmark, Poland, and Germany ... and, unlike the Wembley World Finals, we didn't have crowds of over 80,000.

Halfway through the 1959 season I received an offer from a few UK promoters, led by Trevor Redmond and Charlie Knott, who had got together to try and resolve the stalemate. The ridiculous thing is that eventually Greene and the SCB chipped in to pay my return fare between them.

Having thought that my career was over, I returned to England with speedway far from the top of my agenda, something that was perfectly illustrated by my weight, which was far from ideal. I needed to sort out our record shop in South London and other things that were becoming a real liability. We sold the shop to Pam, a friend of Junie's who had been managing it while we were away.

Despite the intransigence of Ronnie Greene over the boat fare, I always had great respect for the man who gave me my first break in speedway. Even so, our protracted dispute meant that I missed most of the 1959 season and that was a big factor in my failed quest to win the World Championship for a third successive year. I didn't even have my own bike for the final but still managed to finish third behind Moore and Fundin.

Sadly, I thought my speedway life in England was finished and having had all commitments sorted I was now under no pressure to stay. I had had a great time in speedway but what the future holds is the exciting part of your life. But, when early in 1960 an offer to return to league racing in the UK with New Cross arrived, I was a prostitute and money won me over.

A couple of things enticed me back. I enjoyed riding the small New Cross track and I also admired and loved Johnnie Hoskins, who led the Rangers revival.

Another thing was that my youngest brother Wayne wanted to try his luck as a speedway rider. In 1960 he was only 15-years-old, so he had to wait a year.

It wasn't a good season for me with New Cross. The side was weak and I wasn't pushed hard enough to keep up to speed. My old team, the Dons, again retained the league title. The big thing about New Cross was I spent the year sharing a workshop with

Jack Young. My bikes were a bit crappy but my snooker got much better as Youngie had a table in the workshop.

After just one season on loan to New Cross I finally got out of Greene's clutches in 1961 and my transfer to Southampton was finally sanctioned with a £750 fee paid to Wimbledon. It was a great move for Junie, Gary and me and after a year in our own house and having a proper family life in New Zealand the opportunity to live in Hampshire came at the right time.

Junie initially missed her native London, but quickly adapted and we had a marvellous time of getting ourselves sorted. I ended up leaving Wimbledon over money but at Southampton I really got my due rewards from Charlie Knott, who was a very good and astute promoter.

Charlie used to pay me £5, which was a fortune in those days, to deliberately miss the start in the second-half final. I had to pass the other three to win and about 90 per cent of the time I did, as Bannister Court was a great racing track.

Charlie reckoned that the most important thing was to send his customers home happy and waiting for next week's meeting. Even if the main match had been crap, with a great second-half final they left the stadium happy. Charlie was forward thinking and always fair to me. He produced a good track on which the other riders couldn't bullshit you as they could at Wembley, where they could win races just by staying on the right line.

At Southampton they always had to really race you for it. You could manipulate people there, and having another hungry rider alongside of me kept me on my toes. Along with Swede Bjorn Knutsson, we spearheaded the Saints to the National League title at the expense of my former club Wimbledon in 1962.

Knutty and I forged a friendly rivalry, but just scratch the skin and you would find a love–hate relationship and it was a bond that endures to this day.

After the meeting Bjorn, Madeline, Junie and I would have a meal. We would sit down, the girls had had a good time at the speedway and were relaxed, while Bjorn and I were different, our bodies hadn't settled yet and we were both still in race mode.

Sometimes it was hilarious, as messages were passed to each

Beating the Wembley rush, on our way to support Webby and Chelsea against Leeds in the FA Cup final.

other through our wives. Something during the meeting might have pissed one of us off but normally the girls got it sorted. With the racing our relationship was at times paper thin. Bjorn was super, super competitive and it was well-known that my relationship with the Swedes wasn't always the best.

Sometimes when Bjorn was in his English mode his thinking was great but then he would go back to his Swedish ways which I had trouble understanding.

I used to bullshit him that the Swedes have a good but sterile life with everything well organised. But, unfortunately, seemingly having everything is not always the answer, Sweden at that time was the country with the highest suicide rate.

We still talk three or four times a year. Knutty likes to know that he's still earning more than me, each morning he gets up and has his coffee and studies the stock market. I think he's grown up and our outlooks are completely different, at times I feel that I haven't grown up, but he can still be fun.

Playing golf with Knutty is like a war, he wants perfection and even if you are Tiger Woods, none of us can be that good. But knowing him definitely added spice to my life and, of course, Madeline and Junie had no hang ups. We raced the hell out of each other and he was trustworthy. He was like me, if you wanted to pass around the outside, there would be room, but only just.

It was a sad day for speedway when Bannister Court in Southampton was sold for a leisure complex redevelopment at the end of 1963. I would have loved to finish my career as a Saint but, saying that, life is for living and all my following years have been fantastic.

In 1962, the year before handicapping came in, I had returned to the World Final rostrum after a two-year absence when I was runner-up to Peter Craven.

It was my second season with Southampton and when it got near to the final at Wembley all my engines were rubbish due to the amount of meetings I was doing. I knew that with my weight I needed something pretty good to pull me to the first corner.

I did a deal with my German mate, Josef Hofmeister, the European longtrack champion who was also a world-class speedway rider who had qualified for a couple of World speedway championships.

I had first met Hoffy at Wembley Speedway in Johannesburg when we were 17-year-old kids starting out in speedway. I still remember that the little bastard beat me the only time we raced each other there.

The engine deal we did was unbelievable. Hoffy wanted some spare parts I had and they were in five piles on my workshop floor. We had to agree a deal for only one pile, plus an amount of cash. Each pile had a value in Josef's head and mine. I was thinking in English pounds, while Hoffy would be calculating in German marks.

To rent his engine it would take, for example, pile one of the spares plus a certain sum. There was a different deal for each pile. The other part of the agreement was that if I finished first, second or third we split the prize money 50/50. It was a normal Briggo deal! I only had the chance to ride the engine once before Wembley. Hoffy loved high compression motors which spin the back wheel very easily. In my first race I used far too much throttle on the start and dug a big hole. Instead of moving forward, I finished a very unimpressive third.

I clicked my brain into gear and sussed out how it was best for me to gate with this type of engine. I won my next four races in a canter, beating Peter Craven who took the title. Pay-out time between Hoffy and myself was an international transaction. It finished up costing me more to hire his engine than it would have done to buy a new engine. But getting second place in a World Final together was fun for us both.

Looking back, I should have bought the engine from Hoffy and put it on the shelf to bring out for my other Wembley races. Dumb! A museum was opened for Hoffy in his home town of Abensburg, in Bavaria, in 2008. He brought up our 1962 Wembley final together in his opening speech. I hope nobody saw me wince. I claimed third spot behind Fundin and Knutsson at Wembley a year later. I was getting back to my best form after my year away.

Ronnie Moore, Norman Parker, Cyril Brine and Ernie Roccio ... team-mates at Wimbledon.

Ronnie Moore was and still is my hero and I owe him so much

6

RONNIE Moore – or Mirac, the nickname I gave him, short for miraculous – was my hero when I was a young kid dreaming of becoming a professional speedway rider and no-one knows my fellow Kiwi better than me.

I have never gone along with the view of some that Mirac was too much of a gentleman on the track and that his perceived lack of aggression stopped him from winning more than his two World titles in 1954 and 1959.

My favourite Ronnie story goes back to his first year in English speedway when the established riders who were making all the big money at the time resented the new young kid on the block and didn't want him in their cosy club.

Ronnie was a big threat. He was the first of the new breed of riders who powered his bike into the corners and very quickly he was giving the old boys a tough time. They were earning huge sums of money at the time, I can recall hearing that Jack Parker bought a new house in Rugby from his speedway earnings ...

every week! He was one of the old gang who didn't like Ronnie ruffling his feathers.

One night there was a big meeting at New Cross and between races the riders would sit on a church pew-like bench. Ronnie was there, sandwiched between fellow Wimbledon rider Norman Parker and his brother Jack, who leant across and said: "Tell your fucking boy that if he comes near me tonight I will break his fucking legs."

Ronnie was unperturbed, he could take care of himself and there was always his protective dad Les who wouldn't take shit from anyone. Sooner rather than later the old boys had to back off and accept Ronnie into their elite group to have his share of the spoils.

Later, when I came onto the scene in Britain, I was referred to as a "bloody menace" after crashing into the back of other riders and being sent flying through the air. But, more often than not, the accidents were caused by an 'old boy' shutting off the throttle in front of me, which was like someone slamming on his brakes, though of course speedway bikes do not have brakes, and I was in trouble.

If I had tried to get back at them more likely than not I would have been the one getting hurt so I just had to bide my time. Never has the old saying "what goes around comes around" been more true. There would come a day when I would be going into the first corner and, lo and behold, there would be one of the old bullies. So I would say to myself, "he's owed one" and, whack, the debt was settled.

Most of the time the bloke at the end of it knew exactly why he had been whacked, and that was the end of it. Rarely did it lead to punches being exchanged off the track. The word soon got around, and people then left you alone and raced you properly, which is all I wanted in the first place.

However, one night at Bradford things did work out a little differently. I was riding my balls off and scraping the fence at high speed, what a race it was. The only problem was that it was with my team-mate, Bill Longley, for the one point awarded to third place. I was not happy as I rode back into the pits, I got off my bike and threw a punch at the Aussie, then we got tied up in a shoving match. All the time I was telling myself that it was a stupid move … Longley was a PT instructor and would have beaten the shit out of me. But it did fix the problem. From then on, if needed, he raced rather than fenced me.

Getting even using a speedway bike can be extremely dangerous and sometimes you must eat humble pie. At Exeter one night, after scoring a maximum (unbeaten by an opponent), I was in a second-half race against the local hero, Chris Blewett. I got behind him but there was no way I was going to go round him. Exeter was a very fast track with a solid wooden fence and a couple of times he bounced off it and just about knocked me off my bike. I cruised the last couple of laps behind him but when I got back to the pits was confronted by a few Exeter fans calling me a coward and saying "no balls Briggs".

I took off my helmet, offered it to the crowd and replied: "Hey, I am a coward but take my helmet and have a go." Chris was like many riders, a really nice bloke but, when he turned on his fuel taps before a race he also switched off his brain.

A Danish rider, Arne Pander, sustained serious injuries when trying to out-muscle Les Owen. It was a mistake he learned the hard way.

Ronnie could also put himself about when he needed to. He was a very smooth rider, although he might have struggled a bit had he

I've got Ronnie well beat

ridden now rather than when he did. It is so slick round the inside of speedway tracks these days. Nobody could go round the line without losing speed like Ronnie Moore.

The Wimbledon promoter Ronnie Greene would often use Ronnie as a bargaining tool against me when we rode for the Dons together. If ever I went to Greene to sort something out, especially money, he would turn me down and justify his decision by saying: "Ronnie doesn't get that."

My thinking was "well, bad luck Ronnie." After a while I realised that Ronnie probably wasn't earning more than me anyway, which was sad because he deserved to get as much as he was worth.

Mind you, Ove Fundin was probably getting more lolly at Norwich than Ronnie and I put together. Good luck to Ove, a speedway rider can never be overpaid.

Ronnie was his own worst enemy in that he never pushed himself forward to get the financial rewards and recognition his talent deserved.

In August 2007, Ronnie, Ivan and me were given the keys of the city of Christchurch in our native New Zealand. I couldn't make it back to my home town for the ceremony but wrote a letter to the Mayor beforehand saying: "Please remember one thing, Ronnie Moore was a better speedway rider than either Ivan or me. I live in California and Ivan is in Aussie so Ronnie really is your local boy. Please make sure he is looked after."

Ronnie is hard of hearing (we all joke and blame it on the Wimbledon pits) and in my opinion he doesn't get the credit he deserves, especially if Ivan is around.

I wasn't being bitchy about Ivan when I wrote that letter. Ivan knows my faults and I know his but I didn't want Ronnie and his achievements to be over-shadowed. The only thing that Ivan and I had more than Ronnie was the desire to win. Ronnie could and should have won more than two World titles but sometimes he went to pieces when under pressure.

Early in 2009 I turned down an invitation to be inducted into the New Zealand Speedway Hall of Fame. I am a New Zealander, for good or bad, and have been proud to race with the Kiwi flag on my breast all over the world.

So, why did I turn it down? The Hall of Fame had been going for about six years and both Ronnie and Ivan were inducted at the opening ceremony. Over the years all kinds of people, including a starting gate marshal and ACU officials, have had their names added.

I felt that, after six years, I was past my sell-by date. When I replied to the invitation I wrote that they probably thought I was acting like a grumpy old man ... and perhaps I was.

I remember when the New Zealand Sports Hall of Fame opened and legends like Ronnie and Denny Hulme, Formula One champion, were missing while road walkers, sheep-shearers and the like were included. I was so embarrassed but they made it in at the next induction.

My admiration, respect and friendship for Ronnie inhibited me whenever we raced against each other. It held me back in a couple of ways including if he was in front of me during a World final as was the case in 1956. In one heat I was trapped behind Ronnie while Jack Geran was breathing fresh air out in front. By the time I passed Ronnie, gently, I didn't have enough time to catch Jack.

I had so much more respect for Ronnie in those circumstances than with other riders in the same position. If it had been against Ove, Booey (Nigel Boocock), Bjorn or Ivan we would have been thrashing each other right up to the borderline of being fair to win the race.

The saying "you reap what you sow" is very true.

Eric Boocock, Nigel's younger brother, was a really clean rider and never 'put it about'. One night I was behind him at Oxford and was really hustling him. In the middle of a corner I picked up a bit of unexpected grip and, although I had the bike very low, I still went straight for a few yards and passed him in a manner that I didn't think was 100 per cent fair.

My respect for Eric caused me to shut the throttle and let him come through before resuming my 'hell for leather' efforts to get back into the lead.

Once, when not riding, I was helping another rider. He passed one of his biggest rivals and came back to the pits flushed with success and boasted to me: "What about that pass then?" My answer was: "That was not a pass, you simply impeded him as you didn't turn in the corner. You gave the bloke two bad choices, shut off and eat humble-pie or just ride into the fence. Neither was good. Someday you may regret that pass, it could come back and bite you."

Later it did and probably cost him a World Championship.

Me with Ove Fundin.

My relationship with Sweden and Swedish riders was always tough

SWEDEN was the dominant speedway nation for much of my racing career so it is no surprise that many of my toughest opponents came from that country. And, of course, one particular incident involving a Swedish rider left me with a lasting legacy, that I am reminded of every day of my life.

People assume that I blame Bernie Persson for my second ride crash at Wembley during the 1972 World Final which not only cost me a finger but also the probability, at least in my mind, of a fifth Championship win. That particular incident is dealt with in detail in my chapter on the 1972 World Final.

OVE FUNDIN

To mention the name of Fundin and Persson on the same page is giving Persson credibility that, in my eyes, he has never earned. Me and Ove crashed our ways through our racing careers. The biggest and the most important to me was my first World Final win in 1957 at Wembley, where I took the spoils, and Ove finished under the fence. We go into this Championship in more detail, especially the controversial run-off race, in another chapter on the 1957 World Final.

The first I heard of Ove Fundin was when he came over from Sweden to race in a World Championship qualifier at West Ham. We laugh now as we look back, and I can't remember who it was, as they retold the tale of his West Ham debut. "There was this red-headed Swede with a bike painted red, who had trouble turning the corners, and demolished the field on more than one occasion."

I have talked and laughed with Ove about this meeting a couple of times. He had sent his bike over from Sweden and the frame was a homemade job. The bike was lying against the wall in the West Ham workshops. On the day of the meeting, one of the West Ham mechanics saw some cracks on Ove's frame. There was only a couple of hours before the meeting started and Fundin hadn't arrived yet, so the mechanic decided to weld up the cracks that in his opinion were dangerous. A speedway bike frame is a very delicate piece of equipment and it must flex. By welding the frame, it made the bike ride like a 'garden gate', with no feeling at all. That was Ove's story and it makes sense.

The speedway world didn't realise at the time that this night at West Ham was to be the launch pad for this 'skinny, red-headed Swedish kid' aboard his fire-engine red bike who crashed his way onto the speedway scene. This super sensitive kid was to become one of the real superstars in the history of the sport.

Ove was really tough. Our thinking was pretty similar; I think I took my defeats a little better than he did. I'd just kick my bike, but out the back behind the pits, by myself. Racing-wise, Ove would always leave you on your bike. He wouldn't just put you straight into the fence, but there would be only just enough space, if you had the balls to stay there on the outside of him.

He was a clever rider, very difficult to pass. He was a special and unusual rider, not always looking comfortable on his speedway bike. But he was a very good motorcyclist. One time he, Olle Nygren and I went to a motocross course at the Monarch motor cycle factory that produces one of the top motocross bikes in Sweden. We spent the day riding there, and Ove showed that he was in fact a very good motorcyclist, yet at times on his speedway bike you would look at him and you didn't think he was.

He had a very upright ugly style, especially in the middle of a corner, and just for a split second, while he was changing direction he looked like a novice.

But he understood traction probably better than anyone. The only one that I felt was near him on this was Ronnie (Moore). Ove never came into the corner sideways. I would be much quicker than him going into a corner, but halfway around the corner he was there blocking the inside of the track.

This gave you false security. You thought you could pass him on the outside, but just as you made your move, he had got his bike turned, then quickly upright with the wheels in line and was gone. Then you found yourself trapped on the outside, and the bloody dirt hit you, it felt as though you had ridden into a brick wall. You also had to be careful, because if someone was right behind you, they could slip past on the inside while you were fighting the dirt. The force of the dirt hitting you is unbelievable and slowed you down, and bruised the hell out of your body.

Ove was lucky he went to Norwich where they had a good mechanic to do his bikes. I don't think he ever turned a spanner. He rode speedway how we all would have liked. He simply just got on his bike and rode. Unfortunately, my finances dictated that I had to do most of the work myself. But you must hand it to Ove that he still had that hunger for success that was not based on money. It was the same with Mike Hailwood in road racing. If you have money in the bank, why stick your neck on the line?

I am told many times that if I hadn't touched my bikes I would have been Champion more times. Maybe, but I got something extra that Ove and other riders didn't, my success or failures were completely down to me. I think that my successes outweighed my failures quite considerably.

The British Match Race Championship was a big event on the speedway calendar in our day. The champion got paid a fixed weekly sum while he was champion. I was nominated to race the first leg at my home track, New Cross, against Ove. Youngie (Jack Young) and me shared a workshop at New Cross the year I rode for them. We had a lot of fun, but my speedway was not at its best, we spent too much time playing snooker, as we had a table in the workshop. When I got home after a hard day, Junie would ask: "Did you have a good day love?" I felt so guilty. On the positive side Youngie did teach me to be a better snooker player. We were messing around in the workshop the day of the match race when Youngie told me with a big smile on his face: "Briggo, I've been thinking and come up with this great idea. I'll un-nerve the Swede for you tonight."

I laughed and went on with what I was doing. That night I couldn't believe it – I overheard Youngie talking to Ove and telling him "Bloody hell Ove, you'd better watch out, Briggo's in a bad mood today and he'll take it out on somebody. Watch out for him, especially on the first corner."

Youngie had turned Ove into a complete wreck, his face was purple with nerves, he kept brushing the front of his hair, and then quickly rubbing his nose with the back of his hand. Another thing, he kept kicking the front of his steel boot foot with the heel of his right foot. Over the years I've seen Ove doing these things when he is really nervous.

In the first race, I was on the inside start and was a little slow in dropping my clutch. Ove had a slight edge on me and really closed me down into the first corner. I got to him when he was doing his middle of the corner shuffle. I was a foot too far back to move him over, but I went over his left foot, which half took off his steel shoe. Down the back straight, he led me by three-quarters of a length.

He spent the whole of the straight banging his foot down hard on the track, trying to get his steel boot back on – all this was happening while still at full speed. I managed to nudge him a couple of times to no avail. He beat me 2–0 in the match races, and twice broke the track record by over one second.

Coming back into the pits after the second race, I laughed with Youngie: "Well, that wasn't such a bloody good idea was it."

I felt Ove had ridden much better because of the pressure he had been put under. All the excitement gave his body a natural gee-up, hence the big performance. I think that maybe Youngie touched that nerve in Ove that night.

I always believed that in my World Finals I had to get 15 points to win because of guys like Ove, Ronnie Moore, Peter Craven and Bjorn Knutsson. There was not a lot of difference between the five of us. In his book, *Ove Fundin: Speedway Superstar*, published in 2006, the Swede claims that it was impossible to be friendly towards one of your rivals but, not for the first time in our turbulent relationship over the years, I don't agree with him.

I was not best mates with Ove but I liked him. Whenever I used to go over to Sweden I would always stay at his place in Tranas. When I went back to New Zealand for a couple of months, Junie stayed with Ove and his wife Mona for about a month.

But what pissed me off was that after Ronnie won the World Championship, suddenly Ove invited him to stay instead of me, so I had to sleep up the road in a pub with all the other riders instead. It wasn't that I minded, of course not but, as Ove's friend, I felt hurt by what he did then and it wrecked our relationship.

I threw him across the pits at Norwich one night and afterwards he had to come and ask me for a lift to London. He says in his book that he didn't do that!

Ove joined us in the 'World Champions' troupe that Ivan and I set up to race in Australia and New Zealand, finishing in America. He was well-read and took notice of museums and those type of things. When we were in Israel and we were doing the tourist bit our guide was pointing out all the different 'Stations of the Cross' where Jesus did this and that. Ove knew better than our guide … he was smart, not only on a speedway bike.

I have Ove's best bike, the Norwich Track Spare 2, which to me is the most famous one ever in the history of speedway. This is the one that he used to win three of his World Championships, plus of course many of the major championships that you could care to name. Ove and the Norwich Track Spare 2 have won them all at least once. At the Donington Speedway Museum it was one of the most popular bikes in the collection.

Ove had won three World Finals on the same bike! I must have used 20, probably more than that, in my World Finals. I was always changing things. Yet when I won my first World title at Wembley in 1957 I was on a brand new bike that I was awarded on an insurance claim after a truck had run over my car and trailer with my bike on it. It was only three weeks before Wembley, so I didn't have time to change anything … well maybe just a little! It was a lesson I never learned!

BJORN KNUTSSON

Bjorn was a tremendous rider; he was absolutely the opposite of Ove. Bjorn did all his own engines and I have never seen spare parts used for so long. He had a German Mahle piston that he used for half a season. Mike Erskine, who did a lot of bits and pieces for both our engines, did magical things with this piston. When Mike re-bored Bjorn's engine he would get the magic piston and put it in the vice and carefully keep squeezing it until it was perfectly round again. Then he would re-bore the cylinder barrel to the clearance of the old piston. He ran his bikes on the smell of an oily rag and was really, really good mechanically. His bikes were always very good and he knew why. Knutty always said I had sticky fingers and that's why I was always having trouble with my bikes. On my way to the World Longtrack Final in Oslo I decided that we'd make a quick stop and visit the now-retired Bjorn and family. He talked me into using his engine and it didn't come cheap. Now I was on a non-sticky engine. I've never seen anyone in such deep distress, as his beloved 'Special' stopped twice on me. Afterwards he got to feel that disasters are always close to hand with me. Knutty has never recovered.

Our rivalry was intense. If I went to a meeting and got 11 from four rides and he got 12, I wouldn't be happy and classed it a failure. My failure level was very, very high. When I got home Junie would ask 'what's wrong?' and I'd reply that Bjorn got more points than me. Part of the game was to always be as good and better if possible than your team mate. It really keeps you on your toes. I never had that at New Cross and it shows in my records.

Bjorn was a very good starter and tough because he was never beaten, and would have a go at you inside or out, right up until the chequered flag. I remember one grass track meeting we were doing in Kent; it was so dusty you couldn't see where you were going. It was very dangerous because if someone fell in front of you, the first thing you would have known was when you ran over them. I was in second place in a heat and happy with that, when Bjorn came storming past, his head about two feet in front of the handlebars to try and get better vision! He couldn't stop himself being a racer no matter what.

In other ways Bjorn was like me, he had no money when he came into speedway and this was his way of making a few bob. Every time he put on his leathers he was going to earn as much as he could. Our relationship was a healthy one and we have remained very good friends. That sort of competition within a team is good; it worked for Ronnie and me at Wimbledon, with Bjorn at Southampton and with Martin Ashby at Swindon. It is a tough business and you have to try to mentally drive your opposition into the ground, which includes your mates.

Knutsson should have won more than just one World Final, at Wembley in 1965. The 1961 final was the first World Championship held outside of Wembley and Bjorn was the fastest that night. While pushing Ove he slipped off through impatience – he only had to wait as he was the fastest that night. He suffered badly from nerves and quit when still young because his wife, Madeline, who was also very nervous, didn't want him to carry on.

I remember when Jack Cramer first started the professional tennis circuit; they played each other so many times, that there quickly became a pecking order. It was the same at the top of the speedway ladder. Ole (Olsen) hated coming to New Zealand because he had to live with the other blokes, day in and day out, and he didn't want them to think he was just like them, and was vulnerable. Like marriage, spending so much time together, you learn each other's faults. As a racer it's great if you can convince your opposition that you're Superman, but living together over a period of time it will be discovered you're not so super.

There was a long period when Ivan didn't think he could beat me. I have heard him say, when he had managed to beat me, 'oh Briggo was riding his old bike, or the meeting means nothing to him, or it's only in the off season.' He was really paying attention, most of the time when it really counted, I could just pull out that little bit to beat him.

I remember the day I let him off the hook. It was when he beat me in the European Final at Wembley. I did have a bit of trouble which I didn't advertise but he did it and it gave him a completely different mind set. It was always much tougher for me after that Wembley defeat.

One Swedish rider I didn't enjoy racing was Gote Nordin. It still makes me smile when I hear him referred to as 'gentleman' Gote. What a joke. He was a good-looking boy and would always give Junie a big hug when we met, but he was one of the toughest riders around.

I remember one time when I had the Match Race Championship with him at Oxford. Gote was smart, he would come up to you before a meeting and say "how's Junie and the kids," be really nice and then whack you in the first corner. On this occasion I told my brother Murray, who was with him, not to let Nordin anywhere near before the Match Race. I didn't want to talk to him; if he came close Murray was to walk between us.

On the track I beat him easily ... he was no problem because he hadn't lulled me into a weak mental state.

He had an unusual style of riding and to me it was dangerous, really more to himself. If you don't lay the bike over at certain times, you only need to get a bit of unexpected grip then you're straight into someone's back wheel and you really hurt yourself. Gote got hurt many times because of his very upright riding style. He was a good rider but you never really knew where you were when racing him, unlike Ove or Bjorn.

Whether it was his lack of control I'm not sure but he was one rider I had trouble summing up on the track.

I had this little thing in my head that alerted me to certain situations and how I was going to handle it. Sometimes I knew I had the dirty end of the stick and wanted out.

I didn't ride against Anders Michanek a lot, but he was another tough Swedish racer. He was very fit, trained a lot because he wanted to be good, and knew how to get there.

He came to ride in some of my Golden Greats meetings and Junie used to ask why I programmed him in the same races as me. I'd reply that it spiced up my life a little. I knew that Mich would give me a hard time but always leave me on my bike, although sometimes he wanted just a little more room. But it was no more than I would have done to him.

Mich was the perfect professional when he joined Ivan and me in Australia, New Zealand and America. He was always exactly where he had to be and on time. I remember before our first meeting in the Houston Astrodome we hadn't seen Mich for a couple of days. But he knew what time he was required to be at the Astrodome and, right on time, just like magic he sauntered down the ramp and into the stadium.

He did a good job, wasn't a whinger and just got on with his racing. Sometimes the tracks were bad or he didn't have the best of the bikes but he got on with it. Mind you, there was one time when he tried it on. It was one of those Golden Greats meetings at Landshut, Germany. The riders simply drew straws for what bike they had in each race. We had two groups of bikes – the A bikes and the B bikes. The A's were a little better, in the finals we always used them. When it came to the Landshut final we couldn't find the number one A bike. The number one bike always started from gate number one. For the start of the final it was missing Then, out of the darkness, came the bike with Mich already on it. He had hidden it away but we made him get off and we did the draw for the bikes.

Blow me, if Mich didn't draw the number one bike anyway. But as he goes roaring into the first corner Georg Hack mows him down, so the bike didn't help him at all.

Tony Rickardsson was a very, very good rider, as his record of six World Championship wins suggests. The best thing he could do was to turn a bike brilliantly but he didn't have to do it a lot of the time because those he was racing against weren't good enough.

I saw him once during a British Grand Prix at Cardiff perform a brilliant manoeuvre. He got on one wheel in the first corner and quickly was relegated to last position. The very next corner he went from last back to first place. He simply had the ability and the confidence just to rip around the line and through the bumps, that had petrified the other riders, for another win. He was capable of doing that. When he was a bit younger, in my opinion he turned the

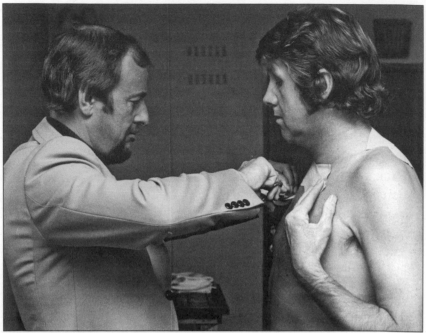

Doctor Knutty fixes my collar bone with a bit of tape.

Neither of us could give up our day job!

bike a little too hard but then he got more feel for what he was doing and stopped it.

In that way I think Erik Gundersen was at times better than Bruce Penhall. He felt the bike and even when he turned so sharply he still had the feel, you go nowhere when you're locked up. Erik got it gripping quickly, whereas Brucie, who was not as soft, just gave the bars a big wrench and got it gripping again.

Scottie Nicholls is a good turner of a bike but loses time by not getting out of the locker quick enough therefore losing speed.

Rickardsson was helped by the fact that he rode during an era when there weren't too many top class riders to challenge him. Erik had stopped, Hans Nielsen was retiring, Jan O. Pedersen and Per Jonsson also suffered injuries that ended their careers prematurely. I thought on many occasions Hans (Nielsen) worked the 'Gote Nordin' on Tony, they played golf etc, we're good mates.

I've seen Hans feed it to Tony on plenty of occasions on the track, not like the best of mates.

Bengt Jansson was brought to England and lived with Knutty in Southampton and went to the meetings together. Bengt was a team mate with Bjorn at West Ham. He was there for over a month but was doing poorly, and the management told Knutty that after next week's meeting they were going to let him go back to Sweden. It was as if Bengt had turned on a light switch and he started to get plenty of points. He had a great, easy style and I feel that he was talked out of his chance to win the 1967 World Final at Wembley, losing a run-off with Fundin.

Swedish official Bergstrom and his gang were in the pits and I felt they conned him. They let him go to gate for the run off while the Fundin camp allowed the two minutes to run down. It's all fair in love and war, but inexperience cost Bengt heavily and Ove won in a trot. Why Bengt went so well in that Final I don't know but he didn't come near to winning it again.

He rode in the Golden Greats meetings and always did well. For the first Golden Greats meeting at Coventry in 1988, the fans came to the meeting to watch the 'old boys' wobble around to great applause from their dedicated fans who remembered how it used to be. In the first race when the tapes flew up, into the lead, riding as he did when he was a 20-year-old, was Bengt Jansson. The fans couldn't believe their eyes. But he was being hunted from behind by the master of hardness, Anders Michanek. Then, on the last corner, Bengt was unceremoniously fenced by Mich to snatch the victory. The fans sat back and enjoyed the spectacle, all of the 'old boys' were riding like kids.

Once you learn how to ride a speedway bike you never forget how to do it. Given good bikes and a decent track the 'old boys' were doing times a mere few seconds slower than years ago.

I didn't race against many Danes. Arne Pander was really top class for a time and then was demolished in a crash with Les Owen that finished a promising speedway career. On the grass and longtracks, Kurt Petersen was a good performer.

Then along came a Dane who had the determination that was required to take him to the very top. Enter Ole Olsen. Tracks all over Denmark sprang up as Olsen moved up the speedway ladder. Everyone has to have some luck to help you to get through the tough road to the top.

Mine was having Trevor Redmond as my guardian and, of course, Ronnie Moore who used to practice with me early in the morning after our meeting at Wimbledon the night before. Ole had exactly the same with Ivan (Mauger) as the man to learn and copy from. Probably me and Ole would have still made it, but it would have taken longer.

It seems to me that riders from different nations have various thought processes. The Swedes were different to the Danes or the Russians. You would have thought that the boys from the then Soviet Union would have been the most dangerous to race against but they weren't. Igor Plechanov was special and had some unbelievably good World Championships, even beating Fundin in a run-off in Sweden. Plus Boris Samorodov was no slug either. They played to the rules pretty well, even the Russian tyre-marks on my back from my Wembley crash were not really the fault of their riders as they really had nowhere to go except over me. I think a couple of the Russians could have raced in England and would have been sensational if they had raced league matches in Britain.

The Poles were much tougher, especially in the first Test match at Wimbledon. It was unbelievably bad planning by speedway's controlling body having the first match at a small track. They were fearless but you had to be bit smarter to ride the tight Wimbledon track and not knock the fence down, which is exactly what they did. My brother Murray and me burnt the midnight oil straightening the bikes the whole team had bent. We were the only ones around with the welding gear needed.

They had a few good riders that could have ridden in the UK. Antonin Woryna twice finished third in a World Final. At one Wembley practice there was a Pole I had never seen before. He was very young. The Polish federation bought him to England for experience, how he got to ride at the official Wembley practice nobody knew.

He was the Polish wonder kid Zenon Plech. He had a couple of near misses in the World Championship and, to me, was screwed at the 1979 World Championship in Katowice by referee Tore Kittelsen when he was caught out at the tapes in one crucial race.

Plech and Eddie Jancarz joined the World Champion's troupe that Ivan and I took to New Zealand, Australia and the USA. They were both very good riders and, when we were having trouble with

Wembley 1972: The crash that cost me more than just my fifth world title.

Ole (which was quite often) we simply loaned Zenon Ivan's bike, with instructions to 'go and beat Ole' and he often did.

As opponents, the Swedes were the toughest. Speedway was big in Sweden in the fifties and sixties … Olle Nygren at the time was a bigger name in Sweden during his heyday than was tennis star Bjorn Borg several decades later. Olle was a model, he was a good-looking boy but he didn't really care. He was a bit Bohemian in those days, was different to everyone else and that hasn't really changed.

He could give out a bit of stick on the track. One night at Swindon he gave me a terrible time, so I got him beside me on the outside and just slowed down and had him in a position he couldn't get out of. We were travelling at near walking pace and outside the pit gate we had virtually stopped. I just looked over straight into his eyes, nodded and then took off again. I didn't fence him but he knew what it was all about.

Nygren was probably one of the best motorcyclists in speedway but he never really had the complete desire, the 'want' as I call it. I would always take a rider with 'want' over one with natural ability. Ivan wasn't the best rider and neither was I – nowadays it's Nicki Pedersen. He is not the best rider, his style is not a good one but he knows what he wants and he will go right to the edge to get it.

Ivan Mauger overcame a tough start in England to take on the world 8

THE easy way to write a chapter about Ivan Mauger is to scan through speedway's record books and simply list all his achievements in a career that struck gold after a false start.

But there will be none of that here. This is my view of Ivan, someone I have known and loved – and occasionally disliked – for more years than either of us care to remember.

All of us, most certainly Ivan and I, have flaws in our characters and there are times when I have cringed at some of the things that he has done.

Many years ago I was staying with Ivan at his house on the west coast of Australia. He was sitting next to his swimming pool nursing his granddaughter Sadie. She was too young to speak but Ivan told her: "Hello my lovely little darling, dad-dad's beautiful little girl, who loves you best in the whole world. Everyone in the world hates your grandad but it doesn't matter my love as I know you love me and that's all that counts."

I just about died laughing. Ivan made a similar comment to John

Chaplin for his *Story of the World Championship* book … "I don't care how unpopular I am as long as I am World Champion."

That's Ivan and he doesn't care who knows it. But you will not find a better family man than Ivan. He and his wife Sarah live at Runaway Bay in Queensland and his three kids and numerous grandchildren all reside close by. Every one of them seems to pass through their front door at least twice a week and he adores them all.

I gave Ivan, who like me was born in Christchurch, New Zealand, the nickname Sprouts when he first came to ride in England in 1956 because, like the American leg-trailing superstar Sprouts Elder, he had his handlebars turned down.

When he and Raye (as we called Sarah) arrived in the UK she was already pregnant with their first child, Julie. He couldn't earn enough at Wimbledon to look after the both of them and he was forced to seek additional work at the track.

He rode for the local cycle speedway team the South London Rangers (he still has the race-jacket) and on Sundays in 1957 he raced for Rye House and a year later for Eastbourne in the Southern Area League.

Ivan was even then never backward in telling people how good he was but amongst his peers at Wimbledon, including Ronnie Moore and me, that wasn't necessary or wise. We had our own eyes and would make our own judgements.

In my view at the time, Ivan had to earn his spurs. He was different to me but that is not to say he was wrong and I was right. But when I was growing up, my motorcycle was a tool that I wanted to have fun with and be the master of, whether it was trials or grasstrack.

I became involved with the local motorcycle clubs in Christchurch and we didn't really like what we termed the 'milk bar cowboys', who were a group of fairly mild Hells Angels types who parked their bikes in Cathedral Square in the middle of the city. Every now and then they would ride round the square or through Christchurch and didn't endear themselves to people in the town or other motorcyclists.

Ivan was a 'milk bar cowboy' and when we spoke before I

started this chapter he admitted he loved it and that he and Raye had some great times in their matching blue leather jackets and on his Triumph Thunderbird machine.

I was lucky in that when I arrived in England I had Ronnie, Trevor Redmond and Geoff Mardon, all Christchurch boys, to look after me, but Ivan's attitude meant that he and Raye were left to fend for themselves.

I first became involved when Junie told her mum Queenie that Raye was pregnant and that they were living in an unfurnished flat in Fulham. Queenie gave Junie a bit of a roasting and told her to get round there and help out.

We took them an old gramophone record player and Junie said they appeared to be really happy together. And they were.

Raye was at Queenie's when Julie decided to make her entrance into the world and we followed them to St. Vincent's hospital in the Fulham Road where Julie was born on July 10, 1957.

Ivan's hopes of being fully accepted in the Wimbledon dressing room were not helped when Ronnie, Trevor and Geoff, all world-class riders at that time, learned that the Christchurch newspapers back home were full of stories about this kid Mauger, who was the real star. We all laughed, we knew it was really Ivan's doing, but we were sure he was making the bullets and his Mum was firing them.

He was a young man with an abundance of confidence who sometimes let his mouth run away with him before putting his brain into gear.

There was a time when my middle brother Murray, who was to become English Grasstrack Champion in two classes, had a practice spin at Wimbledon on a Tuesday morning after the Monday night meeting.

It was his first go on a speedway bike and he was doing okay when he crashed awkwardly and fractured his skull. We were all gathered around Murray waiting for an ambulance to arrive when Sprouts came up and said: "Briggo, you cannot believe what was wrong with my bike last night." Looking up, I barked at him: "Ivan, why don't you fucking piss off and go clean the bloody dressing room toilets."

Me with Jack (Milne) and Sprouts (Ivan Mauger).

Ivan Mauger, Ronnie Moore, me and Ove Fundin.

Once again, there was nothing that he had really done wrong other than open his mouth before his eyes. After a couple of frustrating and unsuccessful seasons in England the Mauger family returned to the southern hemisphere to live in Adelaide.

The Arunui track in Christchurch had closed down but Ivan certainly hadn't given up on his dreams of becoming not just a speedway rider but also a World Champion. He had the guts and determination to settle in Adelaide and be near to a speedway track where he could ride and rebuild his career.

Fate can often play a role in the direction our lives take and speedway in Great Britain was given a boost by the formation of the Provincial League, a second tier behind the National League in which Wimbledon operated. There was a new batch of promoters and a serious shortage of riders and Mike Parker, a Manchester-based businessman normally associated with stockcars, opened Newcastle and gave Ivan another chance. To say that he grabbed it with both hands is the understatement of that or any speedway era.

In retrospect, what happened to Ivan at Wimbledon was probably a good thing and his rejection at the South London track made him all the more determined to succeed the second time around. He was by now much smarter, his ambition burned as brightly as ever and he hadn't lost any confidence in his own ability.

Ivan was by now streetwise in many ways and we often laugh when he says the biggest decision he made was NOT to follow my example mechanically but to do exactly the opposite. What a bloody cheek!

Throughout his career Ivan compiled his own little black book which included all the various gear ratios he used at tracks in the UK and abroad, the best positions in the pits, the best place in the dressing rooms and his own dossier on referees. He was both thorough and meticulous in everything he did and it worked for him. I could never be like that. I only really got my head around it leading up to the 1972 World Final at Wembley where I out-thought and out-raced him but for all that I still didn't win.

From those early days at Wimbledon I really got to like Ivan as

I saw sides of him that nobody else did. He never believed that he lost a race, if defeated there was in his own mind a plausible reason why it had happened.

Ivan was the master starter, especially before touching the starting tapes was outlawed. He could dictate what happened at the starting gate, seemingly able to get inside the mind of the referee and get him to release the tapes when he wanted.

For many years the World Finals were refereed by Tore Kittelsen from Finland, who got the job because he was deemed to be neutral because there were no riders from his own country in the field.

When Ivan met local hero Zenon Plech in a championship-deciding race during the 1979 World Final in Katowice the referee released the tapes before the Pole had even reached the start line. I was watching from the centre green at the time and thought it was ridiculous but just one of those things. But with hindsight it was another example of Ivan out-witting the referee. He hadn't cheated, he had paid attention to detail and just anticipated what Kittelsen was going to do.

We had a great time on our first trip to Poland in the 1960s for an international meeting. Apart from anything else, it was also the first time that we encountered a woman referee.

As usual, Ivan was in and out of the tapes, driving her (and me) mad. We were sitting around during the interval and were starving (food wasn't in great supply in those days and what there was didn't appeal too much) when Mr. Organised Mauger pulled out a Mars bar and was about to eat it. We were all envious and I said: "Sprouts, I will give you ten quid for it."

"Briggo," he replied, "you haven't got enough money to buy it."

"Sprouts, you are such a miserable bastard. I will give you five quid for a bite. In your Rye House and Eastbourne days you would have shared it!"

We were still messing about, waiting for the meeting to restart, when there was a loud bang from the other side of the track. Turning to Ivan I said: "Bloody hell Sprouts, you've done it now, that woman referee has had enough of your bullshit and shot herself."

We were pretty depressed, having no food and racing on a track where you needed headlights to see let alone race. And, of course, we didn't have headlights. Sprouts just laughed, nothing could embarrass him, not even the thought of the referee committing suicide. Many is the time, having listened to some of the outlandish things that Sprouts has said, I have thought to myself: "That's just Ivan being Ivan".

We have been down the same road, both leaving Christchurch to travel halfway round the world seeking fame and fortune racing speedway. After he was settled and going well at Newcastle I saw a big change in him. To me he got better as he got more successful. And, when he told people how good he was, you had to take notice … because he was!

There have been several times during my life when I have thought that if I was in a serious jam and could call just one person it would be Ivan. Not simply because I have absolute faith that he would be there at the drop of a hat but that he would help find a way out.

Ivan Mauger – World Champion for the sixth time.

Ivan followed the trail blazed by first Ronnie Moore and then me and became the third Kiwi to win the World Championship. We have battled it out, head-to-head, in World Championships, league matches in the UK and in continental events across Europe. But that on-track rivalry, as fierce as it was, never dented our friendship forged over so many years.

We have also raced together for Great Britain and New Zealand and jointly promoted speedway events including the 1982 World Final at the Los Angeles Coliseum with Harry Oxley and Jack Milne. We have also staged meetings at Wembley, the Houston Astrodome and ran our own World Champion's troupe in South Africa, Australia and New Zealand, plus a number of grasstrack events in England.

We never had a formal agreement written down on a piece of paper. It wasn't necessary because we trusted each other implicitly. Our respective families were also close but we never lived in each other's pocket. Away from speedway we like different things. Ivan has never really shared my great love of riding all types of motorbikes. He is probably more at home on a jet-ski. I'm the opposite.

Ronnie had all the natural talent to race speedway, Ivan and I had to work much harder at it and that shaped the careers of both of us.

Ivan's life was 24/7 speedway and he worked out all the angles, particularly in World Championship qualifying events when he knew what position he needed to finish in order to have the best starting positions in the following round.

He even put a false number on his rear wheel sprockets to deceive anyone who might take a peek in the pits hoping to glean some useful information. Ivan was driven by a desire to win more speedway and longtrack gold medals than any other rider. That's what motivated him year after year and he didn't really care who he upset along the way.

My brother Murray, English 350cc and 500cc grasstrack champion.

My brother Murray led the way on grass and I was happy to follow

MY middle brother Murray came to England from New Zealand in 1955. He had finished his apprenticeship there as a boiler maker welder and, when he had done his time, he decided to race the grasstracks in England.

At that time you had the chance to pick between three or four meetings every weekend. He worked at various jobs while he got started. At first he had no transport so I used to take him to his races and it didn't take long for me to decide that if I was taking him to a grasstrack meeting I might as well race as well.

I did this for a couple of years and finished up doing a lot of English grasstracks with Murray. At that time the grass bikes were scramblers fitted with JAP engines. There were some special frames but they were of the scrambler-type design.

Hanging on the Wimbledon speedway workshop wall was a strong centre frame diamond for a speedway bike. It had hung there for a couple of years, then it disappeared and it was taken by my Wimbledon team-mate, Alfie Hagon, who put it to better use.

It was the start of Alfie's very successful Hagon Frames business, which for years has manufactured the very best grasstrack and longtrack frames. It was the start of the slider grass-speedway bike. The Hagon frames are still used by 95 per cent of those competing in the World longtrack championship. With it came the start of a new style grasstrack racing, but it was also the end of the thrilling hillside tracks which I loved, which were replaced by the large, roughly shaped speedway-type ovals tracks.

In the meantime Murray had started to race in grasstrack meetings in France and Germany. He was a real good rider and was crowned British Grass Track Champion for 350cc plus the 500 class as well at Mere in Dorset in 1958.

I was one of the first speedway riders to ride on the continental grasstrack scene, mainly through Murray who, when he was riding in France and Germany, had promoters constantly asking him about me riding at their events.

Once I started, I was increasingly in big demand on the continent. I had developed a large fan following and had now established a reputation and was recognised as a star international speedway rider. This made me a draw card for the promoters and clubs, which allowed us all to cash in.

Murray also tried his luck with speedway but a simple crash at Wimbledon resulted in a fractured skull. He recovered at the nearby Atkinson Morley hospital.

When I won at Wembley in 1957 I told television's David Coleman in an interview after the final that I had won the title for Murray who was still in hospital. I showed David my good-luck telegram that Murray had sent to me that morning. I carried it in my leathers as my good luck charm with me to my victory.

Murray was the first to taste the Briggs bad racing luck – it seemed that I had stolen most of the good stuff. He was in a serious car crash in France and lost an ear, which affected his balance, so he had to retire from racing. Later Murray started to help with my Jawa business as well as doing some of the meetings with me. But it wasn't always good as he would at times get more wound up than me.

When I started doing the continental racing it really made it tough to organise transport and the different bikes that were needed, plus it was much harder on the body. It did help make me a pretty adaptable type of rider and, if I had problems, I would just about always find a way to overcome them in the best way possible.

I was always rushing off after Swindon's Saturday night home meetings to ride at the big Sunday grass and sand-track meetings on the continent. It was hard on me and especially Junie, who was a great help to keep my head straight, away from the racing. But most importantly the extra strain and work to do this type of racing started to earn me some real money.

You had to set yourself a high standard and try to be the best at a track where they only staged one meeting a year, especially if you wanted to get invited back.

I was lucky as they normally started each meeting with the Bahn-Record attempt, which was for the fastest five riders from practice, who made a solo attempt to try and establish a new record time.

Even though I didn't always have the fastest bike, I'd grit my teeth and hang on with the throttle flat-out in a real balls-to-the-wall deal! If you did well in the Bahn-Record, it would make up for any problems you might run into in the meeting, and was a major help in securing a contract for next year.

One year I broke my arm just before I was due to race at the grasstrack at Osnabruck in Germany. They still paid me the same money just to start the first race and to appear in person at their track, even though I couldn't ride. It was really just to prove to the big crowd that I hadn't, in fact, gone to race somewhere else, and that I was actually injured!

It was all about building a good reputation for yourself and always giving full value for your start money. It started a trend when all of the world's best speedway riders rode at all of the big meetings with crowds as large as 30,000.

I am afraid that today that has all changed. Now the star riders are riding in Polish and Swedish leagues. I smile to myself when I hear that today's riders are tired, with all the air travel. I would have liked them to have accompanied us on a '1960's Briggs tour' for a month. As well as being the rider, which I found the easiest part, I was the mechanic, mostly the driver, then at the meeting I would grab a local to help fuel the bike and push start it for each race.

I have many nice friends over on the continent who were my mechanic for the day. Luckily, sometimes I was spoilt and could fly to a nearby city. I always got there just before the meeting but prior to riding had to take an engine out of my kit-bag and fit it to the bike. Then came the easy part, zapping around the track for a couple of laps, finding out the position of any dodgy bumps that could prove dangerous when racing. Then it was straight into the meeting proper.

It was tough riding at Swindon on a Saturday, getting to Heathrow for an early Sunday flight to whatever city was nearest to the venue at which I was competing – sometimes it could be 100 or more miles away – racing and then getting back to England for a Monday fixture at places like Exeter, Newcastle or Reading.

I can remember hurting myself before a Test match against the Russians at Exeter. I looped the bike on top of myself, doing a practice start as I went to the tapes for my first race. I was a bit sleepy at the time. A crash at Newcastle occurred when I had just returned that day from racing in America at Chicago. I reared in the middle of the corner and then, on one wheel, cannoned straight into the fence. God only knows what time zone my body thought it was in at that particular moment.

But the different types of racing always stimulated me. In England we raced in league meetings, which meant that you only had to race one or two stars each time. My continental races were always tough as 90 per cent of the time the meeting included all the current and past champions. So, World Championship or international meetings never really fazed me as I had a big meeting every weekend.

The trick was to get myself a sleep pattern that allowed me to get the best out of my body. Sleep is your battery charger. I can now sleep on a clothes-line at the drop of a hat and twenty minutes later I'm ready to roar.

Younger brother Wayne.

Wayne was heading for the top when cut down with injuries

10

WAYNE is my younger brother by 10 years and from a very early age was, like me, interested in motorcycles but never really had the money or a father to help kick-start his ambitions.

I first left our home in Christchurch when Wayne was just seven years old so wasn't around that much while he was growing up. And, as a consequence of our parents going their own ways, my position in the family changed dramatically. I was the eldest of the three boys and had to help steady the ship and my relationship with Wayne was often more like a father than a brother. In many ways he was more like a son who I wanted to look after, than a brother who I would go out with socially.

Wayne had an old 350cc BSA in New Zealand and was really competitive in what there is called miniature TT, a cross between scrambles and grasstrack.

This little story illustrates how seriously I took my role as a protective 'father' with Wayne. Junie was in hospital in Christchurch where our elder son Gary had just been born. It was a Sunday morning and I took Wayne to a miniature TT race near Waikuku Beach.

I made sure he had everything sorted and ready for the meeting, watched him practice and then raced back to the hospital for visiting time which began at 2pm to see Junie and our lovely new baby. Junie was so proud; you would have thought she was the only woman in the world to have given birth. It was great.

When visiting time was over – in those days, of course, even new fathers were only allowed on the ward at certain times – I jumped back in my car and ripped back to the races. When I got there the meeting was over and just a few stragglers were left cleaning up. Wayne was sitting on his fuel can waiting with his bike and gear.

Obviously, my first question was "how did it go?"

"Okay," he replied but that didn't really sound like Wayne. I could see that he had been crying and I quizzed him about what had happened. Reluctantly, he told me that Bob Burns, the father of one of the riders, had arranged for the track to be completely changed after practice because his son David wasn't the fastest, even though he had the latest Tribsa 500cc Triumph, and was slower than Wayne on his 350cc BSA.

Bob Burns was famous because he had broken the World Speed Record on his sidecar Vincent. He was a very arrogant Scot and a bully.

We packed up Wayne's gear and headed home. Wayne was no cry-baby and I realised Burns must have got to him badly as he wasn't very talkative throughout the journey. My fatherly instincts kicked in, I knew where Burns lived and went to his house and knocked on the door, which was opened by Mrs. Burns.

I asked to speak to her husband and when he appeared said: "Bob, what have you been up to with my Wayne?" He went into a rage and started to rant about "that little shit Wayne" who I had left sitting in our pick-up.

I accused him of being a bully and a coward and suggested he pick on someone his own size and with that he lunged at me. He had no chance and, like all bullies, after taking a couple of good hits he had had enough and went back inside, still mouthing threats.

"I'm sorry about that," I said to Mrs. Burns. "That's all right, Barry," she replied.

I went back to the pick-up where Wayne was waiting and we continued on our travels home. After that incident Burns was perfectly okay with both Wayne and I but he had done something that I hate to see fathers doing, becoming too involved in their kids' racing.

There is a line in the sand that should not be crossed but he did, I was not proud of what happened, but I was simply acting as Wayne's dad.

Wayne naturally wanted to follow Murray and me to England and, although he had never ridden a speedway bike, he too made the trip from New Zealand to give it a try. It was 1961 when Wayne, aged 16, arrived on English soil. I was embroiled in a row with Wimbledon promoter Ronnie Greene and the Speedway Control Board and didn't want them to know that I was back in the UK and was trying to lay low while I attempted to get a move away from the Dons.

Junie, Wayne and I were staying with a friend, Brian Johnson, in Kent, an area where nobody knew me.

We built a bike for Wayne and, luckily, Brian owned a grass field that was reasonably smooth. We found some bollards and made different sized and shaped tracks. Every time Wayne practiced we changed the track. Most days we would go there twice and never let the weather, even rain or hail, stop us.

I telephoned Ian Hoskins, pretending to be in New Zealand, to talk to him about Wayne. Ian agreed that Wayne could have a trial the morning after the next match at New Cross.

By this time Wayne was looking like a speedway rider and was really excited that he was, at last, going to have a spin on a proper track. We drove to New Cross and I was dropped off in a back street near the track. I climbed over the perimeter fence and lay down on the ground so I could see under a gate and get a view of the track.

There are many kids who want to be speedway riders who just go thrashing around and around without any real idea of what they are doing or trying to achieve.

A few sustain serious bangs that are not what you need when trying to learn the game. I had my own ideas about how a youngster should be taught and had applied them to Wayne's instruction. We had a plan despite not having a proper track at hand.

Now we were about to see whether I was right or wrong. Wayne was surprised how much easier it was to ride on a proper speedway track than on grass. His times were unbelievable, only half a second slower than some of the races the previous evening and he was on a slower, slicker track.

Ian, the son of the legendary Johnnie for whom I had ridden at New Cross the previous year, decided that he wanted Wayne to ride for him at Edinburgh in the Provincial League, the second division of racing in the UK. Also at Edinburgh was another Kiwi, Dick Campbell, a very classy and fast rider with whom I had spent a season in South Africa. Wayne would be in good hands.

In his first meeting Wayne won three races, admittedly in a weak event, but it did his confidence a power of good. He made good progress and by August was Edinburgh's top scorer and was a challenger for the Silver Sash match race championship – contested by the two highest scorers that night.

I also arranged for him to ride at Southampton, where I was now leading the Saints having secured my transfer from Wimbledon, St. Austell and also Shelbourne Park in Dublin. He was gaining experience all the time and also recorded three paid maximums (unbeaten by an opponent) in a good first season. Readers of *Speedway Star*, the sport's leading publication, voted Wayne 'Most Promising Novice' ahead of Terry Betts and Eric Boocock.

His 1962 season didn't start until June because Wayne required an operation for a detached retina. He started in style, with a paid maximum against Newcastle, won a World Championship round at Meadowbank and broke the track record at Stoke.

He came within a whisker of winning the Provincial League Riders' Championship at Belle Vue, but a 'desperate Dan' last corner by the experienced Len Silver snatched victory away. Wayne was on my bike and rode like a champion all night and it was only inexperience that cost him the title.

In 1963 he began like an express train, only dropping half a point in his first three home matches. In the Meadowbank round of the World Championship he was robbed of victory by an engine failure.

Edinburgh historian Mike Hunter writes: "However, luck then took a fierce turn against young Briggo. He sustained a broken collarbone at Southampton and after only one match back he crashed in a controversial second half race with Doug Templeton, breaking both wrists.

"The Monarchs' captain, Templeton, was strongly criticised. In hindsight that was where Wayne Briggs' rocket ship to stardom ended. He needed a trouble free run of injures to regain his confidence. But instead he suffered his worst injury – a broken thigh at Newport when his frame broke in half. Wayne moved to Poole in 1966, and then on to Exeter 1978–79 and was a fair heat leader for the Falcons.

"In 1970 he was signed by Kiwi Trevor Redmond as a Wembley Lion and had a reasonable year. For veteran fans the name of Wayne Briggs will long conjure up memories of a high-speed spectacular Kiwi kid with the padded shoulders and the wide handlebars who might have been a champion."

I agree with Mike's assessment and it is not just because I am his brother that I believe he was destined to be a truly great rider. It is a shame that we did not live nearer to one another – me in Southampton, Wayne in Edinburgh – because I am sure I could have helped his career more.

He missed having someone to follow and set standards as Ronnie Moore did with me. I would also have helped with his physical training that helps you in so many ways, including bouncing off the track!

Some say that you make your own luck but I am not so sure about that as Wayne had atrocious luck.

The broken collarbone at Southampton was an injury that should never have happened. Wayne was at the track with me and we arranged for him to have a second half (after the league match) race. I had my race and then handed over the bike for Wayne to use.

He was leading the race when the con-rod in the engine broke. Normally when this happens it just smashes the crankcase and the engine still rotates without any danger. But on this occasion the end of the con-rod jammed under the steel cylinder barrel and locked the engine which resulted in Wayne being thrown over the handlebars and breaking his collarbone.

Luckily, Dr. Carlo Biagi was attending and when he got to Wayne used scissors to prise open Wayne's jaw as he was in danger of biting off the end of his tongue. It was my bike that had caused Wayne's injury and had nothing to do with him. Was that luck or destiny?

Then came two broken wrists caused by a cowardly act and, what made it worse it was through his own Monarchs' team captain. After getting a few meetings under his belt following his painful recovery, one day the police came knocking on our front door in Southampton after midnight. On seeing them I thought the worst and that he must be dead. Once again it was nothing to do with Wayne, the frame simply broke off at the steering head, which caused him to crash and break his thigh. More niggling injuries followed.

On another occasion Wayne was in one hospital in Southampton with both eyes swathed in bandages while at the same time in another hospital our second son Tony was being born. I was a full-time hospital visitor, rushing from one to the other. Perhaps it was me who used up all the luck due to the Briggs family. When Tony started his speedway career he quickly found out that the 'luck bucket' was empty.

I only raced against Wayne a few times and was really nervous when he challenged me for the Silver Sash at Exeter when he was riding for the County Ground team. His career never fully blossomed and it is sad that the world at large never came to appreciate just how good a speedway rider Wayne Philip Briggs actually was.

"Believe me, Tone you don't really need a speedway track".

I knew it was coming ... Tony saying "I want to be a speedway rider"

11

TONY Briggs was born in Southampton on March 16, 1962. He was blue eyed, blond headed with the face of an angel. He was small and feisty. But within seconds he could produce a smile that could melt the heart of an ice maiden.

His brother Gary had my brown hair but had his mother's calm brown eyes. He loved books from an early age and, later, he became a reading buff who liked school.

Tony was more mechanically minded and had small, busy hands. He loved nothing better than pulling the alarm clock to bits to see what made it tick. Then he moved into electrics.

Whatever Gary did, Tony wanted to do as well. I spent so much time trying to tell him that his time was coming, or that he was too small at the moment. He accepted none of my answers graciously. School to him was a bind and he felt that it was just wasting his time.

Education was slow for him but it accelerated dramatically when Junie discovered by chance, after watching a documentary on television, that he was dyslexic. Listening to Tony being diagnosed, all his symptoms sounded very much the same as mine. I was dyslexic, too, but not as bad as him. I'd had these problems for years, without understanding the reasons why until Tony's diagnosis, so I had just worked my way around them.

Numbers were always a problem. I must always pay attention when taking down telephone numbers as my brain is ahead of my hand and I'm liable to write them down in the wrong order.

The first motorbike the kids had was a small Honda monkey machine. Gary rode it a few times but felt happier, if he had some spare time, kicking his football against our football-cricket wall that I had built at the end of the garden. Tony was different and, whenever he had time, it would be spent on the bike circling endlessly around the apple trees in our back garden at Chilworth on the outskirts of Southampton.

Our Alsatian, Lady, must have been the fittest dog by far in our area. She did every lap with Tony, always trying to bite the spinning front wheel of the speeding bike.

For quite a few years, the Briggs family went to California for about a month for our Christmas holidays. The weather was almost guaranteed to be sunny and clear at that time of the year. It was great for any outdoor activities, especially riding our motorcycles. And, of course, there were plenty of beautiful shops for Junie to indulge her passion for shopping.

For a couple of years in the 1960s I rode in the American short-track races. The bikes were half the capacity of my 500cc speedway bikes. The engines had been cannibalised, mostly, from motocross bikes. For a while I used a 250cc twin cylinder road race engine that screamed at 12,000 revs and was quite difficult to ride. The fans loved it, especially if I had enough courage to hold it flat out through the corners.

I rode for Yamaha in the States, so I got good deals on our play bikes. A Yamaha motorcycle at Christmas was always a very well received present, especially by the kids. Each year there was an upgrade. As the boys got older and stronger, they could handle the bigger, faster bikes as the engines got more powerful.

Junie's Christmas present was a beautiful new purple Yamaha

125cc electric start model, which came with a matching purple helmet. Junie's smile was big and radiant when she got her present but, for once, I thought that her smile seemed a little fake.

We found out after a couple of test rides in the local hills that it wasn't her cup of tea. Now, looking back, I didn't give her enough personal tuition. We had been around bikes for so long together that something made me think that she could ride one.

The purple Yamaha is now somewhere in Liberia as we took it there for jungle transportation. Junie, finally, did have some good times on her purple bike, not as the rider but as a 'pillion mate'. There were three motocross tracks within half an hour's drive of our place at Dana Point so, if we wanted, we could ride three days or nights every week.

The three of us rode at Escape Country on most weekends. The track was set in beautiful, rolling hills. I rode under the name of Johnnie Hoskins which, hopefully, would stop people possibly recognising my name and putting pressure on my kids.

It was always just fun time when we raced at these meetings. The deal was that half the field received trophies, so the boys have quite a few lying around in California. 'Johnnie Hoskins' even got a few. It was heaven-sent for me to be able to get on a motorcycle and not have to win to pay the rent.

The best times we had on our bikes was on our trips to Baja, which is situated a couple of hours south of Dana Point. Our leader was Bruce Brown whose two boys, Dana and Wade, were just about the same ages as Gary and Tony so they all got on well together.

Bruce made the best surfing movie called *Endless Summer*. He was a very good rider himself and, later, made a very successful motorcycle movie called *On Any Sunday*.

Our two-day trips were great adventures and, after about 100 miles, we would stay overnight at Mike's Sky Ranch, which was in the middle of nowhere. It was great fun for most of the time. Trying to keep control of four kids determined to have fun was not always easy. It was an ever-changing adventure as we all sped along on what was called a road. It was, in fact, just two tyre tracks worn in the sand over the course of time. It wandered through the most enormous outcrops of rocks and boulders.

It was just like the old 'B' rated cowboy movies from yesteryear. This was where the baddies would jump from the top of the giant boulders onto the top of the stagecoach which was loaded with gold for the wages of the people of Tombstone City!

Speedway crept into Tony's life when Lance King's father, Don, gave him a small bike that he manufactured in Northern California. The day we went up to the factory to collect the bike, which had a 200cc Triumph engine, it was teeming with rain. But that didn't put off Lance or Tony from going out for a ride and they both showed great skill in the way they rode the slippery, wet track. Most importantly, they both just wanted to ride. They had big hearts, matching smiles and showed no fear in the atrocious conditions.

Tony was now finishing his last two years of education and had worked really hard to follow Gary to Millfield School, in Somerset, on a bursary. Gary won a bursary for his academic and his all-round sporting abilities while Tony had to get his grades higher to follow him but he buckled down and achieved a successful level.

I had found it difficult to barter for the education of my kids but the headmaster at Millfield realised it wasn't hot air when I told him that both boys had to have the same chance so a deal was struck for Tony to follow Gary there a year later. The school had a reputation that male or female students, who were gifted academically or good at sports but didn't have the necessary money, could still become pupils.

Mary Rand, the 1964 Olympic long jump gold medal winner, who came from nearby Wells, was helped when she was a young girl at Millfield. The expertise and the school facilities helped her to be the champion she became.

When their schooling was coming to an end, pupils were asked by the visiting careers officers what they wanted to do to earn their living. Most of the boys wanted to follow their father's footsteps into the family business. Others wanted to be bankers, lawyers, building contractors, plus many other various types of employment.

Headmaster Colin Atkinson smiled when he heard of Tony's

ambitions. He knew him because his wife had told him he was sweet on their daughter, Sally. Colin flashed a big smile when he said: "That will be a first for Millfield. We have produced many sporting champions, but we have never, ever produced a speedway racer before."

Not long before finishing school, Tony hit me with the words that I always knew were coming. The only thing I didn't know was when, but now the time had finally arrived. "Dad, I want to be a speedway rider," he told me. I already knew my answer.

He certainly didn't give me much room in which to manocuvre. The type of young man that Tony had grown into would be a speedway rider with, or without, me. Junie would have been much happier if he had chosen another type of profession but getting him to change his mind would have been like trying to stop an avalanche with a pudding spoon.

I told him: "Right Tony, this is the deal. For two years you do what you are told, without argument. Then you can take on the world by yourself. One thing to remember is that being a speedway rider is a real tough deal.

"You have seen up close the endless hours of work needed. The travel sounds great, but mostly it's rough travel, in cars or backs of vans. The most important thing is to keep focused and always remember that it's very dangerous. But first you've got to organise yourself."

We had a close family friend called Kevin Holden, who was riding speedway for Poole at the time. Tony replied: "Briggo, I've talked to Kevin about it, and he's going to teach me all the best ways to clean and maintain my bike. School is finishing soon, and he said that I can go to a couple of meetings to help him. This will help me to learn about the deal from close up."

Kevin worked for me as well. His speedway racing was going really well and he had become good enough to represent England on a couple of occasions. He and Tony got on together like a house on fire.

At this time, Junie and I were living in Germany and the boys were boarding at Millfield. We left for Germany at about 4.30 on a Wednesday afternoon. The last thing I did before driving to

London Airport was to have a chat with Kevin about what jobs he was going to do for me the next morning. Then we waved goodbye.

We arrived at our flat in Holzwickede at about 9.30 that evening. As I opened the front door, I could hear the phone ringing. I rushed in to answer it. I was dumbfounded. My side of the conversation was only a yes and a no.

Junie could see immediately from my face that there was something seriously wrong. She stiffened as she thought that it was some kind of trouble with our boys back in England. Putting down the phone I was virtually speechless. It came out as a low whisper: "Kevin has just been killed at Poole."

I went and sat down. Junie was also in shock. But she handled these things better than me, she understood me. After a few minutes she appeared with a cup of tea. I was numb with pain. Why? Why? Why? He did nobody any harm, he had a lovely family. Junie and I would have been proud to call Kevin our son. I just could not understand. Why God, why?

By now it was 10.15 and we knew we must tell Tony and Gary before they read or heard about it, especially Tony. We figured out that at this time of night the boys would be in bed. There was no way that they would find out about Kevin tonight, so we decided to ring them at 6.45 in the morning.

A sleepy Tony came to the phone. When I told him softly, the line went deathly quiet. "Tony, are you there?"

"Yes Dad, I'm just thinking," he said.

"Tony, it's terrible I know. But what happens to you is in the lap of the gods, and I'm afraid there is nothing we can do about it. We were lucky to have known Kevin, as he was such a lovely boy. Let me speak to Gary, and I'll ring you tonight," I said as I coughed and cleared my throat.

It was a watershed for Tony, and it lived with him for a very long time. We thought that he might even reconsider his decision to be a speedway rider. But, of course, he didn't change his mind.

To get started in speedway Tony needed a couple of bikes that would do plenty of laps with the minimum of maintenance. We put together an old two-valve Jawa grasstrack bike and also a two-valve Jawa speedway bike that would run on the smell of an oily rag and was virtually maintenance free.

Weymouth was our nearest speedway track and it was a couple of hours away. Luckily Harry Davis, whose son John was a rider, owned the speedway so it was possible for us to go there at almost any time.

Travel time was valuable riding time lost. When you are starting out, you need as much time on the bike as possible. What you are trying to achieve is to train your brain to accept that it's a completely natural thing to ride a sliding speedway bike at speed, but most importantly in control.

One of the biggest questions that must be answered and once again to be firmly established in your brain is at exactly what point is the control of the bike suddenly taken out of your hands by outside forces. You must find and establish this point in your brain. This is your very own personal monitor and if you overstep it, you are going to crash.

The very best riders in all types of motorcycle racing can find this point quickly. Then they can ride on this ragged edge whenever they need. Tony had to get his brain to understand and accept this if he really wanted to be the very best, but this certainly wasn't going to happen on a few quick trips to Weymouth.

Rider Bernie Leigh came up with the answer. His friend, Graham Biles, owned a pig farm on the back road to Swindon and this was only a relatively short drive from home. So the pig farm was to be the pad for the launching of Tony Briggs into the speedway world. This was where he started to learn his trade. The big minus was that our workshop was the most foul smelling in the world, there is nothing worse than the smell of pig shit! It was like glue. It stuck everywhere.

The most critical problem though, was that Tony was very slim and riding hard through the bumps was really tough on his small body. I could tell when he started to tire and I would get him to stop immediately. You don't learn anything when the bike starts taking control. If you do too much, and don't rest, your recovery time takes so much longer so you finish up with less proper practice time. After a day's hard practice, it's fantastic to get home, unload, and then have that heaven-sent hot shower.

Dinner would be followed by all of us moving to the television room to catch up on the day's news and to simply enjoy our family being together. It was not a frequent happening, though. The news is rarely very happy. One day it was Italy's turn when a massive earthquake flattened houses and flats in the north. Hundreds were feared dead.

Looking at our family sitting together safe and secure in our lovely home made you feel sad for all of the suffering Italians. They were in turmoil with major problems. It was like being on another planet here at home. Boy, weren't we lucky.

For no particular reason my gaze fell on our family's baby, Tony. It is amazing that his grubby face from fifteen minutes ago is now absolutely glowing. It's amazing what soap and water can do … it's magic. Looking at him watching the TV, I think: "What does his life have in store for him?"

Tony had a hard row to hoe, following me into speedway. He's a better rider than me at this stage. Most importantly, he wants to be a winner, no matter how hard he's got to work for it. I can see myself mirrored in his passion and desire.

I wonder if he can have the luck that I've enjoyed all through my racing life. Or have I used up the full quota of the Briggs fortune? I felt a little tired after the early start and all the running about. Plus it's amazing just how much it drains your nervous energy by just standing watching your flesh and blood putting it on the line.

Tony's speedway career was planned to start in New Zealand after the English summer but it needed handling carefully. He had never raced properly so, mounted on his old pig farm grasstrack Jawa that by now had done a million miles, he decided he would like to do a couple of local grass meetings, which I thought was a great idea. The buzz was around speedway that the young Briggs was riding, and I thought it was bad for him to start before he was ready.

He wanted to look good right from the word go, so we came up with a plan which was a variation on the Johnnie Hoskins theme I had used in California. Tony had an old set of leathers from American Brad Oxley before he grew into a giant. He had used them when he was a kid. Being an American, the Oxley name was plastered all over them.

Tony needed a bit of incognito racing to get him going. Too many times I have seen good riders, mostly young, do badly when they have gone to a track for trials. There could be various reasons but the main one was simply that they were not ready for it.

The problem is that if you don't do well after showing your hand it is virtually impossible to get another trial at that track for quite some time – if ever. We thought to put him in the Oxley leathers was the answer. Mainstream speedway wouldn't know about it. So now we had a Brad Oxley with an English accent

Tony didn't set any houses on fire, but he did have some really good races. It was a really good experience for him to start with ten other riders, especially in an organised atmosphere. The only thing that didn't seem to come to him naturally was making starts, but to make a judgment when he was mounted on his 'pig farm' special would be unfair.

The 'Gypsy Briggs Clan' headed off to New Zealand for the launch of Tony's speedway career. We rented a house in Christchurch and settled into the most normal family lifestyle that we had enjoyed for a long time. It was great that for a change everything wasn't geared around me. Now it was Tony's turn.

Gary and Tony got jobs with my best mate, Tommy McCleary, at his motorcycle shop in Christchurch. Gary was in the spares department with Bobo Valentine who would later come to England to try to break into speedway at Swindon.

Tony worked on cleaning and getting bikes to look a million dollars to sell to potential customers. They both loved working there.

Tony's first ever speedway race was in my home town of Christchurch. Nobody had any idea of how good or bad he was so he was put into the novice races on his first night and won them all in a canter. He was moved up into the 'B' grade and, once again, he won all of his races. Finally, he was in the First Division as each week he went up a division. Nobody realised just how good he was, not even us.

The World Championship started with the South Island Final

qualifier in Christchurch. Tony had the chance of riding in it in only his fourth official speedway meeting but it wasn't going to be that easy. Some of the local riders were up in arms as the story had been put around that he wasn't a Kiwi. True, he was born in England. But, unbeknown to them, he had a New Zealand passport which he only produced at the last minute.

It was nice to see who was for you, or against. The most important thing was that he wanted to be a Kiwi. The strangest thing was the revolt was led by an Englishman. One of Tony's strongest backers was Kiwi Graeme Stapleton. Tony was a competitor against him but Staps had known him from when he was a baby and his feelings were if the kid was good enough leave him alone.

He finished in third place but soon learned a lesson when paid his prize money. He thought that now he was a speedway rider he was on the gravy train, he was on his way to a fortune. He was thinking about what type of car he should buy.

Payout time arrived and winner Larry Ross received $45. Ivan Mauger was also in the lolly as his second place finish earned him $43! Tony won $41 so he soon figured that his car would have to wait.

Next was the New Zealand Final at Western Springs, in Auckland, and he qualified for the Australian Final in Adelaide, Australia. David Bargh, another 16-year-old from the North Island, joined him on the trip to Aussie. But when they had arrived the FIM (Federation International Motorcycle) made, in all their wisdom, one of their normal ridiculous decisions that Tony and David were too young to race.

Okay, there is a rule that a rider of 16 is too young to race and could possibly be dangerous. But the FIM, true to form, then said: "They can ride but their points don't count."

Please show me the logic in that. The guts were knocked out of the two boys who came into speedway to race, not to play games.

California was the place where we decided to sharpen Tony's ability

12

WE had to decide, after the visit to New Zealand, on the next step in Tony's speedway career. There was no shortage of options because considerable interest was being shown by the top clubs in England. But we felt he needed more experience before committing himself to the world's toughest league, so it was California where the Briggs tour descended next.

There were four tracks running weekly so there was the chance for Tony to get plenty of racing experience if he could be reasonably successful.

It was really important to have fine control of your bike on the small American tracks because they only measured around 200 yards so there was very little room for man and machine.

A small track created many problems. It was very easy to be knocked off your bike when you were in a bunch of riders or to fall off when your piece of track was taken away. Laying your bike down to avoid trouble was seldom seen so a rider would often find himself excluded for doing it. Speeds were relatively low so, although there was plenty of contact and quite a few crashes, there were very few bad injuries, although good bike control was always at a premium.

We lived in an old ranch house owned by our friend, Bruce Brown. We had five miles of dirt track from the main road to get to the ranch so there were very few distractions for Tony. We had our motocross bikes with us, so when we were fed up with working we could slip on a jacket and a pair of boots to have a good ride in the surrounding hills and fire-breaks.

The sun was just going down one night when Tony thought he'd go for a five-minute ride before bed. He only wore his helmet and he came back ten minutes later covered in blood. He had unloaded in the rocks, cutting and grazing his body, arms and legs. It was more than ten miles to the nearest chemist so we had to take care of him ourselves. He looked like a Red Indian after we had covered him in the bright red of the antiseptic Mercurochrome. The stuff really smarted as well but the boy was tough and rode for a couple of days without complaint.

Tony was charging a little too hard at the start of his California tour but was making good progress.

One bad decision, which was probably my idea, was to return to England for him to compete in the 350cc British Grasstrack Championship. The thinking was that it would be a good thing for him to get a title under his belt.

It was a good idea in some ways but leaving California for England every six weeks or so did his American racing no good. The tracks there were all about tight control and discipline whereas the English grasstracks were much faster and a rider had to let the bike have its head at times in order to keep his speed up.

It would take Tony a couple of weeks to settle down again when he returned to California where he qualified for the US Championships at Costa Mesa. He won his first two races to be the joint leader but a couple of bad starts saw him fall down the leader board and he finished with a well-earned sixth place.

The British Grasstrack Championship was lost with an horrendous start in the final. But, as usual, Tony battled away to take second place. We had an ironic laugh together, as whoever remembers who finished second in anything?

Tony went back to New Zealand for the English winter and qualified for the Australasian Finals but he didn't go through to the next round for various reasons. Mainly it was his starting but the competition was also very hot in the Southern hemisphere at that time.

The point was illustrated by the fact that Tony needed a race-off against top Aussie Phil Crump for the last qualifying place at Christchurch. Crump took him seriously enough to borrow a bike from Billy Sanders, who had already qualified on it, and he beat Tony. It was time to leave sunny New Zealand for the cold of England. Tony didn't even notice the weather. He had the biggest challenge of his young life coming up.

The build-up to the 1980 season posed the difficult question of where was the best place for Tony to ride? Two top English clubs were applying a lot of pressure and offering him good financial deals. But the biggest consideration at this point of his career was to decide what was best for his future.

Nobody had seen how good he was, mainly due to his starting, which was suspect. He was in a terrible position because if he was a big winner people would say: "So he should be with all his dad's money." He had taken some stick like that in America, not always to his face. But, I must say, he stuck in there, even after some pretty good bangs, some being unnecessary.

One day I was reading an article in a baseball book about an American doctor, named Don Teig, whose business was named The Institute for Sports Vision. It was amazing what the eyes can compute. He told the story of the New York Yankees star, Ted Williams, whose eyes were so good he could see which way the logo was spinning on a ball that was travelling at well over a hundred miles an hour.

We visited Dr Teig and he thought Tony's problem at the start of races was related to his dyslexia. He gave him exercises to help his eyes and reaction times. The most unusual was playing table tennis in the dark apart from a strobe light. It was a 'now you see it, now you don't' effect. I think it did improve Tony – but I know that it definitely helped his table tennis skills!

I knew we could create a big problem if we kept talking about

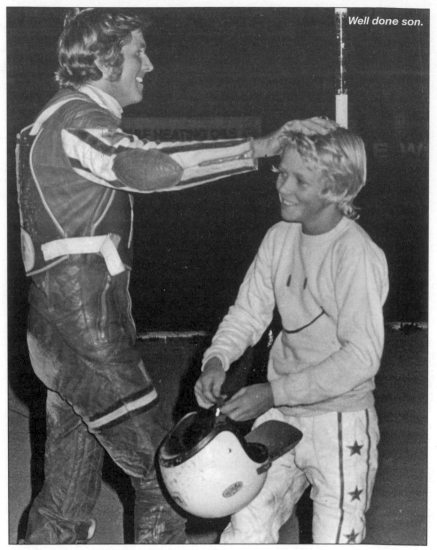

Well done son.

Tony's bad starting because it was liable to become an obsession and that was exactly what we didn't want to happen. If he had stayed in California in the 1979 season, and not kept moving backwards and forwards to England for the grasstrack, I am sure he would have been a big winner in the States by the end of the 1980 season. It was finally time to take the bull by the horns and decide on England or California and, after taking a good look at all the pros and cons, it was England that won the day. The most important question then was where would be the best track for him to start his career.

At this stage, I felt that Tony needed space from me and one of the major reasons for choosing Reading Racers was that my close friend, Terry Betts, rode for them. I felt that Tony would be in safe hands with Bettsy around. Unfortunately, Tony was stuck with me as his father. It helped him in many ways, but it needed special efforts at times for him to overcome the minuses.

What engine he should use was a problem. I was the Jawa dealer, plus at the time we had our own Briggo four valve conversion engine. Using either one made financial sense and it was finally decided to use our Briggo motor.

So, with all the decisions put into place, we waited excitedly for the 1980 season to start.

Tony Briggs was finally launched into English speedway in a blaze of publicity and with the backing of a lucrative Fabergé sponsorship deal.

When everything had been planned, signed and sealed, Reading decided to change their team manager to Dave Lanning. I didn't know Dave that well but there always seemed to be a lot of noise and razzmatazz around him. Full marks to him, though, because he turned out to be good for Tony and was really fair to him.

The big blow for us was the loss of Terry Betts, who had decided to retire. As a father I had to keep my nose out of things. I felt that Tony was suffering because he had the Briggs name. Bettsy would have taken a short cut through all the crap and got the major problems sorted. It would have made it much easier and better for Tony, but we had to soldier on.

Also, with the benefit of hindsight, the engine choice should have been Weslake, the same as the top boys were riding. When Tony had been faced with the decision on the type of grasstrack frame he should use, Don Godden made him an offer that you would think he couldn't refuse – free frames. Godden was one person who saw his potential and realised just how good Tony was on the grasstrack.

But this time the right decision was made on merit, not price. You can buy the same frame as used by the World Champion and then, at the end of the season, it is still worth a minimum of 50 per cent of what you paid for it.

So if you are using the same frame as the champion, then the results are down to you. You have had no advantage, but most importantly you are not at a disadvantage. Tony had managed to sneak up to Belle Vue for a second half race at the end of the 1979 season. He managed to beat their young hero, Andy Smith, to win his first trophy in English speedway. Tony told me that his throttle had stuck. I smiled and told him: "Just don't tell anyone."

Racing at Reading was tough. Tony looked as though he was over the hump at times as he scored some good points but then, bingo, a couple of crashes would put him back. I watched and I could see that the Briggs name was not always good for him. We really missed Terry Betts. I watched as a couple of his partners would stick Tony on the outside gate when his strength was on the inside.

Then, on numerous occasions when he made a good start on the outside, his partner wouldn't look and close the gap against the fence, not only slowing him but also letting the opposition through. One night I heard his partner tell him that he must be patient and serve his time.

I must say I never heard him complain, he just got on with the job. Many was the time I thought to myself: "I wish I was riding, I would quickly sort it out."

Tony was still very small and had enough trouble getting his racing on an even keel without having to sort people out. Bettsy, where were you when we needed you? One night Swindon were racing at Reading and Steve Gresham, the American bully boy, whacked Tony in the first corner. I helped him to the pits with my arm around him as he was a little groggy. I was carrying Tony's crash helmet in my other hand.

As we came to the pit gate Gresham was waiting in a confrontational pose. I wagged my head as we went past him, which was the red rag to the bull. Our brave toughie grabbed me around the throat, ripping off a gold chain, which Junie had given me for my birthday.

I thought Gresham was smarter than he acted, you don't mess

with someone's own flesh and blood. He got in the first move, but then a swirl of Tony's crash hat swinging around his head called for his quick retreat. Then our hero called the police to see me, but when they heard the full story they laughed.

I remember racing against Gresham at Newport. He was easy to beat because of the way he rode. His deal was to run you down so I would do something different on every corner and straight. He would set his sights on me but I would be in a different place. It's really hard to hit a moving target.

After beating him twice at Newport, we met again at Hull. I beat him in our three races, which really drove him mad. He came up beside me on the inside after my third win. He laid his bike low and then gassed it, covering me in dirt.

I just laughed to myself under my helmet and uttered: "Are you happy now you fucking idiot?"

Tony was going great guns away from the Reading environment and had no problems qualifying for the World Under 21 championship. We were together at Moorwinkelsdamm, in Germany, for a qualifying meeting and he was well on the way to winning it.

His next race could swing it his way as he was against his arch-rival, Tommy Knudsen. Tony was off gate four, which we had looked at during the interval. We'd decided the best run to the first corner was from the outside of the gate. But, for some reason, Tony decided to start on the inside of the gate. He missed the start but produced a storming ride to pass Knudsen.

He was well clear when, suddenly at the start of the last lap, his bike ground to a halt. I went onto the track to collect it. The tank was empty so obviously his idiot bloody mechanic hadn't fuelled his bike. As I was the mechanic I felt terrible.

I felt even worse on leaving the track with his bike. The German official demanded a fuel sample. He didn't understand simple English as I told him three times that there was 'no fuckin' fuel to test.' The German fool just kept on but, luckily, Tony saw what was going on and took his bike from me. He qualified easily and I was hoping I was going to be sacked – but no such luck!

Tony was racing for Reading at Wimbledon just a week before

the Under 21 final. It was the second half and he was still racing his heart out when his footrest was caught under the fence on the back straight. He was pitched over the handlebars and was unconscious on the track for a few minutes as there was no ambulance present. My mate, Eddie Toogood, took all the books and *Speedway Star* magazines out of the back of his Citroën Safari to lie Tony down and take him to hospital. He was in for two days but X-rays revealed no broken bones.

I said to him as we left the hospital: "Bloody hell, you must be bionic." He was a tough boy and, even in pain, you saw where his focus lay when he said: "Hell Dad, I really thought that I'd messed up for the final in Pocking next week."

There was never a tougher Under 21 Final as the field included a couple of riders who were to become World Champions. Tony was right in the thick of the action but this meeting again showed that he should have been on a Weslake engine like the rest of the top contenders.

The track was slick, which was unlike a normal German track. Tony was a lightweight so it was very hard to stop wheel spin from the starts. We had made and fitted a retard system to the ignition, which made it a little better.

But, in his last couple of heats, God didn't help us as some drizzle made the conditions even slicker. Tony had been able to pass until then but the dampness and his not-so-good starts meant he started to drop points. Whichever way you looked at it was an unbelievable achievement as in the last week the kid had spent two days in hospital. He had exactly what it needed to be the very best. All that he wanted was a touch of good luck.

Danish star Knudsen took the title with 14 points. Tony was second with 12, one more than Dennis Sigalos and Erik Gundersen. This meeting helped Tony's confidence and he finished with an average of just under five points per meeting for Reading. If his stoppages and crashes were removed from that figure, it was a good first season. I'm sure that he did better than I did in my initial year at Wimbledon.

Tony with England's Michael Lee in 1980.

TONY BRIGGS FABERGÉ RACING

I watched Tony crash but surely it wasn't a serious accident

13

TONY'S speedway racing was making steady progress. He had a great time from May to July 1981 with flashes of brilliance which showed there was an underlying talent just waiting to break out. In May he was New Zealand's only heat winner and top scorer in the World Team Cup at Reading but it was a very under par performance by the Kiwis.

His grasstrack racing was going unbelievably well, he was unbeaten in two European Championship qualifying rounds in Germany. He had spent a week at Manfred Poschenrieder's workshop at Kempten where master tuner Wolfy had been breathing extra horsepower into Tony's Briggo engine.

The best grass circuit by far in Bavaria was at Bad Waldsee, where there was a purpose-built grasstrack arena. The promoters decided to make it tough on Egon Muller, the German World Champion, and Tony, because they were getting big 'start' money and they wanted to make them work hard for it. They decided that the pair must take the worst start positions for all their races.

I believe that in my many years of racing in Germany Egon was by far and away the best grasstrack rider I have ever seen, ahead of riders such as Simon Wigg, Karl Maier and Kelvin Tatum.

Tony was absolute perfection that day at Bad Waldsee. He missed most of the starts but went past all the top riders, including Egon who was on the microphone after every race telling his German public of his supposed problems, blaming everything but never admitting Tony's excellence. No matter what bike Egon used that day, he couldn't beat our boy. They could have kept racing till the cows came home because he wouldn't have beaten Tony on this form.

The big final, with all the best riders, was a non-event. Tony finally made a start and was off into the sunset. Poor Egon wasn't even close enough to swallow his dust. Poschenrieder gave the Briggs contingent a laugh when he translated the report in the local paper. It read: 'Young New Zealander Tony Briggs crushed World Champion Egon Muller in front of thousands of his German fans.'

Tony's all-round racing was improving all the time. We had decided to delay his first longtrack meeting where racing is on a well groomed surface of a 1,000 metres horse racing track. If you haven't got a good bike here then you are history.

Longtrack is one of the nicest rides that you can possibly have on a motorcycle. It's really fast and when you are out in front, breathing fresh air, it's exhilarating. You simply let the bike have its head while you gently guide it to keep your speed to the maximum. But, miss the start, and it's a nightmare. The dirt coming from the back wheel of the bike in front is propelled at you at more than 100mph and is like riding straight into a wall. The speed of the dirt hitting the rider, plus the speed of the rider hitting the dirt, causes an explosion big enough the split the atom!

The longtrack hopes of many riders have perished because of the flying dirt. In our early days we would stuff magazines inside our leathers to try to stop the damage to our bodies. You have a minimum of five lenses in your goggles but when the dirt lands it sticks like shit to a blanket and it's total blindness. Try going down a motorway at 100mph in the rain and turn off your wipers. That's only water, imagine the same thing but with dirt.

Damon Hill, who was a really good motorcycle racer as well as being Formula One World Champion, told me how he would have loved to have ridden on a longtrack. Maybe he's lucky that he hasn't. Even so, I am going to beg, borrow or steal a bike for one last lap at Muhldorf longtrack before I kick the bucket. I might even invite Damon along.

Tony's longtrack debut will always be engraved in my heart. Thank God his mother, Junie, wasn't present. We had held him back for a year from doing his first meeting but an opportunity presented itself for him to race in Muhldorf, a beautiful city in Bavaria.

We hired an engine from Fred Arbel, an old friend from speedway and longtrack racing. Tony was already great on the grasstracks so I figured that the extra speed wouldn't worry him. Fred's workshop was just over the road from the Muhldorf track which was just as well as we only got the engine from him ten minutes before practice started.

I thought, mistakenly, that things would be different by bringing some new organisation into the Briggs camp. However, hiring an engine brought the same old problems, just in a different language.

Some people in speedway, including those around Tony, thought I was pushing him too hard. The fact was that he didn't need any pushing, if anything he needed to put on the brakes a little now and again. He started well in his first practices, half sitting up down the straights, just like a speedway rider on his first longtrack. As he got faster he got lower and lower to help to lessen the wind resistance.

I was lulled into a false security after practice. Things looked good. You don't want trouble in longtrack racing because the danger level is much higher when you are going so fast. I had time to walk the pits and have a bowl of goulash soup. There was a chance to have a laugh with Sprouts, as we call Ivan Mauger, have a cup of tea with Simon Wigg and a chat with Alois Weisbock, whose home track is Muhldorf.

It was good to be alive. Fred was working his backside off and I was glad to be surplus to requirements. The meeting was due to start in a couple of hours. Suddenly, there was some activity in the pits. Shawn Moran had just arrived after racing in England the night before and was getting ready for his free practice.

I was talking to Christian Kalabis, at his Bahnsport stand, when our conversation was broken by a bike on the track. That will be Shawny practicing, I thought. But no, wait a minute, there were two bikes starting out so I strolled over to the track fence to look.

Two riders roared past the fence just in front of me at over 100mph. I couldn't identify them until they went down the back straight. Bloody hell, that's my Tony behind Shawn. At the end of the straight Shawn, who hadn't warmed up to the speed of the track yet, sat up and slowed going into the pit corner. It was obvious he didn't know Tony was behind him.

Tony now thought he was a longtracker but his speed was so great the distance between him and Shawn decreased alarmingly. He was head down, arse up and a little slow in recognising the danger of the rider in front of him.

I had done many years of longtrack racing and had never seen anyone lay down their bike at 100mph. As soon as he did it, Shawn was gone and out of danger but the same couldn't be said of Tony. Was there enough track left for him to scrub off his high speed before hitting the solid, hardwood fence?

My heart stopped and I think everything else in my body stopped, too, as I watched Tony and his bike gobbling up the distance to his Waterloo, the fence. Then I was breathing again. It was just like magic as the sliding twosome finally stopped a foot from impact. I let out a big sigh and relaxed. Now, maybe, I could settle down to enjoy the afternoon's racing.

When I got back to the pits, everyone was putting the finishing touches to their bikes. Tony was sitting there cleaning his goggles. He looked up, he knew exactly what I was thinking and gave me his heart-warming but sheepish 'I've done bad' smile. The ten riders had left the pits for the start and all the crews jostled to get a decent view of their man's first race.

What a baptism for Tony's first taste of longtrack. As far as I could see, he was on gate eight. The roar of the half-silenced engines reached a crescendo and died off as everyone dropped their clutches for the start. As they reached the corner, Tony was in a good position on the outside. I looked as he swept past most of them on the outside. Then, suddenly, a bike appeared out of the pack but it wasn't going around the track. It was like a rocket launch, a missile, and the bike must have shot ten feet in the air.

I didn't need telling who it was. I pushed my way through the pit crowd to get on to the track. I must have broken all running records, as I sprinted about half a mile to the scene of the accident.

Although I was having trouble breathing, my brain was in gear. I knew 100 per cent that the accident had been caused by the wall of flying dirt. It hits you and the lights go out. You have no idea where you are, keeping in mind that you are travelling at over 100mph.

This is what I had been trying to explain to Tony the previous week. I felt like an old nagger, but it normally only takes one practical demonstration to catch your attention and then you know exactly what you were being nagged about. I arrived at the accident and said to him: "You all right, love?"

He'd had plenty of crashes in his short racing career, but this time the message had got through to him big time. He was shaking like a leaf in a strong breeze, I'd never seen him affected by a crash this way before. I simply wanted to take him in my arms and cuddle him, like we had done many times before when he'd fallen out of a tree or hit the deck trying to roller skate. He just needed a big cuddle, but big boys don't do that, do they?

I looked at him, gave him a warm smile and a wink. I ruffled his hair as I went to see how the bike had done in the battle. Both were okay and were ready for the re-run of the race. Tony is an amazing kid; his slim body houses an enormous heart and he is virtually impossible to deflate. But this high-speed crash got to him, and the message was loud and clear. You are in a very dangerous sport, so use your head.

He gained enough points to make it to the final which dazzled me, especially after his couple of mishaps. He was looking like a seasoned longtracker in the final when he grabbed third place behind Alois Weisbock, the current World Champion, and was chasing the hell out of Uncle Ivan (Tony and Gary's nickname for

Just the right amount of traction.

Ivan Mauger) for second place. We drove out of beautiful downtown Muhldorf very relieved, a happy father and son, with many valuable lessons learned.

Tony was gifted as a grasstrack racer but there was another young gun, Simon Wigg, arriving on the scene. If you had the statistics on the results of their head-to-head encounters in their first few years, Tony would come out the winner. Simon rang him once as he needed riders for a trip to a longtrack meeting in Estonia. It was after Tony had broken his neck and he was only riding part time so Simon let him borrow one of his bikes.

Wiggy told me the story, laying it out as a joke. He laughed: "Briggo, I loan that little bugger of yours one of my bikes for the

1,200 metres meeting in Estonia, and what does he do? He beats me, in the Bahn-record, what an ungrateful little sod."

They were big mates until Simon died in 2000. Full marks to Tony, he was full of compassion and didn't like to see what was happening but he showed the same trait as in his racing. He hung in there and spent a lot of time making Wiggy laugh, which came as second nature to him. We still have a beautiful letter from his brother, Julian, which makes me very proud of Tony.

I used to promote Golden Greats meetings and once I had P-O Serenius, the World Ice Racing Champion from Sweden, doing a record attempt on his ice bike at Coventry. I introduced Tony to him and he told me as he shook his hand: "I know him although we have never met. I saw him demolish Egon Muller at Bad Waldsee. It was the best grasstrack performance I have ever seen."

Tony smiled, and even blushed a little, as he mumbled: "Thanks."

It was a lovely summer's evening as Tony and I strolled round the Coventry track, remarking how well it was maintained and an example to others. Tony's speedway consistency was getting better and better so we were looking forward to Reading's match there for the Speedway Star Cup.

It developed into a very close affair with every point at a premium. Tony had performed well in his previous heats but his last race was crucial as the result could hinge on it. He was on gate three which is not normally the best so late in the evening. Thirteen races had been run and 95 per cent of the bikes had passed over gate three on every lap. This meant that 300 wheels had packed it down to make it hard and slick with little grip to the first corner. His Swedish partner, Jan Andersson, was on gate one. Next to him was Coventry's double World Champion, Ole Olsen, with another Dane, Alf Busk, on the outside.

Looking back at this nightmare, it was relatively easy to see what was going to happen on the first corner. Andersson was a brilliant starter while local hero Olsen wasn't going to be beaten on his home track without a battle. And that's how it turned out. Andersson made the start, just ahead of Olsen, and made the most of it by drifting out onto his line going into the first corner. Tony, for once, was up with the action into the first corner but he was about to become the meat in a riders' sandwich.

He had Olsen on the inside while having to contend with Busk squeezing him from the outside. He was seriously running out of space. Then, bang. Olsen's back wheel hit Tony's front and straightened him up. With a large slice of luck, plus a good piece of skill, he stayed aboard his bucking bike.

Looking back, he could have done with a bit of bad luck by being knocked off. It would have saved him from what destiny had planned for him in the next few minutes. By the time Tony had his bike back in control the rest of the field were well ahead but, as usual, he kept his head down, trying as though his life depended on getting a point for his team.

On the third lap he started to rear in the middle of a corner. It looked for a split second as if he was going to get round it okay. But then he made a safety decision and simply laid his bike down. Because you have no brakes, you must put the machine on the ground, even though you might be moving at around 70mph.

As the bike comes off its wheels and slides on its side the rider normally holds on the handlebars. Nine times out of ten he will get dragged along on his stomach and the speed of the man and machine slows dramatically. Every rider has done this many times, either to save himself or to stop hitting one who has fallen in front of him. Normally, the worst you get is a few bruises and a bit of skin off your left hip. Tony's problem was that he was very close to the fence.

Then, for no apparent reason, the left handlebar suddenly dug violently into the track surface. It caused the bike to spin around instead of sliding into the bottom of the fence so the top of Tony's helmet hit an unprotected post rather than his wheels making the contact. The power of the impact was huge. Vertebrae numbers four, five and six in his neck were damaged. In fact, number five simply disintegrated.

I was standing with the rest of the riders in the pits and saw everything. The laying down manoeuvre Tony had performed was exactly what I would have done in the same circumstances. But luck must be on your side and, at that crucial moment, his had run out.

I stood in the pits watching and talking. I expected Tony to bounce up as he normally did but, after about a half a minute of no movement, I ran onto the track to see what was happening. His luck hadn't run out completely because the very able Coventry doctor, Peter Kenyon, was by his side. Tony had lost consciousness for a very short time, but now he was coherent. I wondered why the doctor hadn't turned him on his side to get the dirt and blood out of his mouth.

It was a little luck, but mainly Dr. Kenyon's skill in not moving Tony that saved him from spending the rest of his life as a paraplegic. The best doctor normally is the rider. As you lie there you know instinctively if something is really amiss. To be a speedway father is the pits, just looking at your son on the ground and not knowing how badly injured he is.

It is impossible to convey to anyone the unbelievable feeling of hopelessness. The only good thing was that Junie was at home in Southampton, and didn't have to witness what was going on. Finally, Dr. Kenyon got Tony in the ambulance without moving his head. I got in with him and was scratching the bottom of his feet to see if he could feel anything.

I never got an answer. Suddenly we were weaving and going very fast. I was battling to make sure that Tony didn't fall from the stretcher. The ambulance was careering along at real speed, even passing through a red light. I was sure the driver was under the impression that Tony had a head injury where speed of treatment was the essence. If Tony had fallen out of the ambulance bed, his spinal cord would have been severed and he'd have been permanently paralysed.

It was amazing that when we got to the hospital, the world stopped. The staff knew for sure the source of his injury. When they finally had Tony on the hospital trolley, they stopped at every join in the floor, no matter how small, and gently lifted the wheels to pass over them.

Two nurses tried to give him injections. They both bent the needles trying to put them in. They enlisted a staff nurse who got it done, but not without difficulty. It was as if his body had become coated with steel and was impregnable. I sat and waited for his return from X-ray. I kept trying to remember if he had moved his arms to help the St John's Ambulance men remove his crash helmet on the track.

I was pretty sure he did. But pretty sure was not good enough, I needed to be 100 per cent sure. I didn't want to raise any false hopes. Later the doctor, who was really caring, told me Tony had a broken neck. He also said we were very lucky getting him from the track into the ambulance, and then transported to the hospital, so gently. It would have taken virtually nothing to sever the spinal column. Then we would have had a real disaster.

I had to smile to myself. If that was a gentle ambulance ride, I would hate to be on a rough one! The doctor told me that they were going to take Tony to a specialised spinal clinic at Oswestry, on the Welsh border, at six o'clock in the morning. They were going to close the motorway as the special ambulance must travel slowly.

Finally, I got to see Tony and, in the circumstances, he seemed okay. He told me that he was starting to feel sleepy as they had given him some special pain-killing drug that would help to get him through the night pain free.

I told him I was going back to Southampton. Junie and I would see him at Oswestry in the morning. I gave him a kiss on the top of his head and headed for home.

A newspaper headline shrieked: "Briggs breaks his neck." The story read: "Tony Briggs broke a bone in his neck at Coventry on Saturday and will not ride again this season. The Reading youngster crashed during Racers' match at Brandon and, after spending Sunday at a local hospital, was moved to a specialised unit on Monday morning.

"He faces a month in traction and then a longer period in a plaster cast but has regained full feeling and movement. Early fears that he might suffer some long-term effects have proved unfounded."

Whoever wrote this article had all the wrong facts.

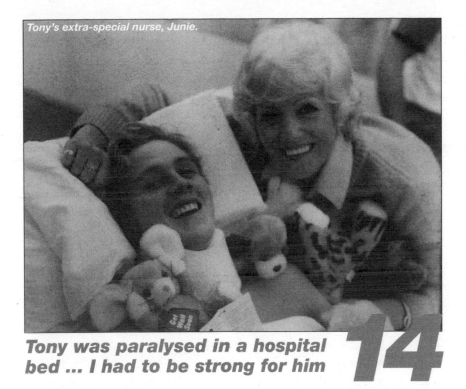

Tony's extra-special nurse, Junie.

Tony was paralysed in a hospital bed ... I had to be strong for him

14

I SPLASHED cold water on to my face and stared briefly into the mirror, trying determinedly to quell the maelstrom of nervous energy churning inside me. Butterflies in the stomach are no stranger to a professional sportsman and, over time, their arrival is greeted with the familiarity of an old friend rather than an obstacle which blocks peak performance.

But this was different. As a speedway rider, the control I had over success or failure provided empowerment and allowed for a level of relaxation. Now, though, what I wanted more than anything rested entirely with the gods, the medical staff at Agnes Hunt Orthopaedic Hospital in Oswestry, and the sheer bloody-mindedness of my son.

When Tony had slid innocuously into the safety fence at Coventry's Brandon Stadium, I did not even move from my vantage point in the pits at first. Having seen more crashes than I cared to remember during half a lifetime in the sport, there seemed to be nothing about this incident that could cause him serious harm.

As I waited for him to bounce to his feet I ran through in my mind what we might need to do to patch up the bike in time for his next race. Except that Tony didn't get up. He didn't move a muscle. Yet, even as I eventually jogged around to the first bend and saw on-site doctor Peter Kenyon leaning over him, I still couldn't believe that there was any major damage. To his pride, maybe. To his body, surely not?

Yet here I was, three weeks later, in the bathroom at the functional spinal hospital on the Welsh border, gearing myself up to present a brave face for Tony, lying completely paralysed in the next room, his future in the balance. The ward had been swamped with Get Well cards, the nurses reporting more than 100 per day over the past week, an unprecedented number for any patient in the hospital's history.

Tony's blond good looks had sent hearts fluttering among female fans even at such an early stage of his career and the racing community had come together to send messages of support. Radio 210, the local Reading station, had distributed a massive card for fans to sign at the previous week's challenge match against a Californian representative side. This stood propped up in a corner, a swathe of cardboard covered with heartfelt words from loyal followers.

However, while the messages were touching, what I wanted Tony to focus on was the battle ahead. Life, at least in the short-term, would be a gut-wrenching, frustrating nightmare. Yet the only way through to that speck of light at the end of the tunnel would be to throw himself head-first towards it, whatever mental and physical agonies lay strewn in his path.

When he had collided with the Coventry safety fence his fifth vertebrae had exploded. The doctors described the effect as being "like a lump of sugar hit by a hammer".

The accident had sent his spinal column into a state of shock and it would be months before the full extent of the damage would be known. By rights, he should not walk again. According to Dr. Jones, the best that could be hoped for was permanent use of a wheelchair and a reliance on some sort of care for the rest of his life.

The long hours spent staring at the austere white ceilings of his ward had already tested Tony's spirit to the max. If it broke, then there would be no way back. The most minor of irritations could provide an infuriating struggle and a tear-jerking reminder of how easy life used to be.

Before Junie and I had arrived for visiting, a fly had landed on the bridge of Tony's nose. A brush of the hand or shake of the head was not an option, and the accursed insect became the latest tormentor to creep into his mindset, alongside the constant companion of pain.

For making his nose its temporary landing field, the fly was now his sworn enemy, consuming his thoughts. He creased his forehead, knitted his eyebrows and puckered his lips in a desperate attempt to shift the infuriating intruder.

His eyes nearly turned inwards in their sockets as he tried to focus on the fly, leaving him with a ludicrous expression that would have been funny in any other circumstances. No other movement was possible. Finally, after what seemed an eternity but in reality was probably no more than 20 seconds, the fly departed, darting off to seek another victim. But that brief episode rammed home to Tony just what his plight entailed.

For now at least, there would be no cleaning his teeth, polishing his shoes, or even sitting up straight in a chair. Those functions may as well have belonged to a different person, a person who may never return. When he awoke that morning, and felt much warmer than normal, he could not even turn his head the few degrees needed to see if the heat was due to sunshine coming through the window.

His world during non-visiting hours was the ceiling above him and, with too much time for solitary thought, the lines of reality were blurred.

A polystyrene tile an inch out of place was a constant source of irritation: 'How could the workman have been so sloppy? Am I going mad? What day is it? They're all the bloody same anyway. I couldn't name the time and date if you offered me a million quid. Will I walk again? Will I ride again? And where's the nurse and those fucking painkillers?'

Sister Jones was the bane of Tony's life in some ways, running her unit with military precision. With her stern demeanour, all the nurses were petrified of her, all the patients were in awe. But she kept everything operating perfectly, ensuring all was spick and span before visiting hours opened. I would try to push my luck by routinely turning up 15 minutes early, always maintaining impeccable manners towards the sister in the hope that Tony would get favourable treatment. But that was about all I could do.

The process of attempted recovery was Tony's fight, and his alone. I knew he would view outside help as an unwanted intrusion, but I believed I could help the process by subtly nudging his psyche in the right direction when needed. As Junie and I headed into the ward we passed by beds occupied by living, breathing tales of woe. These folk, whose lives had been shattered by tragedy, were not action people or thrill-seekers. No car-racers, motorcyclists, sky-divers, mountaineers or hang-gliders.

Folk like Howard, the loudly snoring man in the bed opposite who had been the only survivor in a car crash that had killed his wife and only son. He would need care for the rest of his days, with no family to share his pain and ease it with love.

Perhaps Tony, like all speedway racers, had been an accident waiting to happen. But not Jean, the housewife two beds along who had been pruning her roses, slipped while stepping back to admire her handiwork, and broke her back. Or a young man, also called Tony, who had dived into the shallow end of a swimming pool at the wrong angle and suffered the broken neck that would impair him forever.

Then there was Ian, a man in his early 50s who had taken his wife a cup of tea in bed. Returning downstairs with a cup in each hand, his slipper caught on a stair rail and caused him to overbalance. Another broken back – and he would never use stairs unassisted again.

Worst of the lot was Jane, an 18-year-old blonde whose beauty was still clear, despite the severe lacerations on her face. Her red Triumph sports car had slewed off the road, dived down an embankment, collecting small trees and shrubs along the way, until it came to a sudden halt, bending like a boomerang around an old oak tree. She had a broken neck, broken leg and a fractured pelvis and wrist. All those injuries were treatable but when an elderly couple drove by and, alerted by the eerie scene of steam gushing from the radiator into the upwardly angled headlights, they rushed to help fearing the danger of fire.

By dragging Jane's unconscious frame out of the wreckage her spinal column was severed and she would never walk again. The helpers were kind but fate was not.

Despite being heavily sedated, Jane was in excruciating pain and haunted by medication-induced nightmares and hallucinations. Sometimes she would wake up screaming, and the heart-rending shrieks would pierce into the souls of the other patients, a reminder, not that one was needed, of the desperation of their own plight.

While I made my way directly to Tony's bedside, Junie stopped on the way to speak to some of the other patients.

"Morning John," she greeted one man, another broken neck victim who had become a friend. "I saw Helen in the supermarket. She will be in about 11, she had to go to the electricity people. She woke up to no power again this morning."

It was just like Junie to spread some cheer amidst the gloom. She stopped next at the bedside of a girl named Joanne. As I continued on to Tony's bed I couldn't hear what was said, but when she left, Joanne was smiling.

"Morning," I said. "Have a good night?"

"All right, a bit of pain early this morning but a pill fixed it. Not looking forward to today though, they're trying to wean me off the really heavy painkillers, but hopefully the pain will piss off soon. The hard stuff gives me nightmares and hallucinations and when I wake up I feel knackered."

Tony lowered his voice as his mother came over, giving him a warm kiss and stroking his forehead. "You look good this morning treasure," she said. Junie would have made a great nurse, her personality naturally full of compassion. There had been times when Tony had lashed out in frustration and anger, and Junie seemed to bear the brunt of it.

I put it down to the type of mental screw-up that came with an injury like this. People would take out their feelings on their loved ones. Thankfully, there was no tension today, as mother and son joked about the nurses, from the gorgeous Julie to Akio who, Tony was convinced, ignored his buzzer-presses when he needed more painkillers.

I even toyed with the idea of installing a concave mirror so Tony could see if she was lurking around the corner and pretending not to acknowledge his calls for attention.

As he and Junie talked, I thought of how he had been just weeks earlier, tearing around the Coventry circuit, at full throttle, pushing himself and his machine to the next level.

Even now, as I looked down at him, there was no outward sign that anything was wrong. He was pale, thin but well-proportioned, long-limbed and with a smooth, bare chest. His long blond hair had been freshly brushed as if he was about to head out for the day.

Now Junie was reading Tony an article from the latest edition of the *Speedway Star*. "Fans were still waiting to see if the younger Briggs had the World Championship potential of his father Barry. The one thing he has definitely inherited is his never-say-die attitude.

"That mentality, which helped make Barry the biggest star in the sport during his career spread over three decades, could be the vital ingredient that will help Tony overcome this setback in his life, and hopefully recover enough to return to the saddle. Fans around the world and those of us at the *Speedway Star* certainly hope so."

Junie looked up. Tony had drifted off to sleep and I was deep in thought, remembering some of the good times I'd had on a speedway bike. Would Tony get the chance to experience highs like that? Would he walk again?

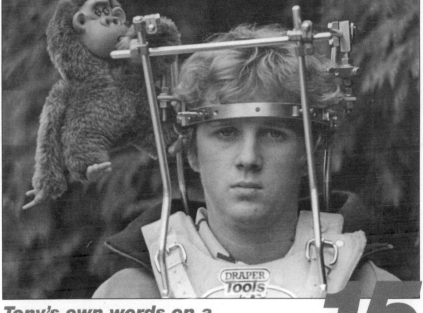

Scaffolding to stop the head moving.

Tony's own words on a critical time in his life

15

IT WAS as though Christmas and all my birthdays had come at once. At last I was home in my own bed. Finally, I'd escaped from that jail that had enclosed me over the last months, that bloody prison named the Agnes Hunt Orthopaedic Hospital at Oswestry.

Well, maybe not quite a prison, but it's really close to it. A noise brings me back to reality. I can hear the movement of someone coming up the stairs, no guesses who it might be. It's my 'angel' mum, Junie, bringing a morning cuppa with chocolate biscuits as well. God it's great to be home. "Good morning love, sleep well in your own bed?"

"It's not too bad, but the mattress is a bit soft compared with the one in hospital," I grumbled.

"Dad had to go to London for the day, something to do with the Clogau gold mine, but he'll be back later today. So I've got you to myself for the whole day. Aren't you lucky? I'm sure Lady (our Alsatian dog) is hoping that you are going to ride around the trees on your bike today so she can chase you and try to bite your front wheel, it is amazing when you patted her last night, her reaction was fantastic. Dogs never forget. I'm sure she is waiting right now for you on your bike or a game of football."

Sitting up and taking my cup of tea, the real world came back into focus. "Juna, what do you think about a trip to South Africa to get some sun on my back?"

"Tony, I think it would be great. I'd love your dad to come as well, but he's got so much going on it would be a couple of months before he could go. I'd love to get you away and all browned up before you go back to the hospital to be signed off."

"Mum, let's go. Briggo is always flat out, especially in the speedway season. Please take the cup, I'll have a shower and come down."

"Are you sure you can sort yourself out? Sister Jones said you must take it easy for a while."

"Stuff Sister bloody Jones, I'm out of there. Please pass me my dressing gown."

It was like magic. Could she read my mind because she was passing it to me before the words had exited my mouth.

"Let's ring the travel agent now about South Africa and get out of here as soon as possible. I want to get brown and fit, so when we go back to the hospital I can show that twat Dr. Jones that he doesn't know what he's talking about after his stupid statement 'Tony, you'll never ride a speedway bike again'."

Junie winced when she heard talk about riding a bike again, especially on the first day out of hospital. Even so, she had trouble stopping a smile from creasing the corners of her lips, definitely a 'chip off the old block'.

The trip to South Africa was fantastic, revisiting old friends and, most of all, the sun burning on my back again. It was heaven. My crash fitness course went well, although it didn't go down too well with Mum. Your body gives you warnings just how far you can push it.

My body movements were bad compared with what they were before the accident, but I am now feeling much better, so it won't take that much to get up to speed again.

Sitting in the hospital at Oswestry brought back all the pain and

Testing the lay-down, the throttle jammed and once again Junie was making hospital visits

suffering of the previous months. I feel humble, as one of the very few who actually walked out of the ward under their own steam after months of suffering, especially with everyone telling you to accept that you would probably be wheelchair-bound for the rest of your life.

That was all except Briggo and Juna, who kept thrashing into my confused brain that things were going to get back to normal pretty soon. The other amazing thing was that everyone in my ward was wishing me good luck, and hoped everything was going to work out for me. I had to wonder why God had chosen me to be released from this hell.

On my return a month later, most of my ex-fellow patients were in exactly the same condition as when I left, some were even a little worse. Ninety-eight per cent are going to be crippled and in wheelchairs for the rest of their lives. Yet their happiness for me had been genuine when they watched me leave. It was a strange feeling because I felt I had moved out of their world.

I was back in Oswestry to see Dr. Jones, a very caring doctor who was always trying to soothe his patients with sweet words, delivered in a singing Welsh accent. With all the talking he did, he just had to be late. Thank God my appointment was not at the end of the day, as I'd be lucky to be away before night fall.

I felt nervous, it was probably just being back. I was told it was only a routine visit, just a formality. Oh, here he comes, be nice.

"Good morning, Mr. Briggs," he said as we shook hands. "Young Tony, you are nice and brown and look well. Give me a couple of minutes and I'll look at today's X-ray to gauge how well you have progressed."

On his return Dr. Jones had the face of a poker player which disclosed nothing on his smiling face, but something made me feel uneasy. He said: "Tony, I know what you have been through over the past months and I am sure you felt that you were coming out of the end of the tunnel. But I am afraid it's going to take a little longer than we expected.

"Unfortunately, your head is falling forward. You will need to come back in and have a bone graft. We will have to fuse discs four, five, six, and seven together for stability. I know how sad you must feel but we took a chance in letting you go home for a month. That gave us the opportunity to check if you needed a graft.

"Your Mum and Dad understood that it was a chance well worth taking. It shouldn't take too long for your neck to stabilise and you'll be much better."

My head spun, I was numb, my world just crashed in around me. What the fuck does this silly old bastard doctor know about what I have been through? Then, worst of all, Juna and Briggo had discussed it. Whose life is it anyway? I couldn't speak and didn't want to anyhow.

The old man took over. I wasn't listening to what they were talking about, I'd had a plateful. What the hell can you do? Your bloody head is falling off, the only choice is you have is to get the fucking thing fixed. The rest of their conversation was just a mumble to me, as dad and the Welshman continued their question and answer show.

It finally ended and I heard the old man say: "I will ring you in a couple of days about Tony's re-admission."

I stood up like a zombie, I only just managed to shake his hand. It was a compromise as I certainly didn't want to. This bloke standing in front of me had just committed me to do more time in this prison. Briggo took me back to the car and left me to myself while he returned to the hospital to ring Junie with the wonderful news.

Normally, a good cuddle from Junie was enough to sort out my pains. But not this time, no way. She was part of the conspiracy. The old man returned to say: "Obviously she's upset. She said to give you her love, and it will better for you in the long run. We can all help you to handle it, and you'll be well again in next to no time. The worst part is past."

I settled down for our trip home to Southampton. I didn't feel like talking at all. I was so upset I wanted to yell out, kick or punch something hard, to help rid myself of the frustration and anger that had built up in my body. As hard as I tried to stop myself, I could feel the warmth of tears starting to flow down my cheeks.

Right from the time I had decided to start riding speedway, I felt as though I was being tested although for what reason I certainly didn't understand. At the beginning I'd had problems from some of the riders, even some of my team-mates, and I could half understand why. They felt I was a rich kid and that everything was planned for me to follow the 'old man' and then cash in on the success and rewards that are part of the parcel. Wrong, wrong, wrong.

Being Briggo's son only had small initial advantages, and what promoters wouldn't give you a chance to see if you had inherited his pedigree to make the big-time. This was a tough time for me because it was then that the comparisons started. I loved speedway the same way as Briggo did.

Having to follow the dangerous, rocky path with extra baggage was bad enough. It was much tougher when you were the son of a champion. Wasn't breaking my neck enough? What was all my bad luck supposed to teach me? Where was all this going to end? Why didn't Mum and Dad discuss the possibility of going back into hospital with me?

One thing, for sure, was that from now on all decisions affecting my life will be made by me, and me alone.

The medical profession never seems to keep the patient in the picture. It's as if they are magicians, and are above being questioned about their magic. If they were plain motor mechanics they would never ever get away with it.

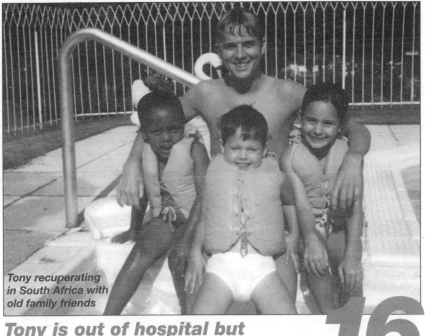
Tony recuperating in South Africa with old family friends

Tony is out of hospital but what are his future prospects?

16

AS I drove Tony away from Oswestry I didn't go south as usual on the A5 to Southampton but turned in the opposite direction, travelling north on the A495 road to Whitchurch. What I needed now was some luck.

Hopefully, we could get another hour's travel under our belts before Tony woke up and started to bombard me with questions on where are we, and what are we doing here. We were both in no mood for arguing.

We had passed Whitchurch an hour ago and Tony was still sleeping. Soon we would be at Stoke-on-Trent and would slip around the outskirts to pick up the A43 to Buxton in the beautiful Peak District. After another half an hour Tony started to wake although it took him a few minutes to take in the small, twisting road that weaved its way up and down the rolling hills that went as far as the eye could see.

"Dad, where are we? Are we lost? I don't recognise this countryside at all."

Broad Steet, Monrovia.

Tony and Gary at our original Loffa river base camp.

"Relax, Tony, I know where we are and, hopefully, we'll be at our destination in under an hour."

A look of bewilderment, with a touch of anger, creased his handsome face. "Are you going to tell me or not?"

"The short answer is no, so sit back and try to relax," I replied.

For the next hour, a sombre silence engulfed us. I watched out of the corner of my eye to his reactions as we passed signposts. He read them carefully, trying desperately to figure out where we were and the purpose of our journey. Names like Pilsley and Baslow flashed by but nothing registered on his now taut face. The sign which read Sheffield, eight miles, relaxed his face a little, but still not a word was spoken. My problems were just starting. I had only been to our destination once before. The information was filed somewhere in the darkness at the back of my brain. What I needed was to recognise something to jump-start it.

Suddenly, the bells started to ring when I recognised an old brown Victorian building that is a Morris car dealership. You would have trouble forgetting this landmark because perched precariously on the edge of this four-storey building's roof was an old British racing green Morris Eight.

Got it, I knew exactly where I was. Three traffic lights down we took a sharp left hand turn into Craven Road. There, low and behold, was the Sheffield Infirmary. Tony spoke up. "Dad, what the hell are we doing here?"

"Patience son, I'll be right back." I darted over to the information desk. When I returned you could have written a book just from that look on his face. I pushed the lift button for the fourth floor and we arrived at Ward Nine. Walking past the ends of the old metal-framed beds, it struck me how very similar in layout it looked to the broken neck ward at Oswestry.

A young male, stripped to the waist, lay on the last bed on the left. He had weights attached to his head, like the old fashioned torture machine, the rack. It appeared that it was trying to pull the head apart from the rest of the body. Now we were close enough to recognise the young man with bolts in his shaved head. I slowed to let Tony get to the bed first.

Turning to me he whispered out of the corner of his mouth: "You smart old bastard, it's Rolf Gramstad. I didn't know this had happened to him."

The small body that had been a picture of misery minutes before turned into Mr. Sunshine himself. "Rolf, how the bloody hell are you?" He leaned in closely and spoke, gently stroking his grazed forehead.

Rolf just about jumped out of his skin, uttering: "Tony, what a fantastic surprise this is."

Tony stepped back and answered: "It's a shock for both of us. But that's a long story and we'll talk about that later – especially interfering fathers." He gave me his biggest smile, and even flashed me a wink.

I said: "Hi Rolf, glad to see you again. I hope everything is on the mend for you. I'll leave you two now and see if I can track down some cups of tea, it's been a long day." I smiled to myself as I went tea hunting.

Rolf Gramstad was a young Norwegian who rode for Leicester. He had broken his neck in an horrendous longtrack accident in West Germany. He was hit from behind by a Czech who didn't see him and ran into the back of him while he was stopped on the inside edge of the track.

Rolf didn't even see what was going to happen so he had no control of his own destiny. He was now in the same position that Tony was in four months ago. His body had hardly any movement, just some in the little finger of his left hand.

Tony had just been on the journey that he was starting. The boot was on the other foot, as Rolf faced a future of uncertainty. Tony could be his expert on what he could expect in the coming weeks. It was a big positive for him when he saw Rolf. He stopped feeling sorry for himself. It showed him how lucky he really was.

There was no guarantee at that time that Rolf would have his luck and get back on his feet. Plus the fact that Tony would be even better after having his bone graft. The help and advice he would be able to pass on would be therapeutic to them both and would also help Rolf to cut out a lot of the worry from the medical bullshit that he'd be told.

Our trip back to Southampton was much lighter than it would have been if we had gone straight back from Oswestry.

Tony takes up the story again ...
The old man (Briggo) did well to point out how lucky I'd been in some ways. I had spent ten weeks in hospital the first time

I'm much happier in my body cast as my smile shows.

around and this visit was going to be better because I knew what to expect. Last time I had no idea what my future had in store. Nobody would, or could, tell me what the outcome would be. That was hell!

I gritted my teeth and got my old attitude going. I muttered the old call: "Here we go again."

The operation was carried out by Dr. Pringle, a Kiwi. He fused the four discs together into one lump. Then I was fitted with a halo, a contraption that is bolted to your skull and braced so that it keeps your neck safe from any bad movements, including bends and twists. The advantage of the halo is that you are discharged from hospital once it is fitted. But it was clumsy and sleep was very difficult.

After six weeks of enduring the pain and problems, I returned to the hospital to be fitted with a body cast for a further six weeks and that made life much more comfortable. My feeling now was that the time had come to get this bloody broken neck problem out of my life.

Briggo had come up with a special speedway bike while I was recovering. Instead of the engine being straight up and down in the frame, he laid it down which gave the machine much better handling characteristics.

However, the throttle jammed when he was racing and testing the machine in New Zealand. His riding ability and quick thinking helped him get rid of the machine but, unfortunately, it was fitted with an engine cut-out affixed to his wrist.

Briggo had hardly ever used this safety device, so it wasn't engrained in his brain. He got rid of the bike as he'd done countless times in his racing life but the killing of the engine's power didn't propel the bike away from under him. Instead it landed on top of him, inflicting internal injuries.

After recovering he decided to take a rest from bikes. He had become involved in a diamond and gold mining venture in Liberia, West Africa, and decided to investigate its possibilities. It sounded like good fun and an adventure so I thought I'd join him. The mind boggles at the thought of two recuperating speedway riders in the jungle together searching for treasure!

Elder son Gary, so much more like his mother than his father

17

JUNIE was keen for us to start a family as soon as we married but we both agreed that it would be best to wait until I had finished my speedway racing.

In fact, Junie became pregnant during the 1958 season and little did we know at the time that I was to quit during the following winter when I had a financial dispute with my British club, Wimbledon, and effectively hung up my leathers.

I threatened to retire over just £30 but learned from a young age that if you go down that road then you must be prepared for the consequences. I was the reigning World Champion, having won at Wembley in both 1957 and 1958, and felt that I was being treated poorly. But nobody believed I was going to stop riding.

Junie and I bought a house in my native Christchurch and were excited at the prospect of our first child. We didn't know whether it was going to be a boy or a girl, it didn't really matter, but there are very few females in the Briggs dynasty … we're a family of blokes!

The days ticked away towards the projected arrival date, time seemed to move so slowly. I was very nervous, and had real trouble putting my mind completely into doing anything, as time just dragged on. Our new house was a lovely home, and in the distance to the north you could see where Larry Ross, then barely out of nappies, lived, and behind that the ocean. To the west was Christchurch and beyond the Southern Alps, a range of mountains that hug the west coast of New Zealand's South Island.

At the time I had an old American car which at times was a suspect starter. So I parked it outside the front of the house on Huntsbury Hill, which was a fairly steep hill, so any trouble with our car we could just simply launch ourselves down the hill and be on our way. I certainly didn't want the Briggo gremlins to strike at such a critical time and made doubly sure that we were ready for take-off at all times and would not keep Junie and her little bundle waiting.

The impending birth was the most important thing that had happened to Junie and me in our lives. The winning of motorcycle races just didn't compare and paled against the excitement of the arrival of our first child.

I was used to spending time in various hospitals and had been hurt many times, but the doctor in me knew how bad I was and if I was going to be okay. It was different for Junie, she had to sit around waiting to discover what the situation was. Now the boot was on the other foot. I was terribly nervous at the thought of Junie going into hospital. When she finally decided the time had come, the old car behaved but it seemed like the slowest three miles I have ever travelled.

Gary actually arrived on January 28, 1960, at the St. George's hospital in Christchurch. He was two days late and has never been punctual since! Junie was ecstatic, she loved the prospect of being a mother and her dream had been fulfilled. Deciding on a name for our first born wasn't too difficult once we had dispensed with the thought of naming him George, after Junie's dad.

We agreed that my own parents had done a reasonable job with Barry, Murray and Wayne and added to it Gary Trevor Briggs. There was another influence that came into play. While I was racing in South Africa and we were on our honeymoon I watched some golf tournaments there and was struck by the style and outstanding ability of a couple of local young players.

First there was Harold Henning, who had a distinctive hair-style, in the mould of Elvis Presley, which I copied when we got back to the UK. But the name Harold didn't roll off the tongue right for our little boy. The other aspiring golfer was the small but mighty Gary Player and the rest, as they say, is history.

Our Gary was never very mechanically minded but loved reading and listening to music. He was also very sports minded and was good at all types of ball sports including soccer, cricket, tennis, rugby and, later, golf. The Player influence eventually came through! Gary did start riding motorbikes and loved it but he didn't know or want to know how they worked. He just wanted to ride.

He was very competitive but, on one occasion, got himself in trouble during a tennis tournament at Southsea when he forgot what he was there for.

Junie and I had gone to see Gary play and he did well in his first couple of matches. Then he met a smaller boy who was not too bad a player.

Some of Gary's mates were playing there, too, and were around the court for his match. Gary started messing around and showing off, and not giving his opponent enough respect. In the end Gary lost and, to be honest, I was quite pleased. By showing that sort of attitude, he didn't deserve to win.

After the game he came to join Junie and me in our car for the journey home. As he opened the door to get in I gave him £1. "What's this for?" he said. I replied: "Gary, that was diabolical. You were just like those other tennis brats, which is not what I expect from my boy. That's your bus fare home, it will give you time to think about it. See you later when you get home."

And with that I shut the car door. Junie was stunned into silence and speechless but regained her voice as we drove away and said: "You cannot do that, it's miles home, he won't know what bus to catch and it will be dark in a couple of hours." There was a tear in her eye. "Junie," I said, "he acted like a jerk. Were you proud of him?"

"No, not really, but he hasn't been on the buses alone before," she reasoned. "Well love, he's going to learn a few lessons on this trip. Relax, he is smarter than we give him credit for, he'll make it."

Once home Junie kept going to the front window looking for Gary. It was dark and about 9.30pm when the doorbell rang and there was Gary with a big smile on his face. "Dad, here's your change." We didn't ever discuss it at all. It was clear that he had absorbed the lesson and the biggest plus was that Junie still loved me.

Both Gary and later Tony learned many things the hard way including life in general through being involved in so many different situations. Often having an actual seat in a car while we travelled from one place to another was a luxury. More often than not they had to sit on or be jammed between speedway wheels and tyres in the seat-less back of the car.

It made me laugh when I heard parents asking people to be quiet because 'little Johnny' was sleeping. My kids, like their dad, could sleep through anything. Gary and especially Tony were always adept at earning a few bob. So they had their chances at my meetings on the continent, it gave them the chance to get into the book selling market. I had done a book for *Motorcycle News* and had some left over which I gave to the boys to sell, while I was racing around trying to win races.

Tony figured he needed a gimmick and he acquired a bowler hat (very British) and glued a small Union Jack to the front to help him get noticed for his book selling. He was under constant pressure, not so much for the books, but everyone seemed to want to buy his bowler.

One of the major problems was that the books were written in English, but had plenty of good colour pictures throughout. Most Germans and Danish have a good smattering of English. The boys quickly learnt to make sure that the book was open on one of the pages showing photos of the local hero. In Denmark, for example, they would have photos of Ole Olsen on display, in Germany it would be Egon Muller.

While at longtrack meetings, where there was always a long gap between races, Tony would often target people in the crowd to sell books to. I remember him spotting a young couple in Germany and while the man wasn't interested and treated Tony like the invisible man, the trouble was that his girlfriend was obviously an Egon fan, so it was an easy touch for Tony's salesmanship.

I felt a little sorry for Gary, as when Tony started riding it seemed that everything was centered on his young brother, but I can't ever remember hearing him complain.

We were all back in New Zealand prior to Tony setting out in his racing career, Gary was working to earn some money with my mate Tommy (McCleary) at his shop Tommy's Motorcycles on the outskirts of Christchurch. Gary had recently passed his driving test and I smiled to myself as I saw a real test for him coming up on the horizon. Up-coming to our local track at Christchurch was a demolition derby series that was travelling through New Zealand. The top prize was a thousand dollars up for grabs. I got the entry form for Gary and I became a sponsor of a racing team.

One of the Christchurch midget drivers owned a car wrecking yard, so we descended on it in search of a winning car for Gary's team. We settled on a nippy, light green Hillman Minx car, and after fitting it with a good safety harness, and with a bit of paintwork, we were ready to rock-n-roll and to win the Christchurch Grand Prix. Our nervous Gary crouched behind his battered steering wheel and was trying to be cool with the radio playing. He was ready, raring to go and uphold the Briggs name. All of our friends, and Ronnie Moore's daughters and tens of girl friends who thought that our Gary was adorable, were there to support our new star.

On the side on the car we advertised Tommy's shop, and on the back we wrote really large in white 'Bobo Pies' … Bobo's real name is David Valentine, who came to England to give speedway a shot at Swindon. He was also Gary's boss at Tommy's Motorcycles and had a pie business on the side.

We sat in the stands with baited breath, waiting for Gary to emerge and tear up the track. There must have been around 65 cars circling the track, but no Gary. They had just started to close the pit gate when suddenly it was thrown open again and chugging

Gary cashing in on his mum's good looks

through the gate came our Gaz, his mighty Hillman only firing on three cylinders. The arena was buzzing with excitement, we wondered how was Gary's nerve for his first ever car race?

You cannot believe the mayhem that went on for the next half an hour as car after car smashed into each other, some spun never to move again, while others just ground to a halt. Some were steaming like a billycan on the boil, others were upside down, some had no front wheels, and it was utter chaos.

Meanwhile, Gary was miraculously keeping out of trouble even though other drivers tried to line him up for a hit. It was probably because he was such a bad driver and new to driving and what you do and not do. Other drivers simply couldn't work out what he was going to do next, on a couple of occasions he just about rolled over by himself without another car near. It was obvious why other drivers couldn't figure him out, Gary didn't really know quite what was going on himself. As the end of the race grew near, there were only three cars left … two large Humber Snipes, driven by pros hunting down the big prize, and Gary. One of the Humbers lost a front wheel and went out and it was now down to two.

Each car in the race had a large white cross painted onto the driver's door signifying that this part of the vehicle was a no hit area by any rival driver in any deliberate collision.

The last guy hunting down Gary didn't seem to care about such niceties but he was having trouble getting his lumbering 'tank' into a position to smash the nippy Hillman.

Then, out of the blue, Gary's car coughed and spluttered and slowed to a halt having run out of petrol. He was a sitting target and had the Hillman's front end wiped out by the Humber reversing into it. There was no justice, the villain had won. But we all had a fantastic night. Gary almost took the big prize but I am not sure even now that I can sleep soundly when Gary is driving … and I can sleep anywhere!

Many years later Gary and Tony, along with Pud, Terry Betts's son, were driving to the old Czechoslovakia. Tony had done most of the driving but wanted a break in the middle of the night and got Pud to take over. He didn't want Gary driving.

Tony went to sleep but woke later to the sound of crunching

gears. Gary had, in fact, taken over the wheel and Tony yelled at him: "Gary, can you not even understand something as simple as a gear change, it is only an H movement."

Gary looked at his younger brother and without missing a beat said: "Oh, you mean a capital H."

They all had a good laugh but it was Tony that climbed back into the driver's seat. Sometimes I wonder if Gary wanted to sleep but first felt he had to do his share … but a little crunch and he knew Tony would throw him out and he'd get his sleep.

Gary rode a speedway bike at Wimbledon and found out the hard way that it isn't easy. He had learned the ways of a motorcycle by riding a motocross bike, and he got to realise that if you get into trouble you turn the front wheel into the slide. Doing that on a speedway bike results in you being dumped on your head. I took him home with a couple of black eyes and Junie wasn't best amused!

Gary was talented at many sports but he really wanted to be a footballer. I took him along to Southampton for a trial but the manager, Ted Bates, said that he was "too leggy, but if he was at war, he would be really happy to have Gary beside him". I liked Ted and it made me laugh but I wondered whether this was his standard line for all the kids who failed.

When my friend Dave Webb took over at Bournemouth football club he gave Gary a job in Public Relations and Youth Development. It was the first step into his coaching and among the first batch of kids at Bournemouth were Jamie and Jeremy Redknapp, whose father Harry was Webby's assistant.

Gary's big chance came when he was brought on for the second half of a reserves match against Exeter. His proud parents sat in the stand, and playing that game helped Gary to realise exactly what was required to be a professional.

Gary continued with his coaching and secured his prelim badge but failed to acquire his full badge. Had he done so he would have been one of the youngest ever to have got through, he would have tried again had his life not taken an unexpected change of direction in a completely new way.

Tony was about to embark on his speedway career in Britain,

racing for Reading in the British League. He had already secured a sponsorship deal with Fabergé alongside boxing legend Henry Cooper and soccer idol Kevin Keegan, who at that time was playing for Southampton.

Fabergé was keen to attract a new young market, and wanted the blond, good-looking 18-year-old Tony to do some photo shoots for various magazines. Tony was nervous and asked Gary to go along with him.

Within months both Gary and Tony had appeared on the front covers of various magazines. Gary was a natural and was snapped up by one of London's top model agencies. He spent the next four years touring the world working for the agency and although he enjoyed it he was never fulfilled mentally.

Fate played a part too. Gary was on an assignment in Japan, modelling golfing gear when otherwise he would have been with a dozen of his model mates on a boat trip. He lost a couple of his close friends who were at the party on the *Marchioness* riverboat when it sank after a collision with a barge on the Thames.

I thought Gary would be bright enough not to let Webby take control.

Tim Blake had been a model before going behind the camera and becoming a top photographer. Howard was a black London lad who had been to visit us at Queenie's in Wandsworth and also in California when Gary and some mates were modelling for the Empire Stores catalogue in Las Vegas.

Both died in the tragedy and it was a huge blow to Gary. He moved to live in California and kept up his soccer coaching there, earning his Ayso badge and was coach at the Laguna High School where four girl players gained sponsorship to go on to University which saved their parents in the region of $30,000 each. His team twice won the league.

In was through one of the girls in his team that Gary became a car salesman. Not just any car salesman, however. Gary sells top of the range vehicles like Jaguars and Aston Martins and his English-style patter goes down very well with prospective buyers in southern California. Gary had a couple of great years coaching young Mexican kids and they won their league in back-to-back seasons. Junie and me liked to go and see them and only a couple of weeks before she went to the hospital for the last time we went and watched Gary's kids play.

Although he never took up speedway, Gary has had a very varied life, loves his music and enjoys coming out on motorcycle rides with Tony and I through the mountains inland from where we live. He has done a bit of acting, playing an Indian prince and a detective in the *Highlander* series alongside one of his modeling mates, Adrian Paul, who plays the lead role.

Gary was always completely spoilt by Junie and her mum Queenie. Tony and I teased Junie that Gary was her favourite but, of course, she always denied it. During her final days Junie would ask Tony and me to make sure that Gary was okay and not left behind. A bit strange that … Gary is the only one of us with a proper job.

Junie would love to have seen Gary in the family life he now enjoys with his partner Amber and her three children, Skyler, Colby and Trevor. As with Tony, he has been a tower of strength for me to lean on whenever necessary over the past few years.

The Briggs family home, Robin Hill, in Chilworth.

TV scenes of atrocities in Liberia capture our attention at home

18

April 29, 1980

THE reporter on the television news spoke of unimaginable acts of brutality, so sickening as to defy belief. His voice wavering, he told a disbelieving British television audience of the bloodthirsty tale of a military coup in Liberia.

Tales of disembowelment, death and gruesome retribution against the former rulers were rife.

Sitting in the comfortable environment of the Briggs family home 6,000 miles away, the sorry tale being broadcast from Africa seemed like a different world.

Little did I know that within a few years my family and I would be right in the middle of one of the world's most volatile nations and get a first-hand look at the mayhem that follows when a country is ripped apart at its political and economic seams.

The reporter's name was Jerry Bryon. We didn't know it then, but he would become a crucial part of our lives.

The Briggs family home was a two-storied Georgian affair,

Monrovia, Liberia's capital city – plenty of action.

nestled in the heart of Chilworth, a small, sleepy, deeply-wooded village on the outskirts of Southampton.

The rural setting of Hampshire, on England's south coast, was my idea of perfect tranquillity and, at the age of 45, the ideal antidote to my former helter-skelter existence as a speedway World Champion.

As I drove my gold Mercedes 350SE – which I knew was ostentatious but I loved it anyway – through the driveway I allowed myself a smile as I passed the gate and saw the red wooden sign for Robin Hill.

The home was named as such mainly as a tribute to the Swindon

Robins speedway team, as it was the club's money that had gone a long way towards the purchase of the property.

As captain of the Robins I had helped the team win the British League title in 1967, one of my finest memories in the sport along with my four World individual titles.

Behind the vehicle was a trailer, carrying two spindly speedway bikes, comprehensively encrusted with red shale. In the passenger seat was my youngest son Tony, who was hoping to follow in my wheel tracks in the speedway business. He was 17, but looked younger, with a mop of curly blond hair and a slender frame, inherited from his mother and in contrast to my own bulkier physique.

Returning from a day's practice at the Weymouth track 80 miles away, we both looked as if we had emerged from the confines of a coal mine and had managed to spread much of our filth on to the Stewart tartan blankets covering the interior of my pride-and-joy Merc.

Inside, my wife Junie and eldest son Gary were waiting, with the television on and the sitting-room fire already roaring. "Go inside and tell your Mum we're home before we unload the bikes," I told Tony, watching him limp up the steps, still in his red and black leathers.

A couple of hours earlier Tony had fallen off his bike at full speed trying to slide through the tight, tricky Weymouth corners. As someone who had seen and suffered more crashes than I cared to remember, I knew he was fine, but his mother would still worry when she heard the toned-down version of his minor accidents.

Junie knew exactly what crashing or even just "slipping off" meant as Tony cleaned up his story for her. She had seen first-hand the kind of pain, injury and upheaval caused by our high-speed sport.

Following me around the world for 20 years, and helping to patch me up and nurse me back to health on countless occasions, the thought of going through the same process with her son was terrifying.

We had both prayed Tony would not follow me into speedway but realistically we knew deep down that we didn't stand a chance.

The youngest member of the Briggs clan had always had a love affair with motorbikes and wanted to be a rider from the time he could first walk.

"Did you hurt yourself?" asked a worried Junie, knowing full well she probably wouldn't get a completely honest answer.

"No, we had a good day Mum," said Tony.

"Dad gets nervous for me but it's unbelievable, he can still get on the bike and show me exactly what I need to do."

A Southern Television crew had been at the track and filmed some of Tony's practice so we hurriedly showered so we could settle down in front of the screen before his clip came on.

I heard Tony joking with his brother as I went up the stairs – with Gary telling his younger sibling how he would make his living as an Evel Knievel-style daredevil instead of a speedway rider.

"He's only got to be ballsy for a few seconds and then he collects his pay cheque," was Gary's take on things.

Back downstairs minutes later, spirits were high in the living room. Junie was teasing Tony that he hadn't managed to get all the dirt off his face and Gary and I were tucking into a giant plate of our favourite bacon sandwiches. The main news headlines were largely drowned out by our chatter until, that is, news anchor Peter Sissons announced: "And now a distressing piece of footage from the West African nation of Liberia …"

Instantly, the mood in our comfortable sitting room changed, the jovial atmosphere stopped in its tracks by Jerry Bryon's words and the pictures that accompanied them.

Murders, beheadings, ritual executions of former cabinet ministers carried out on the orders of Sergeant Samuel Doe.

At that moment, as the clip ended and the programme moved on to sports news and Tony's footage, I would have questioned the sanity of anyone who suggested you would ever find me within a thousand miles of Liberia.

Yet due to a combination of factors it was just three years later when we were thrust into the middle of that hornets' nest and sucked into a series of experiences that were fraught, unforgettable and life changing.

Ray Thackwell with his son Michael.

A chance meeting with an old friend changed our lives forever

19

WEDNESDAY afternoon at the Agnes Hunt Orthopaedic Hospital in the Welsh border town of Oswestry. In the Wrekin ward my wife Junie and I sat on either side of the bed that held our youngest son Tony prisoner. Metal screws were embedded into his skull and held the weights that helped to keep his head in a straight position.

Two weeks had passed since I watched from the pits as Tony was involved in a nothing-type crash at Coventry Speedway that caused him to sustain a broken neck. Now the only movements coming from his rigid body were from his eyes and his mouth.

Across from me Junie was sitting patiently massaging his slender hands with Lanolin. I was busy trying to tell Tony that the doctors were wrong in their diagnosis, and that he would be out of there in no time at all and be back in the saddle once again. I didn't know whether to believe my own words, but I felt strongly that it was what my Tony needed to hear.

From her position, Junie could see the entrance to the ward and suddenly a big smile creased her beautiful face – her first genuinely happy expression in a fortnight. I turned around and just about fell from my chair.

Striding down the ward, larger than life, was a stocky, suntanned man with long, grey hair sticking out from beneath the flat cap perched on his round head. A full grey trimmed beard set off the white teeth of his winning smile.

Enter Ray Thackwell, a fellow Kiwi and speedway's answer to Arthur Daley. I didn't realise at the time that this defining moment of his appearance was to be a big turning point of my later life. Unfortunately it was not all going to be good.

"Thack, what the bloody hell are you doing here?" I asked as Junie got up and planted a kiss on his cheek. Tony, his vision impeded by his lack of head movement, lay wondering what the hell all the fuss was about. "It's okay Tony," I said. "It's the return of the old bandito himself – Thack."

The thought of Thack being there immediately opened up the creases of the laughter lines missing from Tony's face since his accident. The next hour was a laugh a minute as Thack told us about his new acquisition – the Clogau St. David's gold mine in Dolgellau, Wales.

The gold that came from this mine had been used in royal wedding rings, and even the Queen's crown.

Ray had always been an adventurer and mining was something he liked to dabble in, having cut his teeth mining in Western Australia. In the mining world there are no exact prices or valuations, so an entrepreneur like Ray could simply pluck values from mid-air. This suited the Thack way of dealing, with a capital D.

He acquired the lease for Clogau by painting himself as an Aussie entrepreneur riding to the rescue of the troubled Welsh mine. Thack was not averse to bending the truth a little, even if it meant temporarily giving himself a new nationality. Then he had to convince the visiting ministerial official he wasn't liable for any safety standards that could have been imposed.

"Mate, this is the way we do it down in Oz," he said. To seal the deal the simple answer was to give the official his best line and get him on his way.

My immediate question was: "How the hell do you dislodge the bits of gold that cling inside hard rock? This isn't alluvial mining where everything is loose – this is hard rock mining."

His answer was simple: "Blast it out."

"Thack, what the hell do you know about blasting?" I said.

"Not a lot, but we are as sure as hell learning fast," he said with a beaming smile.

Apparently, this blasting was happening 200 feet underground in over two miles of tunnels that zigzagged beneath the surface in an unruly pattern forged when the old-timers of the early 1900s tried to follow the gold seams.

"The first time we blasted we were standing too close," Ray said laughing. "The bloody compression of the after-blast knocked me and my eldest son Kerry arse over tip. We got up looking like we were Africans and we couldn't hear a bloody thing. We are lucky to still be here – we were also stupid enough to have sticks of dynamite stuffed into our pockets."

As the afternoon wore on Thack continued with more adventure stories and an update on the career of his 18-year-old son Michael – then in the motorsport record books as the youngest ever driver in Formula One.

"Well, you Briggs clan, I'll see you all again after I've been to the mine and paid the wages," he said. "I'll swing through here on the way back home on Friday."

"Don't worry," said Tony. "I don't plan on going anywhere in the near future."

As I got up to walk Thack to the car I told him I might take a break from the hospital and pop up to the mine to take a look.

Returning to Tony's bedside I immediately noted the feeling was much lighter than an hour earlier. You don't realise just how important laughter is for your well-being, plus you don't have to go to the NHS or your doctor to get a refill prescription.

It was written all over Tony's face, showing that at this moment he'd forgotten his present predicament if only for a short time. I remember thinking that if you could bottle laughter, it would be the most wonderful medicine in the world.

"Well, Tone, that was a big surprise," I said. "Thack is still a bundle of laughs but I feel that he's right on the line of being a crook. Look at what happened to Ronnie in their disastrous car sales business."

Thack and Ronnie Moore had gone into business together some years earlier, a partnership that quickly turned sour and left Ronnie out of pocket and feeling bitter.

Tony had his own opinion to offer. "I think the general consensus is that he plays the lovable rogue well, and this gives him plenty of slack. I really like him."

At that Tony closed his eyes as the drugs kicked in and sent him into a deep sleep. Junie kept up her massaging, trying her hardest to instil life back into those dainty little hands. At that point it was impossible to imagine them controlling a bucking, sliding speedway bike.

"Juna, let's go for a cuppa while he snoozes. I think that Thack is a bit dodgy, but I suppose it's 'better the devil you know'. He is fun though, even if he is full of bullshit," I said quietly as we got up to go for our cuppa.

June agreed with Tony that Thack's fun and laughter lowered your guard when dealing with him and pointed out that Ray's wife Patsy was constantly worried that one day he would really land himself in trouble.

However, a couple of months later, there I was putting myself up for the Ray Thackwell test, having convinced myself that I could look after myself in business with him. I purchased a 50 per cent share of the Clogau St. David's gold mine. It so happened that I had already put money together for a takeover of Bournemouth football club with my mate, former Chelsea defender Dave Webb, but the project fell through.

Webby had grand plans, including signing an ageing George Best and getting rid of most of the club's under-performing squad. In the end most of his ideas – apart from Best – were implemented over the forthcoming years, but before we got the chance to move, the club closed ranks to keep us out.

A shift from football to gold mining was a pretty major leap – a true case of jumping from 'the frying pan into the fire'. But my feeling has always been that life is a gamble and I knew I needed to follow my gut instinct.

The investment in Clogau thrust me into a whole new world. Early in the piece we got word that an Australian mining public company, Belgravia Resources, wanted to buy into the Clogau mine, so we set up a meeting at London's Savoy Hotel.

It was dress-up time, and I wheeled out my Sunday best to try to tie up a deal with the Aussies. Thack scrubbed and dressed up well and looked a million dollars. To an outsider he had the appearance of a big-time Jewish businessman, which while I knew he wasn't, the Aussies didn't.

Ray carried off his act perfectly. Within an hour we concluded a deal to sell 49 per cent of Clogau St. David's shares to the Aussies.

Clogau St. David's Gold Mine plc was later listed on the London Stock Market. I was voted on to the board of directors, as the biggest single stockholder. But I felt out of my depth. Common sense and hard work were my talents, plus my experience in different businesses. This was about paper money, and definitely not hard work, as I knew it. The common sense factor didn't seem to enter into it and I have seen this virtue overlooked many times.

Money comes in from those who invest in the hope of increasing the valuation of what they have put in. They trust you and your fellow board members to do your best to make money for them, as well as for yourself. I watched as legal and accountancy expenses ate up bags of money.

It seemed to me that people figured gold mining was a gamble. I looked on with bewilderment as board members had everything first class, except me as I didn't really understand the game. I suppose it's called creative accountancy!

My philosophy in life has always been to save money rather than fritter it away. During my racing career I often spent hours at border controls or road blocks to avoid a few dollars worth of fees or charges.

Clogau's first chairman was Lord Harlech, who seemed to me a perfect gentleman, and I was sure he knew how to make a public limited company work.

Even though Lord Harlech lived in Wales, he didn't know too much about mining nor had, I believe, ever been down the eerie

Digging for gold in the Clogau St. David's Gold Mine. The Crown worn by the Prince of Wales is made from Clogau gold.

tunnels and vast caverns that the old boys tore up through the 1800s and 1900s with their picks and shovels.

Unfortunately, Lord Harlech was killed in his Audi in a car crash on the extremely dangerous A5 before he had the chance to show his true mettle as Clogau chairman.

Our next chairman, Lord King, was an even more controversial and tough British businessman, who had been through the school of hard knocks through his career in charge of Babcock and Wilcox bearing manufacturers.

Later Lord King was pulled in by British Airways in 1981 to get the business under control after they had suffered gigantic losses. He took them from the ashes into one of the most respected airlines in the world.

In some quarters, Lord King had a reputation as a bully and he made things happen by his sheer aggression and drive. His first meeting as Clogau St. David's Gold Mine plc's new chairman was worth paying an entrance fee to view.

He obviously was a master at handling meetings, as he had sat on numerous boards of large companies.

Sitting at the top of the table Lord King showed no emotion as he glanced over the top of his half-moon reading glasses at the two Aussies, a Kiwi, and the rest of the directors, all English.

After the formalities of opening the meeting, the Aussies launched their attack. It was obvious that they weren't 'Pommie' lovers, and now with another bloody Lord as chairman, they wondered what the hell was going on.

Across the table sat Collis, one of the Aussie businessmen, who opened his bowling attack with a half-smirk written across his face. He roared in: "Mr. Chairman, could you first of all please explain to me how the bloody hell have we got an Admiral as the Captain of our row-boat?"

I watched Lord King closely. His pale blue eyes peered unblinkingly, showing nothing. But I thought I detected a fleeting moment that flashed across his face that said he was going to have fun with this lot.

Collis' outburst was followed by a dramatic long pause as Lord King readied himself to face this prepared Aussie onslaught.

He was Middlesex-born but had spent a great part of his working life in the North of England so he called a spade a spade. His track record showed that he could handle and deflect this type of inflammatory comment to his advantage.

"Firstly," he said. "We must establish if our colonial friends are in this gold business for the glamour that surrounds it, especially the Royal gold, or are we here to run a profitable business and make money?"

Things went very quiet. Nobody had expected Lord King to counter-attack like this, and his answer knocked everybody, especially the cocky Aussies, backwards.

Lord King 1 Australia 0.

Suddenly all the faces at the table broke into smiles as the realisation dawned, 'hey, this Lord bloke speaks our language'.

The clearing of the air helped the meeting to settle down and good progress was made. Unfortunately, for political reasons, this was the only Clogau plc meeting Lord King ever chaired. It was a pity – he cut away all the bullshit and he would have made Clogau a much more successful company.

Meanwhile, Ray Thackwell wasn't letting the grass grow under his feet, and spent a year setting up deals in Liberia, West Africa. He had acquired gold concessions and staked claims along the Loffa River. These claims had been partially worked, by international mining company Globex in the 1980s, before the coup.

Even Liberia's new leader, President Doe, had worked on these claims when he was a private in the army. Doe used to spend time in Gbeni town and when he became the President of Liberia he rewarded the town with a large electric generator.

After Ray returned to England he told me it was possible and profitable to buy raw gold from the local miners in Liberia and it would show a healthy margin of around 25 per cent. I was nervous – would it work? All Ray's schemes sounded so easy.

After checking all the avenues, I figured gold was better than cash. Transportation was safe and insurance sound. Buyers were plentiful and would pay the world daily rate.

The money would come in on the day of the gold being delivered to their bank vault in Birmingham.

We came up with a set of working rules for any gold transactions involving the company. All deals had to be carried out at our Monrovia Bank under extra security. A gold assayer named Mike Beecham was to accompany Ray to Liberia to ensure the gold content was correct. Once satisfied all the stipulations suited me I felt happy to go ahead. The only thing was that I desperately wanted to go myself, but due to business reasons couldn't make it.

Surely I had all bases covered, so I rounded up the money to buy $166,000 worth of gold.

The money was deposited in our English bank with strict instructions on exactly the direction that the transfer must take.

We'd heard that some New York banks were at times a real problem. So, what did our English bank do? They completely ignored our instructions and they sent the money to Monrovia via New York. Believe it or not, the money simply disappeared. It went into a New York-based bank and never came out.

"What do you mean you've lost our $166,000?" I screamed down the telephone line to the Big Apple. "Are you a fucking bank or not?" All my complaints fell on deaf ears and, frankly, the New York bank didn't care. At this point I was panicking big-time and I went back to our English bank and demanded, tongue in cheek, that they send a second $166,000 – this time as per our instructions.

Realising their blunder, and persuaded by a copy of the letter I had sent them with specific instructions, this time they did send it straight into our Monrovia bank.

So much for our banking systems. How much money do they lose? From then on we dealt in travellers' cheques. You could feel them, cash them, and do what you wanted with them. If you happen to lose them, then it's your problem.

So the start of our gold-buying deals began badly, but hopefully all our troubles would be behind us.

The gold was to be exchanged at our Monrovian bank. But for various reasons the purchase couldn't be carried out as planned. I was thousands of miles away, relying on second-hand information to make such a big decision. I didn't know the people Thackwell was dealing with in Liberia.

If the same situation had arisen in England I would have pulled the plug. But by now we had spent quite a large amount of time and money to set up this deal. Based on the available information I decided to purchase only $40,000 worth of gold.

I had always been a little worried about Thackwell's judgment of people and this deal was starting to prove me correct.

The gold was delivered – and then stolen during the night. The bent Liberian who Thackwell had relied on fled into neighbouring Gambia. The borders between the two countries were completely corrupt and for a few dollars you could take a whole army through the Liberian–Gambia border post.

Information later gained showed the Liberian had started a taxi business in Gambia. A bitter ex-girlfriend told the police of his whereabouts, and we were informed we could have had him extradited.

But dragging him back into Liberia and sticking him in jail made no sense either, as we guessed he would simply buy himself out within weeks.

Most of all, if there was any money left, it would disappear in bribes. It would have been stupid to throw good money after bad. More stories emerged which said that Liberia had been riddled with foreigners coming in to make a 'quick buck' out of the supposedly stupid locals.

My bad experience on this deal was that we were in fact the stupid ones. It proved two things to me. One, you must stay with the money, and you must be the one to handle all the financial transactions. Secondly, that Thackwell had dreadful judgment. Hopefully, this knowledge would prove invaluable in all future dealings with Africans, were I to ever go down that avenue again.

The final lesson was that a bad deal never improves. Blame can only be laid at my feet; it was my decision to carry on. I should have pulled the plug, nobody was twisting my arm.

Money down the drain but we give Liberia another shot

20

THE disastrous affair of the magically disappearing money effectively ended any chance that I would consider conducting future business in Liberia. Any further participation would have to be studied under a microscope and approached with great reservation.

After all the trouble and turmoil and the shenanigans with various police and government departments in our quest for the return of the stolen money, the penny finally dropped. I realised that if I approached business matters in the same way as I would back home or in a western country, I would always be fighting a losing battle.

The saying "When in Rome …" kept filtering through my mind and I was unable to shake it off. I had tried to make allowances for the differences in culture but even then I hadn't gone nearly far enough.

Doing business in most African countries you have no chance of success with a mindset that assumes you are protected by the same laws we enjoy in our society.

While I had some understanding of the Liberian mentality, I didn't do enough to immerse myself in it fully. I failed to totally grasp that this was a Third World country and that I had no option but to play by their rules. It didn't matter if it was right or wrong or fair. It was just the way it was.

Truth and honesty were two words seldom practiced or used in Liberia. It was a public infrastructure built upon bribery and corruption and had, over time, evolved into a system which worked for a select few and drained millions from others.

"You scratch my back and I'll scratch yours," might as well have been a national motto. While such a concept prevailed at all levels of life in Africa, there was not even the slightest pretence at covering it up in Liberia. Even if it was a matter of only one dollar or millions, it jeopardised lives and livelihoods, it didn't matter. Liberia didn't need a monarchy. Corruption was king. Even in our sophisticated world the same happens but it's 'beneath the covers'.

In the course of handling the stolen money issue, I had placed Ray Thackwell on the back burner and took complete control myself.

I was quickly discovering that in Africa you were completely responsible for your own business. If you allowed someone to rob you, there was no question of expecting the law to rescue you. Justice didn't come from a public system, it needed to be meted out personally.

We had allowed ourselves to become exposed, and we were paying the price. I didn't realise it at the time but this modified thinking would serve me well in my future dealings in Liberia. With crooked officials, options were limited. It was a case of either pay up, or expect nothing. Money doesn't just talk in Liberia – it is the only voice that matters.

As hard as I tried to implement this way of thinking, at times something within me rebelled against it. Whether it was my own stubbornness or simply my upbringing in a more legitimised and structured society, handing over my hard-earned cash to those I felt didn't deserve it gnawed at me.

The loss of $40,000 was an expensive price to pay, even for such a valuable lesson – literally a crash course in Liberian business. Offers to help in Liberia rarely came without a hidden agenda. So when I received a fax out of the blue from a security officer working for President Doe's Mansion House group I approached it with a degree of trepidation.

As I read the message from Jerry Bryon, about how he had heard of our problems with the stolen gold and wanted to help, my brain screamed with suspicion and a sense of 'here we go again'.

It took a while for the name to register with me, but after a couple of hours I remembered. Jerry was the BBC television reporter whose horrific clips from Monrovia we had watched in Southampton back in 1980.

Jerry had a mountain to climb to stand any chance of helping me go back to Liberia. But he had a slick line of patter and an earnest manner that came through in print. It seemed as if he could help yet still doubt raged through me. Did I believe him because I wanted to, or because his plan made sense?

Jerry told me he had a friend in the local government in the county of Grand Gedeh. Within this family they had the rights for a large gold concession situated only 40 miles from the regional capital of Zwedru.

Talk of the 'family' sounded good. Even '40 miles' sounded okay. It didn't even cross my mind to think about what the word 'family' could mean, and just how big an African family could be.

Also disregarded was the true meaning of '40 miles', which I sub-consciously associated with a 40-minute drive around the M25. In Africa, a measurement of distance could mean it was taken 'as the crow flies'. With single tracks and mountainous terrain to negotiate, such a journey could take days to cover.

However, I always believed that God loves a trier and there was something about Jerry that made me want to trust him. I peppered him with questions and he had the right answer, time and time again.

He wanted us to go to Zwedru, 200 miles south-east of Monrovia. He insisted that our geologist, John Clutterbuck, be accompanied by gold assayer Mike Beaumont and me, to fly to

Not a lot of room in a Liberian bath.

Zwedru to check out the gold mining possibilities, and the costs of the project sounded reasonable.

Understandably, Junie wasn't too happy with me wanting to take off to Liberia. She was a special woman who understood me better than I do myself and had no desire to see me heading off to an area of such instability. Junie remembered the horrors of the 1980 coup, but I convinced her that the country had now settled down after the new government and President Doe had re-taken control. With a certainty that I didn't completely believe, I assured her that nothing could, or would, go wrong.

Control of the money was very important to me, so I made a very thin nylon money belt, which also held my passport. A small pocket on the left held a $50 bill while the right pocket contained a $100 note.

The severity of the trouble I encountered would determine whether I went to the left or right pocket. Junie knew about neither.

The flight to Monrovia was with KLM, via Amsterdam. I had some decent contacts in the airline industry that had often smoothed things such as excess baggage for me on previous trips. But I didn't know anyone at KLM and, as I had 15 bags of supplies and equipment, there was a major problem looming. That amount of luggage meant coughing up serious money – it would double the price of the plane tickets if we had to fork out.

I figured we would need plenty of smart ideas if things were to go our way in Liberia, so why not try cutting a few corners now? Money saved is money earned, so I wasn't going to lose hundreds of pounds without a fight.

We arrived at the airport an hour earlier than needed, a plan evolving in my mind. Once at Heathrow I studied the airline staff to see who might be sympathetic to our plight, while sending Clutterbuck and Beaumont upstairs for a cuppa. I eventually narrowed it down to two baggage agents. One was a jovial middle-aged woman who clearly loved her job and probably wrote the customer service manual.

The other was a slim Liberian man who didn't seem to care about much, and looked like work was an inconvenience rather than a profession. I'd seen him let one guy through already with at least four overweight bags.

After another five minutes of watching the pair I went upstairs to get John and Mike's passports and airline tickets and as I returned I was surprised at how nervous I felt. I understood that the next few minutes, minor as it was, might give me a good indication of how well I could read people and use my wits.

I had always prided myself on my ability to think on my feet, and now was the time to prove it. I finally went for 'Miss Customer Service'. Striding up to the desk, I greeted her with a big smile and a good morning.

"I've got a problem, love," I said, maintaining eye contact. "I'm part of a group travelling to Monrovia and I have most of their bags with me. They are all coming up from the West Country and, as it's getting late, I'd like to check in three of us and all the luggage. The others will only have hand baggage, I'm sorry if it's a problem."

I had felt her looking me up and down trying to work out if this was all a bunch of bull or a legitimate request. As it was, she gave me the green light straight away.

"Don't worry sir," she said. "I'll check in all the baggage, and when the rest arrive they will just have to check in to get their boarding cards."

Job done – and I hadn't even had to lie. Well, maybe a little white one.

The trip to Amsterdam was short and comfortable. In contrast, the long grinding flight to Liberia seemed to take forever. The uncertainty of what actually was at the end worried me a bit, but certainly not enough to stop me sleeping.

Monrovia International Airport is over an hour from the capital of Liberia. It was situated at an old American air base called Robertsfield. The village has a very strong smell of food, and the locals named it the village of 'smell no taste'.

The flight had been long and mind-numbing but any boredom was swept away within seconds of our arrival. As I stepped from the plane the heat hit me, it was a wall of sweltering air that made breathing a challenge. But that was just one part of the obstacle course that had to be negotiated before officially entering the country.

The packed arrival hall was a sea of humanity with crowds of people all mired in a similar state of confusion. Speedway riders and paperwork don't normally make a great combination and I struggled to get my head around the stack of forms I was told I had to fill in.

After scribbling down my name and date of birth half a dozen times on different coloured sheets of paper, we joined a long line. However, before we had moved a couple of feet a tall local with ill-fitting clothes asked me if I was Barry Briggs. I nodded and we followed him upstairs.

The room to which we were taken was badly air-conditioned, but at least it was better than the oppressive conditions in the main terminal. Standing up to shake hands with us stood a man who looked remarkably similar to President Doe. Bloody hell, I thought during a split second of madness, have we got an official welcome? Later I was to realise why there was a similarity, they were both from the Krahn tribe.

But it was Jerry Bryon, wearing horn-rimmed glasses and dressed casually smart; he had a very open face and a winning smile. He took our passports and papers, handing them to an airport employee who was dispatched to take care of the formalities. Jerry obviously had some clout, and I was suitably impressed.

Five minutes later our documentation was completed and we were ready to go. First though, the madness of the baggage hall had to be survived. To say we were unprepared for the sheer pandemonium of the human circus that greeted us would be an epic understatement. It was like one of those dreams where bits and pieces make sense but everything else is utter confusion.

At the root of it, as we would soon discover, like everything else in Liberia, was the basic human desire for money. Everyone was on the scam … men, women and children, eagerly looking out for the next foreign mug to dupe into handing over some cash.

I spotted one of our green bags disappearing into the distance, carried effortlessly on the back of an athletic young local. And there was another, being pulled off the carousel by another youngster. And three more on the far side of the terminal, being watched over by another unfamiliar face.

At that point I felt there was a genuine chance we would leave the airport without any of our possessions and began to feel utterly helpless. Jerry spotted the anxiety on my face and burst into action to sort out the issue. With a combination of barking orders, finger pointing and authoritative shouting, he managed to round up all of our belongings, and within five minutes they were stashed at our feet by one of the exit doors.

It was an early taste of Liberian life and further proof that we were going to have to fend for ourselves. If we couldn't look after our own business, it was going to cost us, both in terms of real money and convenience.

The level of chaos was nothing short of astonishing and for the first time I truly believed the tales of potential investors getting no further than the airport on their 'get rich quick' scheme before turning round to go back home. The taxi rank provided yet another potential pitfall for the unwitting foreigner, with the kind of scrum that would have done the All Blacks proud, as we converged towards a couple of battered vehicles at the kerb-side.

I saw Clutterbuck's teeth clench as he spotted the scene, but he needn't have worried. Jerry announced he would be taking us into town in his car, a battered old Toyota estate that was clearly his pride and joy.

Jerry was keen to get straight into tour guide mode, pointing out plenty of local landmarks and places of historical importance in Liberian culture, amid the bizarre backdrop of a cassette tape playing the latest preaching of the famed evangelist Oral Roberts.

I'd heard that Liberia was a deeply religious country, yet with my 40 grand having disappeared into a black hole and the manner in which it was handled, I would take a bit more convincing about this nation's godly tendencies.

I was keen to quiz Jerry on his time as a reporter for the BBC, but decided there would be other more ideal opportunities once we got to know each other better. Jerry dropped us off at our accommodation, Julia's Bar in Gurley Street, which was a well-known watering hole and meeting point for westerners looking for some familiar home comforts.

To see fish and chips on the menu at dinner that evening was a bit of a shock – how could I resist? It wasn't too bad either, even if it wasn't quite up to the standard set by our local Southampton chippy, but the cost was just a fraction of what we paid at home.

I went to sleep that night at Julia's with a full stomach. My brain was also full, but not with contentment. My mind wrestled all night, subconsciously trying to figure out what tomorrow would hold for us on our trip through a real jungle.

Arrested in the jungle and we have to pay 25 US dollars for our release

21

WE were up at the cruck of dawn for our trip to Grand Gedeh County, flying to the capital Zwedru, the launch pad for another new adventure.

Because of the shortage of time with the wet season imminent we decided to travel on a privately chartered plane from Monrovia's small Spriggs Payne airfield.

My back was creaking from the long flight from London but I was anxious to get on with business.

As we climbed the narrow steps to board our small high-winged Cessna, we were greeted by our pilot, Roger, a serious-looking Belgian who had been in Liberia for more than a decade.

Looking at this Cessna plane, I had to smile to myself. In my 'Walter Mitty' mind I visualised having rescued myself and our crew when our pilot had a heart attack. I took over the controls and saved our souls when I landed safely. Wake up 'Biggles Briggs'. My fantasy was triggered by the sight of the plane. I had soloed and passed my pilot's licence in a smaller version of this Cessna model many years previously.

As the plane rose from the tarmac and edged away from Monrovia, my spirits began to lift too. I'd been to dozens of capital cities in my time and witnessed the carnage and extremes of humanity they can display. But Monrovia was something else altogether and, flying above the city, you realise why there is a malaria problem as the city is surrounded by water, some of which looked stagnant, the ideal breeding ground for mosquitoes, the transportation for malaria.

Monrovia demanded constant vigilance to avoid falling prey to opportunistic conmen or thieves and the culture shock was quite overwhelming. It wasn't the most threatening place I had been to but it was one hell of a challenge to spend time in somewhere operated by the law of the jungle – survival of the fittest, or smartest.

Strange to say, I found the Liberians to be the nicest of the Africans I had met. Circumstances made them do what they did. They were friendly, happy people, especially when untarnished by booze and dope.

Sitting next to me on the plane was a man of the cloth, Reverend Paul Scott. Jerry had told us that morning that he couldn't accompany us to Zwedru and had lined up the Rev. as his replacement.

While it was a surprise to have a religious man thrust into what was a pretty atheist group, the key was that, like Jerry, Reverend Scott was a Krahn.

Over time I would come to understand the full importance of the tribal structure in Liberia and its significance in everyday life. At this point I was still learning but was reassured nevertheless when I learned of the Reverend's background.

On the flight Scott told us about his position in Liberia – he conducted services three times a week at his local church and was coach of a kids' football team. For all that, he didn't make me feel entirely secure or protected. We would find out in the next couple of weeks just how reliable he was. For the moment he seemed to have things under control.

When we arrived in Zwedru, it was good to find it cooler than Monrovia. The town was surrounded by green, healthy-looking bush and trees covering the rolling hills, some of which were a couple of thousand feet high, but not really mountains.

The local airport was completely different from the chaos of its counterpart in Monrovia. Very few foreigners ventured to this neck of the woods.

We were taken to an old house near the airfield. There we met about 20 young Africans who, we discovered, were mostly students hired to come with us into the backwoods.

Guidebooks will tell you that English is the language of choice in Liberia but I couldn't understand more than the occasional word when the locals spoke. It's referred to as pigeon (or pidgin) English; unfortunately I'm not a pigeon! With clipped words and sentences, and a little dash of the American jive talk, it made for tough listening, let alone understanding.

We needed 15 lads just to carry the bags we had bought from England. Another three large bags were added, filled with all the new provisions to help keep us going for the next two weeks in the jungle.

A trip to Khalid's, the local Lebanese trading post, quickly filled the extra bags. We needed a great variety of goods for our upcoming trek. Rice, water, dried fish, biscuits, plus other food, a couple of hurricane lamps, torches, mosquito repellent and medical kit, plus the most important source to get to the gold – spades. The store thought it was Christmas as we tried to purchase 10 but they only could find eight and that included their own old used one. The Lebanese will never give up a deal.

They are the ultimate traders. Their forebears started a hundred years ago in the rivers of Liberia, trading mainly rice and a good variety of goods from their canoes. They could be found in the most desolate places and they knew how to make money; without them we figured the country would collapse.

The Mandingos are the African Lebanese but are hard to deal with. The Lebanese had a direct line of communication with the President and paid little or no duties on imports and taxes, it all went into the President's box.

It was common knowledge that presidents and their government ministers had sticky fingers – money due never seemed to get to the correct department.

The run-of-the-mill government employees hadn't been paid for four months yet there were no riots from the unpaid employees. Maybe it was the dire consequences connected with the rule of the gun.

Before long I discovered that the Rev's commitment to holy matters didn't prevent him from telling the odd white lie. Time and again I threw out the question of how far we had to walk, but he was as silver-tongued as they come and, what he didn't know, he would have a go at answering with good old-fashioned bullshit.

At all times he tried very hard to tell us what we wanted to hear, not necessarily what we needed to hear. His estimate of 12 miles was hard to believe; just looking at the nearest large hills they had to be a minimum 10 miles away. All our helpers just said our trek was 'longa-longa way boss'.

I didn't share with the group my concerns over whether my body would be able to handle the exertion. Just six weeks earlier I had been laid up in hospital following a nasty crash in New Zealand and I prayed I would be up to the challenge. Not only did I want to get to our destination but I also didn't want to show any weakness in front of the locals.

The accepted method for carrying bags was on your head, which caused a fair bit of laughter as the Africans watched us trying to balance equipment on our skulls before setting off. But we were only play acting, as we only had to carry our bodies to our destination. Our floppy bags were inclined to fold around their heads, and there was much amusement all round before flat bits of plywood were found to cure the problem.

Clutterbuck was an old pro at this kind of situation and kept himself to himself. Everything he needed was packed neatly into a little carry bag and, while I didn't expect any fuss or complaint from him, there wouldn't be a whole lot of humour either.

Mike Beaumont was a different kettle of fish, just happy to be on the trip and not afraid to do more than his fair share when needed.

Beaumont was piled high with gear but looked to have the physique and mentality to shoulder the extra load.

Our mate the Reverend, meanwhile, wasn't carrying anything and had his own assistant to cart his kit into the jungle. Not until our posse had headed out of town and towards the distant mountains did I do a final head count, which came to 23 people. At the head of the group was a girl I had not previously noticed – another expense for Kiwi Minerals?

Kiwi was our new operating name, devised a few weeks earlier when I decided 'Barry Briggs' wasn't right for a company of supposedly international prestige.

As I heard the bag carriers talk about our operation as a 'big American company' I couldn't help but chuckle to myself. Little did they realise that the sum total of Kiwi Minerals staff and directors were standing directly in front of them.

I had no idea which direction we were heading, but we were soon in a deeply wooded area, trekking along a single-lane track. We seemed to be climbing all the time but because of the trees and foliage it was difficult to gauge what kind of progress we were making.

It was as tough on my body as I expected and luckily I was wearing a pair of good training shoes, in stark contrast to all the boys carrying the heavy bags in their flip-flops, with no protection. It was very humid, and we sweated profusely. Luckily the trees lining most of our route gave us shade and coverage that protected us from the overhead sun which was a blessing in disguise.

It was the first time that I realised just how different westerners smell when sweating, compared with the black person with their very strong and acidy aroma. I wondered how I smelled to them? The girl at the front of the party was wearing an African wrap, a simple long piece of material wrapped around her body, and she must have been as hot as hell.

She also wore flip-flops, but she was like a ballerina, even balancing a heavy bag on her head while gliding along. At one point a downed tree blocking the pathway was traversed with remarkable grace.

Jungle, jungle, jungle and more jungle …

Can't find a signpost anywhere!

We exited the forest to the small village of Kali late in the day and it was dark by the time sleeping arrangements had been carried out. Normally you would be careful where you decide to sleep but I was so knackered I just collapsed in a heap without a care in the world.

The next morning we were up at daylight. Across the dirt track from where we had slept, there was a football field. Unbelievably at this time in the morning there were half a dozen kids having a kick-around in the goalmouth with an improvised football. It looked like an old part of the canvas car tool kit, filled with grass, but it seemed to do the job. Illustrating just how small the world really is, one kid was wearing a beat-up tattered Arsenal shirt.

Amazingly my body didn't feel too bad after the extreme workout from the day before but I still wasn't minded to join the locals in their impromptu game of football. The day's trek involved crossing several streams, which I figured meant there was probably some kind of decent-sized river not too far away. I would have asked someone, but by this time I was starting to labour a bit and didn't want to use up any more energy than needed.

It was practically dark when we stopped again and this time I pitched my one-man tent in a clearing. The best part of all this was that I only had to look after myself, so obviously it appeared that the Rev. must be doing a reasonable job. I was secretly pleased to see that I wasn't the only one struggling, as almost everyone looked wiped out physically by the end of the day. By the look of them they didn't need a bed, they could have fallen asleep on a clothes line.

This village was called Dweh Town and was run by a Paramount Chief who came to greet us foreigners before we closed down for the night. The township seemed quite large, and there must have been 300 living there, as they all gathered in the morning to gaze at the 'big American Company'.

Some of the local maidens were easy on the eye and had clearly not yet been introduced to bras. The amazing thing was that here in the middle of the jungle the local maidens knew how to flaunt their bodies, especially to three white men.

I wondered why we were so late in leaving, until I saw all our shovels on the ground in front of the chief's hut. What followed was a half-hour ceremony to bless our shovels, and to ask that God would help us to find the riches from the ground – gold.

Getting ready to leave, the kids were loading up the cases on to their heads when suddenly the entire group erupted with laughter. Clutterbuck's thin vintage cardboard case, which must have been as old as he was, finally gave way. The young Liberian charged with carrying it hoisted it on to his head, the case collapsed, the young lad's head disappeared completely inside and he staggered around for several seconds, unable to see anything.

As everyone was creased up with laughter, it was great to see that the Liberians had a healthy sense of humour. The kid involved made the most of the gag as well, hamming it up like he was on the West End stage with a liberal dose of slapstick and farce.

That incident put the group in good spirits for that day's travels and we made good time. By mid-afternoon we finally stopped near a creek – the area that would be our home for the next two weeks. A flat plateau was selected and all the bags were dumped in a heap.

The Liberian lads were fantastic with their machetes and rapidly cleared an area to house our camp. A fire was quickly lit and the kettle was boiling for my first cuppa in days. "This is more like it," I thought that night. "This is real adventure." And so it was for a few days, real boy-scout stuff. Camping out, working hard and finding gold in an area that seemed rich with the stuff.

At night we sat around the camp table telling tales and sharing food. The locals told us that 10 years before a 50-year-old Dutchman called Jokam Vandenburg worked in this area for gold. He was a wild one and fathered quite a few of the coffee-coloured kids around the area. He lived hard and drank all of the local palm wine he could get his hands on. He had guns to guard his gold and wouldn't be fazed to pull the trigger.

Many times in the middle of the night, the peace and quiet was broken by rounds of gunfire. The wild Dutchman was having pot shots at any passing animals. Anyone even thinking of nicking any of his gold would have had to be a raving lunatic. Suddenly, there was a crashing noise that immediately took our minds from our food, and a giant specimen of a man emerged out of the forest clad in an official-looking uniform. The first thing I had noticed about him was his feet, covered in black boots, which immediately told me that he was a Liberian copper.

The man marched straight to the Rev. and handed him a rolled piece of paper, then stood back glaring, with his arms folded. The Rev. opened the document and his face creased – and he immediately started jabbering away in a tone I couldn't understand. Their words were sharp and their voices raised and I demanded to know what was going on.

The Rev. thrust the paper into my hand and I felt a jolt run through me. I couldn't believe what I was reading and I didn't know whether to laugh or cry. In the end I did the opposite – I got angry. The poor old Reverend hadn't seen me pissed off yet.

The proclamation was dated that day from Dweh Town. It was headed: Arrest Warrant. Underneath, in smaller writing, it read: "To arrest three white men and bring them immediately to the Paramount Chief at Dweh Town."

Even better, we had to pay $25 each for the 'privilege' of being arrested. What a carve up.

When I read it out, Clutterbuck looked glum, Beaumont just smiled.

"Reverend," I yelled. "Tell the bloody copper that we aren't playing and we are definitely not moving from here. If he wants to arrest someone, that's going to be you, Reverend. You got us into this crap, now you sort it out."

I couldn't imagine what a prison cell in this part of the world looked like and I didn't want to find out. I never really expected the policeman to arrest the Reverend, I'd used it as a way to get him to sort out the problem more quickly. But he did, the Reverend stood up and then he just disappeared off into the night with the policeman. The copper looked disappointed to have missed out on arresting three white men, but smug to be returning to base with something to show for it.

After the shock, we had a real good laugh. What if we had a few white fellas over for a barbecue, which three white men would they have picked?

Two days later the Rev. was back. He had to put his hand in his pocket as he had failed to get permission for us to come into Konobo County. Zwedru was in Tchen county. But this was Africa at its best, $25 each to get arrested, and the books were balanced.

Or were they? The next day a goat was sent as a peace offering from the Paramount Chief. The Rev. cooked it that night and it tasted great. But, after paying out $75, it was still a pretty expensive meal.

Just over a week of testing determined that the gold was of good quality and plentiful. However, it was very difficult to get to as it was so deep into the jungle.

The logistics would be a huge obstacle. To put in roads and surrounding infrastructure would need a huge investment and I got the sense that working in this type of jungle and its oppressive conditions would have a bad mental effect on you over the course of time. We had done all we could so we decided to head back to Monrovia and, with a bit of time in hand, we would get John Clutterbuck to evaluate the geology on the Loffa river diamond concession, into which Thackwell had poured a large amount of money for no return.

The Loffa project was completely different from the gold concession at Zwedru and was open and bright, sitting right beside the main Loffa river.

There were large villages on each side of the wide river. On our claim side was Saki Town and, over the river, was the village of Gbeni.

The tests carried out by Clutterbuck determined that all the minerals that are associated with diamonds showed up well. So, after all the travel and work, the old Loffa river deal looked to be the best.

It was amazing. Did Thackwell really think that if the Liberian workers had found diamonds they would ring him in England and tell him? I reckoned they had written off Thackwell as a joke or stupid.

The only way to operate a mine in Liberia is to move to Africa and run it like a proper business. The main thing is that you must be able to hold everything together, no matter what. You and your fellow foreign workers are the only white men within a 40-mile radius.

Boss ... we have a problem.

Packing our gear in England to build our mine in Africa

22

INSTEAD of enjoying a nice, relaxing trip on the plane back home from Liberia, my mind was racing at over one hundred miles an hour. My thinking was all over the place. Did it make sense to even think about returning? Could we find enough diamonds and gold to actually make some money? The answer was probably not because we needed lots of luck to discover some really big diamonds ... we had more chance of winning the football pools! The only chance we had was to prove the potential of our claims site and, having done that, convince another mining company or a large investor that they should buy part of our operation.

I asked my travelling companion, John Clutterbuck, his thoughts on our diamond prospect on the Lofa river. He was positive it was great, but felt that tight control would be needed. He said he would spell it out for me in his report which would be finished and with me inside a week.

The report was really positive. So I decided to give Liberia another go. This time with my younger son Tony, who had physically recovered from his speedway crash although unfortunately it had effectively ended his racing career. He was at a bit of a loose end and wanted to come with me. Being on the board of Clogau plc gave me the chance of meeting people in the mining business and helped me decide how I was going to attack and conquer Liberia.

I needed to raise some extra money to finance the testing that was an important requirement to prove to potential investors that we had something of value that they would want to invest in. That necessitated a proper geological report with samples and results.

The Clutterbuck report was very optimistic and we wanted John to come back to Liberia to substantiate our claims. Unfortunately, he was off to work in Malaysia but he gave us the name of Mike Joll, a fellow geologist he felt sure would do a good job for us.

Sons Gary and Tony and I got some money together and a Kiwi friend, Alan Davidson, who lived in Los Angeles, thought it sounded like a good deal and also put up some hard cash. Mining wise, our resources were just peanuts compared to what would normally be needed, so this operation would have to be on a very tight Kiwi budget.

The trip with three of us to the Loffa project turned out well as far as the final report went. But Tony and I had a bit of trouble negotiating new agreements on the venture. Apart from the deal with the claim owners, Thackwell had given away some bits of the company, which we had to re-purchase to gain complete control.

Previously, those working on the project had been receiving monthly payments simply to make the diameter of the hole in the ground bigger. We needed to change tactics. If we kept making the hole larger we would have no water problems – but if we went deeper we would require pumps and need extra money for running costs. We were only going to find diamonds by going deeper into the diamondiferous materials formed under the river bottom thousands of years ago.

But, back in Southampton, it was all systems go as we started to gather up all the equipment needed for the Liberian assault. The first major purchase was a 1970 Land Rover, ex-Southern

Electricity, impossible to miss as it was a rusty red. A good buy was a small Honda generator that could run all our power tools and, of course, provide lighting when we needed it.

The biggest drain on our budget was the addition of a new five-cylinder gravel pump. It was big, the size of a small car, and was mounted on four wheels. I've always liked a deal with value for money but this time I had to forget the cost. This machine was going to be the workhorse of the whole operation. With the dry season only five workable months long, time was of the essence and we couldn't afford any breakdowns, so paying extra for a new pump made common sense.

We packed up all our camping gear plus an electric welder, which was essential and had to be very mobile, run off our small generator.

The seats from our old Citroën estate finished up as a great idea for our living room furniture – who wouldn't want adjustable backs to their sofas? We also gathered up all Junie's old kitchen gear, pots, pans, knives and forks, the lot. And we took a couple of pump-up mattresses, which proved to be useless.

Taking up a lot of space and very heavy was the hydraulic gear for dredging from our raft. The back yard of our beautiful Southampton house looked like a rubbish tip.

Luckily, we found a special five-gallon earthenware water filtration system at our local junk shop. With water a lifeline in the hot, humid jungle conditions, the earthenware system would prove vital. Being able to keep the water cool and drinkable was worth the cost of freight to Africa.

So, finding bits and pieces went on and on until we figured we had everything we needed. Junie was very happy when all this gear passed through the gates of Robin Hill on its way to Liberia.

Our container was in Southampton so we needed numerous trips to take all the gear there to pack. Two items that would prove to be invaluable were our motorcycles. They would provide transportation on tracks impossible for cars and, even better, having a chance to ride them from time to time would help keep us sane. The most comfortable was Junie's Yamaha, her Christmas present, but I knew she would not be that sorry to see it going to

Liberia and out of her life. The other one was my old Ossa trials bike.

The small budget was our biggest concern. Even stretching it as I knew we could, it would still only buy us a certain amount of time before the cash ran out – maybe before we proved the viability of the project. If we proved it could be profitable, we could then raise more capital on the back of this report. Then all our hard work, plus the buckets of money thrown at the project, would not be wasted.

It was 4am as we snuck out of the front gate of Robin Hill on our way to the Africa-bound container in the Southampton docks. Our old Land Rover was packed so tightly we reckoned you couldn't have got another nut and bolt inside. The trouble was it was dangerous, being so heavy. To exceed 20mph would be like committing suicide. Hence, our pre-dawn operation with everyone hoping the local police force would all be asleep.

When the Land Rover was loaded into the container we were ready for jungle action ... or so we thought.

But, as normal, there was trouble at the last moment. The diving gear, and a massive two-foot cutter head purchased in California arrived that very morning.

We reckoned we couldn't fit anything else in the Land Rover – wrong!

We cut out the passenger's front seat and got it all in, the only problem being when driving you couldn't change gear. That was something we decided to sort out when we got to Liberia. If a thief tried to nick our trusty steed he would have been in trouble as his getaway speed, jammed in first gear, would only be a massive three miles per hour! The travel time for the container by sea was three weeks to the port of Monrovia. Tony and I were booked to fly out in two weeks and we hoped to be there a week before the container arrived.

On our arrival we now knew the ropes much better and survived the airport drama, although I must admit with some help from one of Jerry's men. We then headed straight to Julia's Bar in the middle of the city, where a clean bed and reasonable food awaited us.

It was to our advantage that Julia had taken a shine to our Tony; she must have looked good some 20 years earlier and she was very kind to us.

She worried about us as she didn't like us going to live up in the jungle. Julia said to us regularly: "I wish you boys weren't up there mining."

She had had three separate groups staying at her bar over the past couple of years, all mining up near the same area that we were working. At various intervals all three groups came back from the jungle and simply quit. One was only in the jungle for a week and had had enough. All just left all their gear there and returned home.

Liberia got the name of 'white man's graveyard' because of the oppressive heat, the dealing with people that were on a completely different wavelength and the jungle which could seem to close down on you, if you let it.

To secure the required paperwork from the Ministry of Mines was tough going as everything cost some dash (polite word for bribery, or Christmas present!)

At this point we had to hope that our man Jerry was straight. As he was on our wage bill he should have been protecting us. Certainly I didn't trust the Minister of Mines and was later proved to be correct.

We took a quick trip to Claratown, on the outskirts of Monrovia, to meet Duane Marks, an American who was dabbling in mining.

We went by taxi and painted on the back guard was the slogan 'Jesus loves you baby.' We had to share the back seat with a black girl breastfeeding her baby and, although we didn't know where to look, she wasn't embarrassed at all. The woman in the front seat was trying to nurse a chicken, which wasn't particularly happy and flapped its wings and squawked like the devil. Even this couldn't take our minds from the gurgling and sucking going on beside us.

Duane Marks was one of Ray Thackwell's finds so we knew we had to pay attention. We only found out later that Ray had cut him into the Loffa project deal.

A nice bloke, but with no real idea of what was going on, he was making us a washing plant which was due for collection and would be ready in a week, or so he informed us.

"Great, see you next week," we said as we left the workshop and headed back to town. I suggested we went for lunch at El Meson on Benson Street, a restaurant popular with foreigners that Julia had told us about. I thought we might even find someone there that could help us to have made a tie bracket that we needed to get our generator working again.

Tony promptly agreed and took the lead. One day I would be the leader, then a day or two later he would take over. Liberia was a place that got to you in strange ways, and it was good to have your best buddy to lean on when it wasn't your day.

At the bar, I had my normal coke, without ice which is not advisable if you don't know where the water has come from. Tony had a local Club beer.

We sat enjoying our drinks and politely declined invitations from a couple of the local lovelies to join them. Then I turned in my seat and the bloke next to me smiled and we got talking. Richard Tillin is English and from Poole in Dorset.

"Barry, you don't need to introduce yourselves," he said "I know you and Tony from Poole and Southampton speedway."

It was the biggest piece of luck we could have had. It seemed everyone knew Richard as he was the workshop manager at Elias Bros, the Toyota agents. All of a sudden we had a workshop, plus someone who turned out to be a great friend. When things got tough we would meet up with Rich, who had the perfect cure – 'a laugh a day keeps the Liberian blues away'.

Tony and I felt much more relaxed as soon as he struck up a conversation. As the three of us were talking, a stocky middle-aged bloke arrived in our company. He had a well lived-in face and as soon as he opened his mouth it was obvious he was a worldly tough Irishman.

"Hi Rich, I was hoping to see you here," he said. "I can't come to the golf on Saturday as it's the Cheltenham Gold Cup and I'm on to make a fortune. God's given me the nod."

Richard introduced us to Father Terry and we got our hands crushed by his handshake. After he had finished wrecking our hands, he launched into a joke.

"There was this Irish priest who was sent as a missionary to

Africa. The tribe that was his flock actually consisted of cannibals. He was really pleased with the great progress he had achieved. In no time at all he had convinced them that on Fridays they should only eat fishermen." We all laughed and as Father Terry departed Richard quietly filled us in.

"Lads, he's a really funny man, but sometimes his jokes are crap. He's a real character, he was a jump jockey and, would you believe, also a boxer but he has a heart of gold.

"Father Terry is a Catholic priest and has been in Liberia for more than five years. He loves where he lives, as his church at Bush Road Island is right next to the Club Beer factory and one of his flock is the Swiss manager. He reckons that he's found heaven right here.

"Early in the week he was arrested on two charges. Later in the week he was on his way to town to speak to the police about the problem. He was dressed in his best white and gold gown, complete with all his church regalia. He was driving into town in his battered old green Honda when he decided to stop outside the travel agents, to book his ticket for home leave in Ireland.

"Getting out of his car a policeman asked him for some money. 'No, no money', he replied entering the travel agents. When he came out the policeman was letting his tyres down, because he hadn't given him any money. Father Terry, with his white gown flowing, simply pulled the policeman up, and punched him one in the mouth.

"It turned into a fist fight but the unfortunate policeman didn't know that he was involved in fisticuffs with an ex-boxer. All around the fight, taxis were blocking the road. Most of the drivers recognised Father Terry, and it was like a circus, horns being blown and all the cabbies yelling.

"A large crowd had gathered and everyone joined the cabbies and chorused together, 'Go on father, go on father, whack him one.'

"It was a one-sided fight, a clear winner and the crowd's favourite and hero was the one and only 'Father Terry'.

"The police were always hustling the taxi drivers for money. All the cheering drivers felt that the Lord had come to their rescue, and was at last sorting out some justice for them. Father Terry never had to pay for a taxi ride again."

We all were creased up with laughter, so Rich decided to tell us another story. "The Father liked a drink and at the VOA (Voice of America) golf club after a hot thirsty game he consumed too much drink. The ex-pats didn't want him driving home in that condition. So they came up with a remedy. First they lifted the front of his old front wheel drive Honda on to concrete blocks so he couldn't drive it. The second remedy was to steal his trousers.

"Everyone was doubled up laughing. He had only gone to the golf course to give mass to the sinners. There's always action around 'our Father'. On another day he went jogging, without wearing his T-shirt, and was arrested for extreme exposure.

"A bit rich, when you consider all the 'local lovelies' are everywhere with their breasts bouncing along to the rhythm of their walk."

Rich finished his story with a chuckle. "Boys, drop around and see me, here's my card, I'll just jot my home phone number on the back. Drop around to my work and we will then make a date to come home one evening and meet my wife Anne, and have something to eat."

The next day was full of sunshine when we went to collect our equipment from the docks. Richard immediately proved a great help to get us a large truck to carry all our gear up into the bush at the right price.

We also purchased half a dozen 45-gallon drums for our own fuel station at base camp. We needed plenty of different fuels to run all our engines, plus of course the right mixture for our motorbikes.

Tony and I sat in the front bench seat of the old blue bomb of a truck. It was all a bit rough, but you get what you pay for. On the back with all our equipment, there were a load of young lads, and who they belonged to, we had no idea.

Earlier, before we started out on our journey, Tony grabbed a taxi and ventured into the local market at Waterside to buy food for the workers at our new camp. The market was very close to being even more chaotic than the airport but he was settling into the flow of the city and got what he needed. He bought so much rice it looked like we were going to feed an army or open a restaurant.

Dry fish, cassava (which is like spinach), fufu and cassava roots all seemed to be part of a forthcoming diet.

Two large containers contained the locally produced palm oil and palm butter which sends your cholesterol levels rocketing and is poison to your body. Luckily, we bought a lot of our own food plus, of course, plenty of tea bags.

Our first stop was for fuel and it provided an insight into the workings of Africa. It takes quite a time to fill up six 45-gallon drums. A crowd had gathered and was getting larger all the time. In Africa a friendly crowd hums with fun and somehow there is always music and laughter.

At least 30 lads approached us, wanting to join up as workers. There were no questions as to where we were working, or how much were the wages, it didn't matter. They were prepared to just jump up on the back of the truck and join us. There was no way that they could let their families know of their whereabouts, but that's Africa.

The Rev. Paul sorted it out and the disappointment silenced most of the laughter. Finally, we were on our way again and I was sure there were a couple of new faces on the back of the truck that weren't there at the start of the journey.

Everything was going well and we managed to pass through the UN gate with no dash changing hands. Then we passed Brewerville and got through the check point okay – still with no dash. "Tony, how the hell are we getting through these check points without paying lolly?" I asked. He just laughed.

"Briggo, I wondered how long it would be before you woke up to the fact it was a free trip. I had thought of our budget and got Jerry to give us an official letter on Government paper stating that we were big investors in Liberia and in no way was anybody to harass these special people." Tony laughed – he loved this, as he likes to get one over on his dad. He was right and this letter did in fact get us out of many dodgy scrapes.

The bridge over the Mahe River was no problem for our heavily loaded truck. It was a lightweight in comparison to the real big rigs that passed this way loaded down with three or four massive 30-foot tree trunks.

This was the area of the large Guthrie Plantation. The road was in very good condition and was tar-sealed and smooth. Just past Guthries was Coleman town – some of the locals use the name Swaray Lah.

This was our turn off and, as we were now on mud roads, the real fun started. A few miles in we encountered our first problem as we couldn't clear the Bong Mine railway line with the bottom of our laden truck.

We had to cut wooden strips and place them under the truck's wheels to raise it and give us more ground clearance so we didn't destroy the railway lines. Our driver and his mate impressed me with their thinking on getting us through this problem.

We passed another logging camp, noticing the roads were in good condition, presumably because there was plenty of traffic movement around this area.

We were rattling along and things were going fine. Then on a straight bit of road we came upon a wooden bridge made of large ironwood tree trunks that spanned a 35-foot stream.

Would it take our weight? Then it started – everyone had an opinion as to whether the bridge would hold the weight of the truck with its load. I was in two minds myself and Tony felt the same.

If it had been early in the day, we would have certainly unloaded some of the heavy gear. But, by now late in the afternoon, everyone was getting a bit tired, a bad time to make this type of decision.

We both agreed that it was not going to be our decision. If we were wrong it suddenly would be our fault and our problem. After half an hour of discussion the driver and his mate decided that it was going to be all right. We still weren't so sure, so we kept our fingers crossed.

After lining up the wheels the truck moved slowly forward, with the driver's mate signalling him slowly on. It looked okay, half the truck was on, then three-quarters. Then, at the point of no return, there was a small splintering sound that got louder, followed by a crescendo of noise as a large iron tree trunk screamed 'enough' and snapped.

In an instant the back right-hand wheel dropped three feet as the massive log gave way under the weight on the back of the truck. Pandemonium broke out and once again everybody had the answer. To me it didn't look good and a crane seemed to be the only way to lift the truck out of this unhappy situation.

With the sun dipping behind some large trees on the side of the road, nightfall was on its way. There was nothing for it but to get out our tent from the back of the truck and set it up in the middle of this mud track main road. Once we got our chairs set up and had our kettle on the boil, things didn't seem quite so bad.

Our first night sleeping in our tent that straddled the dirt jungle road was no hardship as it was so quiet. The nearest small gathering of huts was probably 400 yards back into the jungle. We didn't feel at all threatened, and both had a great night's sleep.

New morning at daybreak the boys, armed with machetes and saws, arrived to attack the six-foot diameter ironwood tree trunk, hoping to level the truck so we could move it. It took two days to find it had served no useful purpose.

Our tent proved to be a very popular tourist sight and the local school-kids came out daily to hang out with white men in the middle of the jungle road.

Most of these children had never seen a white man before; Tony, with his blond hair, was especially unusual.

Some of the braver ones actually touched his skin, then stepped back quickly as they thought they would be grabbed by the devil. They were good fun and happy kids. It was a pity that the older ones weren't as happy as the school children.

The driver was quite cool but his six-foot 'truck boy' had trouble with us for no apparent reason. He kept pushing and pushing me, trying to test the 'Old White Man', his name for me. Tony could see it coming to a head and kept clear. Finally, I completely blew up and got into his face with plenty of menace. Until now I had been a relatively quiet old man but, suddenly, I became a football hooligan and got very verbal and threatening which completely shook him and put him on his back foot.

"Hey, you black mother fucker, yes I am your old white man, I'm your honky brother, God made me white, and you black, so what's your trouble brother?" I yelled and was ready to go to war.

The change in his attitude – and our relationship – was remarkable. The glowering threat of trouble was replaced with a real aura of respect for the rest of the trip.

The local chief appeared out of the bushes and wanted paying because his dirt road was blocked. The opposite approach from what we used our brush with the truck boys was needed to calm the chief down.

We told him we were very sorry and would send out our crew within a couple of days to replace the bridge.

A $20 dollar bill saw peace restored but that was far enough and we turned down his kind offer to spend the night in his hut.

After a couple of days it was apparent that the only way the truck could be moved was by crane. So the Reverend Paul Scott set off to walk to Monrovia, 30 miles away.

He figured out that he could borrow or steal a Ministry of Works crane to get us out of the river. Nothing like optimism, is there?

He had been gone for three days and we had all but given up hope. Then down the road in a great roar and out of the cloud of dust, appeared the intrepid Rev. Scott. He assured us that his friend had borrowed a crane and finally we got the truck out of the river. Problem solved but now there was a new problem. Our driver and his mate announced they didn't want to leave. They had got themselves a couple of local maidens. Somehow we convinced them they could be back the following night if we hurried.

That evening as the sun was setting we arrived at Saki Town, only two miles from our base camp. We were once again hailed as the Big American Mining Corporation and were offered a room in the new chief's hut for the night.

Once again though we turned down a free bed with a smile and pitched our two-man tent in the darkness outside of the circle of mud huts. Within 24 hours we would be at our own camp-site and the real adventure would commence.

Tony outside our mansion.

Setting up our base camp on the banks of the Loffa river

23

WE had a brilliant day setting up exactly where we were going to have our base camp. Our tents were on a plateau that overlooked a beautiful part of the Loffa river. Our big watchman's hut was 200 yards away, overlooking the large pit-lake of water that we named 'Thackwell's Folly' after all the money Ray Thackwell had spent to enlarge rather than take it deeper, where the diamonds lay.

A lot of our expensive equipment was being used daily and would stay on site. The hut would also be used for security and storage plus of course our cook-house. To construct the hut, five of our boys went into the nearby jungle to cut the wood. The locals loved a normal corrugated tin roof, which impressed their native friends who thought they were rich. Even in the African jungle you must keep up with the Joneses.

But this Kiwi had no one to impress except our bank manager. So, for the roof we used palm fronds. The hut was built and in use within a week. Amazingly, this was achieved with only machetes and then lengths of reasonably straight branches were bonded together by long strips of tree bark and not a nail in sight.

At the same time they built us a table next to our tents. This was an all-round double shelved table. Its many uses included being a place to eat and to use as our bathroom with all the washing, cooking, and kitchen work as well. At the end of the week it was the office desk at pay-out time.

The bottom shelf was the same as anywhere in the world – Omo washing powder, disinfectants, cleaners, brushes; it was all there including our toilet bags. Boy, it was just like home. Then a load of large stones were placed around for our fire and it served as our outside cooker. It was our most important kitchen utensil, which we kept blazing away on the ground for the whole working day or until we retired for the night. We cooked over it and, of course, made many cups of tea.

Whenever we weren't cooking on it, there would be a bucket of water perched over it to boil. When it cooled, we stored the boiled water and boiled more. It was an endless process. We had a five gallon earthenware filtration water holder. You must drink a minimum of two gallons of water a day to stop getting dehydrated.

We never had any serious stomach problems when we only drank our own boiled water. If the water in town was off, you could even get a bad stomach from the ice in your Coca-Cola.

We learnt another serious lesson on our first day. You must always wear a hat when outdoors. Many times it didn't appear to be that hot, but it was very dangerous to expose your head. The Liberian lads had no trouble. Sometimes we found ourselves acting irrationally and becoming bad-tempered. It meant it was time to just go and sit in the river, to cool everything down.

On our first weekend everyone had left the camp, except Tony, Mano Johnson, our cook-cum-security guy, and me. With no one around we decided to test the diving equipment, as neither Tony nor I had ever dived before using the compressed air system.

After Tony had read the 'How to Dive' manual, it was time to carefully assemble the equipment for our first live test. When we thought we understood it well we moved to the edge of the river.

Tony stood with water up to his waist and we got everything beside the edge of the river. He then fitted his face-mask that supplied the life-giving oxygen when under water. Pulling on his mask he smiled, gave me a wink and then disappeared beneath the surface.

I stood beside the river feeding out the air-carrying tubes as Tony went deeper and deeper. If it was possible this was even worse than watching him race speedway. Finally, with 90 per cent of the air-tube fed out, he stopped. After what seemed like hours, but probably was only a few minutes, he moved again and I started breathing once more. He was on the way up.

I gradually re-coiled the air-tube as he started on his upward journey. He eventually surfaced, and moved ashore. But when he took off the mask it wasn't our smile-a-minute Tony. He looked decidedly second hand. I waited a couple of minutes while he sat down and got his breath back. Then I couldn't wait any longer and blurted out: "Well then?"

Looking me directly in the eyes he said: "Briggo, that scared the shit out of me, especially descending the first 20 feet. After 10 feet I started to lose vision and it got worse and worse. All I could hear was my breathing and I could hear myself getting panicky and then your breathing starts to really speed up. Then you realise that you must force yourself to breathe slower. It is amazing to hear yourself getting your breathing under control.

"It was so dark that when I finally got to the river bed, I felt so happy to be at the bottom of my first dive as I wanted to get moving upwards to the surface as soon as possible. It started to get lighter and lighter as I moved upwards. When I was just over halfway up to the surface my ears exploded, I thought that my head was going to blow to pieces."

The dive had taken its toll, as Tony started pulling and wiggling his ears, at the same time blowing as hard as possible through his blocked nose, just as you do when a plane lowers altitude.

"I think somehow I've messed up my ears," he said as he dried himself and moved towards our seats around the table. "The only way you could work down there is by feel. I think that we may have trouble getting ourselves local divers, even paying them double money, to go underwater. Anyhow, now it all works okay I will have another more careful read of the diving manual."

Later in the evening sitting around the camp-fire Tony told me that he had surfaced too quickly from the depths and should have stopped halfway up to equalise the pressures. I told him that he shouldn't go down again for a week and by the time we had the raft finished and launched and found some local divers he should be on the mend. "Thanks Doctor Barry," he laughed.

My thought was to get Tony's raft on the water as soon as possible and to do this we had to sort the two new Briggs-Stratton engines and get the pumps functional before we could start working in the river.

I remembered that our boss-man David knew a diver named Maurice, who he said we should check out. I had just opened my mouth to tell Tony but, as if by magic, he took the words right out of my mouth.

"B, I'll check David tomorrow about the state of divers," he said. "But after trying it myself, the Liberian boy who is going to be a diver must have real good discipline. Briggo, what do you intend doing?"

I told him I would drain 'Thackwell's Folly' as David was supposed to have 10 workers here first thing in the morning. Then we would try and suck up the material with the gravel pump and put it through the riffles on 'Mark's' dredge, which we could bring to the camp on our next trip with the Land Rover.

Tony seemed satisfied with that and suggested we go and have a fry-up and a cuppa. "Is Mano here today? If he is I'll get him to do us some rice with some of the fish that I saw he caught yesterday," Tony said, as he got out of his diving gear.

"Tony, that sounds great. Even better, we have some olive oil that we could heat up and put in your ears – that may help," I replied.

Hiring workers turned out to be no problem as there was no work here in the bush, so everyone wanted to join us. Generally, it was a lot of fun and it didn't take long to sort out the good workers from the bad.

The Africans were not good at hiding their true feelings on most things. When they saw how hard we worked, they realised we expected the same from them. In the jungle you must get yourself into a daily routine; you mustn't let yourself go without washing, cleaning your teeth, brushing your hair, all mundane things but without doing them you'll finish up with serious problems and then it's all downhill from there.

You must have discipline. You're not going to sit down at lunchtime and watch TV (if you could find one), your ethic is work and you are going to be at it all day. Our workers followed the example that we set and at the end of the day, most of them got into the river and washed. Although their clothes were torn and ragged they still washed them almost every day.

We now had an old yellow painted 15-foot wooden boat to transport most of our workers who came from Gbeni town across the river. The boat was a must and every 'big American corporation' in the area had one. Strangely, ours was the only one I ever saw!

The river was huge, probably a half of a mile wide. The township population was around 700, with plenty of kids. The general store was run by a Liberian family – not the Lebanese, which was very unusual. There was ice-cold Coca-Cola and fresh bread five days a week which was unbelievable when you understood where we actually were, in the middle of nowhere.

A focal point in the town was the football field, where the locals loved to kick a ball around. It was like a magnet, flying everywhere with everybody drawn to it hoping to give it a good kick.

There was a dirt road running in between the cluster of mud huts. We went there one Sunday morning and nearly fell over with laughter when we saw our boss man David in the middle of the road with a lot of his mates having a conference.

He was dressed in a suit, with a collar and tie, and of course he had his briefcase which never left his side. It seemed so out of place, but secretly we were proud for him.

Gbeni is the town where Master Sergeant Samuel Kanyon Doe stayed the night before he brought down the Liberian Government. When he took over the reins of running the country, one of the first tasks he carried out was to send a new electric generator to Gbeni so the village could have lights. It was still lying up against a tree just off the main road and, naturally, many parts had mysteriously disappeared. (President Doe's own lights were to go out on September 9, 1990, when he, too, was a victim of a bloody takeover and was killed.)

At the end of the month everything was working well for us, but there was no sight of any diamonds. We caught quite a bit of very fine flour gold, which had virtually little or no weight to be of any real value.

The system of sucking up the material from the bottom of 'Thackwell's Folly' didn't work that well and was far too slow. We decided we would make a raft to sit on the pit-pond and use the hydraulic-driven American cutter to bore and suck up the material from the bottom of the pit.

We were quickly learning what diamond mining is all about. It is like looking for a needle in a haystack with someone continually moving the bloody haystack. It's tough looking for diamonds and it seems that you must pay your dues – or was it just us? The truth is that as far as the nitty-gritty of diamond mining went, we knew nothing and had only read a couple of good diamond and gold mining books.

The American Duane Marks had been in Monrovia for years working as a mining expert. We even bought some equipment from him. Certainly he knew more than us then. The difference was he did his mining in the city, while we lived it in the jungle, on site. But we must have moved on as, after we had been in Liberia for a couple of years, Duane was having trouble so we got on our motorcycles and went to his mine to sort out his dredge for him.

David Waterhouse, my Southampton works manager, was on this particular trip and came to give me a hand and proved to be a big help. Dave was in shock at first and even from his first day in Liberia he would have loved to have gone back to Southampton.

Dave was a great help but he had to learn what the jungle was all about. One day we were moving a load of material and Dave really wanted to lend a hand but I could see that he was struggling.

Tony and boss man Attia in Gbeni village with some of the locals.

On a couple of occasions I told him to stop and sit under a tree in the shade. But he refused. Suddenly, he went to the tree and virtually collapsed under it. It was though he had turned on a tap and sweat poured from his body for at least an hour. Looking deathly pale, it scared the hell out of him and he never suffered this problem again. He had suddenly learnt in one quick lesson why Liberia is called the white man's graveyard.

Now we had our large cutter we had to build a large raft to float on 'Thackwell's Folly' as this would allow us to raise or lower the raft. It was a big help if you needed to change the water depth, especially when we wanted to bore with the cutter. It was hydraulic driven, which I had built in Southampton but it had never been tested and, as this was my first experience of building hydraulics, I had my fingers crossed.

Our gravel pump was the size of a small car and probably weighed twice as much. All our boys knew it was really heavy as with a dozen of us pushing we could only move it very slowly to the launch pad. In making the raft the trick was to anticipate how many 45 gallon drums it would take to float this beast of a machine. We settled for eight drums per side and hoped that the 16 would do the job.

All our black boys kept telling us that we were crazy and were laughing and joking, the only plus being that they had no idea of floatation – but, then again, we knew only the basics. It was only a guess if it would float or sink.

Launch time arrived and we edged the raft into an area cut in the side of the pit where we could stand on one side. Potentially, this was a major 'egg on Briggo's face' deal. I had to stop the audience laughing. I tried to look calm and confident, but I'm not sure if I succeeded.

Slowly we edged the monster yellow caterpillar pump on to the raft. It was a hard slog, so I got the Land Rover on the other side of our small pit-lake and attached a tow rope to the pump, which helped a great deal. I was in control but badly needed Tony and David to be on top of their game, as this was an expensive bit of kit to fall to the bottom of 20 feet of water.

Show time! With two wheels on the raft and the water halfway up the drums, it was now or never. And we did it. All the boys went mad and when I looked at Tony he gave me a smile and a wink. The boss man Barry hadn't lost face. As a reward we had an hour's rest and I had a real strong cuppa. It was a real happy base camp.

After the festivities it was time to get the five-cylinder engine fired up. Because of our starvation budget, we didn't buy the model with an electric starter but one that required a crank handle like an old-fashioned car.

"Dave, let's have the crank handle and get this beauty into action," I said. Dave looked bewildered. "Barry, we never got a start handle with it," he replied.

"Dave, you've got to be kidding me. Nobody would sell a machine like this without a starting handle. Go and check everything, it's got to be hiding somewhere, look and see if you packed it inside something else, as I'm sure that we must have been supplied with a start handle."

A frantic search found no starting handle, so we had to go into Monrovia to make one. We certainly couldn't purchase one here in Liberia, and even if we air-freighted one out from England, it would take at least a couple of weeks.

Luckily, it was just another time that Richard (Tillin) got us out of the deep pooh. He had a Spanish friend in the engineering business; Tony spent a couple of days there making the new handle.

Two weeks later I was doing a job at the side of the pit when David sauntered up: "You'll never believe what I just found," he said with a grin. And then from behind his back he produced the missing starting handle.

That's why I loved Dave and trusted him so much; 99 per cent of people would have taken the bloody handle and thrown it into the middle of the river, but not our Dave.

What could I do? I just smiled and said: "Dave, you're right – I would never have believed it."

We had a load of trouble with the power of the hydraulics. The need for near perfect throttle control on a wet, slick speedway track was nothing compared to this. You hardly had to breathe on the controls to smash or bend metal as though it was putty.

One day the cutter head key sheared, the head was stuck down a five-foot hole it had just created. With the cutter not turning it was virtually impossible to get it out. It took us two days of hard slog to extract the bloody thing from the mud.

Our California cutter was efficient but, once again, it was too slow. I thought about the old gold rush days in Northern California when they washed away whole hills by hydraulic mining to trap the gold. The gold was part of the slush flowing down into riffles that caught the descending gold.

It was doing so much damage to the ecology that it was finally outlawed in California but there were no such rules in Liberia. So why not try that system here? I recalled that when I was riding at St. Austell Speedway in Cornwall, they used something similar to get the clay for all the pottery that is produced in Cornwall. I vowed to check that out on my next trip back to England.

Before the end of the dry season, and before the rains arrived, we set out to build a four-bedroom mud hut to live in. With this in mind we went to Gbeni and looked for the best looking mud hut. We found the one and then we had to find who the builder was.

We discovered it was John and we explained to him what we wanted house-wise, and finished up doing a deal for an agreed figure of $200 US dollars for the job. John and his gang started straight away.

It was a pity to do away with the tents that had been our little homes over the previous couple of years despite all the problems with the heavy rain that descended on us all too often.

I really mean rain, the river rose about 10 feet and normally it decided to start at two o'clock in the morning. We would be washed out completely and, by the time we got dry and comfortable, there would be another downpour.

Eventually we decided we couldn't beat it. Our tents were our little heaven and, after a hard day's work and having finally retired for the night, you simply zipped yourself in. Then you could mentally transport yourself out of that jungle.

Tony's and my tents were immaculate, bed-clothes neatly folded down, our clocks and Walkmans on homemade bedside tables. Dave was a different case, he lived it as it fell, and had been spoilt by first his Mum and then Grandma so he had problems getting organised which made it tough on him.

The camp was now looking a million dollars. We had painted all our mining gear and washing plants at 'Thackwell's Folly' that looked splendid in caterpillar-yellow. Already the next part of the plan was forming in my brain.

Indiana who?

Everybody was happy, President Doe had been deposed, but ...

24

IT was Tuesday, November 12, 1985 and we were at the Kiwi base camp on the bank of the Loffa river. The early morning mist hung lazily over the water. It was 6am and near sunrise. Both Tony and I had been up early.

I had just started cleaning my teeth when I heard a noise that was increasing in volume every second. It was our workers coming across the river, in the company's boat from Gbeni, which would be about one mile as the crow flies, from our registered claims 25 and 39b listed at the Ministry of Mines.

Even this early in the morning the boys were laughing and joking and the noise would have woken the dead.

I turned to Tony and wondered what it was all about.

"Maybe Liberia has won the Africa Cup," I said.

"It must be something special. They must have heard it on the radio."

The boat arrived and they all piled out: "Good morning boys, whatever is going on?" The question was answered by 10 voices in unison but nothing made sense until our beaming head boy David informed us: "Boss, there has been a coup in Monrovia."

Everybody was cheering. "David, how do you know this?"

"Boss Barry, we heard it this morning on radio ELWA ... Doe is out and Quiwonkpa is in."

Everyone was in a jovial mood with much laughter and discussion on how they were all going to burn their political party membership cards as the new President was a good man.

General Thomas Quiwonkpa was a partner with President Doe in the 1980 coup. But, in 1983, he was forced to leave Liberia or he would have died at the hands of his former partner Doe's soldiers. He had now returned to Liberia to run the country for his people. Not like Doe, who only looked after himself and the army.

Turning on our radio we managed, after a great deal of difficulty, to get Monrovia's Radio Station ELWA. On the hour at seven, just before the news, there was a blast of stirring music. Then followed a statement from General Quiwonkpa: "Patriotic forces as of now have seized power to liberate our country from fear and brutality."

The Quiwonkpa troops were laying siege to the mansion of President Samuel Doe, calling on his forces to surrender. Newscasts were given hourly and every time cheering, laughing and general pandemonium broke out in the camp.

Luckily, we didn't need to go to Monrovia for provisions until the end of the week. Nevertheless, we listened to the radio bulletins with great interest. The attempted coup proved to be a failure in less than 24 hours. It appeared from what we could hear on the radio that normality had returned in Monrovia.

It was now five days since the coup and time for us to go to Monrovia for fuel and provisions. We thought it would just be another normal routine trip. Of course, there would be the usual number of problems, road blocks, traffic violations, and police demanding fines for whatever they could dream up. It was very serious stuff, but if you gave the police officer a half share of the biscuit you were eating, you would be free and clear.

There was nothing too sensational that we felt we could not handle, or so we thought. We could have waited for another week but finally decided to go to town because one of our workers needed to see his wife who lived just off the road to Monrovia.

In great spirits we left our camp on the Sunday at 10 o'clock in the morning. In the jungle around our camp we had no idea what was happening in the outside world or anything about the coup except on the increasingly intermittent radio bulletins, so we did not expect anything unusual to be in store for us.

Our first stop was Bombi Hills, about one hour from the camp along the dirt roads, which included navigating two minor rivers and other streams before arriving at the checkpoint.

Before we got there our security guard Mano Johnson left us to return to his home after a two-week absence. He was loaded down with a bag holding 20lbs of rice and a couple of other bags when we dropped him off at the side of the road. Even after Mano left us we were still pretty cramped as we continued our journey. We had a full load, including empty fuel cans and equipment that needed repair. With Tony, Dave and me in the front seat, Jwah was sharing his trip with the equipment in the back.

On our arrival at our first checkpoint it was immediately clear that things were desperately wrong. Initially, getting used to the Liberian ways was not a great problem and you never really felt threatened. This time it was very different.

As we stopped at the checkpoint, we were aware that all the soldiers were armed with machine guns which they pointed at us. The soldiers should have felt completely in control, as they held all the trump cards in this game. But they were young, confused and nervous and not sure what to do, especially when confronted by three white men.

A very young and nervous soldier stepped forward and, in a shaking falsetto voice, yelled at us to get out of our Land Rover, which we did, but then our boy soldier really lost it, telling us to stand six feet back and open the bonnet. He screamed this ridiculous order five or six times. Maybe he thought we had very long arms. Things were definitely not normal by any stretch of the imagination. What especially grabbed my attention was the twitching of his trigger finger on his machine gun.

Initial reports had insinuated white mercenaries were involved in

Has our raft got enough floatation to carry our enormous gravel pump?

James Wah, butler, tea-boy, gardener and great fun.

the coup attempt and at first glance we must have looked suspicious in our shorts, in need of a shave, and riding in our old 'well lived in' trusty Land Rover. To make matters worse, Tony was wearing his Boy Scout-type uniform with a sheath knife on the belt. Things looked really bad until he gave up his beloved knife.

But luck was on our side when the ensuing search failed to find Tony's other knife or recognised our stun gun.

Eventually we were allowed to leave but things here were in bad shape and would only get worse. Maybe the right thing to do was to return to camp. We spoke about it and decided to push on and hope that things would improve. In the centre of Bombi Hills there were soldiers everywhere and a general feeling of unrest.

The next crisis point though was to be the Sierra Leone cross road checkpoint where we normally bought all our beer and coke from a run-down Lebanese owned shop. This time we decided to give that a miss and try to get through to Monrovia in the daylight hours.

One thing we found a great help in Liberia was to try and adopt the African mentality, staying loose and light-hearted. The problem is that the Western attitude, when confronted with something dangerous, is to get serious. Getting uptight never helps. Another routine we always practised was to remove our sunglasses at checkpoints. We found eye-to-eye contact made us appear much stronger than if we had been hiding behind sunglasses.

After our rocky passage through the two checkpoints at Bombi Hills it was very important we were on our best form for the forthcoming checkpoints. The Sierra Leone control was not normally the most difficult and this day we were blessed as one of the soldiers, along with an immigration friend, needed a ride with us. His house was in Arthington, a village just off the main drag, about 15 miles down the road from the control point.

After moving and repacking all the equipment in the back of the Land Rover, we managed to fit in the two extra passengers, along with machine guns. All the barriers were lifted and we even got waves from their colleagues, so off we went with things looking somewhat brighter. When we stopped to let our passengers off at their village we were feeling much better and even took photos with our two travellers and their armament.

The biggest and the most difficult border was the gate that was a further 35 miles on. We had to decide if we were going to use a short cut we had discovered in 1984, missing out the border control, or continue as we were. We found the short cut when we had no transport of our own – our theory at that time was 'cheapest is best' and, after a lot of asking around, we hired an old Toyota to get us and our equipment to camp eighty miles away, and agreed on the princely sum of $135.

The first time we saw the van we didn't think we would make it out of Monrovia, let alone to our camp over two hours away. All the tyres were right down to the canvas, there was no spare wheel in sight, only one front headlight (and who knew if that even worked) and, of course, no tail-lights.

The front bumper was tied on with a long piece of red electrical wire, the back bumper was non-existent and must have fallen off somewhere along the way. The body looked as if Woody Woodpecker had had a field day. When the old rust bucket was running, the smoke from the exhaust pipe suggested it was on fire. At least the price was right, but to give us this 'deal' the driver and his car-boy had to cut corners to make money on the trip. The picture flashed into my mind of the short cut we used before, returning to base camp. A few miles from Monrovia's city centre, there was a small turning about 800 yards before the Brewerville gate checkpoint. When we turned down this very small road and then through bushes and over a dozen or so dirt mounds, we realised we were detouring though the local dump!

Onwards we trundled with the driver doing unbelievable things to keep this old heap of junk moving on its bald tyres in wet slippery terrain. The driving display was a sight to behold. At one point we thought we were being kidnapped. The driver was very serious and whenever we told him 'this is not the way to Bombi Hills', a smile would crease his face and he assured us 'all okay, boss'.

There was little option but to sit back and enjoy the mystery tour. After 20 minutes through trees, scrub and wasteland, we arrived back on a dirt road and in another 15 minutes we were on the main road to Bombi – five miles past the checkpoint.

When we finally made it to the main road, the driver gave a real loud laugh and a smile that only a Liberian can. He was just like a schoolboy who had stolen his teacher's sweets and hadn't been caught.

The Liberians are hard on their own people. The police, army, or immigration wouldn't have let them through the checkpoint without paying and, seeing us with them would have cost them double. So we were equally happy for them.

As things were so good at the Sierra Leone checkpoint, we decided not to use our illegal detour through the wild jungle and rubbish tip, but to use the normal route. It should have been quick because there was not so much traffic around. Radio listeners understood it was a bad time to be out. Doe's army was trying to round up the outstanding members of the coup who were still at large. Sunday afternoon was not the best time to come to Monrovia.

The vibe at the Brewersville gate immediately smelt bad – even from a distance. When the checkpoint was in sight, I told Jwah to gather up what he was taking with him and be sure that when we stopped he melted into the background. We certainly didn't want any other trouble, as Jwah had no papers. He played his part; one minute we saw him, the next he had simply disappeared.

The welcoming committee at the gate was not good. It was obvious the soldiers and officials had been drinking and smoking weed, a dangerous mixture. They were hanging around in groups, laughing and messing around. A vehicle full of white men was just what they needed for some fun to relieve the boredom.

The greeting set the tone: "Right honky, let's have your papers, and all out of your truck." As I let myself out of the Land Rover I answered: "What papers do you need, brother?" I knew that no matter what papers we had they weren't going to be the right ones.

Talking was getting us nowhere and then I made a dumb move and decided to produce the Jerry Bryon Government letter. Our immigration officer yelled for a comrade. His replacement was even more out of his head than our first interrogator. "These passport control entries are wrong and have been tampered with," he yelled.

Our jaws dropped open and we feared this man was a blind alley and dangerous. We were right, he was trouble in a non-negotiable way. With much yelling we were ushered into a brick-house which was like an empty store room. The soldiers were suspicious of us and had the feeling that we were part of the mercenaries involved in the attempted coup.

Despite the situation we found ourselves in, Tony seemed okay but Dave, on the other hand, didn't look too good at all. I told him not to worry. Try to look strong even if you aren't, I told him.

As we sat on some old beer crates and waited in our makeshift prison cell, I asked Tony if he thought we had, in fact, been arrested. "Dad, I think they are clowns and don't really know what to do with us," he answered. Tony must have been feeling the pinch, too, as he only calls me Dad when he's not sure of himself.

All of a sudden the leader of our captors returned, obviously not in a good mood. "Those fuckin' phones are useless, and are not working," he said. "Get these three foreign arses back into their truck, and you, Johnson and Gontee, travel with them, take no shit, and shoot if needs be."

With that he yelled at a group of soldiers who were kicking a football around. "Hey, you lot, get three vehicles and follow their truck. We are taking the prisoners to Centre Street. Nayh, you drive the lead car and make it fast, brother."

We now had two unpleasant smelling soldiers cradling their AK47 rifles packed in the back of our Land Rover. Strangely, with the back half door closed, they suddenly seemed like a couple of scared young men. There was nothing for it but to sit back and face the music.

We are arrested and put in jail by drunken soldiers

25

HOW the hell had we got ourselves into this kind of bloody crap?

Now a terrifying new nightmare was about to start. We had been bundled into our Land Rover, along with two Liberian soldiers accompanied by their best friends – AK47 assault rifles. Being ordered to join a convoy of armoured vehicles taking us to an unknown destination was not exactly my idea of fun. "And to think the day started so well ..." I muttered under my breath.

Living here in Liberia, we soon understood that information spread quickest by word of mouth. Much of the population had never seen a television, let alone owned one. Tight controls over conventional media such as radio and the newspapers meant the human grapevine was the primary method by which news reached the population. Often stories about events did not become common knowledge until many weeks later. In Africa, nothing travels faster than the spoken word.

The problem was that rumour and fact usually became blurred and what may have begun as sound information was quickly distorted into half-truths or outright falsehoods. In many cases, the lack of clarity was confusing. In the days and weeks before and after Tuesday, November 12, 1985, it was downright deadly.

In 1980, Thomas Quiwonkpa and Staff Sargeant Samuel Kanyon Doe, together with a handful of enlisted men, had wrested control of Liberia by overpowering President Tolbert in a swift and spectacular coup. Doe then claimed the Liberian Presidency, even though many felt that Quiwonkpa would have made the better leader. Instead he was installed in the new regime as Doe's right-hand man, as Brigadier General of the armed forces.

But life stands still for no one and during the following years their relationship was destroyed by paranoia and jealousy. By 1983 Quiwonka's friendship with Doe had deteriorated to such an extent that he fled in exile to the United States, fearing death at the hands of his former brother-in-arms. For two years from that point, Liberia walked a tightrope of uneasy peace. What Doe had not bargained on was that his tyrannical attempts to suppress Quiwonkpa's political ambitions would be the catalyst for a counter-coup against him, led by his former ally.

On the day we came to remember as Black Tuesday, we awoke to the news of Quiwonkpa's return. In a courageous move to overthrow Doe and his cronies, Quiwonkpa, according to reports, had re-entered Liberia through neighbouring Sierra Leone. He linked up with a band of around two dozen loyal and tough soldiers, all obsessed with dismissing Doe from power.

Quiwonkpa's initial move was timed to perfection and his strategy was immaculate. Despite lacking the support he had hoped to gain from the United States government, it didn't deter him. His men struck quickly and soon had Doe and his minders trapped in the Presidential mansion. But Quiwonkpa foolishly thought that he could persuade Doe and his entrapped soldiers to give themselves up.

Instead of using military muscle, and forcing his way into the mansion, then finishing off President Doe and his cronies, he instead tried to negotiate.

History will show that he made a serious military mistake. The lost time that passed while trying to bargain would prove to be fatal. A bloodless coup in Liberia is impossible. Quiwonkpa should have known better, he had personally witnessed the massive bloodshed of the 1980 coup, when he was one of the major players.

His tactics, while noble, were to prove his downfall. Wasted opportunities allowed Doe to buy himself enough time for his army, stationed 20 miles away at its Paynesville base, to arrive on the scene. Quiwonkpa and his followers paid the ultimate price for his error. He and his brave band of would-be revolutionaries were wiped out in a hail of bullets. Blood spattered the surrounding streets. Before long, his disembowelled body lay mutilated and rotting on show at the Barclay Training Centre.

It has been claimed many times since that loyalist soldiers had eaten his liver and testicles as bullet-riddled rebel bodies crashed to the dusty streets.

The news started with an early morning bulletin on Monrovia's ELWA radio. The big early news was that the radio station was now in the hands of Quiwonkpa's freedom fighters. Very few Liberians were in possession of a radio but it really didn't matter and the news spread like a plague nevertheless.

The citizens of Monrovia were overjoyed that Quiwonkpa's coup had been successful and that Doe had been overthrown, or even killed. That sparked wild celebrations in the streets, with a grand carnival-style fiesta of singing and dancing bursting into life to recognise the collapse of Doe's hated regime.

Doe and his cronies had raped the country's economy over the years and had killed thousands, sparing only members of his own beloved Krahn tribe from his attrition.

Entire families of Liberians wept with joy, neighbours embraced. Years of suppressed emotion, created by Doe's tyranny, came tumbling out. Soon though, the real and horrific truth emerged. For coup supporters, or anyone closely associated, even those who had reacted to the word on the grapevine, the repercussions were severe. Now, the real horror started in earnest.

Reports began to emerge of Doe soldiers shooting randomly into the cheering crowds early in the coup attempt. In the days that followed there was an outward appearance of calm but, in reality,

Doe's troops were secretly tracking down those who had shown opposition to his leadership during the premature celebrations.

In particular, many members of the Gio and Mano tribes, who had formed the backbone of Quiwonkpa's support, were ruthlessly hunted down and murdered.

Members of the government, police and immigration officials not of Krahn stock were also silently targeted. This time there would be no public firing squads on the beach. Doe was savvy enough to recognise that a more effective method of extermination was simply to have his enemies 'disappear in the night' – never to be heard of again.

This policy, just as brutal as the mass public exterminations of 1980, actually bred more fear and paranoia than his previous approach. Obviously, the actions of Doe's vigilantes were not widely publicised. Listening to Mano Johnson's battered old radio in the tranquillity at our Kiwi base camp, it appeared that the uprising has been quashed and calm had been restored to the capital.

Five days after Quiwonkpa's efforts ended in failure and death, we discovered first-hand that nothing was further from the truth. It seemed so long ago that we had all piled into our dust-covered, battered red Land Rover, to make a routine run into Monrovia to stock up with provisions and fuel. It was only this morning and so far it had indeed been a hard day, but there was another nine hours left to enjoy. We were now in a bit of strife and where this was going to end nobody knew.

As we passed the turning into Hotel Africa, we would have been much happier to be popping in for an ice-cold Coke and a steak sandwich at the end of a hard day. Roaring over New Bridge our convey raced towards Monrovia's main thoroughfare, Broad Street, which for years was one of the finest stretches of road in the city.

Being there awakened in me the vast difference of living in the serenity of our base camp on the Loffa river than here in the city, particularly with the present turbulent situation hanging around our necks.

In the 1960s, when Liberia was at its most affluent, the traffic flowed either side of the wide grass central divide along Broad Street. A wide variety of large well-established jacaranda and cotton trees were interspersed with the tall palms.

Liberia's high rainfall and equatorial climate encouraged the abundant growth, and Broad Street blossomed with greenery for most of the year. By this stage, however, a lack of government funds had condemned the once attractive sight to something of an eyesore. Barren swathes of dirt occupied the area which had once been the pride of the city.

Anyone looking at the shambolic mess of Broad Street in 1985 would have found it hard to believe that this section of Monrovia had once enjoyed an elegance to match any capital city in the world. Once known as the 'Mayfair of Monrovia', the street's triple-story colonial buildings, complete with majestic balconies, had been allowed to dilapidate into nothing more than a sorry reminder of their former splendour. By the time we arrived in Africa, time, wear and tear, and neglect had taken their toll.

Our convoy, with the soldiers still performing their war games, continued its way north towards the Paradise Hotel on Broad Street where, months earlier our most distinct memory was looking on from the balcony as a local Rastafarian dropped his pants and defecated on the central divide, in full view of the hotel patrons. So much for paradise.

Looking ahead, we could see the infamous, iconic Hotel Ducor, perched on top of Mamba Point. That towering limestone edifice still provided outstanding views of the city and surrounding water, but had seen far better days.

For 20 years the hotel was the choice for Monrovia's elite, but the Ducor had lost its status by the late 1970s. Safety had become a major issue, with local gangsters soon realising that the hotel's permanent collection of foreign businessmen and dignitaries offered ripe opportunities to line their own pockets.

The reception area, once gleaming and glamorous, became a haven for conmen and prostitutes. A series of break-ins meant visitors were unlikely to return a second time.

As awful as the Ducor was, its successor, the Las Vegas-style Hotel Africa, was still in good shape. Built as a status symbol prior to a meeting of the Organization of African Unity (OAU) in 1979 and now run by Dutch investors, the Hotel Africa was a beacon of opulence as the city decayed around it.

It was the last sign of wealth we would see for a while. Things were about to get ugly and I started to develop some real concern.

On any normal Sunday a street in Monrovia would be no different to any other African city or township on its day of rest. Children would be noisily playing football on any vacant lot. People everywhere would meet, talk, and laugh. It didn't matter if they were dressed inappropriately for the weather, or it was too hot for a jacket, because it was Sunday, the day of the Lord, time to strut and show off a little.

Completing this colourful scene would be a musical beat, the pulse of African society. Raunchy, vibrant, and played at a ferocious level of decibels, it would draw men, women, and their offspring like bees to the honey pot. But this Sunday was far from being the normal day of the Lord. Even the Africans in their inimitable laid-back style hadn't yet recovered from the death and destruction that had hit their city over the last five days.

There was a palpable difference to the vibrant scene that had greeted us on previous Sunday excursions to this part of Monrovia. This time the locals spoke in hushed tones, amid furtive glances, instead of chatting and laughing on the street corners, as they prepared to enter their places of worship.

Children stuck close to their parents and were subdued and anxious. No football or frivolity here.

Our convoy did nothing to ease the state of tension. Of the four vehicles, three had hazard lights flashing and their headlights on full beam. Our dirty Land Rover looked out of place among the military vehicles – and we certainly felt out of place.

As this small armada of machinery roared up Broad Street, soldiers were hanging out of windows, or standing together on the pick-up's rear trays. All brandished the American-manufactured automatic AK47 assault rifle.

This automatic rifle was used for violence, revolution and destruction throughout the continent. Also on display were M21 automatic rifles. The screaming soldiers were enjoying the power of the gun to the hilt. The yelling and screaming, mixed together with the occasional static blasts from the rifles, added to the fear and unrest in the area. The locals reacted quickly, some hustling inside, keen to escape the crosshairs of attention. Others remained rooted to the spot, transfixed by the dramatic sight before them.

The military drivers kept their hands firmly pressed to their horns, part warning to pedestrians to stay out of the way, a show of machismo. There was no doubt about who was in charge of this road. The convoy was in no mood to let anyone slow their passage and the locals duly scattered as quickly as they could. The lincs on the road counted for little, as the military men sped along Broad Street with no regard for anything in their path.

An old woman was within inches of being flattened, hauling her creaking body onto the pavement a split second before the convoy raced past. The maverick law of the gun ruled. Cars were forced to swerve hastily to avoid the reckless, speeding convoy. They were travelling on the wrong side of the road.

I wasn't about to play their game though. 'Fuck them,' I thought as I refused to break the laws of the road, and I continued within the legal speed limit, on the correct side of the road. Guns or no guns, I knew we couldn't afford to show weakness to these clowns.

The soldiers, high on drink, dope and adrenaline, pulled alongside our Land Rover, screaming instructions to keep up and gesticulating angrily.

Leaving Broad Street in a state of shock with smoking tyres, we turned right into Centre Street. Suddenly, halfway down the sloping street, the front two cars screeched to a halt in the middle of the road, with tyres still smoking.

Soldiers flooded out into the road, with the third car staying behind the Land Rover, blocking any chance of escape. Yelling and waving their guns in the air, largely for the benefit of the gathering crowd, the soldiers were pointing and shouting to show me where to park.

Paying no heed to the frantic arm-waving, I chose my own parking spot, nestling the front wheels in the gutter, the bumper resting snugly over the footpath.

I could see the excitement and bewilderment among the crowd that immediately gathered around. They knew something was about to happen, but weren't sure exactly what. We weren't that much the wiser either.

"What the hell now, Briggo?" asked Tony. I said: "Now the bullshit starts. Let me do the talking. Have you got any lolly?"

"About two hundred dollars in my body belt, one hundred and fifty in my back pack, plus about fifty Liberian bucks in five dollar coins." Tony was still bending down and counting as he replied.

"Tony, keep the Liberian money close by, we may have to grease a few palms. Hide the rest." Tony twisted his body so he was out of view of the soldiers in the back as he snatched a fistful of coins and notes from his money belt and stuffed them under the seat, moments before an irate gun-toting army man banged on my window.

"Prisoners, out of the car now," he yelled.

"Christ, he looks angry," said Dave, clearly not convinced that the soldier merely wanted to wish us Merry Christmas ahead of time.

"Piss off, we'll be out in a minute," I yelled back at the soldier, still determined not to be intimidated.

A crash on the back swing door of the Land Rover told us that someone was trying to open it to let out the passengers. The two soldiers riding with us from the UN gate hadn't uttered a word since their forced hi-jacking. They didn't look the happiest of passengers, squatting in the filthy dirty back section of the Land Rover, squeezed in between the greasy fuel cans and equipment that cluttered the rear.

They looked very uncomfortable even though they were the ones toting their AK47s.

"Wait a minute, it needs unlocking," I cried out, trying to stall for time before we had to get out and face the music.

After the men outside tried again and failed to unlock the back door, Tony eventually slid over into the back and opened the latches himself, allowing the soldiers to get out. By now, the Land Rover was surrounded by a sea of inquisitive local faces.

"Did you hide the rest of the money, Tone? We'd better move, I think the natives are getting a mite restless."

Truck in the river – B&B in the middle of the highway.

Amazing balance.

"Briggo, the lolly's fine."

Tony seemed to be holding his nerve pretty well, but it was Dave I was worried about. He had never experienced anything like this before and I didn't want him to suddenly lose his rag and say something that we would all regret.

As beads of sweat formed on his creased brow, I said: "Listen Dave, it could be a lot worse." I reminded him of his first days at the Jawa factory in Czechoslovakia, when he had been overwhelmed by the red tape of the Communist machine and the inability to communicate in English. But there hadn't been any guns in Czechoslovakia!

"Just stay calm. And remember, when in doubt, look straight into their eyes and hold the look. It makes them nervous and they don't like it."

Finally, we had to climb out and face our captors. First to step into our view was a six-foot Krahn Commander. His jolly face gave me a brief jolt of confidence that we could appeal to his better nature, but those thoughts were quashed when he barked: "Prisoners get in line."

Neither Tony nor I are the best in the world at obeying orders. He stepped forwards while I stepped back. Despite the guns, the situation and the look of fury on the Commander's face, I could barely suppress a smirk. That's evened the score a bit.

Dave, meanwhile, didn't appear to see the funny side and looked as if he was relieved to be wearing his brown corduroys.

He didn't understand the game, or indeed that it was a game, and who could blame him? This shit wasn't what he had signed up for. Stories of riches, sunshine and adventure didn't exactly fit in with this terrifying sideshow.

Over the years Tony and I had learned not to reveal our feelings, especially when you're in a tight jam.

As the Krahn Commander stared us down, I tried to get inside his head. He looked young to be the boss man, I thought. He must have reached his present position by showing he was steadfast under pressure.

I could sense his dilemma as he now faced something that wasn't spelt out in the army handbook.

He wanted to show he was in charge and not lose face, but he could also tell that this could get messy in a hurry if he wasn't careful. Surely he just wanted the thing dealt with; then he could get on with getting stuck into his latest stash of dope.

The problem was it was three white prisoners. He knew how his fellow Liberians thought and reacted in certain circumstances but this was new territory for him. I could see him trying to sum us up and get a read of how we might cope with the situation.

All these questions were clearly shown by the quizzical look that now sat uncomfortably on his sweat-soaked face. As he opened his mouth to unleash another outburst at us, his words were frozen by a crash at the back of the Land Rover.

Someone was trying to close the back door but could not work out the special knack needed to release the catch. Seeing an opportunity to keep the Commander off guard, I charged to the rear of the vehicle.

"What the fuck do you think you're doing, fucking up our vehicle? Leave it alone, don't break up our equipment," I screamed into the face of an army minion who looked no older than 14.

The Commander didn't like how this was developing and tried to get things back under control. He fiddled menacingly with the holster of his gun as the hapless sergeant who had tried to shut the back door pleaded: "Boss, I was only close de door, not good, no close."

He still held the door, about to try again.

"Leave the fucking door, I'll do it," I shouted, trying to break the Liberian record for most swear-words in a minute.

The Commander had seen enough. "Prisoner in line, you have been arrested, get in line."

"But someone from your bloody army is wrecking our car, I must fix it." Our man wasn't used to being sworn at by a middle-aged white man in shorts and trainers.

"Prisoner, you told me to fuck off ..." He uttered as he moved menacingly towards me.

"I never told you to fuck off. I said you were fucking up our equipment."

Gently, I closed and locked the back door, but the Commander was not happy, and his lip curled into a smile that was far scarier than his scowl. Tony saw anger intent in his eyes and moved between the two of us, while giving the Krahn officer a big toothy smile.

"Where do you want us to go, boss man?" Tony asked.

The Commander didn't like losing face and by now he wanted no more part of us. He glanced around, and saw a way to get rid of us. He pointed at some stairs, situated between 'Ebihams Ritz', the local hairdressers, and 'The Beirut,' a Lebanese restaurant. We went up them.

A beaten-up motorcycle lay nearby, two grubby Liberian boys sat playing in the dirt, completely oblivious to the maelstrom of activity that surrounded them. The kids looked up as we were marched by.

I made eye contact with them and flashed them a wink. Two big genuine African smiles illuminated the depressing surrounding buildings and momentarily relieved the sick feeling of uncertainty in the pit of my stomach. It gave some buoyancy to a dismal situation.

At the top of the small flight of badly decaying stairs was a grimy wooden door that led to the Liberian Immigration Department. Or so the unpolished brass plate, which looked completely out of place, informed us. The door hadn't seen a coat of paint for at least ten years and it badly needed re-hanging.

As a place of incarceration it didn't look much cop. In fact, it wouldn't have taken a crack squad of kindergarten desperadoes to shoot that coop.

The relieved Commander happily passed over the three crazy white men who had threatened to screw up his day and headed back to street level. Needless to say, I wasn't sorry to see him go, but who were we up against now?

We found ourselves confronted by another uniformed soldier, six-foot-six and stood straight as a rod next to a plain-clothed Immigration official.

Tony had got the feeling that I was about to unleash a further salvo at our new adversaries, and he was probably right. "Dad, for God's sake loosen up," he whispered out of the corner of his mouth. "Don't you remember the coup we saw on the television at Southampton? This ain't no bloody picnic."

Tony ... having a mud bath!

No food or water and still the army refused to let us go

26

WE were marched through a couple of bare rooms with chairs scattered here and there along with a couple of broken desks. The smell of sweating bodies dominated the atmosphere as we entered a massive room that was divided in two. One side was enclosed with prison bars stretching from floor to ceiling with a small gate in the middle.

The prison cell was much smaller than the rest of the room. Behind the bars were around 20 Liberians dressed only in their underpants. They had nothing to sit on. Most were squatting on the floor and used the walls as their back rest. Some just lay on the floor fast asleep.

One skinny older black boy was standing and gripping the bars as though he was going to tear them out. His haggard face was a masterpiece of fear. The arrival of three white men in the jail caused a ruckus, the boys sitting woke up their mates. This was unreal, three white brothers in jail, man!

They all thought the coup was a tribal deal and these three brothers certainly didn't look like Krahns!

Our jailers were also embarrassed. What were they going to do with us? It really threw them, should they put us behind bars and make us strip to our underpants? Nobody knew what to do. Finally, one of the jailers told us to sit down on some church-like pews that had been placed along the window side of the room. I chose the seat right next to the bars. Tony glanced at me with that 'what the hell now' expression. I just gave him a wink and a smile.

It was the time to sit quietly and contemplate our situation and it was important to work out exactly who was in control. After 15 minutes the chaos of our arrival had subsided. All of a sudden the quietness was broken when the same two soldiers who had brought us here appeared with two other Liberians.

One was dressed up in his police officer's uniform. The other was in his immigration officer's kit. Any Liberian with authority wore their clothes with pride. But in their underpants they finished up looking just the same as the other prisoners, except the bar clinger. He definitely didn't fit into the rest of the group.

I moved closer to the prisoner behind the bars. I quietly spoke through the bars to him. "What's happening here, brother?" I asked.

He turned and looked me in the eye, then started speaking in a hushed voice. "After the coup we were all in different places around the city. We were all really happy that Doe was gone. But we started to celebrate too soon.

"A company of Doe's troops came from Paynesville and took everything back. First was the radio station that broadcast the news Doe had been toppled. After Doe was back in control, fingers were pointed and they ferreted out who was happy with the government change in the interim period. Most prisoners here are government officials."

"What are our rights?" I asked tentatively.

"You should be okay, boss man. As you can see, nobody knows what to do with you. We have all been threatened ten times that we will be shot tomorrow. After a couple of times you don't even think about it. We go to sleep. If we die tomorrow, we die tomorrow."

My next question was the most important, as you can waste a lot of energy and put yourself in even bigger danger by yelling at the wrong person. "Who's the boss man?" I asked.

"The Commander is a young Krahn lawyer. When the coup started he was enlisted. Biggest problem is that he is being worked too hard, with little sleep. I figure he's on some kind of stimulants to help get him through."

"Thanks brother," I said. "God be with you." I turned and relayed the information to the boys. Even Tony didn't have any questions. During the next hour we learned a lot about the African mentality, how tough they are, the strength of the tribal war. It was going to be played out in front of our own eyes. There was no way in our present predicament that we could escape from watching Africa bare its soul.

We had to stay strong but it was getting to Dave. He was cowering like a beaten dog and he kept looking at the ground. He needed some harsh words. I moved to his corner and got right in his face.

"Dave, this may sound stupid or dramatic but our present situation could become life threatening. You must look strong. Stop looking at the ground and look them straight in the eye all the time. They don't like it. Sit up – you look like a beaten dog. Our lives could depend on it. I'm probably not scared, the better word is apprehensive. We must stay strong as a unit."

"Sorry Briggo," said Dave. "I'll try my best." Finally he lifted his chin to look me in the eye. "Come on Dave," Tony chimed in. "Where's the old British stiff upper lip?"

As time passed I realised we needed to find some sort of sympathetic figure if we were going to get out of this any time soon. But all the officials were so on edge, it would be dangerous and foolhardy to tell our story to the wrong man. I felt strongly that if we could get access to a telephone to call Jerry Bryon, he would be able to bail us out of this sorry situation.

Studying the officials for the next half an hour I found little cause for hope. Anger, resentment, fear and confusion creased every face.

However, I later spotted a chubby, jolly-looking figure wearing an odd hat that for whatever reason had a squirrel-like tail protruding out the back. In any other situation the hat would have been downright comical. The face underneath carried a different look though, leading me to think this guy had a bit more savvy than the rest. I beckoned him over.

"Brother, we have problem," I said, looking down at him as he was a couple of inches shorter. "We have no idea why we are here. All our papers are in order, what's the problem?"

For the first time he met my gaze. "These are serious times with the attempted coup. You can tell the commander your story when he arrives. That should be within an hour."

He turned to walk away. "Brother, will you please call our Liberian friend?" I asked urgently. "This is his number. Please tell him that we are here."

I handed over the number that Tony had rapidly scribbled down. I didn't feel like the encounter had done much good but at least it gave us a bit of hope and I felt better to have actually taken some action.

"Thanks brother," I said to Fatty's back as he left.

At that moment the relative quiet was broken as a Liberian dressed in his policeman's uniform was pushed, punched and kicked through the door, by our original two captors.

Blood streamed down his face as he was ordered to "get your clothes off, you Gio scum" and another flurry of kicks rained down before the prisoner was dragged to an adjoining room. About five minutes later the most piercing blood-curdling scream came from next door.

The inhumane sound of beating and pummelling was non-stop. The screams and groans were soon followed by whimpering – an indication that the light of life was flickering weakly. Looking around nobody seemed to take any notice, except the three of us who were sick with shock.

The scar-faced officer then walked back into the room, a satisfied smirk across his pock-marked face. He nonchalantly threaded his large leather belt, with a monster buckle on it, through the hoops on the top of his trousers.

The next prisoner to arrive was treated very differently. It was a young woman, and instead of being ordered to strip like the others she simply lay down, curled up and went to sleep. Nobody took any notice. It was a strange day and it kept getting more so.

In the evening, a group of prisoners' wives and girlfriends brought in food and drink to their caged partners. There was no emotion, no kissing, or touching, even though their husbands faced the threat of being shot the next day. Even more bizarre was the way the prisoners openly shared their food and drink with their captors, even Scarface.

I knew what I'd like to share with that rat of a man – a round of bullets from a machine gun. How can anyone do what he did to a fellow human being? But this was Liberia and anything goes.

Finally, the Commander arrived. He was in his mid-twenties, well over six feet tall and dressed in the Liberian army uniform. He was a good-looking man but his face told it all – no sleep – and he was virtually out on his feet. Every couple of hours he would go and listen to pleas from prisoners scattered around Monrovia on why they shouldn't die the next day. Few met with a positive response.

Tony kept nudging me to find out what was going to happen to us. "Tone, I think their problems are much worse than ours," I said, gesturing to the other prisoners. "We will just have to wait and hope the Commander doesn't fall asleep in the meantime."

Of the stories told to the Commander, some were funny, others sad and heart-rending. Going by what happened in the last coup these men were really up against it and were arguing for the ultimate, their lives.

The 'bar gripper' was a taxi driver who was just carrying some of the prisoners in his cab. He was simply thrown behind bars with the rest of them. The difference in his mental capacity was vast and much lower than his fellow prisoners. He just stood and held the bars all day. He was petrified. Everyone took advantage of him and he did all the bad jobs, cleaning the toilets, even cleaning up after the beating.

Finally, we got our turn and the commander seemed to wake up. We told him about our arrest and that our papers were in order and we didn't understand why we were arrested. I pointed out that Fatty was given our Liberian friend's phone number, so that he

This was not the place that I wanted my life to end ... our cell in Monrovia (circled), where we were imprisoned.

could come here and get us out. Without answering he turned to Fatty and fired the question at him.

"What happened about the phone calls to the white man's Liberian friend?"

Fatty looked nervous and said that he had tried three or four times with no luck. "Well, try again. And if still no luck, send a car to his house and make sure you find him, as soon as possible."

Turning to us, a smile shone through his weathered face as he spoke. "I must apologise for the trouble you have been caused and I'm sure it wouldn't happen in your country.

"I actually studied just outside of Cambridge for six months and the people were great to me. Sorry once again. Liberia is on hard times again, and nobody is quite sure what is happening. The coup was supposed to have involved some foreign influence and your white faces probably didn't help your cause.

"I am afraid my hands are tied, for the moment. But I promise you tomorrow morning I will be in touch, and make sure you are taken care of. Do you want some food or drink?"

Looking at my watch I realised we hadn't eaten or drunk for over 20 hours. "Thank you," I said. "Also, could you please advise the British Embassy of our whereabouts?" I queried.

"That won't be necessary as it will be sorted in the morning. If there is still a problem we will inform them, but I think this is highly unlikely. Good luck lads."

Our spirits were greatly lifted but, like anything in Liberia, the proof would be in the pudding. The Commander's words were encouraging but I wouldn't really feel better until we were safely out of this miserable place.

"Well boys, another night in this shit hole, but at least we are going to eat and with luck we will be out in the morning," I smiled. We sat around and talked until Fatty took our food and drink orders. He let us go to the toilet one at a time with a guard.

It had been a long day, and now the hunger demons in my stomach had been satisfied, there was nothing we could do until the morning, so I thought I would try to get a bit of shuteye. I lay on the narrow, hard wooden bench, trying for a little bit of sleep that would take me away from this hellhole for a few hours.

But no sooner had I drifted off than there was an explosion of noise and drama. Crashing and yelling jerked me back into reality but my eyes hadn't even got into focus fully when I felt a boot stamping on my head.

As I came out of sleep it took a few seconds for me to remember where I was, then I saw a black boot rushing towards my face. Instinct kicked in and I immediately started screaming "what the fuck" and trying to grab the offending boot.

Then someone grabbed me from behind. It was Tony.

"Briggo, quieten down," he said. "They think that we are the 'peace corps' and that we are infiltrated by the CIA. They are drunk and doped out of their heads."

I then took in what exactly was happening around me. The foot that I grabbed but couldn't hold belonged to a drunken Liberian soldier carrying a machine gun.

My trip had caught him off-balance, he had staggered back in shock, and dropped his machine gun. Suddenly it went deathly quiet. Everyone was looking at me, this stupid old white man. I defused the situation by sitting down. The offending soldier didn't want to know and was trying to melt into the background. I simply eyeballed him and he couldn't handle it. He tried to turn away, but he couldn't stop himself from looking again to find out if I was still staring at him.

My eyes were burning into his, the look and scowl on my face left him in no doubt what I'd like to do to him. It was three in the morning. Hopefully we only had a few more hours to put up with this shit. But with the soldiers in various states of intoxication, anything could happen.

Five soldiers who'd been on street patrol came bursting in. These characters would walk the roads looking for anyone stupid enough to have broken the curfew that had been put in place. It was sport for these boys. Any offenders on the streets could be shot. Any soldier who scored a direct hit was bought drinks by his colleagues the next day.

Now they were bored and had come to the prison to have some fun with the traitors. They didn't expect to see us three sitting there.

After our scuffle had died down, all the attention was then focused back on the 'traitors', the Liberian prisoners. They taunted them, yelling, 'on your feet, now sit down, up again', on and on.

Then the questions, questions, on and on they went.

"Who's the boss?"

"You sir."

"And who's the people's President?"

Yes sir, no sir, three bags full. All the time the soldiers' guns were menacingly pointed at the prisoners, with gestures that they were going to shoot them all.

The atmosphere was electric and we feared we would soon end up in the middle of a bloodbath. It all came to a sudden stop when one soldier actually fired a shot into the ceiling, by accident. Everything changed immediately and the soldiers just melted away, African style.

The one thing we did learn during the action-packed night was

Tony swimming with his mates again.

the enormous difference in the attitudes towards dying between white and black people. Once a Liberian had been told three or four times that they would die tomorrow, their attitude was: "So I'm going to die tomorrow."

If we were told that we would die tomorrow, we would come up with three or four schemes for our getaway. There were guns just lying around, and you wouldn't need to be Al Capone to shoot your way out and get away.

By 8am it was just starting to warm up and so was the smell of unwashed bodies, including ours. The captors changed shift and three new recruits arrived. A new day was dawning – hopefully it wouldn't be like the previous one – which felt 100 hours long.

I knew for a fact that I didn't want another day like that for as long as I lived.

At nine, the moment that we had been waiting for arrived. Strolling through the door was none other than Jerry Bryon. "Where the hell have you been?" I asked right away, part indignation and part relief.

Just as the question left my lips I noticed that Jerry had two badly bruised eyes and his eyes were so swollen they were just slits. Also, there were two teeth missing and a deep gash on his right cheek. 'Barry, why didn't you open your eyes instead of your mouth?' I asked myself.

"Boys, I've just been to a three-day party," he laughed. "Now it's time to get you out of here."

By the look of him, I couldn't bear to think what sort of party it had been, especially having seen how the Liberians treated their own. To think we felt hard done by for a couple of days!

Suddenly, me, Tony and Dave all burst into laughter – we just couldn't help ourselves. Our diabolical ordeal was over. The scary thing was that it was something that we had no control over. Having my life balanced on the knife edge of death now felt much worse when it was all over and the full consequences came into focus. "Let's go," we said in unison.

Jerry looked at our beaming faces in bewilderment. He had no idea of how happy we were to be heading back to the tranquillity of the jungle.

Bedtime reading for Junie in our colourful bedroom.

New partners and new hope for our mining operation

27

AFTER our enforced holiday in Monrovia it was great to be back to the quietness of our 'little old mine' in the jungle with its river view. It was time to take stock of exactly where we were at this moment of time in our search for diamonds.

Tony's river dredge was coming up with all the right messages but still there was no sign of any diamonds. Maybe we were losing some. A dredge is only as good as the operator and the water flow and speed over the riffles on the river dredge is an exact science.

The water and the material that contains the diamonds have to pass over the riffles at exactly the right speed. This creates a vortex that is induced by the speed of the water flow and the heavy diamondiferous materials are sucked down into the bottom corner of the riffles.

We would clear the riffles out very carefully at the end of each day hoping to expose some diamonds. Every hour we would take a sample of the material from the end of the riffles before it flowed back into the river. If there was no diamondiferous material in the samples it could mean that we had to slow down the water flow – because if there were any diamonds in this material they would just be lost and washed straight back into the river.

To work our river dredge we used divers and we had an unusual problem. The air temperature was in the mid-80s. The water was warm but after the divers had been in the water for about half an hour they were getting so cold they couldn't do anything, let alone work underwater. They were still shivering an hour after leaving the water.

We made a huge bonfire on the river bank to try and warm them up but the cold had got right into their bones. The fire made no real difference. Something had to be done, otherwise our operation would stall but salvation arrived from an unexpected source.

After hunting around we discovered that a departing American couple who used to dive and spear the local grouper fish in the St Paul's river, on the outskirts of Monrovia, had left their wetsuits behind in case any of the other ex-pats wanted to try their hand at diving.

It was heaven-sent for our divers and us but unfortunately not for one, as the lady's suit was a brightly coloured pink. Every day when they were diving there was always a fight about who got the pink suit. We arranged a truce and they took turns on which diver was going to be the 'woman for the day', in his pink suit.

After Tony had recovered from his initial test-dive and the subsequent ear troubles he was ready to go down again. To protect his ears for a little longer he rationed his dives and only went down to check the progress of how the mine 40 feet down on the bottom of the river was shaping up. He never wore a wetsuit, he simply slipped over the side just wearing his swimming trunks. The purpose of the mine on the bottom of the river was, of course, to find diamonds, which was a bit like looking for a polar bear in a snowstorm.

First you had to trace the line that the heavy minerals flowed along the river bottom. To determine this path, you had to dive to the river bottom and bring up a small sample. It was a very simple test. If your first sample contained three pieces of heavy minerals, then you moved five feet closer to the riverbank and took another sample.

If you got more pieces, then you were going in the right direction, if less you were going in the wrong direction. When you thought that you had found the right track, it normally would be confirmed with odd bits of heavies, such as old nails or small bits of metal.

Once you were on the right line, it would be time to build a small mining station on the riverbed, which would finish up as an eight-foot square hole.

First the front side facing upstream needed to be sandbagged. This allowed for digging the hole behind the bags and it also meant that you could go deeper without the river filling up the hole with material as quickly as it was dug. The six-inch suction hose from the raft would then be used to suck up the materials from the river-bed.

The previous week, our diver David surfaced and told Tony and his boys this unbelievable story. David said that he was standing on the river bottom, with his hands above his head as he shook the suction pipe that had become blocked. Suddenly, a 'big-oh fish' appeared and bit right through his index finger.

Even though there was blood streaming from the wound, nobody believed him and everyone laughed.

But a few days later Tony went down to check out the mine. As normal visibility was virtually zero, he crawled into the back of the mined hole, and was checking the sandbagging and what progress had being made. Then as he crawled out of the hole over the sandbags, he looked up and his heart stopped. He was nose to nose with this monster-sized face of a giant grouper fish. He got out of there in double quick time.

Finding the guide rope that hung from the raft above, he surfaced, climbed up on to the raft and burst out laughing. Everyone was shocked and the boys were really worried, saying: "Boss, boss, what's the problem?" It took minutes for Tony to get back into control and to stop his uncontrollable laughter.

When he told his story of the 'big-oh fish' everyone burst into laughter, David looked dolefully at his wrapped finger.

A week later we finally found two diamonds from the river dredge. One was small; the other was about two carats. In their raw state there was no glitter, and they didn't look worth all the trouble that we had gone to find them. They were both gemstone quality, but strangely enough to finally find diamonds turned out to be a real anti-climax.

Back on land, our 'Thackwell's Folly' pit was costing us a lot of time and money and if I didn't pull my finger out, we would start running out of money. Then the pit could be renamed 'Briggo's Folly', a situation that I certainly didn't want to happen.

After a couple of calls to England to the works' manager of the St. Austell pottery manufacturer, who just happened to be a speedway supporter, we decided to try the water-hydraulic system. We started to change our gravel pump in readiness for its use in the new water-hydraulic mining.

After we had replaced our California cutter with the new system the results on the amount of material we moved was impressive and it certainly looked as though we had gone in the right direction. Hydraulic mining meant that we pumped water at a very high pressure onto the clay on the inside of our pit. The resulting sludge settled into a well at the bottom of the pit. Then the sludge was sucked up to the ground level. This material is where the diamonds are, this diamondiferous material could be worth any figure you could think of, and therefore must be guarded well. This innocent looking pile of gravel is where all the time and money has been spent.

Throughout the camp there was a real upbeat feeling the day after hitting the jackpot of actually finding real diamonds in the river project. I was going to London the next week for a short trip for a meeting of Clogau Gold Mine plc.

The best thing was that Junie was flying in from California to meet me in her home town, London. Just the thought of being with her again soon put a spring back into my stride.

The Clogau meeting in London had just finished with some really good, positive results. We were sitting around in small groups chatting over a few drinks when, out of the blue, Aussie Arthur Dew, one of the big hitters for Belgravia, asked the question.

"Barry, what are you up to at present?" I was shocked as I couldn't have scripted it better myself. This opened a conversation that I wanted to get into, but I wasn't quite sure of how to go about it.

"Well Arthur," I said, "I've just got back from our gold and diamond mining projects in Liberia, West Africa."

"How's it going mate, found any diamonds, or even gold?" he asked, and carried on, "I read some time ago that the De Beers Company tried to get into Liberia, but couldn't come to an agreement with the Liberian government."

"It's fine if you understand the African way, and you can get most things done but it will always cost you. It's what the Africans call dash, it just means that you must pay a few dollars here and there to get things, and is normally a time saver. It's not our way of doing business but if you need something important enough you must pay," I answered.

Arthur leaned back in his chair and I could see his brain ticking over. Finally he asked: "Have you got any paperwork on your project?"

Quick as a flash I pulled out our two geologists' reports and our caterpillar-yellow photos of our operation and laid them down in front of him. Two hours later we had new partners in Liberia.

I sold Arthur 49 per cent of Kiwi Minerals for $500,000 and life was good. We then changed our name to Kiwi Resources, leaving Kiwi Minerals behind because our new associates didn't know if we had any debts and the new company had to be free of debt and any other encumbrances.

I smiled to myself and reckoned that the money spent on the purchase of the ten gallons of caterpillar-yellow paint had proved quite an investment. The fresh shine had helped in a big way to tie-up our deal; of course this really eased our financial burden. My life had taken a turn for the better.

The highlight of my trip was still to come. My darling Junie would be here in London in a couple of days' time.

It was great to be back in the proper world, especially with Junie, but it seemed to be no time at all before we were on the move back to the jungle. Junie had been there before and wasn't that fazed, in fact she had her own bag of bits and pieces for the kids at our local school in Gbeni, so she was also excited.

When we finally arrived back at our base camp Junie and I had an unbelievable surprise. While I was away, Tony had worked wonders. He had, in some magical way, finished our palatial four-bedroom mud hut, on our riverside location, and most things were finished so that we could move in.

Now it was painted white inside and out and looked a million dollars. The only trouble Tony had in getting it finished was when he was going to paint the inside of all the rooms white. All our boys told him: "No boss Tony, you just light a fire in the middle of the rooms and they will all go black."

Junie and Tony had obviously been talking about the house as she pulled curtains out of her suitcase to put up in our newly painted bedroom. With some glamorous large posters, one of yachting in San Diego and some other feel good posters, and now curtains ... first-class, eh!

"How did you ever get the measurements?" I quizzed her. "Tony just told me to open my arms wide, and then double that and it would be perfect," she said.

James Wah was our man Friday but was really nervous of Junie's arrival. Tony told James that Junie didn't like people around the house and that he would have to let him go as we had no work for him. The day before we arrived back at the camp James had found some plants and had planted them all around our house, then he swept the hard dry clay so that it looked like marble.

James Wah wasn't going to lose his job without a fight. We knew we didn't really want him to go – he was our source of fun and laughter.

I forgot how good our camp was after being away. With Junie at base camp we had to make some alterations, for having a lady in a man's world.

First, we had to put sides and a door on our river-view toilet. We dug out a platform on the high river bank that was about eight-foot high that you could stand beside. We moved a 45-gallon drum onto the top bank, then I made an arm from the drum out two feet from the clay bank. Attached to the arm was a piece of plastic tubing fitted to a plastic coke bottle with ten small holes bored in the bottom. Lo and behold we had a shower.

The water lying in the drum all day in the sun was heated to a good temperature for our evening showers. If the temperature was too hot or cold it was tough luck. This model had no room for adjustments.

We used to laugh with Junie, telling her that the boys from the village from the other side of the river used to queue up at nights to watch her showering. I must admit that at times when I was showering I did try and see if I could see any eyes watching.

In a short time Junie had turned our mud hut into a home, complete with curtains, pictures on the walls and pots of flowers. The place now had a woman's touch and it had completely changed.

It wasn't all plain sailing, though, and every now and then we would get a real life wake-up call that things were very different in the jungle. One day I was having my regular dip in the river to cool my blood down when I slipped on the wet rocks and cut my shin quite badly. It was on my left leg, where I had previously suffered from septicaemia.

I badly needed a shot of penicillin but, although we had our own new needles, we needed to find a doctor with the medicine. Rather than return to Monrovia, our working boss David told us there was a doctor in a village called Gboleken that was not far away.

Tony, David and I loaded our two bikes into the company's boat and crossed the river to start our journey from Gbeni.

It was about 2pm and the sun was losing a bit of its heat. We couldn't afford to be too late as only one bike had a headlight. However, the description of "not too far" provided by David was stretching it. The journey seemed endless as we roared through the jungle. David had never been on the back of a motorcycle before, and didn't realise that you lean your body into the corner. He loved to lean in the other direction and it made me feel like a novice rider, especially when I crashed.

We were on a double dirt track with Tony and I side by side when trouble loomed. My side of the track was washed out. I took immediate evasive action and tried to jump from my lane into Tony's with drastic results.

I landed short of the wash out and the handlebars were torn from my hands. I flew through the air and landed hard on my hands and knees. With my speedway racer's instinct my first thought was to survey the damage. I had badly torn the left knee of my jeans and took a load of skin from my left forearm. Apart from that everything seemed to be all right.

What happened to David, my pillion passenger, was a miracle. He had flown through the air and landed on top of the battered briefcase he always carried. There was not a bloody scratch on him. Tony thought this was all very funny – all part of a lovely ride through the leaf-lined tracks, no gloves, no helmets and then this.

Still fuming, I yelled at Tony that the crash was his fault as he gave me no room, but he just came back with even more laughter. David just stood by, with only a mark on his briefcase and couldn't believe what he was seeing. Being a father, and if our positions were reversed, I would have gone mad at Tony for being an idiot but there was only one idiot around, and he was old enough to know better. Of course, I wouldn't tell him that.

After I cleaned off my precious blood, we started out again. David's directions were hard to understand as he had only walked this way once, and at 30 miles per hour things looked much different.

Finally, more by luck than design, we found Gboleken village, which was a gathering of about 40 mud huts on the top of some dry rolling hills. Luckily for me the doctor had only just arrived back from Monrovia one hour before we got there.

We told him of my problem and he went to get his medical kit, while we all stood outside the back of his house. The word soon got around that there were visitors in town. Within no time, we had 50 or so people gathered around us. Most had never seen a white man before and they were completely in awe, especially of Tony with his mop of blond hair. As had happened before, the kids just wanted to feel the white skin and the reaction is always the same. Two came out of the pack and got brave and came up and touched Tony, then backed off quickly as if he was going to bite them. It was all good fun.

Soon the doctor came back with his bag of tricks, rustling through to find the penicillin to use with the sterile needles that we had brought with us. I was completely embarrassed when he told me to drop my pants, in front of everybody. So much for privacy … there is no such word in this part of Africa.

It was probably my imagination but the crowd seemed to be starting to get really excited as I lowered my trousers and obviously they were starting to enjoy this free show. So, with my trousers around my ankles, the doctor got me to lean forward against the wall so he could get a good shot at my backside.

I could see Tony out of the corner of my eye and he was really enjoying the show along with the rest of the village.

The injection was high in my thigh muscle and, boy, did it hurt. I could have screamed. It hurt so much it brought tears to my eyes. I never turned around as I pulled up my trousers so the crowd wouldn't see what a sissy I was.

The next bit really eased my pain as the doctor beckoned to Tony – now it was his turn and the smile quickly disappeared from his face. Word had spread and the crowd had doubled for the next show and the young local maidens loved it. Tony had no idea that he was going to be on show today and had worn his very skimpy white underpants with red hearts on them saying 'I Love LA', a Christmas present from his mother. The doctor did the same to Tony as he had done to me, much to the delight of the onlookers. We had come into this village as complete strangers, now all the locals knew us intimately!

It was now late, the sun had set and was disappearing beneath the horizon, and darkness had descended on us. The trip back home was a nightmare with only one headlight and Tony had now got himself a passenger, good old 'lean the wrong way' David.

Between us we must have crashed five or six times on the return journey, which took us three times longer than going. Suffice to say that everyone back at camp enjoyed the tales of Tony and I dropping our pants in front of the villagers.

By now, it was time to enjoy the open spaces down here on the Loffa river. We only had a few weeks before the wet season started.

I was never quite sure if Junie liked being on the back of a motorbike with me. Over the years we'd had a few crashes together. We were out riding together one day after work had finished. It was a beautiful day as we rode through the lush jungle heading back to our camp. I'm afraid that I couldn't help myself – when I saw a nice pile of clay I decided I'd give Junie a bit of a thrill. "Hold on love," I yelled as I accelerated up to the mound.

We soared like a bird, but while in mid-air I could see that the backside of the mound had been cut away in the last couple of days. It was too late, what goes up, must come down. I kept control but Junie's head crashed down and her chin was transplanted into her chest. We stopped and she was in tears, I felt a complete heel and knew that I should have known better. When she had settled down, I had to plead with her not to tell Tony or the others. She enjoyed my embarrassment enough to absorb a bit of her pain, before eventually agreeing to let me off the hook by keeping quiet.

Life in the jungle was soon to finish for me as I would have to move back into Monrovia to run the business now that the Aussies had coughed up the money, they expected action for their investment.

After a couple more weeks it was time to get down to business in Monrovia. We went to the beautiful Hotel Africa to set up a deal for a large suite in which to stay before we returned to California for Christmas.

The hotel did us a great deal, it was the best place to stay while in Liberia. It had a swimming pool, tennis courts and was on the beach. Best of all it was a few miles outside of Monrovia and the security was good. Although we now had money, I found it impossible to waste it.

When we were just Kiwi Minerals and struggling for cash I would have stayed at Julia's Bar. Now, as Kiwi Resources and with some heavy finance behind us, we could take advantage of the new monetary injection. Truthfully, though, I would rather have been at our $200 mud hut than the Hotel Africa with all its splendour. I know it sounds stupid but I felt that I was losing what I had come to Liberia to achieve, an adventure. Now money was back as the major factor in our operation, the whole adventure had changed for me forever. Sad, sad, sad.

Junie always loved being surrounded by children.

When is a deal not a deal? When it is done in Liberia

28

TWO Belgravia directors, Australian Collis Thorpe and Englishman Martin Buckingham, arrived in Liberia to look at our prospects and evaluate what was now the best direction to take. They also brought their wives and travelled first class, which proved they didn't mind spending the lolly.

They all stayed at the first-class Hotel Africa, which offered luxury on a par with any in the world. They had decided to only spend half a day down at our base camp. Obviously they knew we had the workings at base camp in the position they wanted. The most important thing to them was their visit to the Minister of Mines, which made good sense.

I sat in on the meeting while they got the information they wanted from the Minister. They told me about their interest in some new northern concessions, and were trying to find out about their availability. The picture that they were painting to the Minister was that our company was an important, serious player.

To work properly in Liberia, you had to fall into one of three groups. If you are a large investor, you would be playing for big stakes. A company must be run properly and look the part for the Liberian officials to take you seriously, which would give you some horsepower and, in some ways, allow you to set some of your own standards.

In that situation, it meant offering 'dash', or financial sweeteners, directly to the President. But that wasn't easy. You must remember the saying in Liberia that things are generally easier for everyone: 'When the President's box is pretty full.' This normally happened when the President had been in residence for a few years.

The other deal with the government was the option of playing it low-key and this had been the way of Kiwi Minerals. We were sneaking under the radar, paying out small amounts of dash here and there.

Acting small-time was an easier way to go while trying to prove and evaluate prospects because we were pretty well left alone. But, unless you got really lucky and stumbled on a real rich find of diamonds, there was no way you would finish up rich.

A company in the middle would have the biggest problems. Such a firm would not have enough money to satisfy the President but would appear significant enough that the Minister would want his whack. I was interested to see how the Minister of Mines now rated Belgravia plc.

I really hoped that he wouldn't upgrade us to the middle group … it's not just the money, it's the bloody hassle of having to deal with people that are basically dishonest.

An American, Bradley Burn, who had been on the fringes of mining and mining deals for a few years in Liberia, decided he was going to get the best treatment by marrying one of President Doe's cousins. Maybe living in Liberia it could be a help, but if you "go bush" then your living standards drop, so everything comes at a price.

We now had an office in Monrovia, rented from my friend Richard at his Toyota headquarters. I soon realised that it was the outdoors of the jungle that I'd come to Liberia for, not really to be locked in an office and dealing with people that in my normal world I would choose to ignore. We had got the Aussie money because we had proved we could do the job, but now my job description had changed.

Tony could handle base camp in the bush better than me anyhow. I had made my bed, now I had got to lie on it.

I had come through many tough times in my racing and business career, but this lot was going to test me to the best of my abilities, and many times I felt that I was coming up short.

After the two Directors from Belgravia had left, my number one job was to get the new concession in Nimba County near the village of Tapeta tied up.

Each concession was 100 square miles. The one that the directors were very keen on was on 1p on Block 77. It was one of the blocks the De Beers Company had wanted to mine and it included the Mano Godua Kimberlite Pipe, which was supposedly rich with diamonds.

De Beers had failed to tie-up with the Liberian Government two decades earlier. An economic geologist from the University of Massachusetts, Professor Stephen Haggerty, had written papers on the diamonds in Liberia. I had read the papers and passed the information on to the Aussies, who then spoke to Haggerty.

He was very positive that there were diamonds in great numbers in Liberia, especially in the north. We completed the paperwork and paid the fees and got the okay for 1p on Block 77 from the Ministry of Mines to start work in those areas. We were told we were only waiting for President Doe to sign the paperwork, but to just carry on, as we were covered, so the Minister of Mines informed us.

I took three geologists to the northern concessions and spent three weeks mapping and sampling in the old De Beers areas. There were many unconfirmed reports of the recovery of large diamonds in this area.

One of the geologists was Dr. John Rottenbury. He impressed me as he got a lot more achieved than others when he was using local labour. It was well known that the Liberian workers slacked off when you weren't there supervising them, they simply downed their tools. They needed constant checking. However, whenever

John just left them alone the jobs still got done. Curious, I asked Dr. John in passing how he managed to persuade his workers to stick to their tasks.

John just about died with laughing when I asked him. He had a glass eye, which I hadn't noticed: "I take out my glass eye and put it on a rock," he said. "Then I tell the workers that I'm watching them all the time.

"It wouldn't work in Birmingham but it sure does here in Liberia."

We made large plans for these new concessions, which were spread over a very large area of rolling hills. There were many mature ironwood trees dotting the countryside. It was a very lush green area with plenty of foliage everywhere. We planned to have our base camp at the top of a small hill, and a building that could house 120 mine and maintenance personnel.

The main road from Monrovia was in very bad condition and was used by many of the logging companies that operated in this part of the country.

The road was very busy with logging trucks. Each truck was carrying four enormous tree trunks, seven-feet round and at least 30 feet long. The loads were massive, but making it worse was that the drivers smoked weed and drank too much.

Revved-up by drugs, and driving on the twisting dirt roads amongst the rolling hills, was a cocktail of disaster. The drivers, of course, thought they were Superman and travelled far too fast, with their unbelievably heavy loads.

Remarkably, they would even disconnect the front brakes on their trucks. This meant that on the downhill dirt corners they could still brake hard without losing steering through locked front wheels. Even so, it was an accident waiting to happen, and there were many serious incidents.

I decided it would be very dangerous for us to use this road regularly when we started mining these northern concessions. With so much danger on the roads to Monrovia we located a large piece of reasonably smooth ground to build our own airfield. Years before the runway was the main street, which was downhill and it was extremely dangerous with many accidents.

Returning to Monrovia I had a message that someone from the Ministry of Mines wanted to see me, and I didn't have to be a genius to know what he wanted. He needed $6,000 dollars in cash to seal the agreement for 1p on Block 77 that was still awaiting the signature of President Doe. It was against my better judgment, but I paid the ransom with a bag full of five dollar coins.

I didn't know if it was a business ploy or simply to heap more pressure on me for the cash, but he half suggested that someone else was showing interest in the same block. I took that with a pinch of salt, as if he had told me it was raining outside, I'd pop out to check.

Work was going fine up in the north. Tony had 'Thackwell's Folly' going well and the hydraulic system was proving to be fast and efficient. They should be getting to the diamondiferous material within the next couple of weeks.

One evening Junie and I were in the foyer of Hotel Africa when an American introduced himself. It was Professor Haggerty, the man our Australian investors had tapped up for information. We agreed to meet for dinner, he had with him a black New York investor and although we chatted freely during the meal I didn't broach the subject of mining.

For some reason, I didn't feel at ease with the professor or his mate, but I couldn't put my finger on why. I would later look back and regret that I didn't get into mining with him.

Jerry Bryon rang me about a week later and said he wanted to see me. He told me that we had lost the concession on block 77. I was livid and took off like a shot to confront the man from the Ministry of Mines.

At the front desk I asked to see him and gave the girl my name. She came back and told me that he was not in today. I decided to call their bluff. "Who is driving his car today then?" I said, angrily. "I'm sorry but I am not leaving this office till I see him." With that I plonked myself down in a nearby chair.

After an hour, the man we'd been dealing with had his secretary bring me to his office. I could tell from the start that he couldn't care less and this was confirmed when he couldn't even be bothered to stand up to greet me. He was completely unconcerned that things had gone bad for Kiwi Resourses and me. He then went into his little speech that "Block 77 had unfortunately been taken out of my hands, by somebody very high up in the Liberian government. It has now been allotted to an American Company led by Professor Haggerty."

I couldn't believe my ears, and was on the point of boiling over. We had worked on that bloody Block 77 for over six weeks with the ministry's permission.

He had personally told me when he took our $6,000 that everything was okay, and we were only waiting for the signature of President Doe. I had handled all money-related affairs for the Aussie and Kiwi investors and at this very moment I felt that I'd let everyone down.

"What about the $6,000 that you forced us to pay you to legalize the diamond concession at Block 77?" I demanded. The man simply shrugged his shoulders.

"Tomorrow morning you will hear from my lawyer," I fumed as I stormed out. My brain was racing and I felt I couldn't trust anyone. How did Jerry know that Haggerty was in town? And how did he know that we had lost the concession? Was our trusted partner part of the doublecross?

The worst part was that it was Haggerty and his mate, our dubious dinner guests, who were leading the new consortium. How could I be so stupid? We later found out it was a Government Minister's wife who had taken the Block 77 concession as a deal for herself, but it didn't make me feel any better, she would just become Haggerty's partner for free!

The truth of the matter is that Kiwi's Liberian connection, Jerry, was weak. He was much lower on the totem-pole than the Minister's wife. For minor problems he was a help, but nothing in the big league. Bad luck Barry. You lose.

The lawyer route cost us plenty, got us nowhere, and we never saw the $6,000 ever again. In the end we still had to go back and trade, with this double-dealing jerk. In England his arse would have been thrown in jail. Wake up Barry, here in Liberia they sing to a different songbook.

I had done nothing wrong. I was the one who lost face. No

matter how much it hurt pride wise or money wise, it was me who took his eye off the ball. I had completely forgotten whose rules we were playing by. We were in Africa, and instead of thinking on my feet I had taken false promises at face value.

In the end we got a deal for another concession. But this time we had it signed by President Doe before we moved. It was in the same concession, Block 77, and it was a huge relief when it eventually went through. The geologists figured that it was similar to the other concession but without the Kimberlite pipe. They also thought it was extremely possible that we would discover a new Kimberlite pipe on the new concession.

Work was now back on track at our new northern concession, and the geologists were coming up with plenty of new hot spots. Much of what we had achieved on the other concession we managed to use on our new area. The planning of the camp, and the airport sites, were just about the same as before.

Meanwhile, the Loffa river project was now in a position to see if we had struck it rich. The diamondiferous material was now ready to be sized and sieved for possible diamonds. To size the material we used an old-fashioned system, the way it used to be done when there were no engines or power around to run the machines. We simply used one-man power.

First, we made a large elongated box, the bottoms of both ends curved like a rocking chair. Then we made three slightly smaller boxes with wire mesh bottoms fitted, so they all slipped into each other. The three were then slipped into the top of the rocker box.

You then rocked it like a baby's crib, then the material was shovelled in, water pouring over the material. The rocking agitated the mix, which would then sieve the material as it fell downwards, sizing itself as it fell through the sizing mesh.

The top box stopped the largest stones from passing through. If you found a diamond in this box it would be so big that you and your family, plus your relations, would never have to work again. The second and the third box each had different sized smaller holes to sort the materials.

One of our fittest boys would stand on the sides of the top box and rock it to a God-given rhythm. The other workers joined in and clapped, hummed and sang as the rocker did his job. Material was being added all the time, and it really was a sight to behold, with the 'Rocker-man' with his muscular body sweating and swaying with the nearby palm trees.

When all the materials had been sized we had to get the diamonds into a position from which we could extract them. This was the most dangerous time for the diamonds to be stolen and all materials at this stage were rechecked and examined by Tony or myself. We could never afford to take our eyes off the workings, even for one minute, as all of the work and money spent was for this one moment.

Standing in water halfway up to their knees, four of our most trusted boys were each armed with a small 18-inch round sieve. These were filled up with the diamond-bearing material, the sieve was then submerged about four inches deep into the water, and then started a continuous pulsating up-and-down motion. At the same time, the sieve was rotated back and forth.

This motion caused all the heavy materials to drop to the bottom of the sieve and, the simultaneous rotating moved the heavies to the centre of the sieve. After a couple of minutes of this drill, the top material was swept off with the operator's hand, and then

Saki Town's Hells Angels.

refilled. This was repeated until the sieve was full. Then the sieve was flipped over on a clean surface and deposited the material over like an omelette. In the middle would be a black circle, about the diameter of an egg cup, of the heavy materials.

All the work finally came down to this. The black circle was where the diamonds would be found.

It had to be done very carefully as an uncut diamond is a dull-looking stone. But, once you have found one diamond, you will always recognise the next one. When the material is being agitated an experienced operator can see the diamonds as water just runs off them just like they are waterproof, which is okay if the operator is honest.

There were plenty of stories about how diamonds had been stolen at this part of the operation. Diamonds had been known to be flicked out of the sieve with the operator's thumb. The operator would then return later to pick up their spoils from the ground. Other tales regaled how a clever operator would flick diamonds into his mouth with his educated thumb and swallow it. Let's just say he wouldn't be using public toilets for a day or two.

The pit next to ours on the Loffa was a joint venture with about 25 locals doing all the work. They were all Muslim and during the holy month of Ramadan would work all night after fasting during the day. Their pit was about 40 feet deep. In the bottom of the hole were two boys shovelling material up onto a step about five feet above the bottom. These steps continued up at intervals of five feet all the way to the top.

In Liberia at night, without the moon, it is pitch black, so much so that vision is a maximum of five feet. Looking out on the scene, the first thing that caught your eye was one solitary old kerosene lamp burning halfway up the pit on its own little step.

The amount of light that the dancing flame put out was amazing, no stage manager could light a scene more dramatically. The flickering flame accentuated the workers in the half shadows as they toiled, moving the diamondiferous materials upwards, always upwards.

They were energised by the very thought that if God smiled on them, and helped them to find just one medium-sized diamond, overnight their life would completely change. Finally, all the material is divided equally between all the workers, and put into bags. It was just like a lottery, did your bag have diamonds or not?

Dramatically they waited for a week clutching their bags of material, and living out their hopes. Then the time had finally arrived and the workers and half the village descended down to the river side. The workers gathered together on the side of the river bank.

The 'most trusted one' was the worker voted by the rest of the group to jig their material. He entered the water amid cheers and laughter. He took up his position in the shallows of the river. The water was just below his knees. When he had his sieve loaded with the first of the materials he started to jig the sieve, in the circular pulsating motion to uncover the diamonds.

Some workers wanted their material done quickly to know if they were going to be rich.

Others never really wanted to know the answer, and continually kept hanging back. They were all laughing and joking, and repetitively they sang over and over their diamond jigging song.

'Hey, hey Mr. Jiggerman spin our wheel of fortune, keep that lighting thumb on the outside, we say on the outside Mr. Jiggerman.'

They sang just to remind their 'trusted one' that they were all watching him, so no tricks please. The singing and chanting went on and on, until all their material had been processed. Great fun, but sadly nobody from our local villages ever went to New York with riches beyond belief.

Even weeks later they were still talking of what they would have done with their life if they found the perfect giant diamond the size of a chicken egg.

Kiwi Resource's jigged material realised the discovery of 226 gemstone diamonds, proving that our Loffa river project could be mined professionally, and had great potential.

Me teeing off at the VOA Golf Club in Monrovia.

A multi-million listing on the stock exchange. We are rich!

29

MOVING back to Monrovia and plonking myself behind an office desk created another style of life for me. Having our office at the Toyota block meant I saw a lot more of Richard. It was great to have someone I could trust, and he had been through the hoops learning the ways of Africa. Most of all it meant plenty of laughs.

The $6,000 dash lost to the man at the Ministry of Mines led to a lot of mirth and Richard taught me how to use such disasters to your advantage. If I had stayed in angry mode I would have loaded myself up with an unbelievable amount of stress and my health and well-being would have suffered.

I came to realise that despite any problems I encountered, I was there to make a success in the mining business. No matter what my feelings were, I would have to deal with the likes of them again. Richard taught me to laugh my way through my Africa problems. The man at the Ministry of Mines didn't think about it twice, he simply turned the page. I had to do the same.

Tony had plenty going on up at the Loffa site and was happy in his work. Partly this was due to having his brother Gary there with him. Gary was the one that had the looks that earned him his living in modelling and mostly a different life to me and Tony. But, despite his good looks (from his Mum) Gary was tough and resilient. He would have made a really good speedway rider but he wasn't mechanically-minded at all. Tony was always there to sort it out for him.

Gary was smarter than Tony and me and was a good actor. Dropping him in the middle of the jungle didn't faze him and he had no trouble fitting in. Also, down at base camp with the boys was Alistair, an old school mate from Southampton. Alistair and Tony were the same age and spent two years together at Stroud School where they had a good time. Of course, I hadn't got to hear all their stories.

I remember years ago reading that Prince Philip went to look at Scotland's Gordonstoun School as he was thinking of sending his boys there. He felt that it taught kids a tougher lifestyle while at school, which would stand them in better stead for the trials and tribulations that come in later life. Prince Charles was enrolled for this toughening up process. People might argue that it didn't work with Charles but I have witnessed first-hand that it did, in fact, work with Alistair who had also gone to Gordonstoun for a while.

I had seen Aussie miners, geologists and that type having to earn their living by toughing it out, at times sleeping on the ground and roughing it. In the harsh Liberian climate it required something a bit special to hang in.

But Alistair adapted better to the conditions than anyone else by far. Tony and I had each other while Alistair did it alone. The Gordonstoun education system definitely worked for him. He was at home in the jungle. It didn't faze him where, or with whom, he had to work. He just fitted in.

Alistair was put in charge of local labour, building a log bridge. The bridge was about five miles from the Loffa base camp and it was a pain taking him there. It was going to take a couple of weeks to complete his project so he offered to stay with the gear in a two-man tent and oversee things from there. One time, when I was visiting the Loffa camp, Tony suggested that we went to see how Alistair's bridge was getting on. When we got there it looked good but his tent was wide open and there were chickens walking in and out as if they owned the place.

A radio had music blasting away and there were washed clothes hanging on the nearby trees and bushes. A couple of the local maidens were doing more washing. It was as if Alistair had created his own village.

Tony and me laughed like hell. Whatever would his school teacher mother think of what had become of her son? Alistair's mum was christened 'Daffy Duck' as her name was Daphne. Alistair's dad was a very serious and successful businessman and wouldn't believe how his boy was teaching the people of his village the real meaning of being laid back.

At times we found ourselves looking at many of the foreigners in Liberia; most seemed to be completely out of place in this tough environment. We would try to figure out what the hell they were doing living in these kinds of conditions. Why were they really here?

At Julia's bar there was a 50-something German who we spoke to on odd occasions. He wore a Swastika ring, was also a pilot and had been there since the end of the war. Does two and two make four? The attitude to sex in Liberia can be very different to what we are accustomed to. We knew of an Englishman living in the north who was well-known for having sex with underage girls – an activity for which he would have been jailed virtually anywhere else in the world. Apparently the parents thought it was okay, but how could they?

One night we went to a party at an American bank manager's lovely big house on the outskirts of Monrovia. He greeted us at the front door dressed in a bright green shiny football shirt, with pink shorts. He was married to a beautiful-looking Ghanaian girl.

During the evening we wandered into one of the living rooms and there was a full-blown porn movie showing on a large television. There were five Liberian couples sitting there watching and laughing. I don't think I'm a prude but we just moved on – maybe their view on sex was healthier than ours?

Easy access to drugs, and especially the local dope, was also a potential pitfall for those coming here. One young guy named Ian, who came from a small Welsh village near the Clogau mine, discovered that soon after his arrival to work for us.

Doctor John Rottenbury assessed him for us: "He's really good at his work, he has just got married and I think he smokes a bit of dope."

Doctor John was correct, he was good at his job, he was also correct with the other part of his assessment. Unfortunately, he 'went bush' fairly soon. He thought he had gone to heaven with the availability of the local strong grass. His joints were the size of Winston Churchill's cigars! Unfortunately for him he couldn't keep his drug use under control.

Ian had never been out of Wales and this complete change of environment played havoc with the chemistry of his body. On his first visit to town he found that he could get valium from the local chemist with no prescription needed. His behaviour became more and more bizarre.

He would get up at two in the morning and start work with the radio blaring. He started to go bonkers, crying and with severe mood changes.

Because of his wild behaviour we were having trouble with our geologists and decided to send him back to Wales. Then what happened? Three days before he was due to leave the country he ran away. Tony was at his wits end, and scoured downtown Monrovia to find him. Then, at great personal risk, he searched 25 of the roughest and toughest bars in town, many of them a no-go area for white folk. But Tony kept pushing on as he tried to find our wayward Welshman.

Tony couldn't find him. He was finally unearthed by the Immigration department, sitting on the top of a container at the Monrovia Port trying to get out of the country. I made myself scarce as Immigration wanted to speak to me. It was the same old story – they wanted money to return our Welshman.

Twenty thousand dollars was the figure they told Tony that they required from Kiwi for the Welshman's return and they kept trying to locate me for the payment. Tony had enough of their threats. Finally he turned to them and thought for a few seconds, then told them to "keep him".

Junie enjoying the adjustable sofa (Citroën-style).

He figured that at least he was safe in jail and we also knew where he was. A few hours before he had to go to the airport Tony went to the Immigration people and did a deal for a hundred bucks. Putting a new T-shirt on Ian, we then put our 'out of control' Welshman on a plane back to the UK. Tony thought it was Christmas to see the back of this lad, who the jungle had tried to destroy.

One of the best parts of being back living in town was that on Saturdays we played golf at the VOA (Voice of America) course. Voice of America built it to help Americans from feeling homesick. To make the club financially viable they needed more players than just Americans. Now most of the members at VOA were ex-pats.

You would never believe how bad the cheating was that took place. One of the biggest culprits was the Nigerian Ambassador, who wasn't averse to bending the rules. On most shots he played from the rough the ball was quickly followed by a tee peg. When playing with him you'd ask: "Was that a four, Mr. Ambassador?" I'm sure that he couldn't count over four.

For many, moving the ball to where it was easier to hit was the norm. Many trophy winners probably had ten or more shots than they had actually entered on the scorecard but great fun was had by all.

Once we were playing a match at VOA and it was getting to a crucial point. A Yorkshireman, who everyone thought was a bit of a pillock, was crouching over his vital putt when his Liberian caddie yelled 'Oyye'. He turned and said: "What the hell are you doing making a noise when I'm about to putt?"

"Boss man, a snake just run over my foot," replied the young man, to the delight of the other players. "That's no bloody reason to disturb me while I'm putting," grumbled Yorkshire's finest.

Mackay & Schellmann, one of the world's top mining evaluators, sent two geologists out to Liberia to check all of the claims and figures in order to launch our new company, Belgravia Resources, on the London Stock Market.

It sounded simple to get all the paperwork together to tie up all the loose ends for the Belgravia listing, but all of the agreements had to be legal outside of Liberia. It was, however, going to be tough to secure a government contract without any dash changing hands.

Everything seemed to be made more complicated than necessary and, of course, this extra work meant more money for the local lawyers. Show me any lawyer anywhere in the world who doesn't know how to charge to the maximum and I'll eat my hat. Only joking … I mean about eating my hat!

The original deal and contract was done by me and Ray Thackwell. As I was now the owner with my boys and Alan Davidson, I had to change ownership on the agreement.

First, I had to find the claim owner, Foday Brown, an old miner from the local Loffa river village of Gbeni who we originally did the deal with. But just to complicate matters, we found that old Foday had died two years previously, so now we had to deal with his brother, Varney.

He was also very old and had no real idea of what was going on. So we had to negotiate with Missu, one of Foday's 43 granddaughters, who worked in the Ministry of Finance. She was a difficult woman to say the least. In the end even her own lawyer lost patience with her, but the deal was finally sealed, and the whole village benefited – so we were told.

Every day somebody would arrive at our mining camp claiming to be Foday Brown's long-lost brother, cousin or some distant relation. The one big advantage of having granddaughter Missu on the scene was that we would just give them her address and she would have to get rid of them. I'm sure it didn't matter if they had entitlement or not ... the jungle drums were beating loudly, telling the locals that they could be rich if they had a drop of the now very precious Foday's blood running through their veins.

Foday must have been a hell of a man in his day to sire so many.

Meanwhile, Mackay & Schellmann's assessors had come up with the staggering figure of $43 million as their valuation of our Liberian project. Yes, 43 million American dollars. Serious, serious money, by anyone's standards. And it begged the immediate question ... what now?

Should we all move to Monte Carlo with a load of money in the bank? Sometime in everyone's life they have dreamed of winning the football pools and having an unlimited supply of money. But what would you really do?

Being couped up in our Monrovia office made it very difficult to dream while surrounded by this environment. Here we were out of touch with the real world. Over the years I have found it dangerous to take 'the money is on its way' too seriously or for granted, in my racing, or the business world. Dream, yes, but get the money in the bank first, then you will know for sure that your dream has come true.

Everything was normal as we worked hard to get the details sorted and to beat the up-coming wet season. All those millions sounded great, but at this point it was just paper money.

The weekend golf was still the highlight of my life. Besides the chips and putts there was always some good stories told and plenty of laughs. One of the golf gang was Arthur, a blunt Scotsman, who had just come back from England. He told us a brilliant tale of how when he arrived at his Monrovian home from his vacation he couldn't find his houseboy. He went upstairs, downstairs, yelling: "Varney, Varney where are you?" There was no answer.

He went outside: "Varney, where are you?" Suddenly there was

We still haven't worked out how to ride on water, so need a boat.

The early years

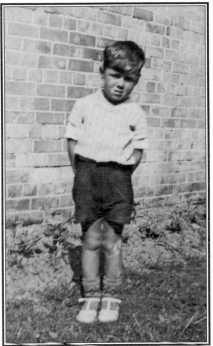

Practising my 'race face'? At home in Christchurch aged four

I'm not really that fat, it's the home-made leathers

The class of '49. I'm on the far left, aged 14. And I thought I was tall!

On my way to England

With Ashton Quinn, my fellow Kiwi racer in Marseille on the way to England

On sponsor Charlie Rosco's bike wearing my home-made leathers

Starting to look smarter in Wimbledon colours ... and I've progressed to wearing 'proper' leathers!

In over my head

My first published action picture ... unfortunately, the only action is me falling on my bum!

Is this the one? The chasing of Junie Rashbrook

Got her! Wedding bells: Wandsworth, London

Have bike will travel

The boot's on the other foot – me running over Ove for a change!

MOTORCYCLE SPORT AND THE MEN WHO RIDE
ON ANY SUNDAY
A Film By Bruce Brown   A Cinema 5 Release   Rated G

I had to buy Bruce Brown's Dana Point house to get in his movie

Me and my shadow. the size of the rear ends tells you which is Tony!

It certainly helps to have spikes as I pass a sailboat

Some success!

First world title, 1957.

A year later ... and another World Championship success

A collection of my trophies and medals

World Champion in 1964, with actress Janette Scott doing the honours

My fourth, and last, World title success in Gothenburg in 1966

The family man

On honeymoon with Junie
in South Africa

Where's Dad riding now, mum?
Junie with a young Gary and Tony

Riding for the Swindon Robins helped me acquire this beautiful family
home – 'Robin Hill' – in Southampton

"Barry Briggs, this is your life ..."

Me and my mates had a great time on the popular ITV programme

My home in California is precariously perched on Dana Point Bluff!

Tony ...

Tony and Lance King, beat the rain to practise in Northern California

Tony finishes second in the European Under-21 Championship to Tommy Knudsen. Dennis Sigalos, right, was third

A Sunday afternoon away from it all

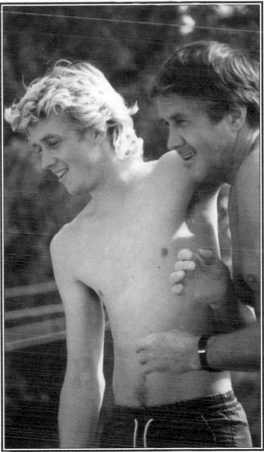

My shadow trying to protect me

Liberia ... white man's graveyard (due to the extreme climate)

Unbelievable – when different tribes can't live together in harmony

My 'Hotel Africa', our base camp on the banks of the River Loffa ...

"I hope Mum doesn't use all the hot water ..."

... and the real Hotel Africa, just down the road in the capital Monrovia

Liberia ... white man's graveyard

We didn't want to give you a free lift, but only an idiot would refuse

Tony ... doing roadside tuning duties   *Rocking for diamonds*

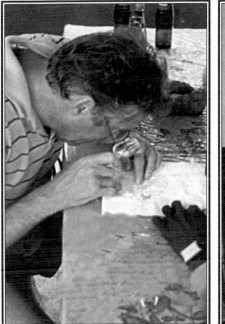

Under the watchful eye of President Doe

Are they real diamonds?

Our pit (top), with the dredge visible. In the foreground is the local miners' pit

Trying to get to the top   *Halfway up Pipeline in the Scottish Trial*

Gary, me, Billy Hamill, Charlies Venegas and Steve Lucero. Tony is the cameraman

At the old Wembley, Kevin (Keegan) asked me: "Do you want a couple of players?". I was flabbergasted when he brought two of the world's finest with him

Champions all at Wembley's 'last round up' dinner before the bulldozers moved in

Janet, Junie's choice, was spot on

Doctor Francisco Contreras and Junie

ABOVE: The loves of my life
BELOW: The 'Adios Amigos' archway frames the Oasis hospital in Tijuana, Mexico

a noise at the top of a large palm tree in the garden and there was Varney sitting in the top of the tree.

"Varney, what the hell are you doing up there?"

"Boss-man, I'm still on vacation."

Tony wasn't interested in the golf, he just wanted out of there, and started the closing down of our base camp for the wet season, which officially commences at the end of October. In our first year Tony and me had tried to work through the wet season. The average Liberian rainfall is 200 inches a year and the Loffa river rises 5 to 10 feet, so it was definitely not the place to be.

By now everything was almost ready for the big launch on the London stock market, which would hopefully turn us into millionaires and set us up for life. All the paperwork was finished and had been sent to London. The good times were ready to roll.

Then, on October 20, a single sheet of nondescript paper was waiting for me in the fax machine as I entered my office. Before I had got through reading two paragraphs I had to sit down.

The fax relayed news of 'Black Monday,' the stock market crash from the previous day that had sent the world's markets into

No job too big or too small at the Loffa river garage.

freefall. The international monetary system was in crisis. Mining companies were folding by the dozen and investment money was virtually non-existent.

It meant that Kiwi's Liberian project had ground to a halt through factors beyond any of our control. All of a sudden, we were back in the real world again. The final blow was when the 226 gem-stone diamonds that we uncovered in Liberia, with the help of loads of money and hard work, were taken to Australia. They mysteriously disappeared and it was a matter for the Australian fraud squad. It seems that all the crooks are not only in the jungles of Liberia!

Tony had finished closing our base camp. After hearing the bad news, he had to take into consideration the prospect that we would never return.

Alistair stayed on with me for a further two weeks as we tried to clean everything before leaving. At that point I was thinking that once back home I might just be able to raise some alternative finance, but all the signs were bad, with a capital B. It was a big disappointment that our mining gamble hadn't worked out as we wanted and it was tough to swallow. So close, yet so far, we were on the brink of a fortune, and then we were crushed by outside forces that I didn't even completely understand, which made it even harder.

But, if everything in your life worked out perfectly, it would mean that life would be a no-challenge deal. How boring, and not too stimulating either. I feel that if you give something your best effort, and you don't achieve your goal, due to many factors outside of your control, then of course it is just plain bad luck.

The most important thing is to give it your best shot.

Stiff luck … move on.

For Barry Briggs, no matter how much money I have it would be impossible for me to buy 'my Liberian adventure' whatever the cost. It got Tony and me, who both had been seriously injured not long before our African adventure, back in life's mainstream, simply by a bit of hard work and tough living.

To both of us Liberia was definitely not a losing deal.

'This is your life', 1974.

When I met my new mechanic with his famous red book

30

I WAS lucky in that for most of my racing career, speedway, unlike now, had a high profile amongst the media. Even so, I never really worked at getting publicity for myself until a guy called Keith Goodwin came into my life. Keith worked in the music business and was the agent for several big-name pop stars and was actually related to Vic Ridgeon, an ex-rider. He was a speedway fan and felt that he could help.

"You don't get enough publicity for what you do and who you are," he said when we met after I had won the World title for a fourth time in 1966. Before long I was making numerous TV appearances on national children's shows and rubbing shoulders with some sporting greats and other celebrities.

I had always thought that people got their names and pictures into newspapers because they were famous through what they had done, but Keith introduced me to the ways of a press agent. He helped me a lot but we never made any money out of it and at times I hardly had time to ride and we had to back off a little.

"Bloody hell, Keith, I am a speedway rider not a tap dancer," I told him.

It is all very well if you can cash in on it, as the big soccer stars do today, but I think it helped raise the profile of speedway. It was fun and I got to meet some of my soccer heroes including Johnny Haynes at Fulham. He was interesting and fun and didn't seem to take himself too seriously, which was good.

Keith was a lovely person and it still pains me that when he died in Malta, where he had moved to with his wife Pat, in December 2003 – around the same time as I lost Junie – she couldn't reach me because she didn't know where I was.

Keith got me on to various TV and radio programmes, including *Desert Island Discs* with its originator, Roy Plumley. It was a live show, I went into the studio with Roy and my list of 10 favourite records and chatted away about my career. I thoroughly enjoyed it and still like it now.

What were my favourite records? I cannot remember them all, I am sure there would have been an Elvis one in there and something by Ella Fitzgerald.

Without doubt the biggest thing I ever did on television, though Keith wasn't involved, was *This Is Your Life* with Eamonn Andrews in 1974.

Of course, I knew nothing about what was in store for me when Eamonn confronted me with his 'red book' but later discovered that a huge operation had been going on, involving researchers from the show, wife Junie, brother Murray and journalist Philip Rising.

Phil takes up the story: *"It was fun helping the guys from Thames Television piece together their tribute to Barry and, along with Junie and Murray, suggest who should figure on the actual show. The big problem was that it was live TV and they only had 30 minutes ... we could have done with a couple of hours at least. Even late the night before Briggo was due back from New Zealand they were still making changes.*

"I was in the bath when I had a telephone call from Frank Hayes, who was orchestrating this particular episode, to say that the programme was likely to overrun and that they would need to

Me and Junie on This Is Your Life, *1974.*

Me, Junie and the famous red book.

cut out Ivan Mauger. I nearly drowned! Not only was Ivan an integral part of Barry's story, he had made special arrangements to get back to the UK 24 hours ahead of Barry. No way could Ivan be left on the sidelines. A very harassed scriptwriter had to go back to the drawing-board and Ivan's appearance was restored.

"For many weeks we had been able to construct the programme in relative peace. Barry and Junie were away and the chances of him realising what was going on, which would have resulted in his programme being unceremoniously binned, were slight.

"But, as the big day beckoned, we all started to get very nervous. This Is Your Life was a huge TV show at that time, with a weekly audience in excess of 20 million. Barry had signed to ride for Wimbledon and the programme was scheduled for the week before the start of the 1974 season. We arranged for a private practice session for the Dons to be held at their Plough Lane stadium on the day BB arrived back.

"With Barry and Junie away, Murray and I devised a plan to keep Barry away from his Southampton home and ensure that he would be at the stadium at the designated time of 5pm. It was planned to shoot some film of sons Gary and Tony that morning and then drive them and Junie, who somehow managed to persuade Barry to let her come home a day early, to the London studio.

"Murray collected Barry from the airport and drove him straight to Plough Lane. Barry is not the sort of bloke you can 'con' into doing things he doesn't want to do. We decided that we needed a very special reason for keeping him at Wimbledon, when he was anxious to get home, and to explain why there were a number of TV outside broadcast trucks in the car park.

"We were banking on the fact that Briggo wanted a run out at Plough Lane before his first meeting as he had already missed the official practice the week before. We also told him that Thames TV wanted to film a preview to the speedway season and that was why the trucks were there.

"Fortunately, he was a little jet-lagged and tired from his long flight and was easier to manipulate than might otherwise have been the case. He did later confess that he was bemused by the TV *units around but thought no more of it. The TV people liked the idea of being able to hook Barry in action before springing their surprise. Hayes, director Peter Webb and his assistant Kay Switser and other members of the Thames team came to Wimbledon for the official practice to work out their strategy and where to hide Andrews.*

"We had to ensure that Barry stopped at a particular place; it wouldn't have looked very good if Eamonn had to chase him around the track! It was finally agreed that Barry should be brought to a stop by the starting gate. But how? Once on the track he would want to do his own thing; practice starts, as many laps as he felt like ... unless he was under the impression that there was a good reason he should stop on cue.

"I told him that Thames needed him to stop for an interview as part of their preview show and that it was going out live. That meant he had to do what we wanted when we wanted.

"By around 4pm everything was ready. Cameras were in position, Briggo was asked to do four laps and then join the rest of his Wimbledon team-mates on the centre green by the start gate. Miraculously, he did exactly as he was told! On the first lap Eamonn Andrews slipped on to the middle, disguised in white overalls.

"Briggo stopped, dismounted from his bike and as he walked to our group, Neil Cameron said: 'Briggo, I would like you to meet our new mechanic'. And, with that, Eamonn walked forward and uttered those immortal words: 'Barry Briggs, this is your life ...'

"The actor Michael Crawford, who at the time was a huge star with his Some Mothers Do Have 'Em *series, was the star guest on the night. I had got to know Michael through the Chelsea footballers, brother-in-law Allan, Ron Harris, Terry Venables and so on.*

"But the man who closed the show, after Steve McQueen had turned down an invitation to attend, was Johnnie Hoskins. McQueen thought that the UK version of the programme was like the one in the US, which he hated, but it wasn't."

So, I discovered later, Hoskins stepped up to the plate to close the show, which was always a big thing on *This Is Your Life*.

Johnnie didn't need a second invitation to grandstand it, he hammed away and did a great job for me and, in fact, the show as a whole.

Looking back, it is quite an honour to be the only speedway rider to have been featured on *This Is Your Life*. I was told later that Thames had received more letters about including me than anyone else at the time. One letter from Sheffield contained over 400 signatures.

The only blemish is that I don't have a video recording of the show. The original tape was destroyed and in those days, of course, video recorders weren't around. I do, of course, still have the famous red book and some precious photographs.

I really liked Johnnie Hoskins, he was such a character. He must have been dynamic when he was young and was a showman throughout his life.

He was a salesman, he always had a trick up his sleeve. He was flamboyant and would have been great to ride for had he any money!

When I did a year at New Cross when he was the promoter a local car dealer had put in some money. He was standing there with Johnnie when I had my first race. I didn't have my own bike and went halfway round the first corner on one wheel before shooting over the fence and ended up sitting on my backside, on the green grass of the dog track. Johnnie's partner must have wondered who the hell he had signed, a guy who cannot even stay on his bike.

New Cross was a gorgeous track but I never really worried enough about my bikes then. I had a great year, it was fun, but I didn't ride that good, probably because of the time I spent playing snooker with Youngie (Jack Young).

Dave Webb, still a great mate.

Some of my best friends have been footballers

31

I HAVE been friends with a number of top footballers over the years but one stands out above all others. Dave Webb, who made his name at Chelsea – remember his winning goal for them in the FA Cup Final replay against Leeds United in 1970? – before moving to Queens Park Rangers and going on to play and manage a number of clubs, is still a big mate and someone whose company I really enjoy.

Dave started his career at Leyton Orient before moving to Southampton in 1966 and then on to Chelsea two years later. When it looked on the cards that he could be on his way to Chelsea from Southampton, Dave gave me a call, saying: "Let's go to Chelsea and see what their team is like."

When we got to Chelsea, Dave went to the office to collect our entrance tickets but there were none for us! We finished up buying a couple from Stan Flashman, the ticket tout. "Webby, it looks as though they really want to sign you," I chortled as we paid Stan.

Dave wanted to move back to London although his preference

was West Ham rather than Chelsea but I talked him into going to Stamford Bridge because I thought their long-term prospects were better. What I didn't know at the time was that he was earning £85 a week and had to drop £20 a week to join Chelsea. It is a wonder that we are still mates! Either way, it was peanuts compared to what the top soccer stars receive now. John Terry, a centre half like Webby, is reported to have a contract worth over £150,000 a week … it would have taken Webby about 45 years to earn that!

Webby and I lived near one another in Southampton and our families became close. It was through him we got to know Michael Crawford and we went to most of his shows in London with Dave. But it was in Los Angeles that we saw him in *Phantom of the Opera*. Afterwards, we went backstage and the lady taking off half his face, needed for the Phantom role, told us she had been a Swindon speedway supporter when she was younger. It's a small world.

Webby and some of the other footballers, including my brother-in-law Allan Harris, his brother Ron, Terry Venables and George Graham, would often indulge in some mickey-taking with me about speedway. Footballers then, as now, are always immaculately dressed off the pitch with a taste for expensive clothes that isn't really like your average speedway rider.

Mind you, none of them wore jeans in those days as we riders did. Now look at photos of the soccer boys and they are rarely out of jeans … though no doubt of the designer variety. It was all good fun and I gave as good as I got.

Born in the East end of London, Webby can be as intimidating off the pitch as he was on it. He is a big guy with granite-like features and a bent nose and quite often he would come to speedway with me. With his crew cut and his camel hair coat, he looked like one of the mob.

There was one time when I was having a bit of a problem with Anders Michanek. Webby was at one meeting when we came face to face. Maybe Mich thought I had brought Dave along as my minder. I had no problems with him that night. Webby liked speedway, so much so that one time when we went to Belle Vue he came along despite having to sit on a wooden apple box in the van all the way to Manchester and back.

It never ceases to amaze me how many top soccer stars used to watch speedway at some time in their lives. Graeme Souness and Gordon Strachan were both Glasgow fans in their youth.

I got to know Kevin Keegan when he was playing for Southampton. I was often at the old ground there, receiving treatment for one injury or another. Soccer clubs can be very helpful when it comes to helping with injuries.

The football clubs have been very good to me over the years. I trained at Chelsea under Harry Medhurst for a couple of years when I was riding for Wimbledon. Ted Bates was in charge at Southampton when I trained there and it was always great fun, especially the six-a-side games. I didn't make many friends due to my limited ability and bad eye-foot co-ordination. Lucky it wasn't my living, I would have starved!

I also trained at Millwall when I was riding for New Cross. The football ground backed on to the speedway stadium and the entrance was actually in the Old Kent Road.

When I was having a bit of knee trouble and Kevin Keegan was manager at Manchester City he sent me to where his players went and it turned out to be the very same hospital that son Tony was in for his broken neck in Oswestry. Later, and still having problems with my right knee, I spoke to Arthur Cox, Kevin's right-hand man, who arranged for me to go to Arsenal to see his friend, Gary Lewin, who was the physio for both the Gunners and England.

Gary and the Arsenal doctor examined me and sent me to Doctor Tim Briggs, a knee specialist. A former rugby player who had played against the All Blacks, he told me that they were dirty so and so's but at least he tempered the blow by saying the French were even worse.

He diagnosed it wasn't my knee but my right hip that was knackered and needed to be replaced, something he was happy to do. Just before they put me out for my operation, I said to him: "Doctor, I know that I sound like a Kiwi, but I'm actually Swedish, I'm telling you this just in case you might feel that it is time for you to get your own back for what those dirty bastard Kiwis did to you." With a Frankenstein-like laugh and rubbing his hands together, he gave me this strange smile and said: "You'll be okay with me mate!"

I first started watching football with my great mate Eddie Toogood (Eddie's Books) who was also my first real mechanic when I was at Wimbledon. We were supporters of Fulham who had Johnny Haynes, Jimmy Hill, Bobby Robson and, course, Tosh Chamberlain. Eddie loved to get into the football banter. At one Fulham match Haynes, our top man, missed a header … "Too much bloody Brylcreem, Johnny." Eddie just couldn't stop himself from yelling out. Haynes, like the great cricketer Denis Compton, advertised the famous hair product. These were great times.

Eddie was always with me at my Wimbledon home matches and came to many away meetings as well. He was always trying to get me into trouble. After I had showered and was ready for our drive back home to London, Eddie always seemed to have a couple of local dollies waiting … for autographs, lucky I was a clean-living lad!

He was put in his place in Hyde Park Lane at 2am one morning coming home from Belle Vue, Manchester. Prankster Eddie, up to no good, said: "Barry, pull over to the kerb beside that Diana Dors look-a-like, and I'll see what she costs?"

Game for a laugh – and nothing more! – I did as he suggested. Eddie wound down the window and cheekily asked the lady-of-the-night: "How much, luv?" She looked at both of us and replied: "Why don't you both go home to your mothers, it's well past your bedtime." I made sure that Eddie was reminded of this incident several times, 'Mr. Cool' being put in his place.

When I had my own car for the first time it lacked a radio so Eddie had to provide our entertainment. I hate to say it but he wasn't that bad. On one occasion, again driving through the streets of London en route home early in the morning returning from a northern trip, Eddie had just finished his very own rendition of a particular song.

While stationary at traffic lights, I turned to Eddie and said: "The two people in the car next to us thought that song was crap."

"What do you mean?" he replied indignantly, turning to look at the car alongside. In it were Lita Rosa and Dennis Lotis, two of the top singers of that period, who were laughing their heads off.

Another time, also in the early hours, we were alongside a car and Eddie again wound down the window to have a go at a guy next to us. Before he could say a word, Harry Secombe, who was in the car, fired a salvo of Goons-type talk at us which left us reeling with laughter. Yet another thrill in the night on the streets of London town.

At times, when something was not going right with my riding, I'd turn to Eddie and ask: "What the hell am I doing wrong?" He knew exactly what to say: "You're not giving it the two big blips on the throttle as you come into the corner."

Sure enough, two 'big blips' as I laid the bike into the corner, I was away again turning like a demon. I hated to hear other mechanics telling their riders how to ride, as most have no idea what the hell they were talking about, but Eddie never volunteered. I always had to ask when I needed it.

Of course, I supported teams that Webby played for or managed. The same with Allan (Harris), I followed him as well and, using a football term, was 'pig sick' when he was transferred because he never got on with Tommy Docherty and was forced out of Chelsea. He moved and he was made captain of Queens Park Rangers, and would you believe it within what seemed no time at all Docherty was to become the manager of QPR, a real bad deal for Allan.

Football is a funny game, Allan and Venners (Terry Venables) grew up as kids and played football together and made a great team in management, with Crystal Palace, Barcelona and Tottenham Hotspur.

I will always remember when they won promotion with Crystal Palace, it was a fantastic night. Alan and Terry lost their closeness, mainly through Terry's divorce, and the partnership broke up, which was sad as I thought they were a great team, with Venners taking the accolades, and having to face the music, and Allan doing the graft.

At one post-match press conference after a game in which Tottenham were off the pace and were having a bad run, I have never seen anyone as quick on their feet and able to deflect bad questions as Terry did that day.

I think that after they each went their own ways Terry and Allan

Me with Harry Redknapp. I admired his skill until he got an own goal at Man. United

Good action ... if only there was a ball!

still missed each other and I wonder whether Jeff Powell, a sports journalist with the *Daily Mail* and someone who thinks Venners can do no wrong, agrees.

I think I have enjoyed watching and attending football even more over the last few years. Along with Jan, we have become supporters of AFC Wimbledon, a club formed from nothing after Wimbledon FC moved from their Plough Lane ground, next to the speedway stadium, to Milton Keynes.

We don't like to stand (too old these days!) but are just like all the other punters when it comes to getting tickets for the grandstand. The only insider I know there is *Speedway Star* Editor Richard Clark, but even he cannot pull any favours.

AFC is one of the success stories of sport, especially now with the outlandish money around football. Wimbledon is just about the game of football, not stars, not monster transfer fees, to me it puts the word sport back into football and I sincerely hope it stays this way.

On Thursday, August 22, 2002, I was in a queue half a mile from the ground trying to get in to watch AFC Wimbledon's home league debut at Kingsmeadow, the ground that the club would be sharing with Kingstonian. They were playing Chipstead and I finally got into the Wimbledon supporters' end behind the goal. Standing in the back row you could watch the athletes training on the quarter mile tartan track behind the football stadium, while waiting for the football action to start.

I was lucky as more than 500 fans were turned away that night and, even though AFC Dons lost 1–2, the club and their passionate supporters who insist that they are the REAL Wimbledon were now firmly into their new era.

Why was this such a special match? In May, 2002 the Football League permitted the owners of Wimbledon Football Club to relocate to Milton Keynes – a move the Football Association opposed in principle. The majority of the club's fans were against it too, but their protests failed to halt this United States-style 'franchising' from going ahead.

At the time, Wimbledon was a First Division club without a home, ground-sharing with Crystal Palace.

The fans voiced their opposition, the supporters then started their very own 'Wimbledon'. In July 2002, an AFC Wimbledon side, cobbled together from hastily arranged trials by manager Terry Eames, a former Dons player, made its debut in a friendly at Sutton United.

On Saturday, August 17, 2,449 fans turned up at the tiny Bottom Meadow ground, home to Sandhurst Town, to set a new attendance record as AFC Wimbledon made their official league bow with a 2–1 victory in their first Combined Counties fixture – then the fourth level of the non-League pyramid.

Four promotions in seven seasons later, AFC Wimbledon are now one rung below the Football League after winning the Blue Square Conference South title in 2008–9 under their third manager, Terry Brown. May this unbelievable success continue, football for the sake of football, the people's game, given back to the people, that's AFC Wimbledon.

Football authorities were always against speedway at the old Wembley stadium. They claimed it ruined the hallowed pitch … well, when there is no speedway there the pitch was still a mess! Sir Arthur Elvin, who owned and ran Wembley for so many years, was a speedway fan, he loved having it there, but these things change when they get into the hands of accountants. If the figures don't add up …

It didn't take long after Sir Arthur's death for speedway to be on its way out of Wembley.

People tend to forget that just after the Second World War over 80,000 people watched speedway at the Empire Stadium EVERY week. There were only a handful of soccer internationals and the FA Cup Final there each season so speedway attracted hundreds of thousands more fans than football every year.

The worst thing that happened to speedway worldwide was losing Wembley as a major venue.

The people who allowed that to happen didn't understand what exactly Wembley meant to speedway, I know that the soccer people didn't want speedway to continue. Now despite the new Wembley being up and running, it appears that speedway will never return to its spiritual home.

For several years I have tried to persuade the authorities at

Wembley that they should include a speedway museum there. I am very proud of the museum I managed to put together at Donington but Wembley was still the place for speedway's history to be in this country.

Before the old stadium was pulled down we had three special bikes on display there … 1936 World Speedway Champion' Californian Jack Milne's old JAP was on show, a model rider was mounted on it dressed as in that era which bought back memories of the good old days. My Jawa two-valver, which was used when I was caught by Eamonn Andrews for *This Is Your Life*, was also proudly standing there.

The third machine was set off with a rider-model wearing the actual riding gear that Bruce Penhall used when he won Wembley's last ever World Final in 1981. The model was posed on one wheel on a Weslake, which Bruce used in the 1981 final. There were also speedway memorabilia including a life-sized photo of me with Keegan, Alan Shearer, and David Beckham, which proved very popular.

How did I ever get this priceless photo? Keegan was England manager at the time and they were scheduled to play an international against Argentina at Wembley. I called Kevin and asked whether he would help me gain some publicity with a photo of us two on speedway bikes. No problem at all, he answered.

Kevin's assistant was Lawrie McMenemy, who I also knew at Southampton, and he suggested that when the England team came to Wembley for a training session we do something then. I arranged to call them when they were on the England coach en route to the stadium. They were running late and the English national soccer press were already waiting for the team to show up. But Kevin said: "Don't worry, I will bring a couple of players round to you."

Kevin didn't want the waiting media to know what was going on and I quickly found out why. The two players he brought were Shearer, the captain, and Beckham, just about the most famous footballer in the world. Keegan, Shearer and Beckham were terrific and posed for the pictures I needed. Beckham was also happy to have his picture taken with a few other people who were hanging around, signed autographs and was very, very pleasant.

I know Beckham attracts some dubious publicity but you can only speak as you find … and I found him to be charming and very polite. He is a bit different from the rest of the pack, and I feel sorry that his decision to join the LA Galaxy didn't quite work out.

My son Gary, who still plays soccer and coaches some local Californian kids, came with me and Jan to see him play on a couple of occasions for the Galaxy but it was never going to be easy for him to make a huge impact on their results. To me, the managers weren't good enough to form a team around him to be successful.

Keegan's concern was that the national press would get hold of a picture and come up with a caption like "Beckham, get on your bike." Anyway, we had the photo blown up really big and people going through the speedway display at Wembley could have their photo taken "with David Beckham on a speedway bike." It worked really well. I watched as loads of people came in and waited to get their chance and it was very popular although some people obviously wondered "What have those bloody bikes got to do with David Beckham?"

I first got the idea about putting together a speedway museum while driving in America. All the big sports there, like baseball, basketball, football, ice-hockey and golf, have their own Hall of Fame. Former players who have made a special contribution to their respective sports are inducted into the Hall of Fame and I just felt speedway, riders and fans, deserved one of their own. The Donington Racing Car Collection near Derby was a great central location, and had plenty of room and it seemed ideal. Tom Wheatcroft already had a car museum there with a fantastic display of racing models from yesteryear. It seemed the perfect marriage.

We did a deal for three years and sadly after six, Tom needed the space. Wembley was the obvious choice but, regretfully, we had to leave when the bulldozers came in.

I haven't given up hope of seeing some sort of speedway museum included at the new Wembley Stadium. With the FA owning the new stadium we can at least hope we can get a good display for speedway at Wembley, its spiritual home.

Bernie Ecclestone loved the World Speedway Finals at Wembley

How I nearly became the promoter of a F1 event in LA

32

LOOKING back it is surprising that my first meeting with Bernie Ecclestone, as explained in his Foreword to this book, should have been such a chance affair. Much of my life had been spent around the fringes of the Formula One circuit. There was a time when the car racers and those of us on bikes mixed often and freely.

I knew most of the star names like Bruce McLaren, a Kiwi, Jack Brabham, Jim Clark, Graham Hill, Jackie Stewart and, of course, those who were champions on both two wheels and four like Mike Hailwood and John Surtees.

McLaren, who was from Auckland, contracted Perthes in his hip as an 11-year-old and spent two years in hospital in traction. He never wasted that time and studied to be an engineer. He drove and raced many differing types of cars in New Zealand.

In 1958 Bruce performed well in the NZ Grand Prix, so much so that the New Zealand Grand Prix Organization selected him as their 'Driver to Europe' where he raced for Cooper cars for seven years.

At the end of 1965 Bruce announced that he was forming a Grand Prix team and drove his own McLaren car to victory at the Spa Grand Prix in 1968. All the McLaren cars carried the 'Speedy Kiwi' logo.

I met Bruce in America where his McLaren team was taking part in the Ca-Am Series, which was a contest for powerful sports cars and the results for the McLaren outfit underlined his flair for design and ingenuity. They dominated the series and in the final year, 1969, they won all 11 races.

I can remember us laughing over lunch in Los Angeles, where Bruce was trying hard to convince me that it was hard to make ends meet in the Ca-Am series even though they were runaway winners.

"I can't believe how much bloody money I have to pay my back-up driver," he said. Sitting with us and laughing like hell was the 'back-up driver', Kiwi Denny Hulme, who was later to become New Zealand's first and only Formula One World Champion.

Bruce was a normal Kiwi who was taught to stretch a dollar or pound as far as possible. Tim Witham, a friend who was one of Bruce's best sponsors, just couldn't believe how much ground he got his sponsorship money to cover.

On one occasion while leading a motorcycle road race at Waimate in New Zealand, I crashed. Our race was after the cars, which had laid a load of rubber all around the circuit. About three-quarters of the way through the race we had some drizzle but it was so light I never picked it up on my goggles.

All of a sudden I got in a God-almighty slide and instinctively thought, 'bloody hell, oil on the track'. On the next corner my bike started to slide violently and there was a solid lamppost right in the way. I laid my bike down speedway style, which was okay for me, as the track was now like a skating rink.

Unfortunately, behind me was the New Zealand Isle of Man captain Noel McCutheon, who had never laid his Manx Norton down ... not even in the workshop! He proceeded to run straight over my head.

On the last lap five riders finished up in the front gardens of the houses lining the course. I was the only rider who knew what he was doing when I laid my bike down but I was the only one who got to spend a couple of days in hospital!

At the next meeting I gave Bruce a bad time about his 'bloody cars' wrecking the track at Waimate by putting all that rubber down on the track. Bruce had actually left the circuit before my race and didn't know about my crash. Just thinking about it still hurts but we both had a good laugh at the time.

In my opinion he was New Zealand's best ambassador and was always available for a chat. I remember a meeting at Brands Hatch, where I found him under his car, doing a gearbox tune. I yelled to him: "Bruce, don't worry I'll come back later." He wouldn't have that, popped out from under the car and wanted to know what was happening.

Bruce was only 32 when he died at the Goodwood track. The rear body of his M8D Ca-Am car came loose, causing the loss of the aerodynamics. Subsequently it lost all of its down-force, causing the car to go out of control. Bruce will never be forgotten. He was a racing car designer, driver, engineer and inventor.

His name will live on as the man who created the legacy that still carries his name on one of most successful teams, McLaren, in the history of Formula One. I will always remember him as a proper bloke and a proud Kiwi.

I knew 'Black Jack' Brabham well. The Cooper workshops were in Surbiton, close to where I was living at the time. They had a valve-facer, so I was quite a regular visitor to make use of it when I was working on my speedway engines.

John Cooper was a very small car manufacturer, his cars were trendsetters. They were one of the first to start the rear engine revolution for racing cars. Originally they did this when they were making their 500cc cars and were using the speedway JAP engine as their power plant.

Their cars were small and had great handling. They completely changed the face of Indianapolis in the USA. When Jack first went there it was in a modified Cooper. The Americans laughed at it and called it the 'funny little car from Europe'. In fact, the actual car is in my friend Dick Marconi's museum in LA. I've had a good look at it on more than one occasion.

Within a couple of years just about all the cars lined up on the starting grid for the Indianapolis 500 were one of those European 'funny little' cars. The Coopers had proved that they made one of the most competitive racing cars and Brabham was a great force behind them, he was an astute and great designer.

He could also jump into the cockpit and do the driving role as well. His World Championship wins underline the fact that he was a terrific driver. He gained most of his early experience of racing cars in the midgets on the speedways in his native Australia.

During his first few years on the road circuits he was inclined to slide the car a little too much, a dirt track habit, but he had tremendous control because of his background and I think he had only one serious crash in his Formula car career.

Jack was a very forward-looking bloke who knew how to get the best out of his cars and he and Cooper worked very well together. Brabham, like McLaren, then went and did his own thing, which was very much the vogue in those days.

It was through his purchase of the Brabham outfit that Bernie Ecclestone began his climb to the very top of the Formula One circuit. Bernie's first love was, in fact, motorcycles. Born in Suffolk, he moved to south-east London at an early age and after the Second World War started a business, Compton & Ecclestone, trading in spare parts.

Later, in 1951, he acquired a Cooper Mk V, and took the Norton engine out of his road-racing motorcycle and fitted it into his Cooper chassis. His home track was the Brands Hatch circuit, and he had some success there on the bike racing.

Bernie's first motorcycle racing was on the grasstracks in the Kent area, before moving on to road-racing bikes.

After a few good results with his Cooper-Norton his luck ran out. He flew off the track at Brands, landing on the top of a spectator's car, breaking the owner's leg. A few years ago I found an article referring to this accident. Bernie didn't know I had it so I faxed him trying to sell him the car, "Bernie, do you want to buy this Riley car? Unfortunately it's got a big dent in the roof and the owner had a serious limp."

The crash prompted Bernie to realise he was on the wrong side of the fence. It was easy to see that it wasn't the competitors that made money out of motor racing. He then concentrated his interests into real estate and loan financing.

Bernie's first foray into team ownership came in 1957 when he became manager of driver Stuart Lewis-Evans and also purchased the assets of the F1 Connaught team. But that didn't last long, either, Bernie withdrawing after Lewis-Evans sustained severe burns when his engine exploded at the 1958 Moroccan Grand Prix.

It was 12 years later when he took over as manager of Jochen Rindt and also partial manager of their Lotus Formula Two team where Graham Hill was the other driver.

Bernie really liked Jochen and some of his stories of their partnership and friendship revealed a side of him that most people thought could never exist. Jochen was leading the championship that same year, in 1970, when he was killed in a crash at Monza and was awarded the championship posthumously.

Early in 1972 Bernie moved from the periphery of Formula One racing to centre stage when he purchased the Brabham team, which he ran for 15 years. As tough and hardnosed as he was, and still is, Bernie's Brabham-Alfa 'Fan car' convincingly won the 1978 Swedish Grand Prix in the hands of Nikki Lauda.

After this victory his controversial car was deemed legal. Even so, Bernie withdrew the 'Fan car' for what he said was the good of the sport. The 'Fan car' really intrigued me, a remarkable idea on how to get more grip and still go faster. It was later exhibited at Tom Wheatcroft's Donington Collection and during the six years that I ran the Speedway Hall of Fame there I would rarely pass it without taking a closer look.

Ecclestone, as the Brabham team owner, became a member and then President of FOCA, the Formula One Constructors' Association, and the rest, as they say, is history. Bernie's foresight in securing the TV and commercial rights for the Grand Prix series subsequently provided the power base that has seen him rule the F1 scene.

Bernie became Chief Executive of FOCA in 1978 with Max Mosley as his legal advisor; together, they negotiated a series of legal issues with the FIA and Jean-Marie-Balestre, culminating in

Bernie's famous coup when he secured the rights for FOCA and to negotiate television contracts for the Grands Prix.

All the teams did well but Bernie did better. But then nobody, except Bernie, realised how important TV coverage was for an event. It was TV audiences, rather than the money they paid for the rights, that was the key to attracting sponsorship and circuit advertising.

In 1982 Ivan Mauger, Harry Oxley and I promoted speedway's World Championship Final at the magnificent Los Angeles Coliseum.

We received over $100,000 from CBS for the TV rights during a tough financial period but Bernie was more concerned with boosting his global TV figures as a way of attracting more lucrative signage deals at the various F1 tracks. In the late 1990s Formula One's TV rights shuffled between Bernie's various companies, the teams, and the FIA. In 1997 he negotiated the Concorde Agreement in exchange for annual payments and he retains the TV rights.

In the 1950s car racing was on a high in New Zealand and Australia with the Tasman Series in which top drivers such as Clark, Hill and Stewart competed against Down Under stars Brabham, McLaren, Hulme, Chris Amon and company. It was a great series.

At the same time I did some saloon car racing in New Zealand in my own car. I messed around searching for more speed but it still wasn't quick enough. With the cars I couldn't even earn enough to cover outgoing expenses.

Once I was at a big meeting in the North Island and the top money was on the last handicap race that I figured was the one to win. I had a pretty boring day, going flat-out around the corners and never going over 70 miles per hour on all of the three straights.

My handicap for the final looked good. I charged in the race as hard as me and the car could, without rolling it over. I got to the last corner and then discovered there was a bigger sandbagger than me. The bastard zapped past me on the run to the chequered flag. Losing was one thing – but to be overtaken by such an ugly beast as a Humber Super Snipe! Well, it simply ended my car racing career.

Well, almost … several years later in the UK the *TV Times* put together a practice day at Brands Hatch for television and film actors, show-business personalities as well as sportsmen and women. It was fun, culminating with a big charity day the following weekend.

It was great, roaring around in someone else's cars, and not having to worry about the tyres I was wearing out. Being a born 'slider', my driving instructor, Gerry Marshall, who was a saloon car champion and held the Brands track record, impressed upon me that in car-racing, unlike speedway, you don't go into the corners sideways.

Gerry was great and explained to me exactly what we were trying to do. He would tell me: "Barry, see that Shell sign on the outside of that corner? Head straight towards it, brake and then turn just before you go onto the grass." It was so much faster, but, compared with going sideways, for me it was boring.

I did have a little smile as, out of the corner of my eye, I could see Gerry brace himself just before the grass. I must take my hat off to him as he sat next to this idiot and let him go so close to the grass. He must have trusted me or had his eyes closed!

Just before the grass meant just that as far as I was concerned. It was easy as we lived, or perished, by fractions of an inch. The sad thing is they didn't let me take part in the Saturday open day of fun; they said I should be a professional. But I had a great practice day and it was good to get top-class tuition from Gerry.

Ronnie Moore had a good run in the cars and spent lots of money on it. Along with Ray Thackwell, who foolishly I later became involved with at the start of my African adventures, Ronnie raced in South Africa and all over the World.

Ronnie was good enough to be an instructor at the Cooper driving school at Brands Hatch. He had a two-seater Cooper sports car. I went round with him a few times, he was very, very good. He would have it flat-out just on the verge of going sideways, it was like being in a tin can as it rattled and buckled at speeds over 100mph.

Car racing was so expensive and when Ronnie was using his own car he couldn't afford to smash it, so he was seldom on the very edge.

You cannot run car racing on a shoestring. I went to a lot of car events with Thackwell and it seemed to me that many of the people involved were always screwing each other over money, for buying or repairing engines.

Ray's son Michael was a brilliant driver and at one stage was the youngest ever to compete in Formula One. He got bored with it and became a helicopter pilot. It was obvious that if you didn't have the right package you would just be an also-ran.

Look at F1 today. One year Lewis Hamilton is World Champion, the next, with an inferior car, he is almost bottom of the pile.

Formula One drivers are so well-known now because of the worldwide television coverage the sport attracts. One night, after a meeting at Wimbledon speedway, I was drying after my shower and noticed a blond boy who was in the dressing rooms with Anders Michanek.

His face was vaguely familiar. It turned out to be the Swedish Formula One top gun Ronnie Petersen who, at that time in the 70s, was one of the very fastest around. Only car failures stopped him from him being crowned World Champion. He had come along to the speedway with Anders but very few, if any, people there realised who he was.

If Lewis Hamilton turned up at a speedway meeting today he would be instantly recognised. The amount of media hype and coverage around the F1 drivers these days affords them a celebrity status that those in speedway, for example, are unlikely to experience.

Unfortunately, Ronnie Peterson was killed in 1978 at Monza in a starting-line crash involving many cars.

The huge success of F1, however much it is hyped, is largely down to Bernie Ecclestone. He is a remarkable man who saw the power of television and built the product up to what it is today. At a pub in Australia a few years ago Ivan Mauger was having a beer with Aussie Formula One World Champion Alan Jones. Jones had his jet-plane parked at the local airport and told Ivan: "The only difference between you and me, especially in the earning department, is Bernie Ecclestone."

Since first meeting Bernie, who in my opinion hasn't changed despite the poor press he often receives, we have tried to put several different deals together. One involved gold mines in Brazil from where, at the time, he couldn't withdraw his money because of foreign exchange restrictions.

I also tried to involve him in a speedway project there, working on the theory that if he had money there we might as well use it!

Bernie agreed that I should go to Brazil, find some local boys to teach how to ride a speedway bike and open three or four tracks.

He had everything out there to make it work. Junie and I booked tickets to be there for the F1 Brazilian Grand Prix but I just ran out of time and couldn't do it, which is still disappointing. There were potential deals with cars, motorcycles, museums, the FIM, TV rights … it was a mixed bag.

One brainwave was a World Production Bike Championship that would run alongside the Formula One events. All the TV facilities would already be onsite, we planned to build a track at the same venue and it would have been similar to the Grand Prix series that speedway has now. The FIM, the Geneva-based organisation that governs motorcycle racing throughout the World, actually liked the idea, but we weren't sure we wanted or needed them.

I produced the bike with a 600cc Yamaha engine and it rode well and definitely had potential, especially the opportunity of getting the Japanese factories involved in our type of racing. We planned to use standard production engines, fitted with special parts to allow them to take the strain that a speedway engine must endure.

With the same engines it would have been up to the competitors to determine who was the best. It was vital that we had complete control of the events and, if things needed changing, we could do it at the drop of a hat. Unfortunately it never got off the ground.

Then we started talking about an indoor series with around 10 venues in places like Paris and Barcelona. We did a lot of work on that one but someone suggested to Bernie that "it could never make money" and it was shelved as well.

The big thing with Bernie is that he can pick up the phone and immediately talk to just about anyone. He can open any door and, although he gave us introductions to a whole list of people, we really needed him to be there with us. However, his time was and probably still is really tight and with Formula One always seeming to have its share of problems, Bernie is the one to sort it out.

Different schemes got shelved for different reasons. Bernie is a very hands-on person and it could simply have been because he didn't have sufficient time. Or, as stated before, because he didn't want to use his own money.

Our relationship became strained for a while and I thought it had come to an end. Then one day, while I was at my home in Dana Point, California, Bernie called and asked if I would go and see Chris Pook, who was running the Formula One races in Long Beach, just up the coast from where we were.

Bernie wanted Chris's views on getting a speedway series up and running in America. Pook is an Englishman who, following the re-launch of speedway in California in the 1970s and '80s, saw the possibilities and tried to start Speedway League racing in many of the major US Cities. Unfortunately, he didn't have any answers.

Later Bernie telephoned inviting me to Silverstone for practice prior to the F1 Grand Prix. He was keen to show me how his organisation worked.

I wasn't that keen and told him that I'd give him a ring if I could make it. Not many people turn Bernie down but he came back again, offered son Tony and I a ride in his helicopter, to avoid the traffic jams, and eventually we decided to go. It was a complete eye opener, the hospitality suites were first-class and, in fact, the whole package was unbelievable.

At that time Bernie also had his own television company handling coverage of the Grand Prix rounds. They went everywhere and would hire their own 747 aircraft when travelling outside of Europe. It was a massive, and expensive, operation that eventually he dropped.

At Silverstone, like other GP circuits, Bernie had his own double-decker motorhome. It was fantastic, like a mobile hotel, with an office that included a couple of TV screens, one of which was focused on the outside of the external door to the vehicle. Bernie could see who was outside and could then determine whether or not he wanted to let them in. Once I made the mistake of leaving my jacket behind in the motorhome and couldn't figure out a way of getting back in.

Bernie has a wicked sense of humour and I am sure he got a kick out of watching people trying to work out how they were supposed to get inside. He later left us at the Williams Team restaurant for breakfast and while there we met John Bloom, who revolutionised the vacuum-cleaner business. He was very Jewish and very funny.

After breakfast Tony and I decided to have a look around the paddock. I have no doubt that Bernie was putting us to the test, waiting to see how long we could survive before being thrown out. Why? Because we had no passes.

As we moved towards the Benetton pit area we were asked by the security guys where were the passes that should have been hanging around our necks?

I told them that we didn't have any but then they wanted to know, not unreasonably, how we manage to get in at all. "By car," I replied innocently but, without any form of pass, we weren't convincing. Eventually I realised we would have to 'name-drop' and told them Bernie Ecclestone brought us here. I am sure they thought we were trying it on but after a few telephone calls and a flurry of activity our passes arrived.

But then, when we wanted to watch practice, we realised we didn't have tickets to do so. Bernie again? No, I didn't want to bother him and fortunately in the Williams camp was Bette Hill, widow of the late Graham, who I knew quite well. She fixed us up with the necessary accreditation.

Once again I learned to appreciate that it is not what you know but whom you know that really matters.

We enjoyed the day, especially from a privileged position that gave us a great insight into the running of a Formula One event.

Tony and I turned down the invitation to return the following day for the actual race. Being in the pits was the most fun for me, meeting people you hadn't seen for years and it seemed many people are there to be seen rather than as fans of car racing.

While we were there Bernie told me he wanted to have another attempt at staging an F1 race in America and that Las Vegas remained a possibility. A friend who I met through the Wheatcrofts (owners of Donington Park) was Ritchie Klein whose father-in-law owned the Imperial Palace hotel in Vegas.

Ritchie was known as the 'king of classic cars' and at the Imperial was one of the biggest collections in the world. Ritchie had helped me out when a museum in San Diego sold my Indy car that I had loaned them without my knowledge.

I was battling to get it back and was constantly being fobbed off. Ritchie is a tough-talking New Yorker and had the other 45 cars there. They could frustrate my efforts but they weren't about to tell Ritchie to take a jump and eventually we succeeded. I had previously initiated a meeting between Ritchie, who was building an Indy circuit just outside Vegas, and Bernie, but they couldn't agree on a deal.

After my visit to Silverstone the time seemed ripe to give Ritchie a call and see whether we couldn't put something together. His Indy stadium was now complete and was a fantastic facility with over 100 hospitality suites that were absolutely first class. I nearly fell over when Ritchie said he would let me have the stadium free of charge, would extend the track and build a pit area … anything I wanted.

I spent a few days mapping out how we could build a proper F1 course, secured a signed agreement from Ritchie and called Bernie to make the next move. I had never thought about being the promoter of a Formula One event but it was getting close.

In the early days of F1, Bernie often had to subsidise events to ensure that they took place and he had enough races on the calendar.

I remember joking with him when he suggested in an ideal world he would run all the various GPs at one circuit just for a television audience and simply change the signage and backdrops to give the impression they were in different countries. Think of how much money could be saved!

It was all tongue-in-cheek, of course, but can you imagine running all the Grands Prix in just one week at one track?

Unfortunately, when I arrived on Bernie's doorstep with my Las Vegas proposal and wanting him to fund it, his policy had changed.

Bernie had big cities throughout the world, often funded by their respective governments, queuing up for a Grand Prix and willing to stump up the required fees.

Bernie explained that his organisation would require a fee of $10 million and would retain all revenue from signage at the track and TV rights. The promoters (me) could keep the gate money.

Even with the Las Vegas tourist board throwing in a couple of million, and that wasn't agreed, I would be a long way short. It was dead in the water. As was my chance of promoting a Formula One race.

Speedway has needed, and probably still needs, a strong figurehead like Formula One's Bernie Ecclestone. When Bernie says jump, everyone in F1 jumps.

Former Ipswich promoter John Berry was put forward for a similar position in speedway in the mid-1980s but, at the last moment, the promoters changed their minds and decided not to put him in overall charge. I haven't always agreed with Berry's views but he is a decision-maker and speedway needs strong people like him. I think he would have been good for me in my racing days because he always looked after the best interests of his riders and fought their corner.

I was reading an issue of *Backtrack* magazine with views from Berry and editor Tony McDonald and I agreed with them on many points. But, as normal with speedway, nobody can agree with each other 100 per cent. I hope Tony doesn't mind me using part of his agenda.

The Speedway Control Board (now Bureau) used to rule with an iron fist, which, at times, bordered on the ridiculous. The World Championship at Wembley was not promoted, it just happened, but the sport was big and strong enough to overcome it. Their handling of my case when I wanted to leave promoter Ronnie Greene and Wimbledon over the princely sum of £30 was the source of my problem. They never spoke to me. All they did was to send threatening letters.

When the British League was formed in 1965, the promoters should have negotiated a seat on the FIM's track committee, the CCP, but they didn't and England were left out in the cold. British speedway was so lucky that one part-time promoter, Charles Foot, knew how to play the FIM game. He realised that British speedway had to grab some proper power and he gave everything to try to bring this about for no personal gain, just for the benefit of English speedway.

After the 1978 World Final at Wembley, he and some dominant figures in world speedway were to confront the FIM, but the pressure was too much for Charles and he had a fatal heart attack. British speedway was so much poorer with his demise. He loved the game and got things done. I saw a lot of him as I was living in Southampton and Charles was my promoter Charlie Knott's accountant. His death left me with a great deal of sorrow.

In a perfect world all the promoters would work together in their thinking and realise they have a great franchise. But, for it to work, everyone must pull together and understand the big picture. Over the years there have been happenings and issues that have been good and bad for speedway so let's look at a few of them.

Speedway's heritage was severely damaged, or even lost, with the closing-down of racing at Wembley Stadium without an apparent fight from the controlling body. It was a massive loss and I feel the sport lost a big chunk of its credibility, especially when it was replaced by that big hole in the ground called Odsal at Bradford.

There were other losses of grand stadiums like Wimbledon, West Ham and Manchester's Belle Vue. Each time one was lost, it was like another nail in the coffin of big-time speedway. Dwindling crowds meant the large stadiums weren't getting enough people through their turnstiles. A couple of thousand fans were nothing in those places and it is better to have a small stadium full, than a large one with a few thousand scattered around.

Speedway needs crowds and atmosphere to make it top-notch entertainment. Look at Cardiff. It is the nearest you can get to compare with the old Wembley days with the hooters and crowd participation adding up to a great sporting occasion.

Evel poses for me alongside the disastrous Snake River Canyon rocket-ship.

A frustrated motorcyclist or the world's greatest performer?

33

WHEN Evel Knievel died I wrote an article that appeared in magazines world wide. It painted a picture of him as the most famous motorcyclist ever.

"The Giant Gladiator finally met his maker after illness in November 2007. Even he would have agreed that he'd had more lives than ten cats but he didn't die the way that 50 per cent of the paying customers thought they might witness. In the end, his tired, battered body cried enough is enough, and he just gently passed on."

I remember my mate Evel sitting aboard his trusty Harley on the narrow runway at Wembley Stadium, fully aware that he could be moments from death after preparing for his final adventure on maybe the wildest of all of his wild rides.

Although he looked calm and collected from the outside, his head was buzzing with what could happen. Why the hell hadn't the mechanics packing the motorcycle in America thrown in a couple of smaller rear wheel sprockets? That would have given him an extra couple of miles an hour and more ramp speed, which would have been so valuable.

It had happened before but, yet again in his chequered life, he'd forced himself into a corner. He reckoned that, at the most, he had only a 20 per cent chance of making it over the 13 double-decker London buses and surviving. The 90,000 fans were cheering wildly, willing him to cross the huge chasm and to back out now would jump-start a riot.

"Balls," said Knievel as he tightened his helmet strap and fixed his gaze on the monstrous target ahead of him. The worst that can happen is to die in a blaze of glory. "Please God just help me one more time, I promise that I won't ask you ever again."

Then, at one of the World's most iconic venues, the greatest daredevil of them all opened the throttle and hurtled his way deeper into immortality. I crossed my fingers for Evel to make a safe landing. I knew myself what it meant to taste Wembley success, to take on the finest men and machines and to emerge victorious. But, while danger in speedway was a constant companion, 13 double-decker buses was sheer madness.

I had first met him in 1967 in Los Angeles where I was helping to re-introduce speedway to America after a break of 25 years. A party with fellow racers was swinging along well. Suddenly, everything stopped as a six foot plus, impressive looking Elvis-type bloke, entered the room.

The presence he radiated was amazing. It was obvious he was one of the boys. I had heard of Evel Knievel, but it was only through the motorcycle world. At this time he was a 500 dollars a jump rider but he badly wanted to be a racer. He had some racing talent, as he had shown back home in Montana, but he couldn't cut it against the top boys. Also, he was too big bodily as most top racers are slightly built.

I got a good look at the real Evel a few days later at the Los Angeles track, Ascot Park. The glamorous centre field was a lake surrounded by swinging palm trees, just like a film set.

This was the hotbed of American dirt track racing on the West coast.

Big crowds and top prize money drew all the best racers. Evel was there to add a bit extra at the end of the night. He had a long wait to collect his 500 bucks.

With a couple of hours left till race time, everyone in the pits was hanging out. Small groups were standing around watching Knievel building his take-off ramps over the trucks parked on the side of the racetrack. My American friend, Skip Van Leeuwen, was joking with him. Then the mood suddenly changed. It was obvious that Evel had said something to Skip that immediately stopped the banter.

Voices were raised and Skip barked back in a threatening voice: "Knievel, you ain't so bloody smart. I'll tell you what, me and the rest of the racers will jump all of your trucks on the last lap of the final race and show what a pussy you are." Evel looked really pissed and he was clearly not amused. Standing up he had a huge presence, he was a big, mean-looking character, especially at that moment. To make matters worse, he was clenching a large wrench in his massive hands to fix his ramps. Really focusing and moving forward so he was close to Skip, he blurted out in no uncertain manner: "Van Leeuwen, I will personally break you or any other 'mother' in half if you try such bullshit."

The gathered crowd fanned out for the impending action. I thought here we go, a point of no return had been reached. Then I saw Knievel give Skip a wink. The riders and Evel thought it was hilarious; obviously this jousting had been performed before. Evel was always thinking of the big-time, even though he was doing okay. In 1968 he came up with a master promotion idea that was to change his life completely. He loved Las Vegas, as everyone seemed to have plenty of cash and he wanted some of it.

Caesar's Palace hotel was one of the latest and brightest hotels on the strip. Evel somehow acquired the private phone number of the managing director. Over the next few days calls came through to him from a reporter asking for the date when Evel Knievel was going to jump the 50-foot high and 150-foot wide gushing water fountains in front of the hotel.

Every time Evel called, posing as the reporter, he pronounced his name wrongly, with each one sounding more ridiculous. Every time he claimed he was from a different newspaper or magazine.

First up was the *Los Angeles Times* and then it was *Time Magazine* on the line.

Finally, when the prestigious *Sports Illustrated* rang, the managing director was beside himself. Who the hell is this idiot with such an unbelievably stupid name? Enter the real Evel. The ploy had worked and the thrilled managing director even patted himself on the back for 'his great idea' of booking him. Caesar's Palace got behind the event and promoted it heavily.

The big day arrived, excitement and speculation was sky high. This crazy stunt had caught the media's imagination and they turned out in full force. The result of the jump would flash around the world in a matter of minutes. Evel mounted his British Triumph motorcycle to fly to his destiny. The take-off speed seemed spot on and he easily cleared the fountains. But his landing was disastrous. Evel and his roaring motorcycle parted company. The spectators stood open mouthed. A full-blooded war started between the rider and the tangled motorcycle which smashed, bucked, and bounced all over him.

The bike was the clear winner that day. When the mayhem had finished he had sustained serious injuries but God was working for him while he lay in a 30-day coma. Evel had finally fulfilled his lifetime ambition of hitting the big-time. The fountain disaster had turned him from a 500 dollar jumper into a true world superstar with untold riches. It was all happening while he was still in a coma!

He had plenty of time to think while he was in recovery. He came up with what he thought was a great idea. Why not jump the Grand Canyon? He figured it would be a sure-fire winner with huge financial rewards. Entrepreneur Evel was not slow to recognise the dollar value of his newly-found fame. The going rate for his jumps had increased 100 fold. Unfortunately, the extra cash didn't stop him from crashing.

Heavy financing was needed to do his Canyon jump and raising the cash was the goal that kept him going. He felt the hand of God was needed to help his success versus crash ratio. He couldn't earn the urgently required finance while lying in a hospital bed. He needed accident-free jumps for the next four years to achieve his dream of the Canyon date.

Suddenly, legalities stopped the attempt but this was only a small hiccup, Evel was never easily beaten. He simply purchased the rights for his own colourfully-named Snake River Canyon in the State of Idaho. Finally, he had the money in place. The machine that was going to propel him was a steam-powered rocket named Sky Cycle X2. The designer was Bob Truax, a pioneer in the rocket engineering industry.

Three rockets were built. The first two failed dismally, smashing themselves against the canyon walls on their way to a watery grave at the bottom of the fast-flowing Snake River. Evel was in trouble again, he was out of money and the rocket design was not working.

Once again he had got himself backed into a non-escapable corner but his drumbeating and promotional skills turned the Snake River Jump into World news. Because of the many delays, the media had come out stating openly that they thought the whole Canyon jump was a massive con and would never happen.

Evel spoke with great bravado, but deep down he felt that this time could be his final journey! In a desperate, last-minute manoeuvre, only weeks before the jump, he gave a post-dated cheque for 100,000 dollars to Truax. A frantic Knievel needed him to come up with a big performance improvement to the rocket. All he was asking for was an even chance of surviving his ride into the unknown, but, with the two sister rocket ships on the bottom of the Snake River, things didn't look good.

This last rocket also had to carry Knievel's weight, unlike the other two. More power was needed desperately to stop him and his third rocket joining the others in their watery grave. Even under this pressure his brain was still working because the proviso was that the cheque to Truax could only be cashed on his safe landing.

Being a gambler, Evel realised that the odds were stacked massively against him. If this was a card game, he would not have thought twice about throwing in this losing hand. This was really a bad deal, the consequence of losing was not about the simple loss of money. No, losing this bet was the ultimate sacrifice, his life.

The media were still sharpening their claws. Many more were now questioning his credibility and he was being forced again into a corner, with no way out. The moment of truth had to be addressed and it finally arrived. Just before he climbed into the rocket he addressed the world's press, many of whom were openly calling the rocket his coffin.

His speech was pure Knievel: "I'd rather be busted into the wind like a meteorite and then just become dust. God made us to live, not just exist. I'm ready."

The blast-off was spectacular, with grass, dirt, rocks and mud blown down the take-off slope. Initially, it looked good but within a matter of seconds the rocket's parachute opened. The ill-fated X2 rocket number three started on the same destructive downward journey previously taken by its two sisters. Knievel blacked out momentarily from the tremendous take-off force. Blood ran from his eyes, ears and nose.

On his return to consciousness, he struggled unsuccessfully to set himself free from the safety harness. The Knievel luck returned in the nick of time as strong winds thrashed the stricken rocket against the canyon wall.

Ten minutes later the searching helicopters found him and the rocket lying in shallow waters. Many felt he had panicked and fired the parachute but he always insisted that the early opening was simply a malfunction, saying: "NASA experience the same problem all the time."

But luck had certainly stayed with him that day. The jump was a failure but he earned in excess of five million dollars. A sombre Evel always said candidly he was convinced he was going to die but, luckily for him, it wasn't planned that way.

Was England ready for Evel Knievel?

His jump at London's Wembley Stadium attracted 90,000 new English fans. They cheered and screamed for their hero in his attempt to clear the 13 buses but Evel was not happy with his take-off speed, it was too slow. His lack of speed wouldn't propel himself and the heavy Harley machine far enough to clear the daunting mass of buses safely.

Disaster struck as anticipated. Evel and the machine became entwined, with the Harley hitting him on every second roll before bike and rider came to rest in a heap in the middle of the speedway

Not pretty and it's going to hurt like hell ... but you can't keep a good man down.

track. A broken pelvis and other injuries couldn't stop the master showman. Keeping him on the stretcher taking him from his wrecked Harley to the medical centre proved impossible. He fought his way free from the medical personnel and, half falling from the stretcher, the wounded hero stumbled, limped, and was half carried to an infield microphone.

The crowd's reaction was deafening. When he started to speak, a deathly hush fell over the packed stadium. The words poured through the loudspeakers: "Ladies and gentlemen of this wonderful country, you are the last people who will ever see me jump. I will never ever jump again, I am through."

Then he fell dramatically into the arms of his helpers. His fee was in excess of one million dollars, which helped to lessen the horrendous pain and recovery. It never worried Evel that he changed his mind after telling the world he had jumped for the last time. Jumping had become his fix.

He pushed himself hard to regain peak fitness and returned to jumping at Kings Island, Ohio, just six months after his Wembley disaster. Lined up were 13 buses, the same number as at his Wembley nightmare.

In the build-up he got the crowd excited with wheelies and practice runs. The public were aware of the significance of the number 13 and he brought the house down when he yelled into the microphone to his helpers: "Hey, bring me another one!"

The man knew exactly what the public wanted. At times he'd get carried away, especially when he got his adrenalin rush leading up to the jump. He would forget completely about his own safety. Evel then mounted up and calmly cleared the 14 Greyhound buses.

The next earner was a jump called Knievel's Swansong. It took place over a tank full of live sharks in the Chicago Amphitheatre. It was a disaster. A cameraman was hit and subsequently lost an eye. Evel suffered brain concussion, plus two broken arms. The injury to the cameraman really played on Evel's mind. Injuring himself was okay, it was part of the job, but hurting someone else was not part of the deal.

Finally, he decided to retire and, after recovering, he set about getting son Robbie ready to be his successor. But you never knew what Evel was going to do next because he was always full of surprises and the next one was on its way.

Evel and I were booked in at the Del Mar Fairgrounds, a mile-long horse racing track near San Diego, California. I had done my demonstration, now it was his turn. Mounted on his Harley Davidson and dressed in his trademark red, white and blue jacket, he made a pass in front of the 45,000 fans cramming the grandstand.

The last of the World's true gladiators was always quickly recognised and the name Evel was understood worldwide. Very

Don't look behind Evel, you are being followed.

few people in the sporting world can be identified by simply one name. A couple spring to mind, boxing superstar Ali and also the greatest soccer player, Pele. Then there's the new kid on the block, Tiger. Like them, Evel remains an icon.

He was on the microphone, doing what he does best. He was one of the best communicators you could ever listen to, a politician on a motorcycle. "Ladies and Gentlemen of our beautiful country," he boomed. "In 2003 I am going to make my farewell monster jump which will be my longest ever!" I was in shock, like the rest of the hushed and visibly shocked thousands.

He continued: "I'm dedicating this jump to all of middle-age America. No matter what cards you are dealt in your later life, you've just got to face up to it. Fight your best fight, and you'll be a winner." The crowd went wild, especially the older Harley Davidson brigade.

With a liver transplant, diabetes, as well as Hepatitis C, he needed daily medication of 25 pills, plus two diabetic injections, to keep it all under control. His message to middle-aged Americans was clearly based on his own experiences.

Evel finished: "I certainly couldn't run and win an Olympic gold medal, but as sure as hell, mounted on my motorcycle, I can conquer the World again." Maybe he looked a little jaded, but Evel thrived on adversity. The crowd and myself left Del Mar all thinking the same: is this going to be one jump too many?

The Las Vegas Harley Davidson dealership presented Evel with their new 100th anniversary Road King Classic model. The presentation was normal for any Knievel deal with big crowds and, as always, the media circus climbed aboard. Crowds and media attention was an aphrodisiac to him. It really lit him up and even his limp didn't seem as bad.

After the presentation, Evel disappeared into the workshop to fit a further 3,000 dollars worth of chrome goodies to his new prize. "Bloody hell Evel, put any more weight on that bike and you'll never get it to move," I chaffed him. He just smiled. He was at his most relaxed in a workshop, fettling his machine with only a couple of mechanics around. Even after having his body thrashed around over the years by an unfeeling pile of metal called a motorcycle, it was amazing that he retained his love and enthusiasm for them like a teenager.

Love is a very strong and emotional word, especially to a man like Evel, who loved and courted some of the World's most beautiful women. But he openly confessed that he loved motorcycles. He really must have done. No woman, no matter how beautiful, could ever put him through so much pain and suffering as a motorcycle and get away with it.

Finally, the chrome hanging was finished and he rode his new toy from the quiet of the workshop back to the front shop. The buzz that he was back circulated like magic. The madness was back and so were the crowds, watching and photographing him. Signing autographs again, you sensed he was on edge and getting agitated. All he wanted was to get out of there. Just twist the throttle and roar off down the open highway. When he was astride his motorcycle, the years melted away and he was a stud again.

Like any good captain he issued orders: "Barry, you drive my pickup, the keys are on the floor, and follow me." His pickup was a special Evel Knievel model Ford, painted and trimmed in the same red, white, and blue as his leathers. The Ford Motor Company had obviously figured out that his name was still big enough to sell pickups.

Virgin Airways chief Richard Branson, who Evel liked because 'he's a real adventurer, a winner and has the balls of an elephant,' confirmed the Ford view. When launching his Virgin Cola to the

American public, Branson chose Evel as his spokesman. Four years later he was still doing the commercials. Finally, we arrived at the RV park where Evel had left his mobile home. This five-star Hilton Hotel on wheels had cost him more than one and a half million dollars and it was real Hollywood. He took a great deal of joy showing off all its great features.

"With just a push of a button this pops out, then look what happens when you do this. It's hard to believe what this small button does, it levels up this great luxurious home on wheels." There was a mirrored bedroom, everything was beautifully lit, and so very comfortable. No doubt you can have anything if you can afford to pay!

"Barry, you must have a ride on my new Harley, it's the real works." I'm not convinced and say: "Evel, I'm not a Harley man. Every one I have ever ridden has shook and bloody vibrated like the end of the world was near. I'd rather not, but thanks anyhow." But after the Evel hard sell, who could refuse? I took a spin on his new pride and joy. The look on my face when I returned must have betrayed clearly how much I enjoyed the ride!

He radiated how much he enjoyed sharing his new motorcycle with another red-blooded motorcyclist and I had to concede: "It's a really nice motorcycle, no vibrations, beautifully balanced. I hate to admit it's superb. But I am sure that it's a one-off Special built just for you because you are Harley Davidson's favourite son."

Sitting in the luxury RV was really nice, especially as you rarely got time with Evel alone. Every man and his dog wanted to shake his hand or get an autograph. Krystal, his ex-wife and now his girlfriend again, was absolutely the opposite to the man she chose and quietly served us with soft drinks.

It was like Christmas for me to have the time and opportunity to ask him all the questions that intrigued me about his chequered life, especially his jumping escapades. For a couple of hours we had a good laugh. One story even saw him stuck for words. Naturally, he loved to brag and we were talking about Wembley.

We were actually blood brothers as we had shared the same experience of leaving the arena by the same transportation. On a stretcher!

He was boasting that he still held the crowd record for Wembley. I had a little smile to myself and replied: "I'm afraid you are wrong, you don't hold that record. The record is in excess of 125,000 and is held by another American who is an even bigger promoter of himself than you are."

"Rubbish," he retorted. "There's no bigger attraction than me." I smiled: "Wrong, Evel, and the guy doesn't even ride a motorcycle." Everything suddenly went quiet. He was thoughtful and a very rare occurrence happened, Evel had lost his tongue! I waited a long second and said: "How about Billy Graham then?"

Slowly, like the sun rising to a new dawn, a smile spread across his face: "God damn it, that ain't fair. He got help from above."

Evel was still working on his last monster jump. He still had his normal up-beat enthusiasm and he also had some big sponsors. Which manufacturer he would choose for the motorcycle for the jump was down to two factories. This time he was taking a very serious look at the landing characteristics of the chosen machine. This had always been the danger point and was the area of more than 90 per cent of his crashes.

Finding the right stadium or arena was proving hard to tie down. He was predicting a crowd of 200,000 spectators so a stadium to handle it was going to be hard to find. Every time Wembley was mentioned his body got a twitch. It was on the stadium list briefly but was struck off on two counts: Would the new one be finished in time and the capacity would not be big enough. He was still thinking big.

A few months later he told me that he and Krystal had crashed his Harley on the road. Luckily, neither had been hurt. It pointed out to me, though, that his body wasn't functioning 100 per cent correctly. I'm sure he got the message as well and the monster jump quietly disappeared on to the back-burner. Years of reading, listening, or watching the media formed a public perception of him which, I believe, was only one dimensional. It was not a fair reflection.

Evel, I will certainly agree, was not an angel in disguise. I am also fairly sure he probably didn't help too many old ladies safely across the street. Knowing what I know about his life, I would like to try to balance the story a little. We all know that he was a larger-than-life, daredevil motorcycle jumper who had broken more than 40 bones. That he would gamble on the drop of a hat. He was a big-time gambler because, for most of his adult life, the stake he put up endlessly was the ultimate, his life.

Let's not forget that, for a part of his life, he was a full-time drinker and womaniser. He tried all the trappings that came with fame and fortune. Cars, boats, planes and anything in between. He also served time for beating up a journalist with a baseball bat.

Here is my humble interpretation of the legacy I feel Evel left when he departed our planet. He was almost fanatical in his love of America. He was a great salesman, motivator and also a great communicator, especially with Joe Public. As a salesman can you name any one person, maybe apart from Elvis Presley, who could get 90,000 fans to pay their hard-earned cash to watch them perform at Wembley Stadium? That is a real sell!

The mention of drugs would light Evel up, they were the biggest hate of his life. Whenever he was on television, on a microphone at a jump, or at any other gathering, he would push the 'no drugs' hard. He was constantly advising youngsters not to wreck their bodies.

His story was likened to the qualifying at the Indianapolis 500, America's biggest car race. He would preach: "In order to qualify some would cheat and use illegal fuel. That would give them five fast laps, then the engine would blow itself to bits. It's the same with your body and life. If you take drugs it is up to you. It's your body, the choice is yours."

He was also involved in the children's Make a Wish Foundation plus various others, including the Child Burn Centers. He stated firmly he never took drugs. Part of his downfall in the baseball bat saga was a drug problem, because it was written that he was on them and that was too much for him. In court he didn't have any problems speaking out about his feelings and it wasn't appreciated. He was severely punished.

Many other charities have benefited greatly because of his generosity and time. He loved golf and played with many World greats. Evel loved to pit himself against anyone at everything and golf for charity was heaven sent.

He hated the Hell's Angels and what they stood for. No proper, normal motorcyclist worldwide would take them seriously. Over the years the Angels and their image has been transferred to all genuine motorcyclists, as if we were all tarred with the same brush. The Angels started to play up at one of his shows at the large Cow Palace in San Francisco.

Evel got stuck in, then some spectators followed his example and sorted out the Hell's Angels problem quickly. The City of San Francisco bestowed the freedom of the city on him for his fearless leadership to stamp out that particular problem.

On a personal note, my wife, Junie, was diagnosed with stage four cancer. Evel rang on quite a few occasions to tell us which pills he thought she needed. The doctors just laughed, they told me that those pills would have blown her socks off. Junie had plenty of laughs, even though it wasn't a happy time, and really enjoyed the thought of her socks being blown off. Even when he was really struggling health wise, he always looked at the positives. He told me excitedly that the Mountain High fun park had named a ride after him.

The Evel Knievel legend had been formed. He crammed more into his 69 years than he ever thought possible. He firmly believed that God rescued him many times. He acknowledged his luck, especially that he wasn't wheelchair bound for life. England's Eddie Kidd was a good friend whose career came to an end with a serious, life-threatening accident.

Evel explained why he must do his monster jump, saying: "Hey, I'm a gladiator and my role is in the arena, not just as a spectator."

On money, everyone speaks of different amounts. He told me he had earned sixty million dollars and had spent sixty-five million. He loved big numbers. Everyone could benefit by the advice on his business card, which read: "You can fall many times in life. But you are never a failure as long as you try to get up."

I'll rest the Evel Knievel case. He did bring some good to the world while he was here on earth. Not forgetting the great, pulse-stopping entertainment he gave to millions.

Burt Munro's 1920 Indian Scout and 1936 Velocette.

Burt Munro was an eccentric character but he was a Kiwi 34

BURT Munro was a motorcycle man through and through, even before he bought his first motorbike at the age of 15. He used it for a few years until he finally sold it to the local blacksmith as he had seen a bike that really caught his fancy at a local Invercargill motorcycle shop. Little did he realise that this bike was going to take up the rest of his life.

The new bike was an Indian Scout that cost him the sum of £140. He could have got the more expensive model with electric lights, but settled for the cheaper model fitted with acetlyn lamps.

This Indian motorcycle went through so many rebuilds and face-lifts in the following years, you would never know what to make of it unless you read the distinctive Indian name on the crankcases.

The bike became an obsession with Burt and his life completely rotated around his old Indian motor-cickle. He loved to read the American motorcycle magazines, and he liked the way that some Americans pronounced it cickle, not cycle.

The word eccentric was often used to describe Burt. The dictionary gives the word's meaning as 'odd' or 'unpredictable'. I don't really agree with that label for Burt. Odd – sure he loved his motorcycles, but he also loved a lot of women, so I don't think he was odd. Unpredictable is completely off the mark, he was so easy to predict and where you would find him, in his workshop or, otherwise, at the local dance hall.

He had tried many forms of motorcycle racing, even speedway in Aussie, but he found that the speed records suited him best. Simply, he could show his true passion by achieving the highest speeds on his record attempts.

The riding was only a small part, the tuning and being able to coax more and more power from his original 50mph bike was a big passion to him. He had got his old 1920 Indian Scout about as quick as he could safely test on the roads and beaches of New

Me at Ramsgate Sprint on Len Cole's Twin Douggie

Zealand, as he needed a couple of miles to get his speed up, then another couple of miles to slow.

A trip to Bonneville Salt Flats really caught his imagination at a rather late date in his life. With his Kiwi frugal handling of money he achieved his dream. He then got this obsession to break the world land speed record on his 45-years-old plus vintage motorcycle. He wanted to challenge the world's fastest, but money was a problem although time was nothing, he had plenty.

His story was later made into a film by Roger Donaldson who, 15 years earlier, had made a documentary on Burt, and was absolutely bowled over by his story. He spent many years getting the money together to make a full length movie about him. The film was called *The World's Fastest Indian* in which Anthony Hopkins played the role of Burt. He did so brilliantly. I can testify to that because I knew Munro well.

He was born and lived in Invercargill, which is just about the end of the world going south, the next stop being the Antarctic. He had worked for 40-odd years on his Indian Scout, now named the Munro Special.

Eventually, in August 1962 at the Bonneville Salt Flats in America, he set a World Record of 178.97mph. Then, two years later, Burt on his now bored-out larger capacity engine, set a new under 1000cc World Record at 183.586mph. Burt was 68-years-young, and the bike was 47-years-old and his record still stands today.

I knew of Burt but never got to meet him until I went to Invercargill a couple of times in 1963. The workshop-bedroom shown in the film was an exact replica of what it was really like. The second time I went to see him, he laughed as he said to me: "Barry, how would you like to come with me and my mate Duncan down to Oreti beach and see the old girl go?" Once there he got this old bike ready to roar down the beach. Burt, being into motorcycles, knew me. I was petrified that he was going to say "take it for a run down the beach".

I was told by many that my bikes were crap but on this one I wouldn't want to go 50mph let alone 150. Luckily he didn't think I could handle it … and he was right!

Anyway, he and his mate Duncan got the bike out and Burt started to put on an old *Dad's Army* type steel helmet. I thought, 'bloody hell, you can't ride with that', and I ended up buying him a new Bell helmet. I also gave him some cash as well. It must have been a good story to get lolly from a fellow Kiwi. I always wondered if I was the only one who had donated him a helmet. He did actually fly down the beach in that steel helmet. I have it all somewhere on 8mm film.

I believe that, as a boy, he would ride his family's horses across their farm to see which was the fastest. His interest in speed came at an early age. But it was his Indian Scout that consumed his life.

Burt had no money and would make most of the spare parts and modifications himself. When I was there it was before he had thought of going to the US of A, as he would say. He was casting his own pistons in an old one-foot square Aulsebrook's biscuit tin filled with sand, which stood on some bricks on the ground just outside his workshop. He made all his own cylinder barrels. The conrods he shaped from an old Caterpillar broken half shaft. Burt loved what he did, and had amazing patience. He would spend weeks and weeks modifying his bike, then go out on it and blow it to pieces in two minutes.

He'd simply go back to the workshop and say: "Well, we are going to make that a wee bit stronger." Nothing seemed to faze him.

I suppose I saw some of Burt in me. I have always tinkered with my bikes, trying to make them that little bit special. Perhaps if I had just used standard bikes and not messed around with them I would have won more … but then it wouldn't have been me!

Burt spent most of his life in his workshop, though he was married and had four children, he was divorced over 20 years before finally setting his world record. He did like the ladies, we all knew that, but all the time his sights were set on that record. He actually did over 200mph in a qualifying run at Bonneville but it was unofficial and didn't count.

Burt died, aged 78, in 1978 and was, in my book, a typical Kiwi. He did it his way and the film is a great testimony to all that he achieved.

Here I am riding Lord Montague's Norton ('Old Miracle') during the London to Brighton run

Some of my greatest moments have been outside speedway

35

I HAVE always enjoyed road racing and have been privileged to know many of the top riders in more than four decades.

One of them was Britain's Barry Sheene. Through my connection with Yamaha in 1970 I was able to buy their TZ 350cc machine, which I labelled the 'rocket ship'. I came to a verbal agreement with Barry to ride it at Daytona, we were to be partners, but around the same time he signed a deal with Suzuki and it didn't happen.

That was a shame ... for both me and Sheeney. The Finnish rider Jarno Saarinen won the race with another mate of mine, Kel Carruthers, second and both were mounted on the 'rocket ship'.

After losing out on the Sheene deal, I sold the TZ 350 to John 'Moon Eyes' Cooper, a big speedway fan and a great mate of Nigel Boocock, the Coventry speedway star.

To compete and win in road racing you cannot afford to be on a bike that is even a tiny percentage slower than those you are up against. Being half a second a lap slower than your opponents may not seem much but, after ten laps, you are five seconds behind and that is a long, long way.

I had ridden a road race bike at Brands Hatch and really enjoyed it. I also competed in New Zealand on a Manx Norton but, as it turned out, the build-up was best. It was the Featherbed Norton and, to get used to it, I rode it for about 100 miles on near perfect country roads through the hills. It was unbelievable, exhilarating fun – and there were no cops around! But, on race day, it sheared a cam key on the first lap!

I rode in a hill climb in the foothills surrounding Lyttelton Harbour, which is over the hill from Christchurch. Because the road had to be closed, the event started at six o'clock in the morning. I won on my JAP Special which had belonged to Martin Tatum, Kelvin's dad. The same afternoon, I was in another road race at the Lake Bryndwr circuit. As the name suggests, it was around a lake in Christchurch. It was a great circuit with some really fast corners and a tremendous amount of banking. After doing well in my early races the old JAP cried 'enough' after it had taken a thrashing in a couple of great races against much more expensive and sophisticated machines.

The JAP was an engine built for speedway and had a total loss oil system. It drops the oil once it has been through the engine, straight onto the track through dump valves, which was okay for speedway because it helped to bind the track, but with road racing it was a bit more tricky. The last thing you want is for the oil to go on to your back tyre for the road races, so I fitted a piece of garden hose leading the oil away.

I was in a race around the streets of Dunedin and was fourth at the first corner. But, as I turned into it, I hit a metal sewer cover and went arse over tip. Luckily, I managed to keep the engine running so, tally ho, I was off and running. The track had about a quarter of a mile of gravel road so I waited for that section.

There was a 90 degree left-hand corner and everyone would queue behind each other on the right of the road before taking it. So I would zap down the left side, do some suicidal braking and pass a minimum of five riders at a time. I had got up to second at the halfway stage but then they decided to black flag that bloody speedway rider for the tube that came out of the bottom of the engine. It had been the same when the bike was scrutinised, and for practice, but now they wanted to throw me out. I don't think the road racing fraternity liked a bloody speedway rider passing their heroes, but it was fun.

The way I tackle riding a motorcycle is not always in my best interests and, looking back, I think that fate looked after me in the Isle of Man. John Cooper and I were watching the racing from the pit area. I can't remember who it was but someone offered Coop a ride in what was called a parade lap on the famous Triumph named 'Slippery Sam'.

He jumped at the chance while turning to me and saying: "Why don't you ride my Seeley Matchless?" I thought why not, I had done plenty of laps around the TT circuit on my 250 Yamaha. I felt uncomfortable even on the start of my first lap but kept going and then fate intervened. The magneto quit as I was exiting Quarter Bridge and that was the end of it. I didn't need to go around the TT course on something I didn't like but there would have been a real danger I could not have stopped the racer in me from taking over, with possibly bad results. It was lucky for me that the decision was taken out of my hands by a dodgy magneto.

Scrambles (motocross) was something I really loved and I did it a lot to keep me fit for speedway. Ronnie Greene, my promoter at Wimbledon, would have killed me if he had known I was racing scrambles at the weekends. That was before I got into longtrack and grasstrack racing as well doing speedway on the continent at weekends.

In those days, at the start of a scrambles race, you stood ten feet behind your bike. Then you ran like hell at the drop of the flag, kick-started your bike and off you went. I used to jump on the bike from the back and tried to kick start it when I was on the way down to the seat. I miscued a couple of times and landed on my manhood but the thrill of the chase was so great you never felt the pain until the end of the race. I had some really bad crashes. One day I was passing three riders on the outside only to run out of track … but I used to bounce quite well when I was young.

There was a track on the outskirts of London called Burnham

Beeches and the 400 yards to the finish was a steep, fast downhill run. In practice I got to know just how fast the 'Aces' were. I was riding as normal, just under being out of control, and then there was some idiot trying to pass me around the outside. The first corner was a very fast sweeper and I lost him, then all of a sudden he's all over me again.

In the end I think he was thoroughly pissed off with me and passed me by being really tough. When he got passed he just disappeared. When I got back to the pits I asked my mate who the bloody hell was the bloke in the green football shirt? It was the works rider Dave Curtis. How bloody fast was he!

On one lap I jumped off the top of the downhill, but this time I was on a different line to normal. I landed on a sheep track, which ran across the hill on an angle The bike went one way, I went the other and the result was a broken thumb. It was a Sunday and on Tuesday we had a league match against West Ham. There was no way I wanted anyone to know because, if Greene banned me, I wouldn't be able to ride my scrambles. Photographs showed me with an enormous cricket glove on my right hand. Strangely, I had a really good night.

I learned the lesson that you didn't have to be a bull at the gate to get points and the lack of perfect grip in my damaged right hand showed me that brute strength was not the answer. The Eso-Jawa was a great engine and I fitted one of mine into Andy Lee's scrambler bike and he got a great second place in the television trophy. I also fitted my engine into Derek Rickman's bike for the Grand Prix de Nations at Brands Hatch. We were warming up for practice when the engine just quit, no sparks.

Derek started to apologise for dragging us all the way to Brands Hatch but he hadn't been around speedway boys that much. I took the magneto from my spare engine in the back of the car and he made the race. In the main final he got stuck behind Dave Nichol who was slower. But every time Derek made a move he got filled in with flying mud and he had to quit three-quarters of the way through the race, beaten by the dirt.

A couple of years later Nichol was working with the Rickmans, Derek and his brother Don, at their factory. Somehow the Brands

Hatch Grand Prix came into the conversation, how they had a great race, and Derek was saying how good the Jawa was and was quick enough to win, especially if it had been dry. Dave told Derek: "You probably would have won at Brands, but that day I had a 600cc engine in!"

The Jawa factory wasn't happy with me putting my engine into a scrambles bike. Maybe there was a political problem because Belgian superstar Joel Robert was way behind Derek on his works CZ before he was forced to stop. I asked them: "Aren't we in business to sell engines?"

I went to a Belgian motocross with Dave Bickers, who was the CZ dealer for England, the same as I was for Jawa. The track was deep sand and I mean deep. Everyone loved Dave, he always gave it everything. If Jeff Smith jumped 10 feet in the air, then they thought Dave would jump 15 feet. If Lampkin went 25 feet, Dave would go 35 feet. Everyone thought Dave was Superman.

Well, I couldn't believe what I saw in that Belgian meeting, which was run over two races. I thought our Superman Dave was going to die after each leg in that sand. I've never seen such exhaustion. On the way home Dave and I were talking about start money for our continental races. I felt like a real con man because we got the same amount, sometimes a bit more, on the longtracks and we hardly break a sweat compared with the scramble boys.

I raced on the American short tracks with most of their road race heroes but, to me, Kenny Roberts is the World's greatest all-round motorcyclist. I have known him since he was 17 and he was the biggest motorcycle star in the USA before he left his own backyard to become World Champion on the road circuit. When Kenny was No. 1 in the States he was riding on the dirt as well as the road. He could ride quarter mile, half mile and TT, they were all part of the American Championship.

I rode as his team-mate at Madison Square Gardens where he also starred, even though the track was on a small ice hockey rink with very slippery concrete. I had some tremendous races with him on the quarter-mile dirt tracks in America and got to know him really well. He seemed like a farmer's boy but had a brain as sharp as a tack, and he did a tremendous job for all road racers.

When he took on the FIM (International Motor Federation) head first, the riders' money and conditions were greatly improved by him being a leader.

My speedway type style, going flat-out into the corners, was very different from the American boys, who shut the throttle, but Kenny would come into the corners with me and worry about it when he got there. Even though he was on his limit, he never knocked me off and I never felt that he would. All of the Yank flat-track riders sat down on their bikes into the corners on a quarter-mile track which gave them little chance against a speedway style.

I reached the American Final in Chicago and got myself up near the lead after 10 laps, after that I thought I was going to die. The 250cc engines made it harder and, when you are riding good speedway, your left foot hardly touches the ground. After 10 laps at Chicago I put more and more weight on my left leg with each lap I covered and, at the end of 20 laps, you could have fried an egg on my steel boot.

On a mile-long track you go nowhere if you slide, but the American boys' bikes are heavy and over a certain speed want to slide or crash, whereas a longtrack bike won't do that, if you ride it correctly. They are very positive and won't dump you on your head like the big old American bike will.

The biggest plus with American type racing is that it is like speedway in the 1950s. Then very few riders could race flat-out, the winner would normally be the last man to shut the throttle and the first to get it back on again. Not so in today's speedway where a 13-year-old kid can ride flat-out. So how do you win? If you don't make the start, with great difficulty!

Kenny did compete in a longtrack event in the UK, which Wally Mawdsley promoted at Exeter and he got England's 1976 World Speedway Champion Peter Collins to race against him. Peter was on his longtrack bike while Kenny was on a Triumph. If I had been him, there was no way I would have done that race. They should have made an exhibition of it but PC went off and left Kenny and I thought that was poor. You just don't do that to fellow World Champions. Kenny deserved better than that.

A few years ago I went to a 1,000-metre horse racing track in San Diego to do a demonstration on my first longtrack Jawa that I built at their factory in Czechoslovakia. Kenny was there on his revolutionary bike, fitted with a Yamaha triple cylinder road racing engine. He had raced it in only one meeting but won on the last corner. He was way over the ragged edge for the whole race, just about killing himself, and the bike was immediately banned for being too dangerous. The organisers suggested we went out together but Kenny would have nothing of it. He knew I could go through the corners quicker than him.

Kenny did try a speedway bike – I think it was Billy Hamill who managed to get him on it – but said: "I'm bloody useless on those bikes, but at least I'm better than my son." Kenny junior went on to be a World road racing champion just like his dad.

Marlboro put up a lot of money for Kenny to establish his riding ranch outside of Barcelona in Spain when he had the Yamaha Dirt Track series. My son, Tony, and I went for a look and had this idea of running some events at the longtrack circuits in Germany where the sport was very big at the time.

We planned to pay Simon Wigg, and the other top longtrackers, to compete on Yamahas. We thought involving a big name like Yamaha would attract a much wider audience. Terry Tiernan, a big mate of mine, was the boss of Yamaha in Los Angeles. I had ridden their bikes for three years in America and I went to Yamaha in Japan and got to talk to the right man about them producing a speedway bike with a lay-down engine.

I had already made one, it was the first I did, and I tried to persuade them that this could be the cheapest World Championship for them to win. But Yamaha had recently had their fingers badly burned by their trials bikes and manufacturing a speedway bike was never going to be a practical proposition for them. It would take about a day to make enough bikes for a year!

I had a dream of kids going into their local Yamaha shop and buying a bike that they could slide around their local baseball diamonds or soccer fields. We would have got an influx of youngsters on bikes from normal motorcycle shops, but it never worked out that way. Many of the top riders from other motorcycle racing disciplines relish the chance of getting on a speedway bike. But, quite often, they aren't given the right information before doing so and get hurt.

On one occasion I showed the ropes to Mark Brelsford, who carried the coveted AMA No. 1 plate, which is the reward for being the overall best in all racing disciplines in America. I had an hour with him on a speedway bike and he then understood exactly how to ride it in a controlled slide. When you are astride a speedway bike, you have to understand exactly what you are actually trying to do.

When I am home in California, I go riding in the mountains, near the ski resorts, with my son Tony and, on occasions, I manage to get my other boy, Gary, out as well. It is a couple of hours' drive away and we could ride for a week without using the same trail twice.

We normally leave home at four o'clock in the morning and try to fit in five or six hours of riding then head home before the dangerous joe-public racers arrive. There are quite a few single tracks, with steep drop-offs, so you don't want to meet some budding motocross riders coming in the other direction.

Also, the temperatures can get up in the 100s, so it's a tough workout when you are getting baked as well. Even today, I still have my share of falls and it still bloody hurts. But now, thanks to my mate Bill Brown of Wulfsports, I've got all the best equipment. I can unload at 40mph but because today's riding gear provides so much protection, I normally get away with it. We've had some scary moments, though, when we've been miles from anywhere, sometimes in areas where mobile phones don't work. You have got to love it to keep going back but despite problems with my knees and hip, that's exactly what I do.

Up in the mountains we are looking over lakes, hills and forests. It is beautiful and it's not like walking where you would only do a few miles in a couple of hours. We cover about 50 miles and have time to enjoy it. Speedway is such a hard form of riding as you have to perform at your best the instant your bum hits the saddle. Now, in the mountains, my body has time to warm up and adjust to the demands of what is needed on a bike, demands that I have spent so many hours grinding into my memory.

When everything in your mind and body are in sync, the pleasure of riding a motorbike just flows. I have often been asked whether there is any other form of motorcycle racing I would rather have had as a profession than speedway.

I've done many types of racing but I wouldn't have wanted to do anything other than speedway for my living. But, by doing all the other different forms, I've met most motorcycle stars on an equal footing. If I was just a fan, I would only be able to gaze at these riders and want their autographs.

I found motorcycle guys much more grounded than the normal car people, although I think the very top car racers would have to be excluded from that statement. Mike Hailwood and John Surtees, who were World Champions on bikes before competing in Formula 1 car racing, told me there was a great deal of difference between the people involved in the two sports.

There are also many differences between the various motorcycle disciplines. I was at Brands Hatch on a Sunday two or three years ago with my friend Mike Smart whose son, Midge, was competing in the British 125cc championships.

There were kids in the pits, from the age of 15 upwards, surrounded by big motor homes and pit bikes while some top riders had two or three mechanics working for them.

To me, it was an unreal world. When Midge's race was over I travelled ten miles to the Canada Heights Motocross track where the World Twin Shock championship was taking place. I was honoured to be presenting the trophies to the winners who included several heroes of mine who were all World Champions.

There was America's Brad Lackey, the dynamic England duo of champions, Neil Hudson and Graham Noyce, plus Sweden's former champion, Bengt Alberg, as well as many other National champions from all the European countries. They all had dirty faces and muck in their teeth. To me, these were the real men of the racing world. I've always felt comfortable in the company of this type of rider, they were straight up with very little bullshit.

I used to meet many others riders in Czechoslovakia, now the Czech Republic. Their Federation brought together many of the top racing motorcyclists from all the different disciplines to take part in three ice shows and the stadiums were completely sold out. It was not normal, but the Federation used the profits to get us all together with no costs to the riders. It was great to see Dave Bickers and Joel Robert playing ice-hockey against the Czech team. Swedes Torsten Hallman, Ove Fundin, Rolf Tibblin and Bjorn Knutsson were all born on skates so it was great fun.

Once again, I took the hard road by doing the ice racing. Not knowing the sport, I made a novice mistake and got my inside boot trapped under the rear part of the frame to jack the wheel and the spikes in the tyres off the ice.

No grip, I was on my arse big-time. The trouble then was that I started to slide across the ice on my backside with very little loss of speed. As I roared towards the solid fence, I stuck out a foot to stop my body from hitting it too hard and, bingo, I had a broken foot. The plaster cast they put on me was out of a comic book. I looked like an old man with gout, complete with a monster plaster and a walking stick. The abuse I had to take from those bloody foreigners was non-stop.

A year later I did a couple of international ice races. The first was in Germany and was the forerunner of many successful meetings to be presented in the beautiful Bavarian town of Inzell. There were no big-name ice racers around then so the organisers decided to look outside the sport.

Ice racing flourishes mainly in Russia and some of the Scandinavian countries. There were six or seven longtracks, which ran at least one meeting a year, within a 30-mile radius of Inzell so promoter Georg Transberger decided to book their big draw-cards. He called me, as I was well known in this part of the country, and he knew that for a pocket full of money I'd do it. I had no bike when Transberger contacted me so I went to the Czech Jawa factory to get one. Then I headed to a big, frozen lake. I cannot remember ever having a more exhilarating ride on a motorcycle as I zoomed around it a few times.

The ice bike has only a two-speed gearbox. Bottom gear is to get you moving from the start. Otherwise, it is rather like trying to leave traffic lights in third gear, it doesn't work. If you want more speed, you fit a smaller sprocket on the rear wheel.

Flying across the lake at 70mph takes your breath away as the air is fresh and cold. If you don't get your foot caught under the rear frame, the two-inch spikes will keep you stable. You can virtually lay the bike on its side but the first thing to hit the ice is your left handlebar. You get tremendous G-forces as you turn sharply at high speed as everything in your body and stomach is forced down. When your left handlebar kisses the ice, that's as far as you can go. If you lay the bike any lower your handle digs in and lifts your front wheel from the ice. The bike stops turning and you go straight on until you get your spikes back on the ice.

The race meeting was very different. I'd been having such a good time that I forgot to do any practice starts. The first I ever made was in my opening race. I did a normal start sitting on the front tip of the seat, with plenty of throttle before I dumped the clutch. Wrong, wrong and wrong! Next thing, in a flash, I was on my backside again and the bike just looped from under me. I hit the ground like a hockey puck but, luckily this time, I never hit anything. I settled down to finish third – and I walked away under my own power!

The meeting was a big success and Georg ran World Championship meetings there over the next ten years.

After my Inzell ice experience, I had a theory that with the ice spikes you can lay the bike down right on the crankcase so why not on a dirt track? But you have to trail your left leg because of being so low and that didn't feel comfortable. Also, I knew it was dangerous after breaking my ankle in Prague.

In Japan they race – and gamble – on half-mile concrete tracks and lay their bikes low because of the banking. To compensate they have the left handlebar a foot higher than the right throttle hand, which runs parallel with the top frame bar.

I felt that with the spikes you didn't need any leverage with the bars, you could lay it right down until your crankcases hit the ground. The only trouble is when you are as low as you can go you cannot turn left any more tightly.

Turning right was even more serious. The old Indianapolis saying also fits riding with the spikes: 'Turn right and you are dead.' Your options with the spikes are about the same but, with the Japanese bars fitted to an ice bike, you could lean it right on its side but keep your foot forward.

I HAD been to Daytona, in Florida, for several years to ride on the dirt short track at the Memorial Stadium and I fancied a trip back there. I spoke to Jim France, who has always been a motorcycle man, I told him that I was now the World's Fastest Dirt-tracker and asked if we could do a deal.

We did, so I thought I had better test my theory and went to the El Mirage dry lake in the Californian desert with friend Johnny Roccio, brother of my Wimbledon speedway team-mate, Ernie, who died tragically after a crash at West Ham. Johnny thought my idea was mad but, after a few teething problems at the lake, it worked out fine and I was lightning fast.

When I arrived at Daytona there were posters everywhere advertising that a 'mystery rider' was appearing as the World's Fastest Dirt-tracker. In the pits a few people recognised me, but they all thought 'what is this idiot up to?' He's well over 60 years old, grey haired and he picks tonight when the cream of America's dirt trackers are here racing for American Championship points.

My bike was sitting in the pits. It was a standard Jawa 500cc ice bike and was fitted with standard dirt track wheels and tyres. I could see by the way people looked at me that they thought I was either mentally unbalanced or on dope! Five minutes before I was due to appear we quietly fitted the spiked wheels and guards. The American Motorcyclist Association knew what I was doing and asked me not to dig up the inside so I took a line a little higher than I wanted.

The public wasn't quite sure what they were seeing. Even with the wrong gearing, and having to ride a little high, I was more than three seconds a lap quicker than the 600cc American bikes. Let me say quickly that this is cheating but it was lovely that, at 66, I could still get a laugh riding a bike quickly, especially when everyone had written me off as having finally flipped my lid.

One of the old racers came up to me later, after he realised that I wasn't mental, and said: "You never told us you were going to use spikes." I laughed and replied: "You never bloody asked."

Mike Smart, who was helping me, joined me in the fun. We had to pack the bike, as a museum wanted to buy it as the 'World's Fastest.' But first they wanted to see if it really was the fastest. They wouldn't buy it before I rode it in case I wrote myself off on their bike and sued! It is now on show at Barbers Vintage Motorsports Museum in Birmingham, Alabama.

My life and my family had been wrapped up completely in me trying to be the very best speedway rider in the world. Here, I had just done something that was fun and, in one night, I had earned more than I did by winning my four World titles. Where is the justice?

I realised how Evel Knievel had felt. He badly wanted to be a top class racer when he started out. Then he changed direction and earned more for one jump than the dirt trackers did from a whole season. It was fun, but doing it just for money doesn't give you that beautiful winning feeling ... money can't buy that.

I rode a couple of meetings on the concrete in America. The first one was at what was then the World famous home of boxing, Madison Square Gardens, in New York. The promoter for the Yamaha Silver Cup was Don Brymer, a friend who I had met at Daytona years previously. He had delivered all the Yamaha race and show bikes, plus all the display materials for Daytona week.

Junie and I were knackered when we came out of the show and were sitting on the side of a street, with our feet in the gutter, when an enormous truck stopped. The driver, who was Don, yelled: "Do you want a ride to the track?" We nodded and climbed in. The joke came later when Don told me he thought I was Phil Read, the Isle of Man TT champion. I didn't know at the time that Phil didn't have a good name in America. I was the second foreign rider to appear at Daytona after Phil and people were going to make me suffer until they realised that I was a completely different kettle of fish and left me alone.

Don got the money from Yamaha to promote the short track event at the Gardens. At the time the movie *The Wild One*, starring Marlon Brando, had earned motorcycling a bad name and image so Don wanted me to live in New York for a couple of weeks to promote his meeting. It was tough, but being dressed smartly threw the interviewers. Most of the publicity was positive and I felt that a packed house at the Garden did motorcycling a lot of good and proved that the people of New York knew about the event.

The small concrete track was very slippery and we were on standard American flat track bikes, so I had to ride the same style as the Americans.

Kenny Roberts and I were team-mates for AA Racing, from Redwood City, near to where Kenny lived. I got to watch him from up close and he was the best. Every man and his dog wanted to ride because the meeting was at Madison Square. Something like

Taking part in a trials meeting along with Sammy Miller.

200 turned up, just to be able to tell their mates they had raced there. Machine examination started at 7am and the meeting at 8pm so it was going to be a long day.

The time trials started at 1pm and, with 200 to get through, it was going to take some time. Luckily I got mine in fairly early. You are timed over one flying lap so there were no prizes for crashing and I was happy to be eighth fastest. It put me in the second heat from gate number two but, with 12 riders in a heat, it was going to be a lottery.

There was no starting gate, like those used in the rest of the world, so huge responsibility was heaped on to the starter. I was ready to go when he held his start flag high but I knew that caution was required. I didn't make that good a start but the race was stopped to be re-run. The starter said I had jumped the flag so I was the one penalised. This was definitely a hometown decision as far as I was concerned.

I formed up on a third row by myself with the other 11 riders in front of me. I had a large Union Jack on the front of my white leathers so I was easily identified but there was no way I was going to take this rubbish lying down. On such a small track, with its slippery surface, it would have been very difficult to pass at the best of times but starting with 11 riders in front of me was doubly tough.

The first corner of the re-run looked like a war zone, with bikes and bodies everywhere. I simply kept both feet on the floor and went into the first corner twice as fast as everyone else. I was not a happy camper! I was instrumental in bringing down 90 per cent of the riders but, obviously, I dropped my bike as though I had been fouled like everyone else.

I was ready to start the third time, when the 'dodgy starter' had the audacity to walk up and caution me. My answer was easy: "Get out of the way or I'll fucking well knock you down as well." He moved! The fans were getting their money's worth and were venting their anger on to one person, that bloke with the English flag. Out of the capacity crowd of 17,250, maybe 50 people were on my side.

When we had the third re-start all the boys in front of me were petrified that I was going to kill them and they left me plenty of room on the inside. But, after the last crash, someone hadn't done their job properly and petrol was left on the floor. When my front tyre hit it, the bike skidded out from under me. *Sports Illustrated* reported that any crashes on the first lap would be restarted, but there was no way the 'dodgy starter' was going to give me any kind of chance.

When I crashed this time I kept the engine running, remounted and chased the field. I only had to pass one more rider to transfer to the next round as I sped into the last corner. I needed to be a little bit closer to the rider just in front of me who I had to beat. I pointed my bike at him but hit him too far back and, once again, I was on my arse.

The 17,000 fans were cheering so loudly that anyone outside would have thought it was a replay of Joe Louis knocking out the hated German, Max Schmeling. I was really mad. I felt I had been done by a unfair official. Don the promoter came up as I took off my crash helmet. All he wanted to tell me was that my effort was worth an extra 1,000 bucks. I gave the prestigious *Sports Illustrated*, the bible to American sports fans, some great quotes and most of their article was devoted to my dragged out one race.

The report included the following: "You need a hero or a villain and the villain turned out to be Englishman Barry Briggs with a sizeable Union Jack stitched to his leathers … not a bit chastised Briggs blitzed his way into the field … when the flag fell, he caromed through on the inside … none could quite match Briggs' cheeky performance."

Don, I think that the 1,000 bucks wasn't enough. What do you reckon?

Twenty years later I was sitting on the pit wall at Daytona when there was a lull in the proceedings. I heard the announcer say they were presenting a special award to one of the AMA starters. Can you believe it, they were talking about 'the dodgy starter'. Despite the years that had passed my anger rose and I wanted to tell the jerk what I thought of him and let down his car tyres. But I am sure that everyone who was at the Garden that night will remember 'the bloke with the Union Jack on his chest'.

Steve was a good listener but had trouble sliding.

McQueen was one of the boys and wanted to slide a bike

36

A SPEEDWAY bike is a very different animal from any other type of motorcycle. The corners are the most important thing when racing a speedway bike. I learned that at a very early age when I went to training schools in New Zealand. I went slowly down the straights and as fast as I could through the corners.

I taught my younger son, Tony, the right way whereas elder brother Gary did the normal motorcycle thing and landed on his head. Once I took Gary home with a couple of black eyes and Junie wasn't too impressed. Gary is still a good motorcyclist but, unlike Tony, he never wanted to race speedway.

There is a system to teaching people to ride a speedway bike. Anyone who has a brain and listens will work it out quickly. I could have got Kenny Roberts sliding near perfectly within an hour.

We were out one day at a motorcycle park called Indian Dunes that had a small speedway track, about the size of Costa Mesa at Los Angeles. I was with Bruce Brown, who had made the hit motorcycle movie *On Any Sunday*. My house in Dana Point previously belonged to Bruce before he moved a little further north. Bruce wanted to ride a speedway bike, so we took one of my Jawas.

Bruce had just finished his movie and Steve McQueen, who starred in it, was also there with Belgian Roger DeCoster, the multi-World motocross champion. Roger was possibly the best ever motocross rider and also McQueen's hero. They were riding on the adjoining track and joined us.

I hadn't brought any riding gear with me, only a pair of speedway boots and steel shoe for Bruce. It's virtually impossible to ride a speedway bike properly without the steel shoe which you need on your left foot to skim across the track surface on corners, and use with dab if you need a bit of propping up. I started the bike wearing just a tee shirt and a pair of shorts. I didn't even bother with the shoe or helmet as I did a few fairly quick laps to check out the bike and track.

When I stopped Roger was standing there ready to ride, wearing the shoe. He had become a champion by his skill and determination, and watching me zoom around made speedway look easy, which it isn't! Roger kept crashing but wouldn't give in, or give up the shoe. The motocross boys can turn somersaults on their bikes but sliding a speedway bike is a different deal.

Finally he gave up the steel boot to Steve, who was now a little bit detuned as he watched his hero struggle. He was a good motocross rider but suffered the same fate as Roger and kept falling. It was time for Bruce to try his luck and while he was steady, he fell like both his mates. Because there was only one steel shoe, and a lack of time, the boys didn't get much of an idea on how to ride a speedway bike.

They were all good motorcyclists. If I could have spent a couple of hours with them I could have got them circling the track reasonably well by using the speedway power sliding technique. I have seen many good motorcycle racers get on a speedway bike and think it was just going to happen. It never did. It's a knack but, like anything else, it takes time.

Many years ago I had a telephone call from a guy in Canada who

had just escaped from the communist rule in the then Czechoslovakia. I learned later he was a cameraman who filmed the Russian tanks storming into Prague in 1968. He took off for America where he made a stack of dough from the footage.

He was Jan Musil and he rang me in California to say he had seen me race many times in his beloved home country. He had the money to open a track in Vancouver and needed me to run a training school for him. I told him that if he could get a couple of speedway bikes I would be happy to make the journey from California. We did a deal and, along with Junie, I flew to Seattle where I got a rental car and loaded our baggage along with a speedway bike in bits.

We drove north across the Canadian border to Vancouver, which is a lovely city, and we were there for about a week. It was the perfect time of year but his idea of a speedway track was, in fact, a horse arena with very deep dirt on it. I tried riding round but it was impossible. The arena was part of a large horse racing track and there was a dirt-covered car park. I told Jan I could use that and got some road bollards to make a speedway track in the size and shape I needed.

To start with I had the boys sliding round a big Blue-gum tree for a day. I got them sitting on the front of the seat, making clutch starts with plenty of throttle on (to get the back wheel spinning). Then, without closing the throttle (which keeps the rear wheel spinning), they had to lean the bike down a little while at the same time stepping forward between the handlebars, planting their left steel-booted foot forward on the ground. Then the bike would slide around your foot.

If they shut the throttle, the bike would stop spinning and then just go straight. They had to keep doing this until they got the feeling and control of a sliding bike. When they could control the sliding bike, they moved back ten feet further from the corner. At the end of the day, they were power-sliding in control.

On the second day, I mapped out a Costa Mesa style track and ran a complete meeting with the 15 riders. It was unbelievable. Many of them were ex-flat trackers and they all raced good speedway. Unfortunately, Jan never listened enough to my advice that the track surface should be hard and smooth to make it easy to slide on. I had arranged for the Costa Mesa track man to come up and sort out the track for his first meeting if he wanted.

The track was deep when it opened so the riders couldn't use their new skills. They just raced around, not sliding, so a lot of money, time and the project itself, was wasted. Once again I had proved to myself that I didn't need a pukka speedway track to teach kids to ride. I taught my youngest brother, Wayne, in a field in Kent. Son Tony learned on a pig farm outside Southampton.

Dave Nichol, a top motocross rider, told me that when he finished he would race speedway. "It's easy," he said. But, believe me, it isn't. I have ridden and raced just about every type of motorbike. And, in many ways, speedway is the toughest of the lot. You need a lot of balls to do it. You have to rely on the other riders in the race with you, as I found out so painfully in the 1972 World Final at Wembley when I was sent flying by an idiotic move from Sweden's Bernt Persson.

I know that is also true of road racing but the surface is much more predictable and consistent than a speedway track which can be grippy and then slick as ice ten feet later. It can catch you out in a split second. New Zealander Hughie Anderson, the World Champion road racer for Suzuki, helped me one night when I was racing at Western Springs in Auckland. He said afterwards: "Bloody hell, you blokes are just like a heart attack." Looking up I replied "You've got one minute to get it all together, otherwise you finish last."

You have to know what you are doing and have absolute faith in that. The JAP bikes were dangerous because with the long-stroke engine it was hard to keep the back wheel spinning, which is how you keep control. Otherwise they just took off by themselves and horrendous accidents happened because they were bastards to ride. Then the Jawas came along and were much easier to handle. Put today's speedway riders on JAPs and they wouldn't know what hit them!

It's tough to say who is the best motorcyclist I have seen. There are so many disciplines and it's a blurred picture when you think of, say, Ivan Mauger versus Kenny Roberts. There's Malcolm Smith, who has won more than his fair share of six-day gold medals as well as all the Baha-type races.

Dave Bickers was brilliant at motocross, he did it with a lot of balls and heart, and then there was Roger DeCoster with the number of championships he won. Sammy Miller won everything in the trials world before becoming a top class road racer. Arthur Browning hit speedway as a top motocrosser and became really good. Now he's road racing. No motorcyclists have achieved what John Surtees did by being the World Champion road racer and then changing sports to be crowned World Formula One Champion.

But my top man has got to be one of the American boys. If they wanted to be the AMA national No. 1 they had to be a dirt-tracker over a quarter mile, half mile and mile as well as being a TT dirt racer and, of course, road racer.

The winner, in my opinion, is Kenny Roberts. I have seen him win at a variety of races and he was one of the best on the tiny, slippery concrete track at Madison Square Gardens. Then, of course, he was crowned World road race champion more than once, taking on and beating Barry Sheene and the others in their home towns. American fans thought he was special and every time he appeared on the cover of *Cycle News* its circulation increased by more than 10,000 copies.

I used to do scrambling (motocross) a lot and I still have photographs of me going up the hills on one wheel and with no helmet. I just got on a motorbike and felt good about it. It's the same now. There is a tremendous bond between those who ride and race all forms of motorbikes. I've known and been mates with some of the biggest names in the sport.

Geoff Duke was one of my biggest heroes and I was excited when I first met him. He was an unbelievable road racer, as were Mike Hailwood and John Surtees before they went to race on four wheels. I was brought up on the opposite side of the world to Geoff and he was someone I read about in the motorcycle books. You just latch onto heroes and it is the same with all sports. I was into all sports as a kid, including cricket, and Aussies Ray Lindwall and Keith Miller were big heroes of mine.

I used to play soccer in the morning, rugby in the afternoon and then hockey as well. The only thing I didn't like was boxing and that was because Skinny McClintock kept hitting me and wouldn't let me get a blow in! But I am the biggest fan of riding a motorcycle off-road and, as long as God gives me enough strength to hold on to the bloody thing, I'll keep doing it.

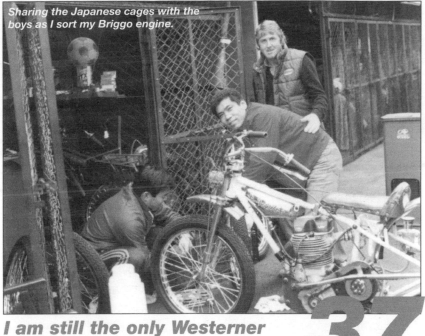
Sharing the Japanese cages with the boys as I sort my Briggo engine.

I am still the only Westerner to tackle Japanese speedway

37

I FIRST got to know about Japanese speedway when I met their Champion, Jimmy Ogisu, in Australia while racing there. It was in the most bizarre situation. I was standing on the inside of the track at Newcastle Speedway chatting to Jimmy in his broken English. The local promoter Mike Raymond walked up saying he needed to speak to Jimmy. After a couple of minutes he was back discussing his clutch.

Later we were told that Jimmy's wife had been killed in an accident back in Japan. I told him how sorry I was at hearing his tragic news and he replied that it was no problem and "I get another when I get back". I hoped something had got lost in translation with his bad English.

Japanese Speedway is as outlandish as Jimmy's apparent reaction to losing his wife. Imagine living in a compound for 120 days a year. Around you are 100 other riders, all working in their own cages, trying to beat you and everyone else. I went to Japan quite a few years ago and met up again with Jimmy. I thought it would be a challenge to make an engine for their speedway racing. Everyone had to use the old Triumph twin-cylinder engines, which were wearing out, although they were mostly running on parts copied from the originals.

I had a couple of trips there with my Briggo four-valve conversion mounted on the Jawa two-valve bottom end. During my last trip there I had the engine bored out to 620cc and it was on petrol not on alcohol as we run on speedway. The final test was to see how my single-stroke fared against the Triumph twin cylinders.

It was a big potential market and was very interesting. The Japanese federation insisted that for the last test I complete 200 laps to prove the speed and reliability of the engine. I shared the 200 laps with Massy Ilzuka, the six-times Japanese Champion. He had been to Aussie once and rode for a couple of months there to gain experience. The track was damp and the old triangular Dunlop type tyres meant you had to commit yourself to the corner. As you fire the bike into the corner it drops onto the slides flat surface, there is no mid-point – the bike is either fully upright or fully cranked over onto the flat on the side of the V shaped tyre.

You must ride it like road racing and be soft on getting on and off the throttle while cornering. The stupid-looking handlebars are just fantastic as they allow you to lay the bike very low, and at that point your hands are level. So when you are on the straights your left bar is up by your armpit and your right bar is down by your bum. One of the best things, it still allows you to keep your left foot forward. In ice racing you lay the bike very low so you must leg trail but with the Japanese bars you can ride foot forward.

Between us we reeled off the 200 laps pretty quickly and I was really embarrassed when I stopped because all the other 15 riders clapped me. They knew who I was, did they really think I was going to slide it? The engine stripped down perfectly but the Federation wanted to buy only this single engine from me and then manufacture their own … the Japanese are sellers, not buyers. It was a lot of work not to acquire any business but racing around this semi-banked track with perfect grip was a real experience. I am still the only westerner to have ridden on these tracks so to me it was a great deal.

Speedway was brought to Japan in 1934 by the American Putt Mossman, It was an instant success right from the off and particularly attracted gamblers, with the first races taking place on horse tracks. The dirt tracks resulted in many riders being injured, which wasn't good for the gambling industry as training the riders took a great deal of time and money. So they finished up re-surfacing the tracks with asphalt.

The huge amount of money involved quite naturally attracted the criminal element in the shape of the Yakuza – Japan's equivalent of the Mafia. The riders are under very strict control and in the early days were jailed for race fixing. It is also alleged that a few who crossed paths with the local gangsters ended up at the bottom of Toyko Bay!

The six special tracks stage meetings around nine days each month. Each is of three to five days duration and all the riders are housed within the stadium compound throughout the event. No communication is allowed with the outside world. The Government make it very clear and state 'that Autorace speedway is for gambling not bikers.' Understand that and you will realise what it is actually all about.

Because of the massive sums of money generated through gambling, the riders are paid very well in return for their discipline and commitment. To appreciate just how well they are paid, go to the riders' car park, which is full of top of the range Mercedes, BMWs, Toyotas and Porsches and even a vintage Bentley. Just like at the training ground of a Premier League soccer club in England!

To become a rider and earn the riches that come with it is tough. The selection process is rigorous and is only open to men of certain ages, height, and weight and they must have been born in one of the six 'home' (track) towns. Also, they must pass intelligence, fitness and co-ordination tests, which have nothing to do with the riding of a motorcycle.

The 24 lucky ones from the 1,500 applicants are virtually set up for life. The special ones then go to the isolated training track at Tsukuba in the mountains for 10 months. They are only allowed home twice in this period of time. If the newcomers think that initiation into the armed forces is tough, then they are about to discover that their teachers are not called the 'Instructors from hell' for nothing. Discipline is the end word. They must do 100 laps a day. The food is basic, they also have no pocket money. All spare time is spent working on their machines.

To keep racing close and the betting difficult, every rider is mounted on identical self-maintained 650cc Suzuki-engined machines using identical Dunlop triangular section racing tyres. Minimal alterations in gearing is the only change allowed. All races at the meetings are handicaps and a rider must perform within a small percentage of his handicap times.

At the end of the season there is the Japanese Championship, open to 88 riders to qualify for a slot in the Golden Race Final. All races here are scratch, and the final is over 10 laps – the normal races are over six. The start of the race is obviously very crucial, stopping cheating is of the upmost importance.

The start line is on the exit of the corner, so the riders have the full straight before arriving at the first corner. Mounted above the

Tony and me became masters of straightening frames for the Japanese boys.

15-foot mesh fence is a 12-foot clock divided into five increments. It takes one second for the large orange hand to move to each of the five numbers.

When the referee is happy that he has the attention of all of the riders, he flicks a switch that lights up five green bulbs, set besides the clock, in sequence. When the first light is turned on, the riders select bottom gear in their two-speed gearbox. When all of the lights are lit, the clock automatically starts the countdown. The middle of each rider's front wheel must be exactly on the start line under the watchful eye of the colourful starting marshal. The front of the tyre is now synchronised with a laser beam only visible on a television monitor in the referee's box.

We watched the race winner on the day, the local favourite, 26-year-old Mitugu Takahashi, collect his cheque for 23,000,000 yen … or $200,000 … or … $1,200 per second. But this was chicken feed to what the government received over the five days of racing – a staggering $49,365.720 ! What could the FIM learn from this?

Massy Iizuka, six-times Japanese champion, gives me the low down.

The implementation of strong rules and the threat of severe punishment ensures that nobody steps out of line. Standardisation of engines is good and keeps the costs down for the riders. The best rider wins simply because he is the best.

There are a new wave of riders on the way through. One rider we met there got off his backside in the short off-season and went to California, bought a two-valve Jawa and rode every day for a month. His name was very difficult for us to pronounce so we simply called him 'Jawa boy'.

He was rated number 32 in his nation and did gain from the trip to California. He asked me if I could train him if he came to England. We agreed and his mate, who was number seven in Japan, came, too. We sorted out a couple of two valve Jawas and descended on King's Lynn for a week. We had plenty of crashes and bent bikes but we managed to keep everything rolling. Jawa Boy was becoming a good speedway rider quite quickly. I thought that he had more potential than his friend who was ranked 25 places ahead of him.

'Jawa boy' went on to win three Japanese Championships, which was worth millions to him, but he had the initiative to go outside the box to improve. Over the years 'Jawa boy' has earned more than all the other riders that I have helped put together.

The riders are well paid but I think it is better to be married to a Japanese speedway rider, as he makes a fortune for you to spend and he is locked away for 120 days a year!

Floyd Landis, 2006 Tour de France winner, was later disqualified.

My dad was a pro cyclist.
I admire the two-wheel boys

38

I HAVEN'T only enjoyed riding bikes with engines. Even now, approaching my 75th birthday and whether at home in either England or California, I still ride a pushbike. It's good exercise and can be a lot of fun.

My dad was a professional cyclist in Christchurch and was the winner of one of the big races there.

English Park in Christchurch had a concrete, banked cycle track where they held schoolboy races and I did a little and then got into cycle speedway and motorbikes. One time I returned to New Zealand and learned that my younger brother Murray, who was a good cyclist, had the sulks about something and wouldn't compete as he was supposed to in a 10-mile race.

I said to him: "Give me the bike, I'll do it," and managed to finish. The sprint to the finish was really scary, there seemed no room with pumping legs and whirring pedals as 15 other guys with no protection and on skinny wheels were throwing everything into it to be first to the line. When there is a crash and they go down they go down big time.

I could imagine me being a bit of a demon downhill racer on a pushbike because, when riding motocross, it is coming down the hills that I most like. I can only imagine what it must be like coming down from the mountains on a pushbike in the big races with hundreds in a bunch.

The Tour de France has to be one of the toughest sports challenges in the world. I was fascinated by a story told to me by Tommy Simpson, who subsequently died because of what he did to his body in order to compete at the highest level.

I met Tommy at a Sportsman of the Year dinner in London and he talked quite openly about taking drugs. He said that you could ride with somebody for nine days, then on the 10th day he's out of the saddle and gone, disappearing as though he has an engine in his bike. He told me that you needed the right drugs to race and he got all the information from a friendly doctor, who was also a fan, from his local hospital, including how to administer it properly.

He made me laugh when he told about a pro-am race in Paris. His partner was a chemist who, Tommy said, he never saw from the start to the finish ... and Tommy was the pro! I have watched the film of him during the Tour de France falling off his bike, getting back on, and falling off again before eventually collapsing and dying. It is so very, very sad because, despite the drugs, he was a tremendous sportsman.

I have read the Lance Armstrong book, how they go out in all weathers, continually training and pushing the limits all the time. It must be tough mentally as well as physically to keep doing that, day after day. In fact, I think that the Tour de France is beyond the normal limits that your body can withstand.

If a fellow racer beats you, or is faster, and you know that he is taking something to achieve this, the question is, do you join them, or be a loser? Unfortunately it seems that Tommy made the wrong decision. Years ago Junie and I were on holiday in Tenerife and staying in the same hotel were Hughie Porter, four-times World Pursuit Champion who was also a top road professional cyclist, and his wife Anita Lonsborough, who won an Olympic gold medal

On one wheel, though not for the first time.

for swimming in 1960. We quickly teamed up and had a great time. Anita taught me how to tumble-turn underwater, all that clever stuff. Hughie was a typical pushbike racer, fit as a fiddle, as you need to be to compete and stay at the top of this really tough sport. He had lost a couple of his mates while training on the open road. He had also suffered being knocked about himself while training.

In 2006 I was watching the Tour de France on television and witnessed what I thought was probably the best sporting accomplishment I have ever seen. I was in England and I phoned Gary in California, telling him to make sure that he watched stage 17 – one of the toughest mountain stages. American Floyd Landis had worn the coveted leader's yellow jersey prior to stage 16 but, for some reason, had a meltdown and completely lost it.

In fact, he had lost a staggering eight minutes on the new leaders and everyone had written him off. Right from the start he attacked and attacked. Finally, the other riders let him go as he was so far down on the overall lead. Not for one minute did they ever think he could keep up that blistering pace.

From then on he simply just rode away from all of his opponents. He continually drank water, also pouring it over his head non-stop. Landis clawed back time spectacularly and by the end of the stage he had actually reduced the deficit by seven and a half minutes. It was unbelievable but, unfortunately, his achievement then became clouded in controversy over whether he did or did not take drugs.

He was subsequently disqualified and had his tour victory taken away, although he has always protested his innocence. I sat glued to the television that day, watching him clawing his way back into contention; I wanted to believe that he did it just by human endeavour, not with the help of stimulants.

Once a year they close the roads in front of our Dana Point home in southern California for a fun-day cycle race. But most of the day is taken up with California's top professionals, including Landis, competing for a fair chunk of money. This year one of the contestants, who was also a motorcyclist, came up and introduced himself as I was watching. We got talking about Landis, who lives locally, and he told me that even when they go out training together and stop for a drink, a cup of tea, or even a chocolate bar, Landis wouldn't have anything in case it contained a prohibited substance.

I like to think that he wasn't cheating that day in the mountains because what he did was just outstanding and will always live in my memory.

No, no, Bernie the track turns left.

The 1972 World Final changed my life but not for the better ... 39

I SET great store by trying to regain the speedway World Championship at Wembley in 1972. It was to be my watershed year. I had ridden in every World Final between 1954 and 1970 but that record-breaking run ended in 1971 when I was knocked out of the championship at the British-Nordic Final stage.

I had been trying to do too much that year and was really a part-time racer. But, in 1972, I decided if I wanted to be World Champion one more time I had to get back my complete focus and re-organise for a serious title assault.

I stayed away from my Jawa agency in Southampton for three months. David Waterhouse, who I brought in to help during the 1960s, ran it for me. I knew that I couldn't run the business and simultaneously expect to win the World Championship. Many times before, while heading out on to the track for an important race, I'd be stopped by a rider or mechanic and asked: "Hey Briggo, your David only sent me one set of valve springs and we had ordered two sets."

It was no good hearing that sort of thing when I was about to race a Mauger, or a Fundin. I had to get fully focused on just winning all my races.

The five riders who had qualified for the 1972 World Final from the British Final at Coventry were Ivan Mauger, John Louis, Eric and Nigel Boocock and myself. During the weeks leading up to the Final we were embroiled in a pay dispute with the Speedway Control Board in the UK. We argued that as we would be appearing in front of a 70,000-plus crowd, the ITV cameras and a worldwide TV audience, we deserved a bigger slice of the financial pie.

We realised that the revenue from the meeting considerably boosted the SCB coffers, which in turn helped to keep a number of British tracks in business.

But the amount of money earmarked for the riders was scandalous against that raised from the meeting. It was daylight robbery. We requested £200 each, a total of £1,000, which even in those days was, frankly, peanuts.

The SCB turned us down and averted a threatened strike by agreeing to raise the issue of appearance money at the next FIM congress. I recall that we met to discuss the situation and to realise the pressures that we were going to be put under by each of our individual track promoters by holding out. The five of us said we were sure we could handle it.

I can still remember having a good laugh at the time as Nigel declared: "If we don't get what we want, I'll go and open a bloody fish and chip shop." However, on the Monday of World Final week, we were dead in the water. Only Ivan and I were left standing against the authorities. All we wanted was £200 each, 200 quid to ride in a Wembley World Final, we were being financially raped!

For me this Final was very special and, for once, the money wasn't the real issue. I was concentrating on winning for a fifth time because I knew it was going to be my last World Final. Having delegated the running of my Jawa business, I was working harder than ever to get myself fitter than ever. My burning desire was to give one more World Championship my 100 per cent attention, to win the title and then ride off into the sunset, just like in the movies.

Unusually I had time to ponder on my strategy, something normally I wouldn't have worried about, I'd just play the cards as they fell but, this time, it was going to be different. Normally, if I won my first race I would take some stopping. Looking at the riding order for the Final I knew it could actually be won or lost in my opening heat. The bookies' favourite, Ivan Mauger, was on the outside of me on the start in Heat Two, and obviously he was the danger man.

But every rider who reaches a World Final is capable of winning races, if not the Championship. You can never, ever underestimate the opposition. But this one time I was ready and felt on top of my game. I felt that the two Russians in my first race wouldn't be a problem as long as they left me on my bike. They would be nervous in front of this partisan crowd and would be unlikely to produce their best at this early stage.

A little soul-searching was also taking place, looking back trying to figure out how Ivan had beaten me in past encounters. The answer was simple, he did so by beating me from the start. I could count on the fingers of one hand the number of times he had passed me from the back.

We had never done well riding together as team-mates, our World Pairs results were dismal. His messing around at the start, the pushing of the tapes, the tapes being held as the referees tried to stop or catch him out, really knackered my concentration.

The referee at Wembley that Saturday night in 1972 was a German, Georg Transberger, who knew both Ivan and me very well. I formulated a master plan in my head. I had come up with the exact tactics that I was going to use to win Heat 2 and which would, hopefully, unnerve Ivan.

As the meeting approached I kept my body weight to a minimum, it was the best I could do. My strategy was also to keep the weight on my bike to an absolute minimum. I wore no tee shirt, only my jockstrap and a pair of thin nylon socks. I used a pair of thin goatskin car driving gloves, which were light but offered no protection, but, why worry, I didn't intend being behind at any time during the meeting.

The dressing room at Wembley that night was surprisingly quiet with just a greeting between some of the foreign riders. I had got my position in the tunnel, where the pits were situated, for my bikes. This was the same position I normally had at Wembley.

Watching the first race, I felt that the referee seemed quite quick releasing the tapes after the green light came on, which indicates to the riders that the race is about to start and the track looked a little greasy.

Then it was time for Heat 2 and my first appearance on the track.

I was pushed off first from the pits as usual and rode slowly to my allotted number one starting gate position. As this was only the second race of the night I had no problem finding myself a clean bit of dirt closer to the inside of the gate. I wanted as much room as possible on my outside so the Russian rider there couldn't nail me before the race had even got under way.

The one thing I would have liked before this crucial race was just a quick look at Ivan's address book under the letter 'T' for Transberger. If I could have seen this, my plan would have been even more secure.

I thought back to a time in New Zealand when I had to get a phone number from Ivan's address book.

I noticed that many of the entries had a 'P' against them and, looking closer, I realised it was always alongside the names of speedway referees. I asked him: "What is the 'P' for that you've got against these names in your book?"

"Oh, Briggo, I shouldn't have let you into my filing cabinet. You can see it's all the referees that we race with around the world. The 'P' denotes whether he is a prick or not, which tells me whether he will mess me about on the starts."

We laughed until our bodies ached. Later, at tracks when the stress level was high, I'd just say: "Sprouts, is this idiot today a 'P' or not?" He would just laugh and shoot back: "Tomorrow I'm going to add another 'P' to his name because on today's performance he's definitely a double 'P'." Immediately we would burst out laughing, which blew away all our stress.

Sitting at the Wembley starting gate, in front of 70,000 people, with the two Russians and I ready in our positions but with Ivan still to arrive, which was his normal tactic, I couldn't help but wonder whether the name of Transberger had a 'P' against it in the 'Mauger guide to referees'. Was Transberger a 'P' or not? I was about to find out.

Ivan finally arrives at the starting gate, feeling that he is in control. I smile under my helmet as I think to myself: 'Right, Sprouts, let's see if you can handle this lot?' He is up to the tapes, then he's back, again and again digging all the time trying to unnerve his three opponents. The starting marshal finally has enough and signals us up to the tapes.

Ivan and I have been in this position a 100 times before and he knows that I go straight up to the tapes. But this time I am sitting well back and not moving. Glancing across I can see he is nervous and asking himself: 'What the hell is Briggo doing?'

He takes another couple of crafty looks, the poor Russians have been ready to start minutes ago. Then, unlike now, there is no two-minute time allowance after which any rider not ready is excluded.

Finally, I've broken him as he pulls into his starting position before I do the same. My eyes are glued on the green light.

On this occasion my starting technique was different. I sat forward on my bike with loads of throttle on. My eyes are on the green light, my peripheral vision will pick up the slightest movement of the tapes and then I'm gone. Within split seconds I will know if Georg is a 'P' or not. As I approach the tapes, the green light comes on and almost immediately Transberger hits the start button and I'm away.

Yes, he is a 'P'. I've outfoxed Sprouts as Georg was watching Ivan and he didn't give him time to do his double shuffle. A new Wembley track record with Ivan blown into the weeds and left trailing 25 yards behind. That was the first race under my belt.

The black number five on my back seems a good omen, hope it's going to last. I am thinking clearly and am supremely confident but not overly so and can only hope that luck stays with me.

Beating Ivan in my first race didn't surprise me. It has taken me a long time to work out his system. A small movement on the start means a couple of crucial lengths to the first corner. Ivan was smart and always got the referee's attention and would normally

Me with Dave Waterhouse, who was such a huge help in running the Jawa business in Southampton.

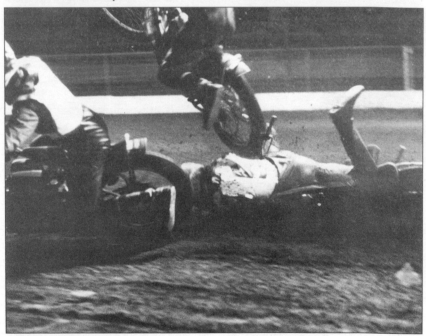

Ouch! Lucky it wasn't my head.

beat even those he categorised with a 'P' because he worked out what they had in mind. It was a sort of double bluff.

If the referee was a 'P' who was always trying to catch him, Ivan would anticipate his move and beat him to the draw. He would have made a lethal gunslinger in the old days as he simply worked out all the angles.

The race, fair or foul?

Heat 5 was my next race and featured two more Russians and a Swede, Bernt Persson. I didn't have any preconceived strategy for this race, just make the trap and get out of there. I made a pretty good start and stayed a little off the white line into the first corner that, at Wembley, cuts back sharply. I wanted to turn early to get speed exiting the corner. Just before the middle of the corner, where I was about to turn sharply, a bike appeared out of nowhere. Without hitting me and helping him to turn, the rider wouldn't have made the corner.

I immediately thought it was one of the Russians as a bike going in a straight line is always faster than one sliding. Sometimes you can misjudge and pick up unexpected grip when you don't want it. If this happens you must respect the safety of the other riders and, as a professional, you should be able to control your bike and not just knock down your fellow competitors.

However, it wasn't a Russian as I thought, but the bloody Swede, Persson, who simply mowed me down, taking my bike and part of my hand with him. The race was immediately stopped with me laying in a heap on the track. Persson was not excluded from the rerun by referee Transberger, as he should have been, and there was a long delay while I received treatment from the first-aid guys.

Just 15 minutes earlier I had felt everything was going to plan. And now this. Ivan came running over to me while I was laying there on the track and said: "Come on, tape your fingers together, you can still make the re-run." When I looked down I didn't expect to see half my hand almost gone … it was a real mess.

I have a big heart and if there had been even half a chance of going out for the re-run I'd have been there. "I'm afraid I can't make it Sprouts," I said, "but you can do one thing for me. Make sure that fucking Swede doesn't win it."

Sprouts just smiled and said: "Briggo, I'll sure try, and good luck, see you at the hospital later." And with that he disappeared out of the craziness that was surrounding me at that moment.

When I looked back later at the TV replay of the incident, I can see that I wasn't too smart. I left a little too much room up the inside after making a decent start. I know that I was a tough and determined rider but I also knew right from wrong and just how far you could legitimately push your opponents without going over the top.

During my 20 plus years of racing, you would have trouble finding any rider that I have deliberately knocked clean off his bike. Mind you, we need to forget my first year in England when I was learning the ropes and occasionally had rushes of blood and got in over my head. I am not claiming to be an angel as I'm not.

The TV replays reveal how lucky I actually was when sent crashing to the ground directly in front of the two Russians, who couldn't avoid hitting either me or my bike, as both were laying there in the middle of the track.

Valeri Gordeev used my back as a launch pad and did well to jump off his bucking mount as it flew through the air, lurching violently towards one of Wembley's lethal steel lamp standards. His bike bounced over the wire-mesh safety fence and ended up on the greyhound track, just inches from the crowd overlooking the exit to the first corner.

Somehow, Gregori Chlynovsky and his bike managed to stay upright but his back wheel struck me a glancing blow as he squeezed past me on the inside. As Chlynovsky came into the corner he threw his back wheel at me which was the right thing for him to do in those circumstances and I have no problem with how he handled the situation. I believe that the back wheel of Persson's bike inflicted the serious damage to my left hand.

Over the years I had taken my share of hard knocks but this immediately looked serious. Being taken off the track on a stretcher and into an ambulance is not a good sign. As the ambulance doors slammed shut I was surrounded by quietness as it was driven down the famous Wembley tunnel. It then dawned on me that the dream of adding a cherished fifth World title to my name was in tatters. I had got myself into a position to emulate old rival Ove Fundin's then record of five World Championship victories and who's to say that I wouldn't have done so, but for the reckless intervention of Cradley's favourite Swede?

While I was on my way to the operating theatre at the Mount Vernon Hospital in Ruislip, having initially been taken to West Middlesex Hospital where they were not equipped to deal with my serious hand injuries, Ivan defeated Persson in a run-off to equal my tally of four World crowns.

I lost a World Championship but I was fortunate not to have suffered a far worse fate when those two Russians hurtled towards me as I lay helpless in their path. I dread to think what might have been the outcome if Gordeev was three inches either way and my head had been the launch-pad. I could have so easily suffered serious head or back injuries. Riders have been killed in less serious-looking crashes than the one that stunned the Wembley crowd into silence in 1972.

I have never spoken to Persson about that Wembley crash and

Tommy Jansson, the Swede who was told by Bernie Persson how to 'beat' me!

my regard for the Swede hasn't been enhanced in the 37 years that have elapsed since my last ever World Final race.

The one printable comment I made about Persson was that he is a "jerk". There were rumours that Bernie Persson had said that the only way to beat me was to knock me off, which I believed. A week before the meeting I saw I had Persson in my second ride. I knew that I must be on my guard, as in my mind I knew he might be an over-the-top danger to me, a dirty bastard.

The only problem was the computer in my brain had switched off and completely forgotten these crucial thoughts of only a week ago. If it hadn't, Persson would not have got me at Wembley. So, the Wembley crash was down to me as I wasn't up to speed in my thinking. I didn't blame him at the time because I knew I'd made a mistake by giving him room. I let him off the hook. I shouldn't have done but I did. I was fair. He didn't need my bit of the track.

He has never spoken to me since which, in my view, confirms my opinion of him as a jerk. I also think he is a coward because he withdrew from all the subsequent meetings in which he would have to face me. But a few years later Ole Olsen ran a meeting in Denmark for the old champions. Persson was there and the bikes Ole provided for us were crap. I was doing okay but nothing special.

In my race against Persson I was cruising round when, all of a sudden, he came ripping under me again. But this time he couldn't escape and I hit him so hard he just about went into the North Sea. You don't have to run people down to show how tough you are. I hit him hard and he stayed on his bike but I never saw him again.

A broken neck zeroes Tony's thinking as regards the safety fence.

Speedway is a tough sport and safety must come first

40

THE most dangerous thing about racing a speedway bike is when it's wet and you can't see. You can always find a way around other problems. Speedway must be a regular event and Wimbledon promoter Ronnie Greene thrashed it into all of his riders that he wanted to run his weekly meeting no matter what.

We had very little say but, to me, riding a speedway bike in the wet is no real problem as the throttle works two ways, on and off. All I wanted was to be able to see where I was going while Ronnie didn't want to give his supporters the chance to find anything better to do every Monday night.

Nowadays, even with the help of the dirt deflectors, the tail seems to be wagging the dog. The Grand Prix meetings run no matter how bad or wet it is but, at some of the normal league meetings, there can be a rain-off because of the whims of the most outspoken riders. If you go through the records I am sure you will find there are significantly fewer accidents on wet nights because every normal-thinking rider has a fear factor.

There have been many safety improvements since I stopped racing. I have a scarred body to recommend the first, the ignition cut-out, which is a great idea. It has become mandatory and I cannot understand why someone never thought of it years sooner. Once, when I was being admitted to the hospital in Invercargill, New Zealand, there was a piece of soiled cord hanging from my right arm. If my brain had registered this simple piece of cord into my memory, I wouldn't have been in hospital that day.

My crash occurred when testing my new lay-down bike. The throttle jammed when it was flat out. I was only doing starts, trying to find out what was wrong with the engine. A jammed throttle caused me to have an horrendous crash. My bike was fitted with a cut-out which was quite new to me. Looking back, I think they were being used in my last year of racing in English speedway. I don't ever remember having to use one, as you need to crash to gain the benefit.

Whenever I was in trouble I would try to throw my bike away because that is what does the damage. While the wheel is still spinning and you throw your bike away, it will fly away from you, but when the cut-out is pulled it kills the engine and the spin and the bike doesn't leave you but loops on top of you. A real bad deal. What I did was an automatic reaction, which had been ingrained into my brain over years and years of racing. This was my act of survival and I had become pretty good at it, saving myself from serious injury on numerous occasions.

If I could have turned on my brain, for just a split-second, I could have saved myself the hurt and pain, plus recovery time, simply by pulling the cut-out cord tied to my wrist. Instead, I got into a fight with my out-of-control bike which ran out an easy winner. It really thrashed my body. If ever, God forbid, you see me in my swimming trunks, you will see an 18-inch scar on my back where they opened me, to have a peep inside. A small piece of bloody cord could have saved me from that.

Chain guards were also really important. There is more than one speedway rider wandering around with fewer fingers than they were born with due to accidents that happened before the guards were compulsory. I'm afraid, though, that if all tracks had to be completely safe, there would a shortage of them. Most are not purpose built and it's tough to fit them around football pitches or inside dog tracks. It is extremely difficult to get the safest track shape.

I did a deal to run a special Golden Greats meeting at Wimbledon. Their greyhound track is sacred so the position of the safety fence determines where the track must be. The Control Board track man came and spent a load of money putting in a beautifully shaped inside corner which would have been great if you could have put the fence where you wanted. I tried to work out how I could fix it. I ran out of ideas so I got Alan Bridgett, the best track man in the business, down from Scotland. Even by spending a considerable amount of money, we still couldn't come up with the answers.

The damage had been done when the inside and drains were laid. So I had to cancel my meeting, a sure winner financially. There was no way I was going to ask the boys to race on a track where it was virtually impossible not to hit the fence even by yourself, never mind when trying to race on it.

There were a couple of other tricky tracks, which I felt were potentially dangerous. One was my old home track at Hull, which was terrible to try and pass on. For the first couple of months there, I hit the fence hard a few times before the penny finally dropped. Then I realised what it was all about, after the first corner, passing was virtually impossible except if your opponent made a very bad mistake.

The best thing as a home rider was that no visiting rider really liked the narrow Hull track. When a top team came to the Boulevard, co-promoter Bryan Larner would come into the dressing room and apologise to us all for the state of the track. He would say: "Sorry lads, a truck came in late with a load of new dirt and just dumped it in piles on both bends. We've tried to smooth it out the best we can." You could visually see the visiting team squirm.

In my heart, I hated Newport. It was square and not nice to ride but the minute you admit something like that to your inner man, you're halfway to defeating yourself. I would mentally convince myself that it was okay, and I had some good meetings there.

Exeter is the other one that a lot of riders didn't fancy all that much but I did all right there. It was funny the night in 1973 when New Zealand faced Poland at the County Ground. You would never ride the inside line at Exeter fast. Except local Goog Hoskin, who held the track record for many years. He was a real white line man but he was an exception. The high banking on the corners got steeper the further you went outside right up to the fence, and was the fastest way round. Our Kiwi team got together before the meeting and agreed that we would con the Poles, who hadn't seen the place before. We decided, no matter what happened, we'd only ride round the inside white line.

All was going to plan as the Poles tamely followed us round for the whole match, which we won comfortably 53–25. But that all changed in the second half when Zenon Plech, their best rider, hit a bump and suddenly found himself out wide where he discovered the dirt. Then the heat was on because the Poles realised that the outside was where you needed to be riding at Exeter all of the time! We had to laugh as Zenon was fast enough to win the second half final, but was not a winner in the match.

Track safety can only get better. I look back in horror at some of the tracks I have raced on. The riders need safety but, unfortunately, when speedway was at its best, with enormous crowds and plenty of money coming through the turnstiles, nothing was put back into tracks, especially the safety fences.

When I did the Donington Museum's Hall of Fame, I made up a list for the 'Lest We Forget' memorial. More than 100 riders had given their all, their lives, for speedway. I'm sure that if you checked the statistics, you would find that over 90 per cent of them were victims of the killer safety fences.

If anyone appreciates the need for the highest possible safety standards, it's my younger son, Tony, whose promising career was cut short at the age of 19 when he broke his neck on a post in a crash at Coventry in July, 1981. It was halfway through his eventful second season with Reading Racers. The problem was the uncertainty of this type of injury. We didn't have any idea whether it would take weeks or months for him to recover. Doctors didn't even know if Tony would ever walk again. For what felt like an eternity the only part of his slender body he could move was his eyes. Thankfully Tony, now 48, had inherited the Briggs' fighting characteristics and made a full recovery.

We were going to run some indoor races in Europe. The first thing needed was a fence that was flexible and yet safe. Tony, after plenty of attempts with different designs, came up with an air-fence second to none. He attacked this project with gusto, fuelled by remembering the pain and heartbreak from his broken neck.

I have seen some bad crashes in which, if they had happened in my times, the rider would have been seriously injured. But, with the presence of an air-fence, the rider simply stood up, dusted himself down and was ready to go again. The air-fences are so good that even the bikes can come out of a horrendous crash without a scratch.

I think that racing has improved, too, because now a rider can afford to take chances of passing around the outside, right on the fence. If anything happens it's no problem as there's a big soft mattress there to catch you. However, I don't agree that you should be rewarded only by scraping around the fence on every lap. The best and smartest rider is the one who is able to get around the inside without losing his speed. There is a new kid on the block who is a future World Champion, given the touch of luck that everyone needs. He is the Russian Emil Sayfutdinov, a born racer who is dynamic around the inside. He sets himself up perfectly going into the corners and he simply uses any bumps for added grip without losing any control. It's just unfortunate he's not British. A rider that constantly roars around the fence is not going to make it. To me you should only throw in an outside pass as a shock move when it's absolutely necessary.

I have gone into the dirt deflector in more depth in another chapter. For it to win the 'Gold Medal Approval' from such a great starter as Ivan Mauger, who stated publicly that the deflector was one of the biggest major improvements to come into speedway, was praise indeed. Of course, I wouldn't disagree because I was the smart arse who invented it!

I wouldn't say that the four-valve engine was as bad as painted. I feel that to have the best racing on the English-type tracks you need an engine with about 55 horsepower. The old JAP engine produced around 45bhp. You could get more but it stressed the engine and then came the troubles, and blow-ups, which put a big dent in your back pocket. The Jawa two-valve engine was as near perfect as possible, but to be perfect you needed about five more horse power. A 550cc engine, rather than 500cc, would make the difference, giving you the flexibility to make a pass on the outside more possible.

When I started running and riding in the Golden Greats we used Jawa two-valve engined bikes. First of all I tried to slip around the outside of the rider in front, which I could have done with the four-valver, but Terry Betts just roared past me on the inside. I was trying to travel a longer distance by going around the outside and, simply, the two-valver ran out of power and speed.

Nowadays, you have so much power and speed that not only can you pass your opponent on the outside, you can go around the outside of the stadium without losing speed. Today's bike has around 70 horsepower, which is far too much and dangerous. Riders tune their engines for the best performance and then they have to find a way of detuning it to get what I consider their most important ingredient in riding a speedway bike, which is grip. That is the reason I came up with my first lay-down. Horsepower is one thing, but what wins in my book is grip. Ronnie Moore and Ove Fundin were the masters of grip but the rider I think was the best of all was my old Wimbledon team-mate, Gerald Jackson.

Jacko, at times, wasn't even flat out until halfway down the straight. I learnt my lesson early on at Wimbledon. I would have just had a good meeting there and thought I now had the answer to speedway. Then I went to Birmingham, which was really slick. I kept the throttle flat-out for all my races. Not only was I last every time, I was so far behind that I didn't even need goggles!

I have gone more deeply into the lay-down bike in another chapter. I made one simply as a personal deal to give me what I thought was an unfair racing advantage. Looking back, their introduction was one of the worst things to happen for speedway. They have pushed up the running costs ridiculously and don't add one thing to the show while giving the riders big headaches trying to balance their books.

Thousands and thousands of pounds are spent to get the bikes to go faster. If the rider parked next to you in the pits is spending this type of money, and you want to beat him, you are forced to spend to try to be competitive. It is a complete waste of money which, in the end, has to come from the spectator's entrance ticket. Getting fewer and fewer paying customers makes it tougher for everyone involved to balance their books.

When everyone has the same powered engine, the best rider would still win and the worst wouldn't. If I could have the money that I have wasted on tuning, and I did most of it myself, I would be rich!

The Golden Greats worked this way. All the bikes were the same, all the engines were standard and all were serviced or tuned at the same time. All the frames were straight, every bike had a new tyre at the start of the meeting, but by the time the final came all the bikes had knackered tyres. No matter what, the winner was the best rider 99 per cent of the time. The Golden Greats provided great racing at minimum costs. All of this was done by us 'old farts'. Just imagine what a job the kids of today could do.

To me, the perfect answer to lowering the high costs of speedway, while producing the best racing, is for each track to buy 20 engines, detuned Jawas, or GMs producing 55bhp. All riders should arrive at the meeting two hours before the starting time. The referee would make the draw, with the two team managers in attendance, to select each rider's engine for the night. Then the mechanics would bolt the engine into the rider's own frame for the meeting and, afterwards, the engines and carburettors would be cleaned and returned.

These detuned engines would run without any maintenance for a minimum of 15 meetings. The cost would be low to the promoters, the riders would have virtually no cost, and the best man would still win. The savings would be unbelievable. All the engines would have to be logged properly with all tuning being carried out at the same time.

The Golden Greats meetings proved it works perfectly with very little aggro from some of the best riders and egos in the world who had won more than 50 FIM gold medals between them.

BRITISH speedway has gone foreign with many teams not including even one Englishman. The question everyone asks is: Where's the new English World Champion coming from? When I came to England the rule was two foreign riders per team although I think that being a Kiwi qualified me as a Commonwealth rider so we were okay. I think a rule should be brought in now to limit how many foreign boys can be in each team because, as the number increases, so the chances of an English champion decrease. In today's world there is probably an EU rule that makes it impossible but, even so, the Swedish and Polish leagues restrict the use of foreign riders. With so few places available in the teams for young English riders, their chances of making it to the very top are nil.

A couple of years ago the Poles had what I thought was a good idea – every team had to include two home under-21 riders. Then it was moved to one of any nationality. The system made sense but, in practice, there was a problem because the Polish under-21 riders were treated like superstars. All tracks courted them as a good young rider meant team success. The rider was being paid ten times his worth and had all the trappings of wealth. Then it was back to the real world when they weren't eligible for the under-21 team spot any longer and their whole life changed. Some had serious crashes, trying to up their pace to save a team place, but much more serious was that at least two riders committed suicide. You may ask, is speedway that important?

At present Denmark seem to have the best youth policy with Erik Gundersen doing a great job. The respect shown to him by all of his riders is terrific and respect is a thing that is very difficult to find in today's world. I'm still waiting for someone younger to give up their seat to me on a bus!

The Swedish youngsters are not far behind the Danes and there are a few Aussies coming through, even though they don't seem to come from any set training schemes. But where are the English? Everyone points to Tai Woffinden, who is climbing up the speedway tree, but he has still quite a way to go yet.

In the 1970s England had a wealth of talent and there were two outstanding talents who were going to bridge the gap in a carry over period left by the retirements of top riders. There was the loss of the controversial Kenny Carter, who was British to the bone and who could have carried his country's hopes on his shoulders for many years. He got under a lot of people's skin, but one thing for sure was that he went to a speedway track for one reason – to win, not to pussyfoot around. He would do whatever it took, he certainly wasn't there to make friends.

Then his head was turned by something which, to this day, nobody can quite understand. It turned a special speedway rider into a murderer, who then committed suicide. It was a sad end for England's big hope.

Mark Loram won the 2000 World Championship Grand Prix but then his luck took a seriously bad turn through injury. In fact, it was worse than bad, it was diabolical. Whether we'll see Mark racing again is not clear but his outstanding talent and big-heart are missed badly today.

The Grand Prix is desperate for an English challenger. The championship could be full of Scandinavian riders in five years time, plus a couple of Aussies and the Russian, Sayfutdinov. Polish speedway went crazy with the wages they were laying out in recent years and it forced up the money being paid in all countries drastically.

Don't get me wrong, though, because I don't think a speedway rider can be paid too much. But if the sport falls flat broke on its face because of these costs, then it has helped no one. Promises are one thing, but getting the money into your bank is a completely different story. Many riders who were promised the big money have not been paid so, in many ways, it was just fool's gold. England was where my full-time job was. Maybe, at times, I wasn't getting paid my worth, but it made me a far better rider.

Also, it was in this country where you made your name and you could cash in on that by racing abroad. I think it is sad when boys leave England for the greener pastures. Then I smile when I see them slinking back because they need English speedway. It's a pity that, sometimes, they don't return the favours that English speedway has done them by making them stars.

We had to go to a practice session the day before a World Final but, for me, the only reason for it was to help the media get bums on seats and to make the event successful, which it always was. You did wheelies from the start and would try whatever was needed to help the sport. We all knew that when race day arrived everything would be different anyway. If there was a meeting the night before the Final I would be there riding. It may sound stupid but I was a speedway rider, and I tried to treat the Final as just another Sunday international meeting.

WHEN I compare the old-style 20-heat World Final with the Grand Prix series, which is spread across the season, I believe that while most fans and promoters prefer the one-off event, I appreciate the bigger picture. I think that for the sport to grow around the world, the GP is the better way to decide who wins the championship.

I think it was harder to win world titles in our day before Ivan came along in the late 60s. There was Ronnie Moore, Ove Fundin, Jack Young, Bjorn Knutsson, and Peter Craven, so you had to be in top form and make no mistakes, because there was very little between us all ability-wise. Of course, an engine failure was fatal, everything had to be right for you to be the No. 1.

The GP would have suited me much better as I would have had the chance to grind down the opposition over the course of a season. Even on my off-nights, I feel I could still have managed three or four second places and won the race that matters at the end of the night, which is what the GPs are all about.

To me it is unfortunate that today's stars, and future ones, will never savour or experience the thrill of racing and, of course, winning World Championships beneath the fabled twin towers at Wembley in front of 80,000-plus fans as I did in 1957 and 1958. I must say though, it certainly was far from being one of my favourite race tracks, it was tough to race and win from behind there.

I won my other two titles in Gothenburg, both with maximums, in 1964 and 1966. The latter was when I created history by becoming the first rider to win a World Final aboard the Czech Jawa-ESO machine. It ended the JAP's stranglehold on World speedway.

LOOKING at my life it looks pretty full. As well as winning four World Championships, I enjoyed being on the other side of the fence when I was co-promoter at the 1982 Los Angeles World Final, and then came up with the idea of the Golden Greats, which was great getting all of your friends and foes together.

It was your's truly who came up with the idea of having the throttle cable over the top of the handlebars rather than underneath. On many occasions I have stumbled across these modifications as the direct result of pain stimulating my inventing juices. During my first World Championship meeting I went roaring under Kiwi mate Peter Clark and was about to run into him. I thought 'bloody hell' and shut the throttle to stop me flattening him. Unfortunately, as we parted my throttle cable was caught over Peter's back lifting handle.

As the distance between us increased it pulled the cable which opened my throttle flat-out and took both of us through the Wimbledon fence. Next morning I re-routed my throttle cable over the top, which is how it is done by all riders these days.

The dirt deflector was invented from necessity and the Wonder Wheel (track grader) is, I think, a great idea. The swinging footrest came about because of my long legs. A low footrest would dig in and cause me to crash into the rider inside of me. I could have shut the throttle, but I didn't fancy that, so the swinging footrest was born.

When I first made it there was a photo in the Motorcycle News. I shudder when I see it now, it looks as though it was made by a caveman but it worked. The Briggo silencer made a huge difference to the power of a speedway bike. I was the Jawa agent, and their silencer was rubbish, but worked well on the Weslake. So with my mate Roy Forfitt, an ex-grasstrack sidecar racer, we came up with the first Briggo silencer. It also helped that Roy worked at the Southampton University sound vibration department.

Then came the American Carlisle tyre, which was the best. It was consistent and, if you wanted grip, it was always there. The FIM and Barums didn't want it and I had to get a court injunction for it to be able to be used at a White City World Championship qualifier. Then the Carlisle was deemed to be too wide, so I made a machine using a grasstrack swinging arm and David Waterhouse – who worked for me – ground them down. At the end of the job he looked like an Indianapolis winner with his face covered in rubber and beautifully clean were the goggles that covered his eyes.

They were undoubtedly the best speedway tyre but were banned when a top rider did a deal with Barum and the FIM. In my view it would have been good to have had the big motocross manufacturers involved, so we came up with a motocross-speedway bike to be used exclusively in a championship series, with 10 or 12 riders in a race, that I was going to run without any interference from the ACU or the FIM.

With just five changes we could change it from a motocross bike into a speedway one. We would find our own riders and make stars of them. I would make all the rules and if they didn't work I could change them. Then I looked in a mirror and asked myself if I wanted to spend the next three or four years getting it up and running. The answer was no but the bike tested well and the whole project stood a chance.

I have also had a record shop and a driving school in South London and, of course, gold and diamond mines in Liberia. At times I have felt like the 'Mad Inventor' but it is all part of the fun and the spirit of the chase.

More recently I have invented a special putter for golf which I call the 'magic wand'. Fighting the R&A, golf's governing body, was like battling the FIM in days gone by, but I finally got approval for it. Looking back, perhaps the name wasn't quite in keeping with what is required in golf but I have had a request from a professional to make him one.

I have had a finger in more pies than Mr. Kipling. I must admit though that not all my countless business ventures have been roaring successes. But who cares …

I now understand better, after losing Junie, that life is for living. It's a one-time experience and not a rehearsal. The globetrotting and adventuring that I've done over the years have always been interlinked in some way with my unquenchable love of riding motorcycles.

I still love nothing better than to put on my crash helmet and all my Wulf motocross crash protection gear, jump on my 250cc Yamaha and take off up into the mountains near my California home. My Kiwi upbringing, which made me careful with money, dictated that I made it tough even on myself throughout my life, especially when it came to spoiling myself. When riding for fun I would always get by with any old bike that I had lying around.

But, for my 70th birthday, things took a turn for the better when my boys and Jan treated me to a brand new enduro-style Yamaha machine with an electric start and a special suspension system. Sometimes, when I'm back in the States, I'll ride twice a week and some of the places where I go can be physically difficult.

I ride in places where I shouldn't really go – on the fire-breaks in the mountains, up really steep hills that are full of large, loose rocks. It's quite easy to get into tricky situations. Now that I have grown up (hey, I'm only 74), I can stop and pull myself out of the situation and look at it more clearly to plot how I'm going to get out of my current, self-created problem.

The last time I went out riding by myself I encountered a steep and rocky two-mile uphill run. I was so completely knackered at one point that I had to stop. After a five-minute rest, and having taken off my helmet to cool down, I managed to get out of this tricky situation. Later that day I spoke on the phone to Tony, in England, about what had happened. He laughed and said: "Briggo, don't feel bad. I tried three times to get up the damn thing and, in the end, I turned round and went back down."

There is nothing like a 74-year-old fool. I never once thought of turning round and going back down the hill. Sad, isn't it! Luckily, I have no problem laughing at myself. Is it too late to learn? I thought that my hip replacement in 2007 might slow me down a little but, up to now, it hasn't affected me that much.

To me the greatest gift in the world is to retreat to the hills on two wheels with my boys, Gary and Tony. That's really living.

My football connections came in handy for my hip problem as I got to know Arthur Cox, Kevin Keegan's former assistant at Newcastle, Manchester City and England. He put me in touch with the then Arsenal and England physio, Gary Lewin.

He has been really great and with the Arsenal doctor, Ian

Beasley, I got everything checked out. The answer was that even though my left knee was knackered, it was my right hip where the trouble lay. It would take some believing but the rugby-playing Arsenal surgeon was a fella called Tim Briggs. He had played against the All Blacks and loved telling me that they were really dirty players, but brightened me up by adding that the French were even worse.

I've fallen off my bike a few times since but it hasn't done any harm to my new hip. I put extra padding over it in my motocross pants and it seems to work well with the extra protection. My left knee is still bad, but I've been managing the problem as best I can

This is the same climb as used in the Briggo Sports Relief Charity Ride.

by doing a series of specific exercises every other day for the past six months. But I should get it operated on soon.

Looking back, I have been so fortunate to have emerged relatively unscathed from what I guess has been something like 15,000 speedway races.

I've always loved riding bikes and I will until I kick the bucket. I also loved racing my speedway bike even though you were expected to win, just like magic. How lucky can you get? And to get paid for doing it, too! The California hills will be seeing plenty more of me for as long as I can remain fit enough to sling my leg over the bike.

I HAVE sorted out another tough task for myself, which will probably be my last appearance in front of the British speedway public. I was at the meeting at Sheffield this year for the Speedway Benevolent Fund but had already decided to do something for charity.

While in California I passed through the ranch where Tony and I lived when he was starting his US speedway assault. Bruce Brown has since sold it to Dick Marconi, a former sports car racer and a very successful businessman. Dick had a car museum, near Costa Mesa Speedway, and I think he had more Ferraris than there were at the Italian factory. He also promoted boxing matches at the museum for the Children's Charity and raises more than $1,000,000 a year.

It got me thinking. What could I do to make some money for something that I believe in and where the money would be appreciated by the recipients? America was not the place to do it, as speedway is very small there. It would have to be England. That day at Sheffield provided the answer. I saw these young men, who should have been at the peak of their physical life. But it had been snatched away, causing them to spend the rest of their lives in a wheelchair. There was the answer, our boys in the wheelchairs. They all are inspirational and, for them, life goes on.

One year the BBC organise and promote the Red Nose charity, then (in 2010) it's the turn of Sports Relief. I talked to them about doing a charity ride and secured an agreement that the Speedway

Riders' Benevolent Fund would receive 25 per cent of the money we raised.

Often money for charity goes into a big hole when it is distributed but I wanted to be able to determine exactly where some of it went. I'm sure that those who contribute will be happy, too. The SRBF will allow me to divide our 25 per cent take into equal amounts for all our boys in wheelchairs, so I feel really good about that.

How am I going to raise this money? Well, it's quite simple. It is all in my head and a couple of the major parts are in place. The response has been fantastic.

Starting in March I intend riding, off-road as much as possible, from John O'Groats to Poole Speedway. I will be stopping on the way south at about 10 speedway tracks, making collections en route wherever possible. There will be a special meeting at Poole where I will try to establish myself as the fastest man ever around the track. I will re-start out of Poole in June and will hit another five tracks on my way to Cardiff's Millennium Stadium and the British Grand Prix on July 10.

I have been asked by IMG, the Grand Prix rights holders, if I would like to finish there with a couple of laps. I thought why not, plenty of good speedway people are going to be there and I am sure they will have no problem putting hands into their pockets for such a great cause.

It will have to be well organised to secure the dates and permissions from all the tracks for it to work. A major motorcycle manufacturer is supplying the bikes and, when I come into most stadiums, I will have a well-known personality from another sport riding with me as well as our own speedway champions.

The main thing is to raise as much money as possible, and for me to squeeze one last hurrah from my well used body. Recently, I did 350 miles in three days in the Cumbrian hills. I managed it quite well but I will have to get myself together pretty well to complete 10 to 12 days on the trot without too much trouble.

I am also trying to arrange a day's ride in the north, and another in the south, where supporters will have the chance to ride with us off-road for the cost of a pretty expensive T-shirt.

A close-up of the Briggo Dirt Deflector.

Ivan reckons I deserve a medal for inventing the dirt deflector

41

I'LL never forget the day I had to call off a Golden Greats meeting at Swindon, even though the sun was shining. I wouldn't ask the boys to ride in the conditions we had that day and, at the same time, it wasn't fair on the public to cancel, especially as two coach loads of fans had come all the way down from Edinburgh.

The problem was that the track was waterlogged after heavy rain and Swindon was notorious as being dangerously slick when wet. The throttle work two ways, on and off, when you are racing. But you have no choice with your cyes, either you can see or you can't, and once you are filled in with dirt, that's the end of your race. This rain-off at Swindon inspired my idea for a dirt deflector, a device to prevent the riders behind from being blinded by flying, wet shale.

The deflector has been a major factor in the improvement of speedway in recent years. Even Ivan Mauger, who was a great starter and less likely than most to need one, has stated that it has been one of the best things ever invented for speedway. It has saved promoters thousands of pounds through not having to rain off so many meetings. The riders have also benefited in several ways. Cleaning their bikes is easier to start with and all of their equipment has a much longer life because of the disappearance of the sand blasting effect from the spinning back wheel of the rider in front. The most important aspect is that the rider's vision is near perfect in all conditions and therefore cuts the danger of racing in the wet dramatically.

I fell out with so many people over the deflector. Then, of course, officialdom allowed others to copy my idea and they produced inferior imitations. The reason was that you 'couldn't have a monopoly'. Are they saying that if someone invents something that is beneficial it can't be used until someone else does the same thing? That's rubbish! I only wish we had had the deflector in my racing days, especially when I was one of the five riders on a 20-yard starting handicap in the mid-60s.

The deflector has saved many Grand Prix meetings from being cancelled. That is very important as they must be run if at all possible because of television coverage, which is worth a lot of money to everyone involved. The deflectors would be even better if the stated rules on measurements were enforced. Just watching from the sidelines I can spot the badly adjusted ones. Also the rubber 'O' ring should only be passed for racing if they are at the proper tension. The 'O' ring is very inexpensive and, if I was organising the Grand Prix, I would issue each rider with four 'O' rings each in a special GP colour, which would be returned after each GP. The blinding dirt would be considerably lower with better vision for the riders. With the new 'O' ring and the correct adjustments all riders would be hit by the same amount of dirt as their opponents.

Where the deflector is not as its best is when the track has a lot of water laying on top. Although it is still forced down by the flap there is still a lot of spray flying, even from the rider's front tyre.

The approach to riding in the wet was different when I was a kid. Promoter Ronnie Greene's attitude, when he brought us up at Wimbledon, was: "Hey, you've got to race. If you don't ride this Monday, people are going to find something else to do the following week." He was tough on us but, in the end, you just think to yourself 'okay, it's wet, but it's the same for everybody'. I rode as hard in the wet as I did in the dry.

When I introduced my first dirt deflector I encountered opposition not only from promoters but also from many riders who, I feel, should have known better. The hassles I had over my deflector were an unhappy part of my life. The Speedway Control Board, the British Speedway Promoters' Association and the International Motor Federation (FIM) never troubled me too much because they didn't really understand the racing, bikes and equipment. Many are just pen-pushers who change the rules for the sake of it.

What upset me most was the opposition from the riders who got them banned for a year because they were blamed for causing crashes. It was also claimed that if you were following another rider you could run into them. Those complaining were a couple of crap riders who really needed kids' outriggers so they wouldn't fall. Whoopee, now they had a scapegoat for their crashes, the dirt deflector!

Looking back, I think I was very badly treated as thousands and thousands of races have been run with none of the troubles the riders said were going to happen. I don't think the name Briggs helped me either! Tony found that, too, when he came up with his No Pain Barrier air fence which is now used at many tracks all over Europe. While people accept you in speedway as a rider, they don't want to know you as a businessman.

After doing the FIM tests on the longtrack deflector at Herxheim, Germany, I got back to England and was bothered that three or four times in a race a bike would suddenly propel dirt 10 feet into the air. Something was badly wrong. I had designed the deflector for a speedway bike with a solid back end. I finally worked out that the problem was the upward movement of the deflector's swinging arm. It was really dangerous.

I told the FIM about the problem but all I got was a letter from their lawyers telling me it was the wind that was blowing the deflector up, and everyone was going to use Jawa's speedway deflector. I withdrew my speedway deflector for longtrack use.

Who was I to tell the FIM technical committee what was needed? Hey, I was only the bloke who invented the bloody thing. How could I possibly know better than them?

Tony asked me: "Dad, your speedway deflector is the best by far so why not forget the hassle and do just as Jawa (the Czech bike company) have done and use the speedway deflectors with the modifications to fit the longtrack machines." There were two answers to that. The first was that with the speedway deflector fitted on a longtrack bike, every time the suspension worked, by hitting a bump or a rider dropping into the seat, the rider behind could be blinded by the dirt.

The art of riding longtrack was missing the dirt. If it 'got you' you were in serious trouble. Many boys had been killed by the lethal, flying dirt. The moral is, if you know where the dirt is coming from, dodge it in all circumstances. But if a machine in front of you is fitted with a deflector you were lured into a false sense of security that the dirt isn't a problem. Wrong, as I had seen and proved. I made a longtrack deflector that worked perfectly. The present FIM rule would have needed only one word added to make sure the longtrack deflector was 100 per cent perfect. The missing word was 'maintain' 35mm clearance from the ground.

The second reason was the legal liability. If someone was seriously hurt, and it was known that there was a deflector that worked properly, and they were using your speedway deflector, you'd get your pants sued off. Business is one thing, liability is another.

Jason Crump came moaning to me at New Zealand's World longtrack championship: "Briggo, look at my bloody bruises?" Jason, don't tell me your problem, tell Jawa. It's their deflector. It is sad because I have watched longtrack racing virtually disappear but deflectors are only one small part of the problem.

Years ago most of the World Champions rode on grass and longtracks at the weekends, which was fantastic for the sport. Nowadays, the top speedway boys ride in leagues in Poland, Sweden, and Russia at the weekends and are normally spoken for.

To me, grass and longtrack racing made life more interesting and profitable. It was part and parcel of your trade. Sometimes you encounter riding problems you must solve instantly. Just watch Crumpy do a longtrack manoeuvre, which comes from his early grass and longtrack days.

The German grass and longtrack scene really misses Egon Muller but where are his successors? Love him, or hate him, Egon was box-office wherever he appeared. Unfortunately, to me, longtrack is basically a game of who has got the most to spend on their bikes is a winner.

The main ingredient is the engine and its power from the gate to the first corner. The most important type of power is needed when you select second gear because it's then that the engine must retain its horse power. Also, the overall weight of the rider and bike is very important. The lighter the total load, the less weight an engine has to accelerate.

The Jawa factory once told me that it takes one horsepower to propel one kilo of weight. To bear that out, Denmark's Erik Gundersen, who had done very little or no longtrack racing, came to Herxheim in 1980 and beat the hell out of all the longtrack champions. Gundo was a great starter and so light the bike thought he had fallen off! It made the pull to the first corner so easy.

I loved the longtrack, but I was too big and heavy to be a serious threat for the World title. I just about made it in Yugoslavia once but lost out to the lighter Muller. If I had got my nose in front I would have made it because the leader out of the first corner can normally dictate the race. A good longtrack race is just a fantastic fast ride on a motorcycle.

FOR a decade and more Ivan Mauger and myself, both New Zealand lads born on the South Island at Christchurch, had been the cornerstone of Great Britain's World Team Cup challenges.

The competition was introduced by the FIM in 1960 and it was obvious from the outset that the English Auto Cycle Union would rely heavily on their colonial cousins for the bulk of their points. Indeed, had New Zealand existed as a World speedway force in their own right during the mid to late 1960s, there's no doubt a team including Ivan and Ronnie Moore would have brushed aside one comprising only English riders.

I became the first Brit to score a maximum in the Final at Vienna, Austria in 1963. I had a good day and scored 12 of our team's 25 points as Ove Fundin's Sweden maintained their dominance. When the Brits were crowned team champions for the first time, at Wembley in 1968, Ivan led the way with a maximum while I managed to add seven. The scores of the English trio in the team were Nigel Boocock ten, Martin Ashby eight and Norman Hunter three.

After victories for Poland and Sweden in the following two seasons, Great Britain regained the crown at Wroclaw, Poland in 1971. Ivan and myself, along with top Aussie Jim Airey, more than played our part but it was the solitary Englishman, Ray Wilson, who deservedly grabbed most of the plaudits with an historic maximum. The six points I scored that day took my tally to a record-breaking 71 from 10 final appearances. The hand injury I had sustained in the 1972 individual World Final at Wembley ruled me out of the team event in Germany later that month. But Mauger's 11 points did much to ensure back-to-back successes for the Brits.

But the Kiwis and Aussies, who had done so much to put Britain at the top of the World speedway tree, were discarded completely from 1973 onwards. I was taking what proved to be a year out of league speedway, but Ivan was aghast at being dumped by the British powers-that-be in favour of the new generation of rising young English prospects, spearheaded by Peter Collins.

We did have the last laugh, even if we had to wait for six years after England had decided to go it alone to pull off one of the biggest shocks in the history of the sport.

No-one gave little New Zealand any chance of winning the World Team Cup in 1979. I was retired by then and the team was led on track by the 39-year-old Mauger and managed by Trevor Redmond – my legal guardian when I had arrived in England in 1952. We used all our powers of motivation to produce superhuman efforts from the less celebrated Kiwi riders and New Zealand rose to unprecedented heights.

After knocking out England at the first hurdle in atrociously wet conditions at Reading, we took care of the emergent USA in the

Inter-Continental (semi-final) round and then beat defending champions, Denmark, in the final at London's White City.

It remains the most sensational upset in the competition's 48-year history and is one the now depleted Kiwis are never likely to repeat. Larry Ross top-scored with 11 and was beaten only by Denmark's maximum man, Ole Olsen. But there was strong support from Mitch Shirra (10) and Mauger (9), while Bruce Cribb (5) weighed in with crucial points.

We were very motivated in the pits where Trevor, myself and the non-riding reserve, Roger Abel, drove the boys along with smiles, abuse or a kick up the backside. They were unbelievable. We won it with virtually the only five riders available. We got Mitch steamed up by saying how Olsen was always messing him about and, just think, you are better than those bloody Danes. Mitch walked out onto the track feeling 10-feet tall.

Cribby was a bit different. We told him: "Hey, take Sprouts's (Ivan's) bike and go and beat them up for us Kiwis, not forgetting your Maori brothers." He was colossal, his comment when the Kiwis were declared the winners was priceless: "Fucking hell, five points and I'm a fucking World Champion!"

The points Cribby scored made a massive difference to us as we were crowned Fucking World Champs. Larry didn't need much firing up as he was in top form and was half expected to get points, but encouragement has never hurt anyone. It was just so unreal and, in fact, it was the real deal. We won two qualifying rounds and then the Final itself.

Ivan didn't score a maximum in any of the World Team Cup meetings that year but his bikes were used by everybody else in the Final. He got knocked off in one race at White City but, when the others saw him bounce back up again, they were really pumped up and responded accordingly. In those days the boys would listen to people like me, but now they would just say: "Who the hell are you, you old so and so?" It took such a great, collective effort from everyone involved that it couldn't be repeated. You couldn't possibly have motivated the guys as well as we did that day ever again.

After 16 hard-fought races, New Zealand emerged four points

clear of defending champions Denmark, who were the huge pre-meeting favourites. A cheeky grin always lights up my face when I talk about winning the World Team Cup. It was a lot of fun – and it pissed off Ole, too, didn't it!

THE rumour had got around that I was going to ride again and, finally, I announced a comeback at the start of the 1983–84 Australasian season. I also unveiled the first lay-down speedway machine and declared that I would re-enter the World championship.

Back on the old trail again! I was 49 and had ridden my last British League match, for Hull, eight years earlier. I spelt it out that it was no straight-forward return to big-time speedway and I wasn't just coming back merely to go through the motions. The comeback, brief as it was, heralded a mechanical revolution in the sport that wouldn't fully evolve for another decade.

My idea was to switch a standard Italian GM engine from the conventional upright position to a horizontal angle. I was racing in New Zealand and staying with one of my best mates, Tommy McCleary. It was bed time and, as I like to read before I go to sleep, I found a book called 'Tuning For Speed' by Phil Irving which caught my interest. There was a chapter on the lay-down Manx Norton motorcycle which, at the time, had never raced.

I already knew about the success of the Italian lay-down Moto-Guzzi and, seeing the Norton lay-down, I wondered why not for speedway. I couldn't find a piece of paper quickly enough to begin mapping out the design of a special lay-down speedway machine.

I re-entered myself for the title race for the first time in seven years and my build-up, back home in New Zealand in the winter of 1983-84, was shrouded in secrecy. I wanted to keep this as much to myself as possible. The sport's previous mechanical revolution, which had happened just over a decade earlier, never got the success that it deserved for the designer and rider, Neil Street and Phil Crump.

Nobody knew anything about the lay-down engine I'd built especially for speedway. It was a bit like when Crump suddenly appeared with Street's first four-valve Jawa conversion in the mid-70s. They brought it over to England and proved that they could thrash everyone.

If Streety had kept riding it, and doing well, I don't think it would have done any harm. But I think it was a mistake for Crumpie to continue using it because he started to get beaten, not very often but often enough. Rivals realised that he wasn't unbeatable on the new four-valver after all. If he'd ridden it for the first month of the British season, then put it away and brought it out again just before the World Final, the other riders would have been at a serious disadvantage mentally. They would have thought that the only time they had raced Crump and the four-valver, the duo were unbeatable. He could have been World Champion that year if he had kept his unique engine under wraps.

As I was retired from active racing, the only time that anyone could beat me, and see how good the lay-down was when they raced me. Nobody had seen anything like it before, although plenty of people kept trying to take photographs once I started to race it. I was convinced that my horizontal motor and our purpose-built, aluminium-plated frame had the beating of all the standard upright speedway machines. I was sure and confident that my revolutionary new-style bike could help me win my fifth World title in 1984.

It handled much better than the standard upright machine but I gave away a little of the handling and made it short, for grip to the first corner. My feeling was that if this bike was as good as it felt out of the start, then even at my age no one could pass me. But I fell into my normal trap, too much habitual experimentation, which was not needed. This flaw was to prove my undoing again.

The lay-down idea was the best, but then I changed too many things. Instead of it being chain-driven, like all other speedway bikes, I made it gear-driven. I then made a slippery clutch, like they use on a dragster, to reduce wheel spin at the start and, to cap it all, I decided to move away from the proven tube frame to a non-tubular aluminium frame, which gave me plenty of headaches.

I had got myself together pretty well fitness-wise and was ready for the battle. After being in retirement for seven years, I felt good as I flew through the South Island final at Christchurch early in '84, dropping my only point to Larry Ross. The reason I was riding again was that I felt I was going to make every start, and was going to win by using my experience and by being smart. But every time I dropped my clutch the engine virtually stopped. I would then quickly dip the clutch and it was away like a rocket. But, by then, I was behind and having to take chances to pass people.

In the New Zealand Final at Wellington, Mitch Shirra and Ross qualified while I finished fourth – behind David Bargh – on 11 points. The overall level of competition was not high but I had to ride really hard, and was forced to pass more riders than anyone on the night. I went close to going by Larry when we met in our first race but you don't get prizes for being the nearly man.

The problem was the carburettor, everything else was good. The short frame and the low centre of gravity of the bike was great for passing. I would lay the bike very low into the corners and the grip was great once I picked it back up. I don't think I was living a dream about winning the World Championship again. I'd got myself very fit and was ready for another serious crack at the title. Larry only just beat me in the New Zealand Final and everyone was wary of what the machine I was using could do. It was fast, but not off the start.

In hindsight, I desperately needed to have got through from the New Zealand Final, as then I would have had the time to sort out the carburation problem. The next round, at Belle Vue, was still another five months away. The lay-down idea, fitted with a normal clutch and chain driven, was a winner. It was not until the mid-90s, when Hans Nielsen and other top-liners switched successfully to lay-downs, that my theories were proved correct and bore fruit on a grand scale.

Looking back, the lay-down bikes have probably been the worst thing to happen to speedway, for a long time. They have pushed the costs right up and now riders are paying £500 just for a carburettor, which is absolutely ridiculous.

Why I made the lay-down was purely to have a last fling at the World Championship and to give me an unfair advantage. It was an expensive, new trend that didn't help speedway one bit. I'm sorry now that I started down this road because of the added expense to the riders.

Me with Dorothy Charles-Batson.

Handicapping the 'big five' was a major deal but did it work?

42

IT was decided to spice up the domestic scene in 1963 by making the world's top five, Ronnie Moore, Ove Fundin, Peter Craven, Bjorn Knutsson and myself, start our league races off a 20-yard handicap.

But I had reached the end of my tether midway through 1964, despite the extra start money we were being paid. We were being beaten by riders who would never have done it under normal circumstances. This, in turn, had the effect of boosting their confidence, which was the last thing wanted by the handicap riders whose number eventually dropped to three.

It wasn't just the psychological factor. It put even more strain on my motors and it was becoming more dangerous having to chase and try to pass the other three in every race, especially in the wet. Who wanted to spend all day cleaning their bike, leathers and boots to get ready for a meeting before driving to the other end of the country knowing you were going to be showered in shit at the first corner?

I didn't think about the effect these defeats were having on my average – I never worried about averages – but I'd had enough of it all. The handicapping was bought in to quell the old saying that 'first from the gate is the winner'. I felt it was good for speedway, but not for us five. The other riders thought we were being paid a fortune but I would have been happy if there was no handicapping.

It was surprising but most of the boys were fair in the year it was introduced. However, it was diabolical in the second year with everybody fencing you or really closing you down. It wasn't racing. To pass anyone at Coventry was more than difficult. Bjorn and myself had to get under our opposition and generate the speed and grip to pass. That meant we had to get half our bike over the concrete white line, which is legal. They fixed us one night by placing the track rakes just inside of the white line around the whole corner. All hell broke out!

From five riders, first Ronnie broke his leg and retired and then, tragically, Peter Craven died after crashing at Edinburgh. Any racing is about confidence and, when Peter died, I felt he was down. Without it you don't react the same as you do when in top form. It was a complete accident, so we don't really know whether or not he would have reacted differently.

Peter's death hit me really hard. It was made even harder because George Hunter, who was involved in the accident, was staying overnight with us in Southampton when they decided to switch off his life support machine. Obviously, Georgie was crippled with grief so it made a big dent in my life.

Ove and I were riding crap and my overstretched bikes were constantly breaking down. The only one it hadn't affected was Knutty. He was riding on a wing and a prayer and I thought he was next on the list.

I was at Swindon one wet night and I'd had enough. Cecil Telling was the referee and I trusted him. He assured me that if I rode that meeting, he would speak to the Control Board on the Monday morning about abolishing the handicap system. Thankfully, they did. I would definitely have retired there and then if they hadn't scrapped it.

I think, in its way, it did help speedway. I hope so as the price paid was too much.

I was one of the first speedway riders to race on the continental grasstrack scene, mainly through my brother, Murray, who was riding grasstrack in France and Germany. The promoters over there were constantly asking him about me riding in their meetings.

Once I started, I was in increasingly big demand on the continent. I had developed a big fan following and with this established reputation as a known international star rider, it allowed the clubs and me to cash in. I was always rushing off after Swindon's Saturday night home meetings to ride at the big Sunday grass and sandtrack meetings all over the continent where I earned some real money.

I had to try to do well at every track's annual big meeting as I wanted to be invited back the following year. I was lucky because, before each meeting, the fastest riders in practice had to make an attempt to establish a 'Bahn Record'. Even though I didn't always have the best bike, I'd grit my teeth and hang on with the throttle flat-out in a real balls-to-the-wall deal! If you did well in the Bahn Record, it would make up for any problems you ran into in the meeting and it really helped to secure next year's contract.

One year I broke my arm just before I was due to race at Osnabruck, but they still paid me the same start money to appear in person at the track. It was to prove to the big crowd that I hadn't gone to race somewhere else instead and that I really was injured! It was all about building a good reputation and always giving full value for your start money.

THE Swedish city of Gothenburg hosted its first World Final in 1964 at the magnificent Ullevi Stadium which had a great track for a racer. Nobody could beat you by bullshit, they really had to race. The starting gate was a long way from the first corner and, as I was quite a bit bigger and heavier than most of my opponents, the pull to the first corner was tough for my engine to get me there in first place.

An amazing experience visiting Buckingham Palace to receive my MBE.

I had been to the workshop of Sammy Miller, one of the World's best ever trials riders, in New Milton, which is 30 miles from Southampton. I was admiring his famous Ariel trials bike and he pointed out how light he had got it with the clever use of a titanium and aluminium alloy. So I got to work and I got my bike's weight down by 25 pounds.

I had to sit carefully as the seat was a thin piece of titanium with virtually no covering. The engine bolts were aluminium and all steel bolts were wasted away. Also I had no fuel taps, everything was cut to a bare minimum. I won the meeting easily with a 15-point maximum, two ahead of Fundin.

This victory catapulted me back into the limelight and introduced me to a world beyond speedway. I was voted into second place in the BBC *Sports Personality of the Year* show amid protests that the Beeb had rigged the viewers' poll to ensure a win for Mary Rand, Great Britain's first female Olympic gold medal winner and the darling of the Tokyo Games.

I had been at the top of my sport for a good many years and plenty of people knew me because speedway was great on TV and there were only two channels at that time. Supporters from all clubs were in broad agreement that a vote for me was also a vote for speedway and I felt the BBC treated our sport with disdain.

Mrs. Dorothy Charles-Batson, Wimbledon's best-known supporter, led the protests, claiming I had been cheated out of the award. Her suspicions had been aroused initially by a set of voting figures provided by a helpful BBC administration clerk. But then Broadcasting House closed ranks. Mrs. Charles-Batson's persistently probing questions were met with an impenetrable wall of silence so she asked high profile TV host, Bernard Braden, to take up the matter on his weekly late-night ITV *Braden's Beat* show, which investigated consumer complaints.

But neither Braden, nor anybody else, wanted to fight the cause of a leather-clad speedway rider when the rest of the nation was happy to celebrate the achievement of the Olympic Golden Girl. I was embarrassed, as I thought the Olympics were the pinnacle of amateur sport. Speedway was a professional sport, like golf, football and motor-racing. It was second to football for the number of spectators who paid their hard-earned wages to follow their chosen sport.

I was back to haunt the BBC mandarins two years later after regaining my World crown at Gothenburg, mounted on the new Czechoslovakian Jawa-ESO machine. Again their annual sports award bash sparked cries of fix from the speedway public as I had to settle for second place again, this time finishing between the England and West Ham United star duo of Bobby Moore and Geoff Hurst.

I was proud of my standing in my sport and that, even by the BBC's admission, I had polled more votes than the celebrated hat-trick hero of England's greatest soccer triumph. Some sceptics suggested that, possibly, I'd even had more than the iconic World Cup-winning captain, too.

As viewers were deciding whether to cast a motor-sport vote for the likely 2008 winner, Lewis Hamilton, I chuckled when I was reminded of the conspiracy theories that abounded around the BBC's flagship sporting awards show in the mid-60s. I think I won it the first time, in 1964, when Mrs. Charles-Batson complained.

But, as much as I love speedway, I don't think it's bigger than football, especially the World Cup. That was really big, even to me. I can only guess the votes were split between Moore and Hurst in '66 because they played for the same club, whereas speedway fans got together to vote for me.

I have a good appreciation of most sports. I was a keen, all round sportsman when I was young, and now a twice-a-week golfer. I got to know many footballers, and met ex-England football captain and manager Kevin Keegan in his playing days at Southampton.

There is an amazingly ironic postscript to the 1964 BBC *Sports Review* business that left many people in speedway feeling cheated. One of my neighbours in California, and now a close friend, is a certain former long-jumper and British Olympian. Mary Rand!

My Junie was Mary's bridesmaid at her last wedding and we got to know her well. She's great and was a real heroine to Junie, who was a good high-jumper herself in her youth.

I felt humble when the *Retro Speedway Magazine* wrote: "To be called a sporting celebrity really embarrasses Barry, and his name helps people to remember him. The alliterative name and BB moniker conjure images of a child's all-action superhero. Imagine what modern-day marketing experts would have made of Briggo, how they could have projected his name in lights had he been at the top of one of the mainstream sports today."

They also wrote: "British speedway is 80 years old this year and, though we've championed a number of greats in that time, none have quite made the lasting impact that Briggs has. It's been said before that if you conducted a survey along any High Street in Britain, and asked the general public to name one speedway rider they've heard of, Barry Briggs is the name most would give first. Not Mauger, not Moore, not Fundin, not Craven, not Olsen, not Collins, not Nielsen, not Rickardsson. And certainly not Pedersen."

Yeah, I think when your christian and surname begins with the same letter it helps people to remember you more easily – like Mickey Mouse, Donald Duck and Bally Bliggs don't you think?

EARLY in 1973 I became the first speedway rider to be awarded the MBE in the Queen's Birthday Honours list. The invitation was for only three people but our request for a fourth was granted so we could take both of our boys.

The pomp and ceremony was great. The large room where the presentations were made was regal and had a balcony halfway round. An orchestra was playing all the while, the paintings and décor, everything in fact, was first-first class. Even the toilet handles were gold. The upkeep must be unbelievable as every nook and cranny was spotlessly clean. It was an experience of a lifetime.

I also appeared in front of millions of ITV viewers as the subject of *This Is Your Life*. You could get carried away with yourself with all this going on and I probably did change a bit with all the extra publicity and attention I got. But I hope I didn't change too much.

My Wimbledon promoter, Ronnie Greene, was very good at keeping my feet firmly on the ground. He'd have me in his office every month and tell me: "You're getting big-headed and this and that." I didn't think I was getting too big for my boots, I was just a kid who was having a good time. I've got photographs of me on my speedway bike leaping off jumps that I'd made in the Wimbledon Stadium car park, which was made of gravel.

Now I look at them, and other things I got up to, and think 'you idiot!' But Greeney used to get on to me about stuff like that. He would never let me get too carried away with success.

By trying to be normal I got to meet and know a lot of people from other walks of life. I'd go to different sporting functions and people would say 'he's all right'. But I didn't know what they were expecting me to be like in the first place. If some of my best friends told me I was acting big-time it would get to me. Luckily, I have plenty of pretty loyal friends who could tell me that stuff. It's also a two-way street. That's what proper friends are all about.

IN summing up my on-track career and my life in general, I believe that winning the World title was much tougher in the days of the one-off final because there were so many other genuine contenders.

When I hung up my leathers after a last fling with Hull Vikings in 1976, only Ove Fundin had won more world titles than me. Since then Ivan Mauger and Tony Rickardsson (mostly in the Grand Prix era) have surpassed Fundin's haul with six to their name, while Hans Nielsen has equalled my tally of four.

Now I'm getting on in life, I have found the biggest thing is your health and losing my Junie bought that sharply into focus. I am content, I've enjoyed myself and have had a very interesting life. I have given everything I could to my sport which has helped to make me financially secure.

I think I was a good rider who could do more than most on a speedway bike. I was always flat out – half the time in trouble – but the people liked it. They stood by me because they knew they would always get my best efforts. Promoters hated paying guaranteed start money but they didn't mind paying 50 quid, or whatever it was, to me because they knew that I wouldn't just turn up and cruise through the meeting like a lot of other blokes.

It wasn't ripping off the public when we used to split the money in second-half finals because it was the last race of the night and a chance for us to put on a good show. What did annoy me was when other riders didn't try in the final, especially those who pulled onto the centre green after only a lap. I was probably giving away the money 80 per cent of the time because I was good enough to have won most of those rider-of-the-night races anyhow.

To split the money with people who couldn't even be bothered to try was unacceptable to me.

Some would accuse me of being a tight bastard but it wasn't a question of being careful with money. My attitude was that if I was prepared to race hard and put on a show for the fans, then why shouldn't the other three in the race do the same?

The boys who did that were mainly the journeymen riders who treated speedway like a normal job and to bank their money without spending too much on their equipment. That was okay by me, but they should still put in the laps as it's the public who were paying their wages every week. The worst thing personally was that I felt they were taking the piss out of me. I was born to race but I always believed it was my duty to give my all every time I left the pit gate.

I don't look back with special fondness on any particular period

British Olympic Champion Mary Rand presents me with the British Championship. Junie later became Mary's bridesmaid in California.

in my long career. There is not one special moment, nor one World Championship victory, that I would single out as the happiest day of my life. I feel I was very lucky to make it through the minefield of speedway racing virtually unscathed plus the fact I was given the opportunity to make a living by riding my motorbike. That made me very happy. I had a hip replacement last year, my left knee is a bit knackered and I might need that doing. But I still ride in the hills near where we live in California whenever I get the chance.

When I started out, it never entered my mind that I'd become World Champion one day. Once, when we were in South Africa, I think it was the Aussie rider, Alan Quinn, who I overheard saying: "And, of course when Briggo becomes World Champion." I thought to myself: "What the hell is he on about?"

I remember being injured before I ever made a World Final and I was watching one on television. Ron How reared at the start every time and I remember thinking: "If ever I get there, I wouldn't do that." I never thought it was a case of when I get to a Final. Before I made my debut in 1954, it had always been to me a case of 'if ever'.

Just before Paul Newman died of lung cancer in September 2008, he asked a couple of friends to take him to Lime Rock raceway in America so that he could fulfil his dying wish to have one last blast round the track at full speed in his favourite Corvette GT-1 race car. They carried him to the car and, after he'd completed a couple of laps, they lifted him back out again. Newman had that big smile on his face. He had obviously got 'that feeling' just one more time in what was his last roundup.

It's one thing fulfilling a last wish in a racing car, as Newman did, but riding a bike might be something else altogether. Perhaps my boys will have to fit stabilisers to keep me upright! Well, that's how I feel about motorbikes.

Speedway has been great to me and, even now, I can't believe that I was lucky enough to get paid for doing something that I would have paid to do. As I said before, I feel blessed.

Swindon, British League Champions in 1967: Back row, left to right: Barry Duke, me, Mac Woolford, Dick Bradley, Pete Munday and Clive Hitch. Front: Boby Kilby, Mike Broadbank and Mike Keen.

Happy days at Swindon in 1967 and back at Blunsdon in 2009

43

REDUNDANT Southampton riders were forced to go their separate ways when the track closed in 1964. Bjorn Knutsson joined the West Ham revival while I had my pick from two or three tracks. I chose to remain in the much more convenient south, and in our Southampton family home, by signing for Swindon where I was a Robin for nine years.

I won two more World titles while I was there, in 1964 and 1966, and hope I helped to put the unfashionable Wiltshire town on the international sporting map. Also, I was lucky enough to lead the club to their first league championship in 10 years in 1967. We had a great bunch of people there. Promoters Bert Hearse and Ted Nelson were good to me and I gave them my all. I liked the track because I could race blokes around there, it didn't matter who they were.

I enjoyed great individual success during Swindon's reign of supremacy. I had six consecutive victories in the British League Riders' Championship, from its inception in 1965 to 1970, as well as six British Championships. I always tried to lead from the front, just like Ronnie Moore did in my early days at Wimbledon. Winning Heat 1, and beating the opposing No.1, struck many a psychological blow in your team's favour.

Swindon also had some ordinary seasons in the bottom half of the British League table during my time with them. To have a winning team takes a lot more than me scoring a maximum. I still think I was a better rider than Ivan Mauger with everything level, but I wouldn't argue that he was a better team man. He usually had two or three bikes with him, which he could lend to his team-mates if necessary, and he had the time to gee up the other boys.

If you were a good starter, like he was, you could come in after a race and not have much to do other than just wait for your next outing. I was not a great gater so I usually came back covered in two feet of dirt. I always seemed to be busy cleaning the shit off my bike and changing bits on it. I was always in too much of a rush to get ready for my next race to be pussyfooting around with the other blokes in the team.

My stay at Swindon was another good time in my life because my team-mates and the fans were a great bunch. My barometer was my two boys who loved going to Swindon. I'm not sure what they were up to when I was racing but they certainly liked it there.

I can't leave my days at Swindon without praise for Martin Ashby who, like Terry Betts, never won what his abilities warranted. Martin was a good rider technically and understood how to pass people without just hooking them up on the fence.

I DON'T really get to visit many speedway meetings in England these days but watch it on Sky Television whenever I can. The 2009 Elite League Championship play-off final between my old club Swindon and Wolverhampton was, of course, of great interest to me.

I was lucky enough to be in the Swindon team when the Robins won the British League championship 42 years ago. It seems like a lifetime for a top club like Swindon not to have been crowned champions again since those misty days of the past.

I knew by reading the Speedway Star that the Wolves were a

very strong team and had a tactical genius in Pete Adams, the old crafty Wolf himself. Being a Swindon man right down to my core, I was trying to be realistic and thought that with the leadership of Leigh Adams we would run the Wolves very close on their home track in the first leg.

After I had watched the Sky coverage I certainly didn't want to dwell on the Wolverhampton meeting.

Swindon weren't just bad … they were diabolical. Dead men would show more fight! I just couldn't believe my eyes. But it did make me chuckle when I saw the Swindon team manager, Alun Rossiter, being interviewed.

We go back a long way. When I was at Swindon in 1969 we were told that we were going to have a new mascot. No problem I thought, it won't really affect me, so why worry. I met the new mascot's mum Anne and dad Colin, a Welsh couple who were really nice, and it never alerted me to what their son was going to be like.

When he first met me Rosco came straight up and introduced himself. The kid certainly wasn't shy or backward; his biggest saving grace was that God gave him this cheeky, angelic face. But what a little menace. He'd get in your toolbox, sit on your bike, he was having a good time, he had a new playground, he was one of the big boys!

Many is the time that I chased him to give him a boot up the backside but, even with his abundance of self-confidence he wasn't quite sure how to take me. When he was old enough he did reasonably well as a rider, but forget the riding, the rest of the package was definitely cut out for stardom.

I had a laugh with Poole promoter Matt Ford when he told me this terrible cry-wolf story about Rosco.

As a kid I remember a teacher telling me about the cry wolf who told everyone that he was ill simply to get attention when there was actually nothing wrong with him. After using the same ploy a few times, the wolf suddenly found that he had something seriously wrong with him. This time no one took any notice as they thought he was only messing around again. Sadly this time he was bad, and he died alone.

Matt said that Poole had a double header at home and lost one of their top riders in the first race. They were on the borderline of having enough riders to get through both meetings. Rosco had a big crash and really knocked himself about. Returning to the pits he spoke to Matt who wasn't listening to Rosco's tale of woe as he had seen and heard it all before.

Matt told Rosco to just keep doing star jumps, to keep everything moving in his body so he didn't get cold and seize up. Matt was in real trouble if Rosco couldn't ride. In the re-run Rosco made the start and was leading for three-quarters of a lap. Suddenly he swerved and rode onto the grass of the infield and fell in a heap. Matt thought he was again playing the drama queen ... but Rosco was to spend two months in hospital. Matt felt so bad, especially after making him do star jumps. But, to be fair to the kid, he was really brave to get back on his bike again in the first place.

Swindon had done really well throughout the season to fight their way into the play-off finals with Rosco at the helm. But, at Wolverhampton, they were so bad that after five heats the writing was clearly on the wall. The team looked as though they were simply going through the motions.

Rosco's interviews were surprisingly negative: "They are all top professionals and they will sort it out," he said unconvincingly. This wasn't the dynamic team manager's 'call to arms' that I expected from Rosco. To me the riders needed a rocket up their arses. I was so disappointed at Swindon's lack of fight.

The following day I was on the phone with one of my mates when he told me that I was due to be at Swindon for the second leg of the final. This was news to me as I thought that going to watch my old team, 16 points behind going into the second leg, was a non-event.

Thinking it over, it brought back memories of New Zealand's astonishing victory in the 1979 World Team Cup when we only had the bare four riders.

I had finished riding, I was the motivator. We won every round plus the final against the world's finest teams. It was achieved by the Kiwis' unshakable belief in themselves, it could never be repeated.

But ... why not try and help Swindon? Trouble was, the only Swindon rider I really knew was Leigh Adams, who I admired greatly. To motivate properly you have to know and understand the person or persons that you are dealing with to get the very best from them. Some need an arm around their shoulder, some need to be told how good they are, but most really need a kick up the arse. The key is to get them to produce their best when it is most needed.

Of course, there was also a huge age gap. I am a hundred years older than any of them! How many of the present Swindon team knew that I rode pretty good and that for two years around Swindon I was giving everyone twenty yards start in every race and managing to win from this position most of the time? I really must have known the best and fastest way around the Abbey Stadium track.

The news is full of how today's kids are this and that, and that respect is a thing of the past. I was really nervous to put myself forward. For what? I don't think that I really understand many of today's youngsters, with their caps on backwards, tattoos, goatee beards and hair looking like it's never been touched for a month.

I hate to see old men making fools of themselves and I was terrorised by the thought of entering the Swindon dressing room and facing them. But in the end I thought 'to hell with it' and went ahead.

I rang Terry Russell and told him my idea of having five minutes in the dressing room before the meeting. My rules were simple ... only the riders should be there and nobody was to know in advance what I was doing.

It all sounded okay but thinking about it I realised I should have spoken to Swindon captain Adams first. I wasn't sure that someone like me from a million years ago could talk to and be taken seriously by the kids of today. I am a person who doesn't live in the past and I certainly didn't want to embarrass myself or the riders.

I called Leigh and he understood immediately. Sixteen points was a mountain to climb and his performance at Wolverhampton was a big part of the problem. He really was very enthusiastic about the idea, so I was happy but still very nervous. More so when I arrived at Swindon, as the first question thrown at me was by Sky's Steve Brandon asking me if they could put a camera in the dressing room for my rider get-together.

"Steve, nobody should know about this, what's going on?" I asked. "Briggo, I get to know everything, so what's the score on having the camera in the dressing room?"

"Sorry, Brando, it's only for the Swindon riders, it's no ego deal."

A passing Pete Adams asked: "What are you doing here?"

"Just to beat you," I laughed, he smiled and kept rolling by.

The dressing room door banged shut and seven pairs of eyes were all focused on me. All of a sudden I felt like an old fart living in the past and out of his depth.

"Boys, you have done really well to have got to this year's final." Now I went for the throat: "Your performance at Wolverhampton last week was unacceptable, especially from professional sportsmen. A newborn baby has more fight than you boys showed there that night. I know it's been a long season but you worked so hard to get here into the final and to throw in the towel now without a fight is ridiculous.

"Leigh, I thought at Wolverhampton you were running on cruise mode and to me you were just going through the motions. You were riding but not racing. It's exactly why the Russky Emil is winning in the GPs – he's racing not just circulating on auto-pilot."

I knew that I had picked on the one rider in the room that had his pride dented and that he really cared. He reacted exactly the way I thought. "You're fucking right Briggo, I was crap, and looking back bloody pathetic and I'm sure that most of our boys feel that they also were just going through the motions."

After some more self-examination all the riders were convinced that they were ready for the battle that lay ahead. Just as we were breaking up I wanted to lighten the mood and reached into my bag and pulled out seven cans of an energy drink and gave one to each rider and told them it would help.

The naughty name of the drink is Pussy, which to me is a real fun name. Why did Swindon win … because they all had a Pussy? Momentarily the serious race faces disappeared.

These young men were just the same as the likes of Ronnie and

Ivan when we were young. They just live with the times with their dress and hairstyles. An old bloke like me had trouble taking them seriously but now, at close quarters, we are all about the same.

That night they all buckled down, and in my opinion produced their very best. Over the course of a few meetings I think I could have helped at least three of them to perform better. There was really only one who thought he was okay and had everything sorted, but, if he would listen, he has room for improvement.

Swindon lost on aggregate, not helped by what I thought was a dodgy refereeing decision at a vital time, but what a great team performance they produced at Blunsdon. The difference between the two legs was like night and day. In the first leg they were like a pathetic team of kids, in the second the team was all grown men putting it on the line. It is my opinion that if we could re-run the two meetings Swindon would emerge as comfortable winners. Come on Wolf Pete, put your money up!

Six years ago I was going to ring Leigh as I thought I could help him to become World Champion. After that night at Swindon I was convinced that I could have done something for him.

Leigh Adams, runner-up in his last Grand Prix.

Little did I realise that an opportunity was just around the corner. I wasn't due to go to the final Grand Prix of the 2009 season at Bydgoszcz but found myself in Poland that weekend for a very different reason. Son Tony and I went to Friday's practice and decided that we would return the following evening. By then I knew, along with everyone else, that Leigh had decided to retire from the Grand Prix and that this would be his final appearance.

Originally I intended sitting in the stands and was grateful that Paul Bellamy of BSI came up trumps with a ticket for a meeting that was sold out. I was walking through the pits when I saw Leigh, leaned across to wish him 'good luck' and moved on. As I did so Leigh called out: "Well, are you not going to kick my arse tonight?" I laughed and kept walking. I hadn't gone far when I thought, "it's Leigh's last Grand Prix so why not try and help him finish on a high note?" I turned and asked: "Are you sure you want that?"

"Bloody hell I do?" he answered. I said I'd come and speak to him after he had got changed into his leathers. Now Barry B, look what your big mouth has got yourself into. Now we will see if you're as good as you think you are.

I got myself a programme and marked Leigh's races. His first was off gate four which normally gets better later in the meeting when the dirt moves out. I had heard at practice that in his first heat Gollob was off four with Crumpie on the inside. The rumour was that gate four was doctored to help Gollob. After saying that I would help Leigh, I pushed my luck and went across the track, (hoping that Ole Olsen never caught me) to look at gate four. Yes, it was grippy from the start to the first corner.

Ten minutes just before the parade I had a general talk to Leigh, telling him he had nothing to fear from any rider as he had beaten them all many, many times, a lot more than any of them had beaten him.

I decided to hold back on telling him about gate four, waiting to watch what Gollob did in his race. Tomasz flew to the first corner and four definitely was a great advantage. I walked with Leigh to his bike, telling him to look where Gollob started as the gates had been doctored and not be fooled by the wide track. Just make the start and glue yourself to the white line. Don't get too clever, ride your fastest, nobody could possibly pass if you stay on the line, especially going into the corners.

In his first race he did make a great start and rode okay although a little bit hesitant. But most importantly, he had a win under his belt. In his next ride he was against Gollob on his inside. My thoughts were for him to get right over Tomasz's front wheel, to be really tough and to not allow the Pole to force him off the line. Leigh made one of his great starts, but then missed the line and Tomasz steamed through on the inside.

I sat quite a bit away from his pits after this race, from where I could observe him, and waited five minutes for him to sort out his head. I knew what I was going to say and it was tough so that he would take in what I said. "Well, Leigh, that was crap," I told him and as he started with his reason I just talked over him. "That was crap, you could have driven a London double-decker through the gap you left." He looked a little shocked, so I quickly added: "Okay, you've had your one mistake of the night, any more and we'll shoot you." I laughed and moved on, it wasn't a discussable matter.

In my head I was thinking that he must win all his remaining races but then realised that wasn't necessary to get through to the semi-finals. It wasn't the end of the world but I felt I shouldn't give him a lot of slack.

I was really proud of the way he battled to get his total of nine points, which got him into the semis. The only negative was that he would not get a pick of the good starting positions. I thought it was time to take the bull by the horns.

Desperate times need desperate measures. It was simple, either transfer to the final or transfer to your van. It was time for changes. "Leigh, shorten the bike up, you've got to make the starts." One of his mechanics did as I suggested but I didn't point out that the back-wheel could have gone still forward by another link.

It was obvious the change I wanted meant moving into new territory for the Adams camp. But I was convinced that the extra grip that Leigh would get, although it makes the bike, which reacts quicker, a little harder to ride, would pose no problems to him.

In his semi all of a sudden he was fast and was just about running over Sebastian Ulamek on every corner. I am sure had it been the Final he would have passed him.

But he kept his cool and kept his bike in the perfect position so that there was no way for anyone to get past. The Final saw him left with gate three, the worst with only one win from 20 heats. Now it was down to see what Leigh was made of. In the Final he made a bad start, which was not his fault as the gate was still crap.

But, after missing the start he rode fantastically and pushed his way through like a teenager to an unbelievable second place in his final Grand Prix.

He was faster than Nicki Pedersen and I wished when he was side by side with Nicki, who closed him down halfway down the straight, that I could have taken over the controls for just a couple of seconds going into the corner. I think we could have done it. If only we could turn back the clock to the time when I thought about calling him …

Bydgoszcz proved to me that it was bullshit to say that Leigh was too nice to be the champion. Riding-wise, that is wrong, which he proved with his dynamic display in the Final. Yes, Leigh is too nice as I observed, when I watched him from a distance. Every man and his dog came and wished him good luck, plus an odd tip to help him ride better. You don't see people wandering up to Jason Crump, Tomasz Gollob, or Nicki Pedersen telling them what to do. A certain Barry Briggs wasn't the nicest person to wander up and chat to when I had my race face on.

When Tony and me first helped Ryan Sullivan years ago to win his first biggy at Coventry we didn't make a lot of friends when we kept everyone away from him. You don't need an overload of useless information.

All this may sound like a lot of input to make a winner but, if the rider can't ride, or handle what he is being told, you have no chance. Leigh is a great rider, it's all there. All I did was to put my hand on his shoulder and mostly just reminded him what he probably already knew. He had to do the bloody hard work and ride the bike. In my opinion, Leigh Adams could have been World Champion.

Breakfast time at the Briggo ranch

Meeting Junie was the most significant part of my life

44

THE whole of this book could quite easily have been not about my life but my wife, the woman who was with me for most of my motorcycle racing career. She helped me get back on my feet when I was down and then keep them firmly on the ground when I was a winner and a World Champion.

She could sit in the passenger seat as we did a hundred miles an hour to get to meetings on time all over the World. She would step out of the car after a 500 mile trip, a quick change while the car rocked and rolled at high speed, looking like a million dollars.

How do you find a girl that is needed to put this balance into a life that at times looks completely out of control?

First they must be young, and think that everyone lives their life the way we do. They must be special. To have so much love for her lover and best friend to hang in when times are bad and not want to be centre stage.

June was of that very special breed. She provided not only love

Making sure that my boys would get to love motorcyles like I have.

Gary can't believe how good I am!

Wembley and **beyond**

but was my best friend when things were good or bad and never sought to be the centre of attention.

She had a presence, a beautiful smile that captivated those around her which frequently helped to take the focus away from me when I was somewhere I really didn't want to be.

She was also able to handle the considerable task of forgiving a moody, miserable, self-motivated boyfriend who later became her husband and fathered our two lovely boys, Gary and Tony.

Let me recall how I got to meet June Elizabeth Rashbrook. I had made the long journey from my hometown of Christchurch to join the famous Wimbledon speedway club. At that time, in the 1950s, most speedway tracks regularly held supporters' club dances and while, as a rider, you were not ordered to go, it was frowned upon if you didn't. It wasn't a problem and the dances were usually fun.

During my early days in England I was constantly amazed at the number of young girls who came to watch us, there seemed to be hundreds, and it was before the rock-n-roll craze.

While growing up in New Zealand I loved getting autographs, especially of some of the big name wrestlers that were around. I used to hang around after the local bouts to secure autographs of the likes of Earl McCready, the World Champion. I now realise that there were probably a hundred World Wrestling Champions but I didn't know that. Some didn't like being hounded by me and my mates and would yell at us to "piss off". I didn't quite understand why.

Now, here I was in England, a speedway rider and not very good, yet kids wanted my autograph – it didn't make a lot of sense to me. All the riders seemed happy to sign autographs so I just followed suit. As I got a bit older I felt it was part and parcel of my job, these kids and the grown-ups were the people who paid our wages and it seemed to give pleasure to a lot of people.

It gave me a sense of achievement when I got a signature in my autograph days and I often wonder what has happened to all the scraps of paper thrust in front of me to be signed? What has happened to those few shapely boobs that I had signed, has the Barry B scribble still not been washed off 30 years later?

My initial meeting with Junie came about by chance. The

Wimbledon Speedway Supporters' Club held a dance at the Tooting Co-op that, for some particular reason, I couldn't attend. I was probably at home licking my wounds as I was getting knocked about quite a bit. At breakfast the following morning Ronnie Moore and Geoff Mardon went out of their way to tell me that by not going I missed a really pretty young girl. They rubbed it in by saying she wasn't my type and I'd have no chance of dating her.

I accepted that I was no James Dean but surely if she went to watch the speedway at Plough Lane she would know who I was. Hopefully that would at least give me an excuse to talk to her. At the time I wasn't particularly interested in chasing her. But Ronnie and Geoff had thrown down a challenge which sparked me up. In my book there is no such word as can't.

I had a very busy racing schedule and put her out of my mind but, a couple of weeks later, the boys in the Wimbledon dressing room had some pictures that photographer Alf Weedon had taken at the dance. There she was in all her sweetness, even showing off a bit of knee. We all had a laugh, and she certainly wasn't too bad looking.

It was a Monday night and we had just finished racing a league match against our London rivals the Wembley Lions.

I had just finished having my shower when Weedon came in and told me that the young lady in the dance photographs had been at the match. I hurried myself up, went outside to my car and after signing some autographs, I didn't see her anywhere. As I left the stadium, I saw two girls walking together and one looked like the girl in the photograph. I drove beside them and tried asking a question but they completely ignored me and just kept walking.

Persistence eventually paid off and they stopped and listened as I offered them a ride home. It was politely declined but it didn't stop me and finally they accepted my offer. They felt with safety in numbers it was okay. I wanted to speak to Junie alone but that didn't work out. I dropped them both at the turn-off to the house of June's friend but did manage to get her telephone number. It was a hard-earned success. I hadn't spoken to her for any length of time, so how could I decide if she was worth the trouble?

Wembley and *beyond*

Junie, meanwhile, couldn't take me too seriously. She later told me why and we laughed about it many times.

The previous year, when Junie was still at school, she had gone to another dance at the speedway and remembered that while in the ladies toilet a girl burst in and said: "Does anyone want to go home with Barry Briggs?"

Junie said she thought, 'what a wimp, he cannot even get a date for himself.'

She rubbed salt in the wound by saying that a not very attractive girl volunteered. She was probably right, Ronnie had the car and got first pick so I had second choice or no choice at all! Oh for the day when I had my own first car.

I was flat out racing for the next couple of weeks and never had the chance to make use of her phone number. I finally got to take Junie to the movies, but the continuing secrecy of where she lived made me think she would probably bring her mum, as a chaperon. Even after a few more dates I was still dropping her off on street corners. It was obvious that I wasn't the apple of her eye. She had just left school and had a job as a shorthand typist at the Yorkshire Copper Works in London.

However, it didn't take me too long to appreciate just how nice this little girl was. What you saw was what you got, there was no bullshit. She was kind, caring and wasn't bad looking, either!

I had to forgive her one thing, though. She had had a photo of a speedway rider under her desktop at school but of course it wasn't me but my team-mate Reg Trott. That told me a little bit more about her. Reg was a good choice. He was quite laid back and just a nice bloke. I would have been a little concerned had she picked one of my other team-mates with the 'love 'em and leave 'em' attitude to life.

A friend of mine once told me that if you want to see what a young woman was going to look like later in life, go look at her mother. Well, Junie's mum Queenie was a fabulous woman in all ways. Later we used to call Junie our 'little Queenie' but she made out she didn't want to be called that but on this particular point she was a very bad actress. It was easy to notice that Junie really loved it, even if Queenie was a little bit on the heavy side!

Looking back now, I realise that she was my life; the rest was just a fill in. Every time I see my boys, they both have parts of their mother written all over them. I don't feel sad and I still get a beautiful warm feeling for Junie.

I wish I could say that I was the perfect husband. I wasn't. If Junie thought I was telling a porky (porky pies – lies) she would push me to "say God's honour" or I would make her say it if I doubted what I was being told. We used this saying for the whole of our life together. It may sound childish but it was really tough to lie when confronted by it. I tried crossing my fingers or muttering under my breath, "I don't really mean it" but nothing helped, only telling the truth.

So, if I saw something heading my way, and I needed to tell a small porky, I'd rush to the toilet or shout, "I've left the water running down in the workshop" and then get out of there and not face "say God's honour" trial. She always knew she had me, even when I'd say softly, "that's true love, on YOUR life'."

Having to put up with the various moods of a speedway racer and clean his muddy leathers and boots while, at the same time, bringing up a family was quite a challenge. Junie actually had three boys to mother not two. Her third boy was quite a bit older and required more attention than the other two put together. She never moaned or complained and, at times when I returned to thinking like a normal person, I'd feel guilty of my take-take attitude.

Then I would cave in and do whatever she wanted and spoil her just like I should have in return for all she did for the boys and me.

She was smart and figured out that, if she didn't rock the boat, somewhere along the line I would fully appreciate what she did for me. Then, when the time was right, she would get what she wanted from a loving husband. When I left to go racing and, if she wasn't coming with me, she knew that I had to leave home with a clear mind to tackle the dangerous profession that I had chosen for myself. If not, I knew that if anything happened to me she would blame herself for not sending me off with a perfectly clear head between the two of us.

Wembley and **beyond**

Appearing on World of Sport

Retirement and a chance to get away from racing

45

I HAD virtually decided before the start of the 1972 season that it would be my last in the British League and I confirmed it at the end of the year.

Top riders like Jason Crump and Scott Nicholls spelt out their decisions to drop out of British racing in 2009 via the *Speedway Star* magazine and the internet but I announced my intention to quit Swindon after nine seasons to a TV audience of millions. I did it on ITV's Saturday afternoon *World of Sport* programme when I was interviewed exclusively by Dickie Davies. Britain had not seen the last of me, though, not by a long chalk.

The British Speedway Promoters' Association (BSPA) subsequently blocked my bid to compete in the 1973 World Championship as in those days the Aussies and Kiwis had to qualify through the British rounds. But I returned that summer to strengthen New Zealand's team for the *Daily Mirror* international tournament, which took place in the UK.

I also featured in the televised *Daily Express* Spring Classic, an individual meeting at Wimbledon in April, when I was a commentator as well as a rider. ITV showed highlights three days later and, as a result of this, they employed me regularly as their expert summariser alongside commentator Dave Lanning.

The decision to prevent me from re-entering the World Championship, as a non-contracted freelancer, left a sour taste in my mouth. What made it worse was that I received this cold-shoulder treatment just when I had become the first rider to be awarded the MBE for services to speedway. It was a great honour for me but I felt like telling them to stuff it when the BSPA wouldn't let me compete in the World Championship.

The MBE was not only for me as it was also recognition for speedway as a whole. It was nice for me but it didn't change my life. I didn't go out and put MBE on the side of my van, or have it printed on my letterheads. The only time I used it to my advantage was in America of all places.

The local authority in Orange County was trying to close down Costa Mesa Speedway in California and at a public meeting one night I spoke up for promoter Harry Oxley.

A woman councillor was painting speedway riders as Hell's Angels so I asked her: "Have you ever heard of the Queen of England?"

"Of course," she replied haughtily.

I told her: " I am a speedway rider and helped to start the sport here more than 20 years ago. The city of Costa Mesa is known worldwide because of speedway." She coughed as she stood up to butt in. I held my hand up and added: "I have one more thing to say. You have acknowledged that you have heard of the Queen of England and you also know I am a speedway rider. Well, these two things go together."

I paused for a few seconds. The poor, deluded and ambitious woman had no idea what was about to hit her when I continued: "Madam, the Queen personally awarded me the MBE for my services to the sport of speedway. I think the actual words you used were that 'speedway riders are Hell's Angels'. Are you saying that the Queen of England made a very bad mistake in awarding me the MBE?"

Everything went downhill for her from that point. And Costa Mesa is still running today over 30 years later. Otherwise, the MBE hasn't done a lot for me!

My fellow New Zealander, Ivan Mauger, always laughs about the fact that the Speedway Control Board had a file on him. It was several inches thick after all the strife he'd been in with the authorities over the years. I was no angel in my racing days, either, but I thought I did a reasonable job for speedway as a whole. Suddenly, though, they just closed the door on me and I felt that was completely wrong.

I'd ridden in England since 1952 and had given British speedway my best, wherever I'd raced. Every promoter had his pound of flesh and I thought that if I was good enough to have qualified through the World Championship rounds in 1973, then they should have let me try. Today they allow certain riders back into the Grand Prix just to pull in crowds. Why couldn't they have allowed me to ride? Fans would have come along to see if I was still good enough to qualify through to the British Final and beyond.

But for my infamous crash at Wembley involving Swedish rider Bernt Persson, I could well have been World Champion again the year before so, clearly, I still had plenty to offer. They should also have taken into account that I was coming back after a bad injury. It was a sad situation. I don't think I would have been frozen out if Ronnie Greene, who I'd ridden for and respected at Wimbledon for years, had not retired from the BSPA a year or so earlier.

AS well as denying me the chance to enter the 1973 World Championship, the BSPA also drew a line under the use of the top colonials in what was called the Great Britain World Team Cup squad. Ivan Mauger, Ronnie Moore, myself and Australian No. 1, Jim Airey, had been mainstays of the GB team in previous years.

Ray Wilson, who scored a maximum in 1971, was the only one of the English contingent to produce an outstanding performance at that time. Ivan, in particular, was dismayed to become surplus to requirements once the BSPA had a growing list of talented young English riders, spearheaded by Peter Collins, to choose from. All five riders who won the World Team Cup with the Union Jack on their body colours at Wembley in 1973 were English.

After their follow-up victories in 1974 and 1975, there was no doubt that England were worthy World Champions in their own right. I didn't share the indignation of my fellow countrymen over the BSPA's revised Team Cup selection policy. I had been the first to score a maximum for Great Britain, in the World Team Cup Final at Vienna in 1963, as well as being the all-time leading points scorer for GB/England but I really didn't mind at all. Great Britain had needed us to help them along but, at the same time, I appreciated that I was earning a good living from racing here.

In turn, making a name for myself in Britain enabled me to earn really good money on the continent. It was swings and roundabouts, so I could understand it when the promoters turned to the English riders who were coming through. I want England to do well at all sports and, even when they are up against New Zealand, I feel divided loyalties. I love it in England. I just wish it had Californian weather!

New Zealand and Australia broke away from Speedway Control Board jurisdiction in 1974 and their respective governing bodies became independently affiliated to the FIM (the International Motor Federation). But there was another storm brewing that August.

Ivan and I found ourselves at the centre of controversy when we withdrew from the UK round of the World Team Cup at Ipswich. It was a rearranged meeting after the original staging had been rained off three nights earlier. The depleted Kiwi team struggled to a meagre six points while Ivan and I were in Denmark and Germany respectively fulfilling longstanding individual racing engagements.

Several prominent British promoters condemned us for missing that hastily rearranged Sunday meeting but we always insisted we had the (tacit) permission of the Control Board representative at Ipswich that night to go abroad, as we usually did on the Sabbath to cash in on our reputations. I already had an agreement with a Danish promoter to ride in Copenhagen that day. It wasn't a question of going there for the money, it was all about honouring my commitment to appear.

The fans had read about me being there to race so they paid their entrance money and expected to see me. In this type of show business you must honour your word, or you'll be out of bookings.

THE World Champions' Speedway Series was the early forerunner to the Master of Speedway competition launched by Ole Olsen in 1978 and the Grand Prix that has decided the World Championship since 1995. Ivan Mauger and myself embarked on our part-time promoting careers as instigators of the Champions Series and it caused a growing resentment from within BSPA circles.

I named it the WCSS for the special reason that it clearly advertised the fact we were selling World Champions like Sweden's Ove Fundin and New Zealander Ronnie Moore as well as ourselves. It stopped interference by the authorities and we weren't hoodwinking the speedway public.

We had a scaled down launch in front of record crowds in New Zealand in 1973 and then, at the start of 1974, we assembled champions and international stars for a series of meetings in the USA, Australia and back in New Zealand. We had a fantastic troupe of riders, including Ove, who we tempted out of retirement through his love of travelling, and pulled off a major coup by persuading the Polish authorities to allow their two top riders, Zenon Plech and Edward Jancarz, to come with us.

Poland was still a communist country at that time, of course, in the grip of the Soviet Union. Negotiations over visas and payments for the riders went on for weeks and, even when we thought everything had been cleared, including the fact that we also had to cough up for a Polish official (he was, in fact, a 'minder') there was a last minute snag.

Zenon and Edward had all the necessary paperwork for Australia and New Zealand but we hadn't bothered about the UK. Why should we, they weren't riding there. But, they were coming to London and staying overnight before catching the flight to New Zealand. It was only a last minute intervention from the British Embassy in Warsaw, providing temporary visas, that allowed them to leave Poland.

The troupe also included, at various times, Ole Olsen, Anders

Michanek, Tommy Jansson, John Louis, Egon Muller (what a handful!) and the much less troublesome Jimmy McMillan and Bert Harkins.

We also took our star-studded travelling road-show to Israel and South Africa. Many people thought there had been more of an exhibition feel to our groundbreaking WCSS meetings but they didn't lack an edge.

But, as in the Grand Prix, it was important to keep qualifying without knocking yourself out. It wasn't cut-throat racing in the heats because second places were good enough to go through. The only time you had to be in first place to be crowned champion was in the winner-takes-all final, the same as in the current Grand Prix. Ronnie Moore will testify that it was still the real thing.

The relationships between Ronnie and me, and Ivan and me, are very different. Ronnie and I have been very close for so many more years and I had real trouble coping with the serious situation he was in when he crashed and was seriously injured in Australia. But Ivan was brilliant. He cradled Ronnie's badly bleeding head in his arms and made him as comfortable as possible until the doctor arrived.

Even so, it still looked grave for the former double World Champion. We were awoken at two o'clock in the morning and asked to go to the hospital where Mirac had been taken. We were told that Ronnie was going to die. He had been taken to a small, church-run hospital in Newcastle but, thank God, the doctors saved his life against all odds.

The general public probably see Ivan and myself as a couple of hard, uncaring bastards, but Ronnie's crash was a terrible blow to us, even though he was snatched from the jaws of death. Within days we moved him to a special hospital in Sydney a couple of hours away. Saving our mate was paramount to both of us. But, once the dust settled and reality set in, we had to tie up the loose ends, which meant paying the bills. The amazing thing is, Ivan and I just settled up the large expenses incurred by Ronnie's lack of proper insurance cover without really discussing it.

We twice took indoor speedway on shale to the famous Houston Astrodome in Texas with some riders from our troupe in NZ and

Oz being joined by others, like Ray Wilson, Terry Betts and Josef Angermuller, coming in from Europe.

But the series never fulfilled our early dreams, mainly due to escalating costs and a lack of decent big sponsorship. It was tough on Ivan and myself as we paid everyone what we had promised but ultimately we never made a lot of money and were the lowest paid riders of the series by far. Overall, the series made its mark on international speedway in a big way because it allowed people to see speedway in countries where, otherwise, they wouldn't have had the chance.

I WANTED to promote a series of motorcycle events where I retained complete control, over the rules, bikes, tyres, everything. And, of course, I wanted to get the big Japanese motorcycle companies involved.

I made a speedway bike with a 600cc Yamaha. England star Terry Betts and I tested it at King's Lynn and it worked well. It looked a bit top heavy, but it didn't ride like that.

The extra capacity of the engine gave it pulling power but some of the standard parts would have to be changed for it to work reliably in speedway. The commitment I would have to make, both in terms of time and money, worried me as did the aggravation that would come with it. Surprisingly, the FIM was completely behind the idea, except they didn't realise about me being in complete control. I have seen the FIM do so many wrong things over the years, mainly through ignorance rather than know-how.

The riders are normally the victims, having to buy new carburettors, silencers and tyres. You name it and I have seen it all in my years of racing. They never listen to the experts. My best example is dirt deflectors, especially the longtrack version, which I go into elsewhere in this book.

I WAS tempted back into the saddle in 1974 after a year out of British speedway. I returned to Wimbledon where it had all started for me in 1952 as a snotty-nosed kid who crashed a bit trying to keep up with the other blokes.

I can't remember how they managed to persuade me back. It sounds corny, but it was probably because I simply loved riding bikes and still do. I was past my best but I've never been a great believer in that old saying that you should always try to go out at the top. If you've got enough talent to do what you most enjoy doing, and can still make a few bob, then why not carry on?

I set my own standards, which, if you look at my averages over the years, have remained high. And, if my dnf (did not finish) races were deleted, my average would be much higher. I never worried about my average. If the team needed it, I would ride three races on the trot no matter what the opposition.

I remember talking about when you should quit with Rod Coleman, a Kiwi Grand Prix road racer, on a month-long boat trip back home. He rode works AJS machines and was the first New Zealander to win an Isle of Man TT in 1954.

He told me he had retired too soon in order to run his successful business. He said: "Don't retire if you haven't got racing out of your system. You can't go back and do it again properly when it's too late. Boxers are probably right to get out while they're at the top, before their brains become scrambled, but there is nothing wrong in earning a living at speedway as long as you've still got the talent to do so."

Swedish riders, who commuted to the UK and were very expensive, had been banned from competing in the British League in 1974 by the Promoters' Association who were delighted to welcome me back to their senior tracks. I think the words they used were a 'household name and major draw-card'. I proved there was still enough in my locker to hold my own amongst the elite. I was also happy to re-establish myself as Wimbledon's No.1 with a near 9.50 average.

I returned to Wimbledon in 1975 but it was the last year I would be seen in the famous red-and-yellow race-jacket. As far as the speedway world was concerned, I had taken off my familiar, full-face crash helmet for the last time and retired to a new, relaxed lifestyle in the Californian sunshine. The arrival on my front doorstep of the smooth-talking Hull promoter, Ian Thomas, started Rod's words of 'don't finish until it's out of your system' ringing in my ears. Everyone who knows me will agree that I am a restless character and never idle for long.

Thommo is a part-time magician and has pulled some rabbits out of the hat in his day. But he did a trick that I didn't think he had any chance of performing by luring me back for one last hurrah with the Vikings. It was a coup that no-one could have contemplated.

The 1976 season was about to start and the East Yorkshire club had finally accepted that they weren't going to sign Ole Olsen, who wanted to leave Wolverhampton and had been allocated to them. Olsen refused to go to Hull and was digging in his heels that he would only ride for Coventry.

Thomas and his then Hull co-promoter Brian Larner refused to budge … unless they had a suitable replacement. Which turned out to be me! I turned down his audacious proposal to start with but Thommo wouldn't leave. I couldn't get rid of the stubborn Hull boss.

Junie and I thought it was fabulous to be living a proper family life again with the chance to enjoy the fruits of our labour in our idyllic, cliff-top home overlooking the picturesque Dana Point harbour on the beautiful Pacific Ocean coast.

To make his offer acceptable Ian arranged for me to fly in from Germany, where I was based for tax reasons, to Manchester Airport every Wednesday. Hull would provide me with a bike that would be prepared and maintained by Bernard Harrison, the reputable former mechanic to Eric Boocock. All I had to do was turn up and race. It wasn't on my mind to go racing again, so I started playing games with Thommo, but I didn't realise just how serious he was.

Junie kept bringing us tea and biscuits and just kept smiling at me. She knew what I was going to do, she knew me much better than I knew myself. He was slowly wearing me down but I thought my last requirement would stop him in his tracks. I just about fell off my cliff top, when he said yes to buying me a new Mercedes straight from the factory in Stuttgart.

Normally, you take the money and stick it into the bank where it disappears. Riding for Hull was very different from any other years, this was the way fans think stars should travel, in a luxury car.

This wasn't really me, except that with the big mileage we clock up it took some of the strain away, especially with the power to pass slower cars. Then, when you've had a bad meeting, the trip home was better, surrounded by the luxury of your car. Coming out of retirement didn't seem quite so bad. I did quite well and scored 300-odd points from 34 official matches to finish as Hull's No.1 with an average a fraction under nine points a match.

I bowed out by leading Hull to its first major honour when they beat Wolverhampton in the Inter-Divisional KO Cup Final. It may seem irrelevant in the context of my collection of silverware in a career spanning 24 seasons of full-time league racing but it meant a lot to me. It was great to see the success-starved Vikings supporters enjoying themselves as winners.

It was nice to read that Thommo described me as speedway's Peter Pan in his book, *Wheels and Deals* (Pinegen, 2006), and added that I was his most popular ever signing for Hull and the £750 loan fee he paid to Wimbledon to secure my services was money very well spent. I really liked the Humberside fans and they seemed to like me as I always tried my best. It certainly wasn't because I was winning all the time, because I wasn't. Ian was a good promoter to ride for, very strong on publicity at all his tracks. He liked to stir things up a bit. He was very clever and enjoyed a fight – like a frustrated lawyer!

IVAN Mauger and I had started running the World Speedway Champions Series in New Zealand and Australia. One year, on our way back through Los Angeles, we stopped to help regenerate speedway that had all but closed there for the last 25 years.

Our tours were so successful at promoting young racers that, in the end, the Costa Mesa track took over from Christchurch in New Zealand as the home of the most World Champions.

We had three champions (Ronnie, Ivan and myself) while another couple of riders finished in the medals. Costa Mesa became the home of four champions (Bruce Penhall, Sam Ermolenko, Billy Hamill and Greg Hancock) who came after our tours and you mustn't forget Jack Milne, the World Champion in 1937 and runner-up in 1938.

Brad Oxley was having trouble with the Costa Mesa Fair Board from whom they rented the speedway track. The Board wanted all tickets for our meetings to go through them. Brad used my family name, telling them that without me there would not be a Costa Mesa speedway so there was no way they were going to turn down people like us. I had never thought about it like that. But it was true because things could have been so different if Ivan and I weren't nosey. Once, when we were coming through LA, we rode at Whiteman Stadium, which was going broke. So much so that Jack Milne sent Harry Oxley, his motorcycle shop manager, out there to make sure that we were paid.

Probably all of the American World Champions, and the other great riders who hailed from Costa Mesa, would have had different employment if it wasn't for Ivan and I venturing to ride at Whiteman Stadium. We also ran a couple of training schools for Harry and helped to discover some unbelievable talent.

Once, when Ermolenko was giving me a load of crap about dirt deflectors, I felt like telling him: "Hey buddy, without me you'd probably still be working in a motorcycle shop so give me some slack." We were passing through Los Angeles doing these meetings and the sport was growing in leaps and bounds with plenty of tracks opening up. If you wanted, you could ride speedway every day of the week.

I have stated elsewhere that I feel speedway riders cannot be overpaid. To me, though, Harry was over generous and gave the riders a percentage of the gate, which was great until greed came into it. This style of payment is open to discussion, and argument, and it caused at least two tracks to be closed by Harry as the riders thought they were being screwed.

We had roughly the same problem when running meetings in Rhodesia (now Zimbabwe) years ago when I bought some shopping clickers so we could count accurately the number of spectators coming through the turnstiles. There were no discussions as the riders' wives were on the gates with the clickers.

The riders miscalculated by more than 50 per cent their

estimation of the crowds. They always thought there were more spectators, of course.

It became quite common for Ivan and I, along with the riders we took to Australia and New Zealand, to return to the UK via California and to take part in a series of America versus the Rest of the World meetings there. We also brought over a few other top names, including Peter Collins, from England.

But, in 1974, Harry Oxley and his fellow southern California speedway promoters, were involved in a dispute with the American Motorcycle Association over the licensing of riders. The AMA refused to sanction our meetings and were backed by the FIM.

The meetings were cancelled, at great expense to Harry, Ivan and me.

We decided to sue the FIM, who hired some very expensive Los Angeles lawyers to argue that as an organisation based in Switzerland the courts in California had no jurisdiction over them. Wrong! Harry had a hotshot lawyer of his own and when the case finally went before the Californian Supreme Court it was thrown out. We were free to sue motorcycle racing's governing body.

The FIM would have had to disclose their assets and, had they lost, could have been in financial difficulties. They weren't prepared to take that risk. And we didn't want to break them ... we just wanted compensation for our financial losses and damage to our reputation as promoters of international events.

We settled out of court and, as part of the deal, were allocated the 1982 World Final, the first to be staged outside of Europe.

Ivan and I, along with American speedway supremo Harry and pre-war World Champion Jack Milne, formed a company to promote the Final at the LA Coliseum. It turned out to be one of the most explosive finals in history and is still remembered for the ferocious clash between Bruce Penhall and Kenny Carter.

The FIM certainly didn't make it easy for us. We had to run a trial meeting at the Coliseum to prove that we could install a suitable track and had the necessary expertise to present a World Final. It was a very costly exercise but, with Harry at the helm, we passed with flying colours. We did, however, have a major piece of bad luck when in the days leading up to the Final it was announced that the Oakland Raiders, a NFL franchise on one side of the bay of San Francisco, were moving their operation to Los Angeles ... and the Coliseum. And that their opening game would be on the day after the speedway World Final.

Efforts were actually made to force us to abandon our speedway meeting. But we had a watertight contract with the Coliseum and, despite all the obstacles that were continually put in our way, the Final went ahead, in front of 39,000 people who witnessed Bruce Penhall announce his retirement (for a career in the neighbouring Hollywood) from the top of the podium after securing his second world title.

It was a tough job and it was poetic justice that three ex-World Champions and America's best promoter shared in the spoils. Harry, the legendary Milne and myself remained business partners for the USA's two other major FIM meetings, the World Team Cup finals held at Long Beach in 1985 and 1988.

I HAD the idea of putting together a speedway Hall of Fame museum while driving around in America. All the big sports there, like baseball, basketball, football, ice hockey and golf, have them. Former players, who have made a special contribution to their respective sports, are inducted into the Hall of Fame and I felt that speedway, riders and fans deserved one of their own.

The big problem was finding a suitable home. The answer came through my friendship with Ian Phillips, a journalist who I got to know when I was doing the rounds watching Michael Thackwell, who, at one time, was the youngest driver in Formula One.

Ian promoted the first meeting that Tom Wheatcroft staged at his Donington Park circuit, despite having no planning permission. He and Tom were always ready for a fight. I met Tom in February, 1989 and he loved the idea of a speedway Hall of Fame joining his World's Greatest Collection of race-cars at his beloved Donington Park Museum.

Tom had lived near the famous speedway rider, Squib Burton, a local Leicester lad. His enthusiasm was infectious and the end product was tremendous. A great deal of that was down to him because he spent time and money to make sure it was the best.

It was a great central location and there was plenty of room. It was ideal. I had to spend a lot of time at Donington, collecting bikes and bits and pieces and building the exhibition.

It also gave me a chance to give some time to my other business interests in the area. Joe Hughes was one of my major agents for the Briggo dirt deflectors and he was just down the road in Derby. One day I roared over to Joe's to deliver some urgently needed spare parts. I had been to his house many times before because we were great mates as well as business partners.

I screeched to a halt outside his house as I needed the toilet badly. I roared through his kitchen and yelled to his wife, Lorraine, who was working over the kitchen sink. "I'll just use your toilet," I said as I went up the stairs two at a time. As I was standing there, and the relief was surging through my body, I thought: "Bloody hell, Joe's done a lot of work in his bathroom." It slowly dawned on me this wasn't Joe's bathroom.

A very subdued Kiwi slunk downstairs to grovel to Joe's next door neighbour. Of course, I have never been allowed to forget it and we've had plenty of laughs about it. Just imagine if I had been in America, someone would have shot me!

The Hall of Fame opened with a blaze of publicity, and was described in the magazines as a great thing for speedway. I was very happy with how well it was received. It was not me alone who did all the work and had the ideas but I was the one who received the accolades. Visitors over the years have written their comments into the book we put out and some startling thoughts have been noted, especially some complimentary observations by the car racing enthusiasts.

Tom didn't know much about speedway but we quickly did a deal. Together we paid for all the original outlay, and it cost a lot, but unfortunately the whole of speedway never really got behind it. Tim Swales, who was Chairman of the BSPA at the time, arranged a dinner there. It was great to be in good company and surrounded by the speedway bikes, plus some of the sport's colourful history which included the famous Wembley tractor.

Pride of place was, of course, for all of our honoured World Champions who had graced our sport from the 1930s. The feel within the hall was magic and helped to revive the memories of years gone by. The speedway section even dazzled people who went there to see the cars. We had more than 30,000 visitors a year and although I had only agreed a deal for three years, we stayed there for five.

Sadly, Tom and his son, Kevin, then needed the space and I had to find a new home. Wembley was the obvious choice and we had a great display there for three years, preceding the arrival of the bulldozers. Every time they had a soccer international there we had to move all the bikes and display material, which was a bind. But I was looking to the future of the new Wembley museum. Speedway was second only to football as one of the major contributors in keeping Wembley's doors open pre-Olympic Games time.

It has earned its right to be a major attraction at the museum because of the history of the famous Wembley Lions' speedway team. In addition the majority of the World Finals were raced there. The stadium was known as speedway's spiritual home. I still haven't given up hope of speedway being a major exhibitor at the new Wembley museum. Sir Dave Richards, one of the top dogs at both the Football Association and the Premier League, is someone I know and can talk to, but nothing has happened as yet.

The one ray of hope is the speedway museum at the Paradise Wildlife Park, owned and run by ex-rider Pete Sampson who once was my riding partner at Swindon. Pete loves the sport and speedway is lucky that he was there to step in after George and Linda Barclay had done the groundwork in raising the money to build the facility. The day-to-day operation of running a museum is a financial problem but, in conjunction with the Wildlife Park to help cover the expenses, Pete can make it work.

I have noticed big improvements each time I have visited the museum. It is a first class facility so, hopefully, our history is in good hands.

I AM not a person who dwells too much in the past as I love the unknown of the future. But I enjoy the history and nostalgia of speedway so there was nothing better to preserve fond memories of track legends than the Golden Greats series.

My idea was sparked by a veterans' golf tournament I was watching on TV. The easy thing about organising this sort of thing in golf is that all the old players have to do is turn up with their clubs. In speedway the logistics are so much more difficult. If the riders bought their own bikes there would be a mish-mash of machinery and the true riding ability wouldn't show through.

I launched the Golden Greats in front of a packed crowd at Coventry on Sunday, August 14, 1988, when Ove Fundin, Anders Michanek, Bengt Jansson, Terry Betts, John Louis and other former stars returned to the track. I had built four virtually new two-valve Jawa bikes, identical to the one I pioneered in Britain as the sole UK agent for the Czech machine in 1965, to all the same specifications. It required a large investment as I needed all the bits and pieces, spare wheels, tyres and spare parts to maintain the four bikes, which were being raced in virtually every one of the 20 heats. Some riders also needed riding gear such as leathers, boots and gloves. It was never ending.

We dressed Ove Fundin completely. Then he just undressed after the meeting and left it lying there so my son, Tony, had to find the gear so we could use it in the next meeting. I think Ove was the only rider to have the same measurements as he'd had when he was racing. Talk about skinny! Although the stars were older, they retained their racing characteristics. Their bodies were in a slow decline but scratch the surface of any one of them as the action started and you would find there was still going to be a massive battle of egos.

To me, the most important thing was that all the bikes used in the Golden Greats were alike, so no one had an unfair advantage. If the public thought the meetings were going to be the old boys cruising around in the sunshine, they were in for a shock. The first race saw Bengt Jansson lead till the very last corner when Anders Michanek hung him out to dry on the fence and claim the victory. Yes, it was just like old times. Wherever we promoted the Golden Greats the public knew they were going to get a full meeting of competitive racing from some of the greatest riders ever to grace a speedway track.

It cannot be true ... Junie is diagnosed with cancer

46

WHEN I finally retired from the hurly burly of English speedway, I had an idea that sounded good. I was going to spend quality time with Junie, do a few continental race meetings in between and make a few bob along the way to keep the caravan rolling.

In retrospect, it was never going to be that simple. There was no way that I could take guaranteed start money and do anything but my best, no matter how big or small the meetings were. It was the nature of the beast that is Barry Briggs.

Junie and I had been married for over 20 years, she would listen to what I was going to do, say 'great' and smile, as she knew that a leopard never changes his spots.

"Well love, I must do a little bit of running and lift a few weights just to make sure I'm sharp for Sunday's grasstrack as Ivan and PC are there," I would mutter. She would smile but her look showed that she was thinking: "Does he think that I'm an idiot?"

The stress level was still there, but only at weekends which made it a little easier to bear. It was great and the travel schedules were

Luckily my Junie loved motorbikes as well.

much more flexible. We had nice meals in beautiful locations throughout Europe as we meandered through countries like Germany, Sweden, Denmark, Austria, Italy, Hungary and the then Czechoslovakia. We had a load of quality time together while still doing what I knew best … racing a motorbike.

When I originally decided to write this book I persuaded Junie to make some notes for a chapter on being a wife and mother of the Briggs 'boys' … all three of us!

I've cleaned it up a little as she had a wicked sense of humour. Some of it has been covered elsewhere in the book but I'm sure it's of interest.

Junie's view of the men in her life and their pursuits.

"Barry, you are going to do what? But you don't know anything about it. Of course I'll come, what time do we leave? What, today?"

1. Normal life, schoolboy sweethearts.
2. Meeting Barry, not sure what I thought of him, never let him drop me home, always around the corner from our flat.
3. We got engaged then, just before he was off to South Africa, he decides we should marry. Chaos to fit in wedding, no passport, complete change of life. I never realised that this was the way life was going to continue for the rest of our lives.
4. Terry Betts christened Barry 'Captain Chaos' about which I laughed. It always looks like it. Trouble is, Barry tries to fit two lives into one, so many things can happen. I can't believe at times where he gets the energy to do so much.
5. This type of life turned me into a great reader. I must always have a book at hand as sometimes I have to spend hours and hours sitting in our car waiting while Barry collects engines or delivers bits and pieces or has business meetings, but I found it was better to be together whenever possible.
6. Barry had built up a very hard exterior to cut out the hurt of losing fellow racers, the pain of accidents, disappointments and to race real friends into the ground to win. Luckily, I learnt to read him pretty well, not speaking doesn't mean we have fallen out, he's just planning something.

7. I have never thought of losing Barry through his racing, but I really worry about him on the roads, the thousands of miles he travels at high speed.

8. Then the arrival of our two lovely boys. Luckily Gary loved music and all sports; the work that motorcycle racing required didn't interest him.

    Tony was different, very similar to his dad, never gives up. He lived for the racing, I thought that he had it all to be a Champion, but he was missing the one vital ingredient – luck.

9. Watching Barry and Tony battle the odds, whether it was speedway or in the middle of the jungle, gave me this beautiful warm feeling to see the love between the two. They have views very similar to each other, but there are plenty of heated discussions. Anyone foolish enough to take sides quickly finds that the two have joined forces against them, it wasn't war, they were only giving their views.

    Barry and Gary's relationship is much softer, mainly due to Gary's more patient, placid nature, as Barry loves music and sport they are never short of something to talk about.

10. Life in the jungle without my rollers, impossible! But Barry sorted out the generator for special occasions. He also made a special dryer, so I put my rollers in when we left the camp, and an hour and a half later when we arrived in Monrovia, lo and behold a quick brush and it looked that I had come directly from a hair salon. What was the special dryer? Barry cut a hole in the roof of the Landrover just above where I sat, with a deflector so that I could adjust the warm tropical air directly on to my hair … the perfect hairdryer!

    Just before I arrived the boys had to build sides onto the toilet. I was always scared that there would be large snakes hiding down the hole. Barry also built, with the help of a 45-gallon drum, my personal shower. It was an open design, the boys were always teasing me that all the men from Gbeni village hid in the forest to watch me shower each evening. Must admit I found myself at times scouring the jungle forest for faces, June concluded.

For a number of years Junie and I had a flat in Holzwickede near Dortmund in Germany. Our local tennis champion was an East German doctor who had a surgery in town. Amazingly, he was at least ten years older than his opponents.

Our friend Joe Joy was a former British soldier who married his German sweetheart and stayed there after the war. First they opened a laundry and then a motorcycle business. Even today when Joe speaks German he still sounds as though he has only been there for five minutes.

However, Joe is no longer English in his thinking, as his garden shed illustrates perfectly. All his garden tools are lined up as if on parade and I would tease him about it all the time. I have known Joe for over 100 years (well, it seems like it) and during this time I had used and abused his workshop along with using his cars and just about anything he owns. He's a real mate.

It was Joe who first told me about the tennis playing doctor who had this special Ozone-Oxygen treatment. At the time I didn't understand the significance as I hadn't listened to the complete story, otherwise I would have discovered this was also considered

The two ladies of my life.

a great treatment for cancer sufferers. All I took on board was that he was the local tennis champion, was years older than his opponents and had this unbelievable energy.

I thought about this and finally said: "Joe, I need a treatment from Dr. Spock," and we laughed about it for a while. Back then this unconventional treatment was not as sophisticated as it is now. It is undertaken over a minimum of three sessions and requires a minimum of 24 hours between each session otherwise the recipients would be so hyped they would be unable to sleep,

When I saw this treatment used on Junie many years later, at the Oasis in Mexico, my mind was transported back to Holzwickede in Germany.

The Joy family took in the 'Briggs lot' many times and treated us as their own. There was nothing better than sitting down to a 'Aunty Helen' feed although, being German, she imposed strict rules on being punctual for the feast she had prepared. If only I could have transferred the 'Aunty Helen' time control to my racing schedule I would have been unbeatable!

Sadly Helen died in August, 2009. She will be sadly missed.

I was at Heathrow Airport at the end of May, 2003 waiting for a flight back to Los Angeles. As usual, I went to the bookshop to buy all the newspapers and some English chocolate that would earn me a pile of brownie points from Junie when I got to California.

Junie would still be on a diet but would always manage to fit a few bars of chocolate into her calorie count. Gary, who lived with us at Dana Point, wanted the papers to catch up on all the stories concerning English football. He kept up with soccer via the television but it wasn't quite the same as the English press having a go at all and sundry.

There, right before my eyes in W.H. Smith's, was the autobiography *It's Not About the Bike*, by the American Tour de France hero Lance Armstrong, which I had been searching for.

I read Lance's story of guts and determination against all the odds and how he beat cancer, during the 10-hour flight. Little did I realise at that time that within less than a month my Junie would be facing the same ordeal.

Capistrano Beach to watch the sunset

Mexico and the chance of alternative treatment

47

I first started writing this book in 1989, which was two years after we finally pulled out of the mining game in Liberia. The original format stood gathering dust for twenty odd years, the rough layout was just about the same as you are reading now.

The massive difference between then and now is that the mainstay of the Briggs family, my wife Junie, has left us. Nothing in the world will ever be the same.

Since I decided to re-invent this book it has been bugging me as to how I was going to approach the most important passage, her untimely death. What would she want me to write?

I can even hear her now saying, "It's your book love, I'm only just part of the pit crew, it's you that the people want to read about."

Without her, I couldn't have reached the heights I did in speedway. She was my strength, and when things were bad and I thought the whole world was against me, she would always be there to pick me up. A kiss, a cuddle, even a pat on the head, she knew what it took to keep me going.

Finally, after bouncing it off the boys, I have decided to tell of her struggle against cancer the way it was. She'd like that.

We were all in complete shock when we were told that Junie, who was seldom ill, had been diagnosed with stage four cancer. What has happened to us could happen to anyone, so Junie's story might be a small help and an insight to someone who also gets trapped by this dreadful disease.

The first thing is that we knew very little about it, so we quickly gathered as much information as possible. Time was of the essence, particularly as her projected life span was very short. We wanted to try and retain for her a comfortable life with or without cancer for as long as possible. Junie very much agreed with this decision.

Hindsight is a wonderful thing, of course, and if we had changed two things months before, they could have made an enormous difference to our lives.

One was that when Junie had a small woman's operation in Southampton in December, 2002 blood tests were taken but not for cancer. If only we could have turned back time.

The second missed opportunity of spotting her illness was when the school Junie worked for in California had an arrangement with their insurance company for all of the teachers to have a colonoscopy. Unfortunately, Junie adopted the 'British Bulldog' stance, stating that 'nobody is going to put their finger up my bum'. This was one year before she was diagnosed with cancer. But you must play the cards as they are dealt.

Nobody had any idea of what was happening inside Junie's body. Cancer is nicknamed the silent killer, it doesn't fight fair, as was proven in her case. I was away in England at the time and, during one of our near daily telephone calls, she excitedly told me that she had joined Curves, a new exercise club, and that after only a couple of weeks she had lost over 10 pounds. Not being in Dana Point, I couldn't get the right feeling or information as I might have done had I been there. My immediate feeling was that Junie was sticking to a more strict diet plus, of course, she was getting plenty of exercise.

Looking back, we now know it wasn't the magic of Curves, but the phantom big C that had found its way into her body, with no fuss or pain.

To me it is always fantastic to get back to Dana Point. Once there I feel that I am on a super non-stop holiday. The saying 'that absence makes the heart grow fonder' summed it up pretty well both for Junie and Dana Point.

While I was away alone, talking on the phone was one thing, but being there with Junie in our own family home made it real. Beautiful Dana Point is home. Being there, with the sun and the sea, allowed me to feel that all the banging, crashing, and the near impossible tasks that I had set myself in my life had been worthwhile.

It is hard to get the same feeling while in a foreign country battling against traffic in the rain, or on some back road in the middle of Poland that is snowbound.

Junie was always the master of turning a house into a home, whether it be Dana Point or a mud hut in the middle of the African jungle. The two are poles apart but Junie managed to achieve this with our four bedroomed $200 mud hut in the middle of the Liberian jungle. There is only a slight difference between the two words a house and a home but to me, the 'Kiwi Gypsy', the difference is massive.

No matter how good life is, the normal things still need doing and on June 3, 2003, which was a beautiful, sunny day, Junie had an appointment with our local female doctor, Dana Mason, who was from Poland.

Junie had a rasping cough, it was not really a problem, but she didn't like being around her children at school with something that sounded so bad. Dr. Mason gave her an antibiotic prescription that would clear the problem within days.

Junie had actually stood up to leave, when the doctor asked: "Is there anything else June?"

Junie stopped for a couple of seconds and a quizzical look flashed across her tanned face. "Well, actually doctor, I do have a small twinge of pain here in this part of my tummy but it doesn't really worry me that much."

Doctor Dana felt gently around the area. "Have you felt anything different or any new pains in the last few weeks?" she asked.

Junie presents Brucie P with his induction into the Donington Hall of Fame.

"Nothing really, I feel good, I have joined a new exercise club and I've lost over ten pounds in a couple of weeks, which I'm really happy about."

On hearing this, the doctor re-examined the stomach area. As they both stood up, she said: "June, I'll arrange for some ultrasound scans and a chest x-ray. These can all be done at the San Clemente Imaging Center just off the 405 Freeway. Give my secretary a ring tomorrow morning and she will give you the address and the appointment time.

"Try not to worry, it could be nothing, but it's better to check these things out," she added as she walked Junie to the door of her surgery. Dr. Dana had seen the lighthouse flashing its danger message, even if she only picked it up by sheer luck, and five crucial words, 'June, is there anything else?'

I hadn't gone with her because, or so we thought, she only had a troublesome cough but when she arrived back she dropped into my arms as I opened the front door, she was confused and nervous and told me what the doctor had said.

I tried hard to deflect the problem, but I had a terrible, heavy feeling in the pit of my stomach. "Juna, Dr. Dana was just making sure that you are okay, she likes you, it's much better to be safe than sorry. When we get the results, you'll see that it was a waste of time. If it wasn't our doctor, who we both trust, I would say they are just out to make an extra few bob.

"Anyhow, let's go and see that Jack Nicholson and Adam Sandler movie *Anger Management*, remember we saw the shorts and it looked real funny. We both could do with a laugh."

After all the initial tests and blood samples had been concluded the results were on Dr. Dana's desk within a couple of days as she chased them relentlessly.

The doctor had the right idea of what the problem was all along and now had the results, which confirmed everything.

Junie and me were sitting down holding hands in front of the doctor when she picked up a sheaf of papers, glanced down at them and uttered the worst words that I would ever hear in my lifetime: "June, you have cancer of the colon."

It cut right into my gut, I felt like kicking out or smashing something. Why? Why? She's never hurt anyone, whoever said there is a God? My body was in turmoil but for Junie's sake I had to bottle it. How the hell must my love Junie be feeling?

Calmly Junie spoke quietly to the doctor, trying gamely to find a reason. "Doctor, the last time I was here, I forgot to tell you about something that may have to do with the colon. Three weeks ago, I had two sessions of colonic irrigation. I could actually see all the bile and rubbish that had gathered in my colon being washed out as it passed through the large transparent pipe that ran beside the bed that I was laying on."

Doctor Dana was furious and went crazy saying: "These people should be put out of business, what they are doing is very dangerous." This was not the response that Junie had expected. I just sat there numb, I didn't know anything about this, I couldn't even think of a question.

Colonic irrigation was made famous by Princess Diana using it supposedly for health reasons. I could see Doctor Dana's point, Junie had colon cancer and this type of treatment, if it went wrong, could have proved fatal. It is ridiculous to say that Junie was lucky. But looking at the irrigation treatment, it luckily hadn't harmed her. The plus was that her colon was now cleaned out.

Down the road, if this treatment hadn't been done, she probably would have had to have an operation and necessitated the fitting of a bag to carry what the stricken colon couldn't carry.

The doctor spoke again, now in a much calmer voice: "June, I have booked you to see two different oncologists on Wednesday and Thursday." We left the doctor's office numb with shock. Our world had just completely fallen apart. Tragically, Junie's first visit to the doctor had nothing to do with the 'small pain in the stomach', being only an after-thought. If the doctor hadn't asked, she would have never known, until the very end.

Gary was at home in Dana Point while Tony was in Europe trying to sort out a deal with the BSPA to fit his air-fences into the top tracks in England. When he heard the news he dropped everything and was home within days. When he arrived back, he tackled Junie's problems as though it was his personal war.

He would never forget how she gave up her life completely and sat by his bedside non-stop for three months, never going back home to Southampton, after his speedway crash that threatened to leave him paralysed with a broken neck. We rented a small cottage outside Oswestry so she could help and just waited and prayed for the day when we could take him out of his hellhole.

We had a very sad and restless night, things were that bad that even I couldn't sleep. In our present dilemma there are very few positives around at this moment of time. We sat huddled together outside on our back deck, clutching our steaming cuppas, and even a breathtakingly beautiful sunrise was completely lost on us both. Words were not needed as we sat clinging to each other, sipping our tea, both lost in our thoughts, wishing the world would stop, and not move on.

Rousing ourselves to get ready to visit the clinic for the first time was a real drag. We were to be there when it opened at 10 o'clock. First we were sent to the Mission Hospital on Crown Valley Parkway, where we had an appointment with a Surgeon Oncologist who was to carry out a colonoscopy. After that had been conducted we waited nervously until we had the results after an hour. It was like a re-enactment of the War Crimes trial at Nuremberg when the judge gave out the verdicts. He showed no emotion at all as he read out the death penalty to me, luckily while Junie was still getting dressed.

He told me brutally: "Her chances are bad and the best that she can expect is two months." He carried on: "Today is Wednesday and she must have surgery by this coming Saturday at the latest. That will take care of the colon. The cost will be in the region of 50,000 dollars."

I was out of my depth and my response drew a curt reply. "Okay, so the operation will take care of the colon but I believe the liver cancer is what is going to kill my wife. What do you do about the liver?"

He answered me abruptly. "We will first get the operation over with and then face that problem."

He must have seen my jaw drop, he didn't waste words, neither did I as I grunted back to him. "We will get back to you."

The second oncologist was so busy that he couldn't see us for a week. But, by using her woman's gentle persuasive powers, Doctor Dana arranged for us to be fitted in at the end of the afternoon clinic.

This doctor was very different to the previous one. This man really cared and was lovely in front of Junie. He didn't actually lie but he gave her a grain of hope. Afterwards, speaking to me and Tony, he explained in relatively simple language that we were fighting an enormous problem with Junie's cancer, especially in the liver.

What a difference between these two doctors. One was from the Middle East, while the other was Japanese. The wonderful gift of life meant something completely different to these two men. Not just a little, but 180 degrees worth.

The seriousness of cancer is rated one to four. Junie was diagnosed with stage four cancer, the worst. The CT scan showed that the primary tumor markers were in the colon but the cancer had in fact actually spread to the liver. I was led to believe that the colon was operable, with an 85 per cent chance of success, but her biggest problem was the secondary in the liver, which is the killer.

I don't know if I had read, heard, or simply wanted to believe that if problems with your liver are caught soon enough and brought under control it can, in fact, regenerate itself by a massive 90 per cent. But the clock had started ticking and we didn't know when it had started. Time is of the essence.

Two months seems such a short time. We were still scrambling, trying to find the right answers. I phoned everyone, everywhere, who I thought knew anything about cancer, through their loved ones or friends who had suffered the disease.

Most people, it seemed, just rowed along with what their doctors had prescribed for them. Then they sat by and watched their loved ones decline. Some suffered in very bad circumstances after chemotherapy or radiation or both. For some it was slow, whilst for others it was a rapid deterioration.

The hardest part for me was that Junie hung on to my every word, as she was sure that I'd sort it out, like I always had. Whether it was in front of 70,000 screaming fans at the Wembley Empire Stadium, with half of my hand hanging off or in the middle of the African jungle, handling the wrath of the Paramount Chief with his wrecked bridge by our lorry.

It was the same in Czechoslovakia when the Russians were trying to take over and our Czech driver decided that he was going to help the cause by running down two Russian soldiers crossing the road.

Junie knew that I had always managed to come up with the right answers. Here I was with my boys stuck in this dark tunnel, which didn't seem to have an exit, as we thrashed around not really knowing what to do next.

One evening I committed a cardinal sin. Junie found me downstairs. I had really lost it and had gone completely to pieces. It shattered me and I was disgusted with myself. She had never, ever seen me like this before. I vowed there and then to myself that I'd never, ever show her any weakness again. It was the toughest assignment that I had ever imposed on myself.

I was supposed to be her strength and here I was folding up. Seeing me like this, how could she ever believe me when I'd told her that we could beat this devil together?

Relaxing looking out over the Dana Point Harbour.

Other problems started to rear their heads when Junie's family wanted her to return to England. After speaking and e-mailing our doctor in England with Junie's diagnosis, he consulted with an oncologist friend in Southampton. I was expecting to hear something better from the other side of the world. I was gutted and surprised that the English medical profession were talking the same language as the Californian doctors ... just operate, stand back and then worry about the liver.

I was surprised and angry as nothing was ever mentioned about the quality of the patient's life.

Here we were, talking about only a two month span of life and the answer was to thrash the patient's body with operations and tough treatment. It seemed brutal, to subject that to a body that had such a short time left here on this planet.

To me it seemed that everyone had lost sight of the fact that they were dealing with a human being, still with all of their God-given qualities intact. Nobody was taking into consideration that her life and feelings was the last thing on their list of priorities. I thought that was inhumane.

To move Junie from our beautiful, sunny home in Dana Point to cold and grey England, and into temporary accommodation, or to live with relations, was not what me and the boys wanted for our Junie.

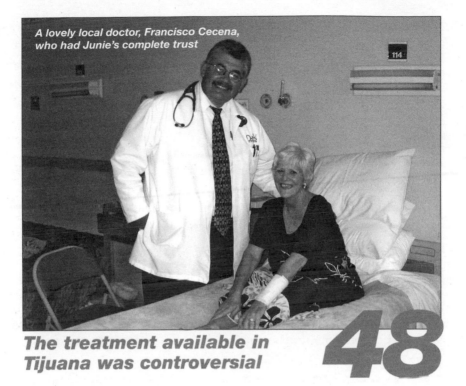

A lovely local doctor, Francisco Cecena, who had Junie's complete trust

The treatment available in Tijuana was controversial

48

REECE Facoory, a New Zealand friend of Junie and me, travelled with his wife Dorothy to Tijuana, Mexico, in 1994. She was suffering from Chronic Myeloid Leukaemia and the treatment she could receive there was not available in New Zealand.

His decision to take Dorothy to the American Bio-Logits Clinic in Tijuana paid off. Nine years later she was fit and strong and living a near normal life. After listening to Reece, Gary, Tony and me took a trip south from our Dana Point home and over the Mexican border to check it out.

It was located in a pretty run down area of Tijuana but the clinic itself looked nice and so were the people in charge. We spent well over three hours there talking to the patients, finding out about their problems and how they faced up to them. Of course, the most important question was: why did they come to Tijuana for treatment?

Some of their answers were exactly the opposite of what we had been led to believe. Most had had their bodies torn about by all kinds of treatments and drugs before they arrived here. They all told us to make a positive decision as Junie, unlike them, had a virgin body, treatment wise, which they considered was an advantage.

The biggest shock was that 99 per cent of them told us if they could start their cancer journey over again, they definitely would not have had chemotherapy. Many also felt the same about radiation. Their reasoning was that while chemo attacks the tumour, it doesn't kill it and the side effects are horrendous.

The main attraction for coming here was for the Laetrile treatment, which is banned in America but is legal when carried out in Mexico. Laetrile attacks the tumour but it doesn't thrash the body. It was all very interesting.

We realised we didn't have time on our side and that a decision would have to be made quickly. Crossing the border back into America, I turned to the boys, and asked: "Well, what do you think?" They were both smiling as Gary answered. "Well dad, if we blindfolded Juna until we got right outside the clinic I think it would be okay."

We all had a laugh, but we did not have that much time to determine our next step. Most Americans would consider having medical treatment in Tijuana as laughable, but to us it was certainly not a laughing matter. The question we faced now was critical, either we take the tough road and go with chemotherapy and radiation, or follow the alternative therapy that would be less abusive and abrasive to Junie's body.

With the latter we wouldn't have to uproot Junie from her Dana Point home, where she felt safe and secure, surrounded by all her normal bits and pieces. "Barry, we must remember that we are not the one that is going to make the decision. We must give Junie all the facts and options, it's her life," Tony said and we all agreed.

"I think we must make a decision of what we think is the best as we are on the ground, and have the advantage of being there and seeing the place. Junie will listen to us and then base her decision on what she hears."

Taking a swig of Cola, I changed lanes onto the 5 Freeway heading towards LA. It was unanimous that we felt it was Junie's call and her decision if she wanted to go the Mexican route or not. She made the bullets … we just fired them.

Gary spoke up: "Now that we have decided on the Mexican route, I think that when we get back to Dana Point we must all be positive and cheerful about the Tijuana alternative therapy and try to give Junie some positive hope."

"Tony, ring Junie and tell her we are on the way home with good news," I said as we passed the coastal town of Carlsbad. When we got home I entered the house as usual via my office in the garage. As we did so I noticed my answer phone was blinking. The message was from Reg Fearman, an English friend who had been through the same drama as us.

"Gary, find your Mum and tell her that I've got to make a quick phone call, keep the Mexican thing a bit general till I hear what Reg has got to say." Over the previous six months he had scoured the world searching for a way to clear his wife of cancer. He had tried the best that England had to offer but, unfortunately, it was not good enough and he lost his beloved wife Joan.

In our little world, the Briggs family was known to be fairly resourceful and we were our own people. In my profession you needed to be. Getting it right for Junie in her battle against cancer was proving to be a real challenge but, maybe, we were just starting to see some light at the end of the tunnel. We all hoped that Junie felt the same.

I had been trying to contact Reg for a couple of weeks and hoped that he was not going to confuse the whole issue again.

Finally, I got him on the phone. I had expected a long, drawn out and detailed conversation, as Reg loved to talk, but he was very short and right to the point. "Briggo, if I was you, I'd just go out of your front gate at Dana Point, turn sharp right and head to Mexico and down the coast to the 'Oasis of Hope'. It is a cancer only hospital on the coast. It's on the outskirts of Tijuana and you should easily find it on the opposite side of the road to the Bullring.

"I will give you the hospital's telephone number. I have spoken to them a few times; it is where I was going to take Joan just before she died. They seemed the best to me and what I really liked was that their number one concern was what is best for the patient's quality of life, not just getting rid of the cancer at any price. Anyhow good luck and let us know if you need anything else."

We went upstairs to find Junie and Gary having a cuppa. She was buoyant at the news Gary had explained to her. Then I told her about Reg's call which to us all sounded even better. Early the next morning we were back in the car on our way back to Mexico. The border-crossing point was almost empty. The previous day it had taken over half an hour to get out of the USA and into Tijuana. But now, 15 minutes after clearing the border, we saw the large Bullring silhouetted on the horizon … we had made it.

There it was, the 'Oasis of Hope', and what a difference it was to the clinic we were at 24 hours before. It was a big, modern building and stood in its own acre of ground with a large car park at the back. We went into the offices and the registrar was already there to meet us. The hospital is purely a cancer facility and has 68 rooms for patients. Each room was designed to accommodate a patient and their guest, which I thought was a great idea.

Normally the first half hour of a hospital visit is spent asking 'how was your night?' but this way you were there so would know. Sharing the room with the patient meant that if he or she couldn't sleep and wanted to talk, needed their tummy rubbed or a drink of water, you were there to help.

After the registrar had answered all of our questions, he told us that the earliest that Junie could be admitted was in ten days' time. We asked if he could hold everything until the next day and we would get back to him before 11am.

We gathered up all the available literature for Junie to read before making her decision. We got back to Dana Point just after noon but, because of the eight-hour time difference between London and Los Angeles, I had to wait until early in the morning to speak to the BUPA insurance company to ascertain what coverage we had in Mexico.

We all chatted about the options and it was great to see that Junie was sold on the 'Oasis of Hope'. The most important thing now was to get Junie strong, especially in her mind, so that she could handle what was going to be a huge, physically and mentally taxing ordeal.

The next morning BUPA took a load off my mind when they confirmed that we were covered 100 per cent. That was a big plus because medical costs in this part of the world are an arm and a leg. For BUPA, having treatment in Mexico was probably the better of the two options … it would cost them less than half compared to the USA or England.

We were fighting for the life of someone we loved and money was not the issue but, at the same time, I didn't want to feel that we were being ripped off.

When we were kids, and growing up, we were always taught that you never questioned the police, the vicar and, of course, doctors. Unfortunately, in today's world who can you really trust?

First you need the truth, especially medically, and then the human factor must be considered on which to base your decision.

Alternative cancer treatment was world news when film star Steve McQueen travelled to Tijuana to undergo the therapy on offer there. Initially, he was treated by Doctor Ernesto Contreras for six months and he responded well.

But, it appears that when Steve returned to California he just carried on as normal. Things were starting to go wrong again so he returned to Mexico for further treatment. In the meantime the Mexican government had closed down the Dr. Contreras clinic for political reasons and McQueen had to go elsewhere. He was operated on and unfortunately died soon after. The full story of McQueen's visits to see Dr. Contreras to receive the 'Mexican Alternative Cancer Treatment' was never revealed.

Later Dr. Contreras opened the 'Oasis of Hope' for cancer patients, specialising in Laetrile treatment, which is banned in the United States. The official reason given is that Laetrile can cause cyanide poisoning. Over the span of many years the Contreras family has treated more than 100,000 patients and have never had one case of cyanide poisoning.

Dr. Contreras's son, Francisco, is now the Director and chief surgeon at the Oasis, taking over from his father when he died four years ago. Doctor Francisco Contreras was Junie's doctor. In hindsight, it was our best move in the circumstances and, to my mind, there was no alternative.

God, and Mexico, gave us Junie for an extra four months and the bonus was that nobody messed about with her body with chemotherapy or radiation. These type of problems, at this stage of your life, confuse and scare. If the decision was about your life, and you get it wrong, then bad luck for you. But, dealing with someone else's life makes it twice as tough.

The patients at the first Mexican clinic we attended told us how they thought they had initially got it wrong when they followed the normal chemo route that their doctors had told them was the best way to be rid of cancer.

Luckily, I had the strength of my sons behind me and we were strong enough to tough it out with the American doctors, especially with the added veiled threat that it was imperative that Junie should be operated on within days.

We now had the money behind us for the operation at the Oasis. The first glimmer of hope was when the Oasis Tumour Board decided to use the non-surgical approach. We were really elated, as they really seemed to care about the well-being of Junie, not the money.

On June 24, 2003, the Briggs clan moved into the Tijuana area. I stayed at the hospital with Junie while the boys were over the road at a Mexican motel. Gary had to go backwards and forwards to his job at a Jaguar dealership.

At the Oasis each patient is allocated their own doctor. Before we came to the hospital, Tony had made a comprehensive file on all of Junie's tests, x-rays, in fact everything. We all shook hands with the doctor and Tony gave him Junie's special file, explaining what it contained. It looked to me that he didn't really care what it contained.

The first question he asked Junie was: "Do you smoke?"

"No, never," she told him.

"How about drink?"

Junie answered: "I have an occasional glass of wine."

"How much?" he quizzed. "A glass of red wine after my evening meal," she replied. "Then you are an alcoholic," he blurted out.

We were all in shock. He then felt and looked at Junie's pride and joy, her hair. "Oh, you dye your hair … it is really bad for you." Then he made some smart-arse comment about Junie's hands. I watched Tony, he was boiling over. He hadn't even bothered to open, let alone look at, Tony's specially prepared file.

Tony asked him some specific questions about Junie's condition and it was obvious that Tony knew more about the cancer than this so-called doctor.

The doctor was now trying to leave, he wanted out of there, but Tony wouldn't let him off the hook and told him to just sit down and explain what's going on.

"What is your actual job, are you a doctor, an x-ray man or what?" There was no answer, he just mumbled that he wanted to go. After the interview the three of us descended on the hospital administration and told them that we didn't want this doctor to be in charge of our Junie. Gary and me were in shock but we realised that Tony was right.

Our next doctor, a large Mexican man, was nice and soft and he had the vital 'simpatico'. His name was Doctor Francisco Cecena. At first he had a little trouble shaking all our hands whenever we met. He also knew that he was going to be quizzed, on all

Junie's doctor, Francisco Contreras, was one of us, a motorcyclist.

occasions, but he had no problem with that. We felt that at all times he was up front with us, with good or bad news. Our initial encounter with the first doctor was really the only problem of any consequence that we encountered at the Oasis of Hope.

Was it luck? Or was someone up there trying to help, as Junie's allotted room faced out the rear of the hospital which over-looked a small canyon. Could you believe it, on the other side of the canyon was a pre-school, named 'Highland Prince' with kids up to 10-years-old. It was an action-packed environment and Junie was in heaven. Most activities took place in the back yard, which was only 100 yards from her room.

Kids were her life, she always had stories to tell me after school, she loved the innocent honesty of them. She was a great storyteller and I had seen her telling them tales while even the naughtiest kid never moved. Then it was my turn to listen intently as she told me the day's tales.

"You can't believe what I was told today by Jason. He said, teacher, you've got a moustache, then worse still, Rebecca told me that I had dinosaur's breath. I think I had a sardine sandwich for lunch," she chuckled loudly.

The first of July was Junie's birthday. After she had finished all of her day treatments we went out to celebrate. We were told that there was a lovely little Italian restaurant within walking distance of the hospital. The one good thing, despite Junie's illness, was that our family could be together and strong right behind our leader. We thoroughly enjoyed our little birthday party for Junie, who was looking well. This was not one of the eateries recommended by the hospital with its organic fruit and vegetables-only menu. At the hospital we all ate the same meals as Junie, but I thought the food was very bland.

On our way to her birthday bash we met two sisters from Leicester. Sue, the elder, had battled with her cancer for two years and was banned from her local doctor's clinic. Her doctor only knew one way to treat cancer, but she was a rebel. He didn't want to help with anything. Boy, this girl really wanted to live and fought hard to beat her cancer. She knew all the treatments and was a walking encyclopaedia on cancer.

As we passed them, we quipped: "Are you girls off to a dance?" They both stopped and laughed, saying: "We're off to Colonel Sanders' for a chicken and chips pig out." Here was one of our inspirations, 'Organic Annie' who had given up her fight for one night.

Our three-meals-a-day schedule meant that we ate and mixed with just about all of the patients. It was a real family atmosphere. No one went too far from the hospital, the rooms were very light and airy, there were plenty of lounges in which to read, and if needed to have some time alone.

The hospital was aptly named the 'Oasis of Hope.' The translation of the word HOPE is, 'an expectation, or desire, a trust in a person, or a thing, that encourages hope'. Yes, it is the right name, if you haven't got hope you haven't got anything.

There were always stories being circulated around the hospital, most of which were good. You could not find a more positive group of people anywhere else in the world. Most of these patients had been told they were going to die but none would believe or accept it. These are different people who have stepped out of the box. Trying to make their own assessment of what they should or could do to beat this dreadful disease. They had obviously decided that their best chance was at the Oasis of Hope.

The patients and even the hospital are battling to find the solution to ridding themselves of cancer but nobody knows the exact answer. Some will realise that they made the right decision by coming to the Oasis. Others would find that if they had followed their own doctor's prescribed treatment they would be in a worse physical condition from the chemotherapy and radiation but, maybe, their life expectancy would be longer.

We believe that Junie's quality of life while undergoing the Oasis methods was good. And we were to enjoy three times more good quality time with Junie than we were told we would by American doctors. At the start of the cancer treatment everyone wants to completely rid their body of this deadly affliction. Then you realise that if the cancer is not racing away you can live a good life together with the cancer in relative harmony. You must decide what you consider a victory. Is a shorter period of time with better quality of life the winner? We decided that the longer the better, but in the end quality is the most important thing. The loss of a couple of weeks, I felt, was better for Junie and her loved ones.

The hospital was only a couple of blocks from the sea and we spent a lot of time walking there when Junie wasn't having treatment. Stories circulated the hospital daily, some of amazing recoveries, others with cancer completely gone, but of course there were the heart-breaking ones as well.

Following the death of Dr. Ernesto Contreras, the most famous pioneer of the Laetrile treatment, in October 2003, we all went to a memorial service at the church just around the corner from his hospital and it was full.

Something happened there that made Junie very happy and made her feel very special. Dr. Contreras's son saw Junie in her wheelchair and walked the full width of the church to give her a hug. With the church filled with his friends, family and many patients, we all felt good for Junie.

Not all patients were like her, she had words of comfort and a radiant smile for all, that's how people remember her.

Ernesto Contreras and his son Francisco were loved by the patients they cured and criticised by doctors who don't believe in Laetrile therapy.

The other treatment that interested me was the Ozone oxygen therapy, which my friend Joseph Joy told me about when we were living in Germany. If I had listened properly I would have heard him say that it was good for the treatment of cancer, which hates oxygen.

We were approaching the time that Junie was going to be discharged to return home. This was bothering me, as it meant within the next couple of days I was to become Junie's doctor for the next 45 days of treatment at our own home. I really didn't pay much attention to the hospital notice board and Gary brought it to my notice that there was going to be a class for home treatment in the library the following afternoon. This proved to be a great help, but I was very nervous about giving injections and was told to be positive and to practice on an orange. But there is a massive difference between sticking a needle into an orange, and your darling's bum!

Now I was 'Doctor Barry' and having to care for Junie

49

The next 45 days were probably the most nervous of my entire life. Junie required 30 different tablets a day starting at 8am in the morning until 9pm at night.

Three times a day she had to drink two different types of drinks. One was a blended organic carrot juice, the other was a greens drink made with organic spinach. Not difficult for a woman to conjure up but quite a challenge for Doctor Barry!

While Junie was strong enough we would go on the shopping expedition together and she would do the blending and then things were not too bad.

Giving her the right pills at the right time was a nightmare, especially as my Gestapo-like assistant staff nurse Tony was unbelievable. His non-stop questions – are you sure, how many, what colour, etc, etc? – were driving me around the bend.

After puncturing plenty of oranges, I got pretty good at injections. I had it figured out, as long as I thought when looking at Junie's bum that it was an orange. But if you lost your mindset and realised that it was actually your loved one's bum you were injecting, and then tried to do it with feeling, it just didn't work. You had to be sharp and decisive.

Being married for over 45 years you would have thought nothing could shock us. But it was very odd and really tough on us both to start and finish the day with a shark enema. Strange as it seems that after a week, we even started joking about it. "Junie, I think you're a strange person, most people want to start the day on an egg but, no, you want to start the day on a shark."

The final task of the day was to check her weight and we were delighted that it remained the same throughout the 45 days.

We returned to the hospital for four days at the end of August for follow-up treatment. Everyone seemed to be quite happy, especially as there was no significant weight loss. It seemed as though the colon problem was no worse and we were holding our own. But the liver was still bad and a real concern.

As the 'home doctor' I was happy to hear that the patient thought our Dana Point brew of the 'green drink' was better than the Oasis counterpart. One thing was that everyone said how well Junie looked. She did look well, but it was the smile that was the sunshine.

It was back across the border and home to California for another six weeks. Back to being Doctor Barry, the constant washing of my hands plus, of course, those bloody pills. Now we had a couple of other problems. Junie was having trouble drinking her carrot juice and was on the verge of gagging every time she tried to swallow the concoction. Being her doctor I told her just to drink what she was comfortable with. I watched as she struggled with it but I would say nothing.

During the time of Junie's cancer I read and listened to many things about this cruel disease. One thing that came up regularly as a possible cause was stress.

I was my own worst enemy and constantly heaped plenty of problems on to myself and obviously this overflowed on to Junie. I will never know, and she would never tell me, or anyone else, if she ever felt the unbelievable stress that surrounded her, and if the hectic lifestyle, had in fact contributed to her illness.

A big part of my life was full on stress, probably caused by the danger and apprehension of racing. Without being too dramatic, to be a winner you have to put your life on the line many times. I had to learn how to handle and live with it. I am convinced, without outwardly showing it, Junie quietly shared much of my stress, too.

I would get wound up and at times even abuse myself for being an idiot or for doing something dumb. But, by letting it out, I think it released the stress and tension that had built up inside of me. The near silence before meetings, when I would cut out the rest of the world from my mind, the changing of her clothes in the car just minutes before our arrival at the stadiums ... it was an unreal world.

But, most of all, she was always concerned about my driving on British roads, especially before the introduction of motorways and we faced long journeys up and down the country many days of the week. Too often I would be running late for a meeting and had to drive too fast. Many, though obviously not me, would say it was dangerous driving but often it was necessary to ensure that we got there on time.

Junie stated publicly on many occasions that she never feared that she would lose me as the result of a speedway crash but her one big fear was a fatal accident on one of my hectic car trips. I must admit that during my racing career in the UK and Europe I had some close calls. If I had written myself off, to me that was part of the deal, but if I harmed anyone, especially Junie, I couldn't have lived with it.

Everyone could see and knew how calm and caring my Junie was under the worst conditions during my racing career. She even suffered abuse herself, when an idiot Norwich supporter whacked her at a Wembley World Championship Final.

Junie would always get a good laugh when she told her favourite story about my driving. I always thought that my driving was completely under control, though not everybody would agree with that. Two American friends were visiting us at Southampton. I was racing at Swindon that night and, with the bikes loaded on the trailer, we took off for Blunsdon.

We went along the back roads, it was a journey that I had done

June Elizabeth
BRIGGS

England 1937 - Mexico 2003

The ultimate Wife , Mum , Sister and Babcia

Forever in our hearts

Junie's Polish headstone for her grave in Epsom came in Tony's van from Poland. Junie would have loved this special treatment.

over 100 times. It was etched in my mind, I knew the fast places, the dangerous places, which corners were dodgy, it was just a normal trip. After the meeting we had everything packed and loaded for our return trip home to Southampton. We found our Americans friends and told them we were ready to go. However, I got the shock of my life, and I thought they were joking, when they said they were going back to Southampton by train.

No matter what was said, they wouldn't change their minds. Junie tried hard to do so but, in the end, she just smiled. Looking back, with all this stress around me, what was it doing to the inside of my darling Junie? On the outside she was the picture of calmness and serenity. I pray that my stress and driving didn't help to destroy her.

Eventually the big day arrives, it's the tenth of September. "Come on love, we are getting out of here and we are going to have a celebration pig out at the local Sizzler." She keeps asking what are we celebrating, I just say, 'you must wait until you've got your glass of red wine in your hand, then I will tell you'.

She was making a real effort, getting ready to go out. She kept looking at me as if I'd gone off my head. Luckily the boys weren't around, because she would have got one of them to tell, by fair means or foul.

She had her favourite glass of wine in her hand, looking incredibly beautiful despite what she was going through, her unforgettable large brown eyes just bored into mine. Looking into the depths of her eyes, I started my speech.

"Darling, you are very brave, and today is really special, I thought that maybe you would have worked it out. Today is one day over the two months that the bloody jerk doctor told us that was all you have left to be with us.

"Look at you, looking like a million dollars, whatever does that idiot doctor know. Just remember one thing … only the good die young, so you must have years of living left in you." She laughed, aren't you talking about yourself, she jived me. "Who me?" I answered, trying to look like the injured party. I never could fool my Junie.

Our bedroom was upstairs and we had a discussion that maybe

we should bring Junie downstairs as the stairs wore her out. From her bed she could see the Pacific Ocean, the yachts and the Dana Point harbour. There we had two 'tall ships' from the old days, they go on trips out to sea and allow the schoolkids or tourists to help put up the sails and other seafaring jobs.

They are a fantastic sight to see when the wind blows and the three sails are in full flow. We decided that it was much better to continue her life without any change. To help her get up and down the stairs we fitted a new type of the 'Briggs Lift', which was simply a good, solid chair.

Junie sat normally in the chair while one of us took the front legs and the other the back of the chair. Then it was laid back like some type of stretcher. First of all we had difficulties because, as normal, Junie thought that she was causing too much trouble. In the end she really enjoyed getting out of our bedroom. When she was outside she would have to move at different times to keep out of the sun.

We were spending plenty of time down in the harbour. The highlight of her day was when we went down a back alley, which ran along the back of Junie's old Montessori school, where she had been for the last six years.

Twelve years previously she worked at a small pre-school. Julie, the young owner, and Junie became great friends. Eventually the school had become too much for Julie, whose large family was needing more of her time. Her kids were the most important thing to Julie and when they got home from school there wasn't anyone to meet them. It was not what Julie wanted for her family.

The new owners hated that the parents went to Junie, as all their kids loved her. After six weeks she still wasn't happy with the job, it was simply that she loved children, money had nothing to do with it and she would have done it for free.

Picking her up from the old school, she was just about in tears, she had had enough. We sat in the car and I asked: "What do you want to do?" She explained she couldn't get on with the new lot, they had no manners and tried to stop her doing the stuff for the kids that she had done for years.

"Do you really want to work?" I added. "Of course, but only

with kids. As you know I have no special qualifications, also I'm at an unemployable age."

"Bullshit, do up your safety belt," I said as we moved off. When she realised we weren't on our normal road home, then the questions started. After no more than five minutes we stopped outside what was a beautiful old Mexican home on a large piece of land. In the front was a large car park, the back had been turned into a playground. It was only a couple of months ago that it was converted and opened as a Montessori school.

Junie celebrating her birthday at The Oasis Hospital.

As we stopped, I was hit with a barrage of negative questions and even more negative answers. When she stopped, I simply told her: "Right, get your arse into gear, clear that misery look off your face and get that winning smile back." She opened her mouth to comment again, I gently leaned across her and opened her door, giving her a peck on the cheek, saying, "good luck, go slay 'em."

Twenty minutes later the big, hand-carved, wooden Mexican door swung open and there with a smile even bigger than the door, stood our Junie. "Well, love, when do you start?"

"Monday! She really liked me, and she is lovely, I can't believe it." I was the one that couldn't believe it. Here was a woman that had been on this planet for over 60 years and still had that naivety that she had when I first met her when she was only 17-years-old.

If you didn't know her, you would think it was a put on. On the other hand in some ways she was streetwise, that was our Junie. I have said before, what you saw is what you got.

Now it was a different ball game, she still wanted to be with kids but her body wouldn't allow it. It was two o'clock in the afternoon when the kids were released into the playground to let off steam. The alley runs beside the play area. In the middle of a hedge is a single gate where you could see into the playground.

The kids would hear us stop and they all run over to the gate, they made no mystery of how much they loved her. There was a chorus of 'hello Miss June,' each trying to talk over the other. I could understand by watching Junie and the kids the great trust and love was there for all to see.

Then Miss June would take over, she would be asking the questions. "Michael, how's your bad foot? Mary, that's a beautiful new dress," Their enthusiasm was infectious, they all wanted to speak at once, she could have stayed there forever, but we had to move on. "Bye children, see you later", was followed by a chorus of "bye Miss June" from over 20 young kids. The happiness enveloped her radiant face for all to see and a couple of times I detected a little tear waiting to slip out.

She still looks beautiful.

Junie's brave fight continues but we face tough decisions

50

WE were now due back at the Oasis Hospital on the new date of October 10. Because of the change, Bill Brown and his wife Jeanne arrived in Dana Point just a day before we left for our new appointment.

I was embarrassed and told Bill that he should stay at our house and use it as his base. But Bill and Jean wanted to come with us to Tijuana. It turned out to be great as Bill is a natural story teller and had hundreds of jokes on the tip of his tongue.

We had a great time, we would all gather around Junie's bed for joke time. Between Bill and Junie's jokes it was laughs non-stop, some of Junie's I think she got directly from the old Tony Blackburn show on radio back in the UK.

In a cancer hospital there are not a lot of laughs going on but laughing is infectious and everyone around us at these times had trouble keeping a smile from invading their faces. The world doesn't seem a bad place when all your troubles are swept under the mat.

We had to meet the doctor so left Junie and everyone behind, but at the end of the corridor I could still hear the laughter. We all loved Doctor Contreras as we felt that he was one of us. When he was younger he had ridden in the Baja 1000 off-road race. I did a little better than him as I did manage to finish. He laughed that he kept crashing his Honda and finally retired. He was not on his own as a crasher, I had my moments as well.

At that moment he had a big 1098 Ducati road racer and had ridden on most of the Californian tracks. He was a very straight talker and, most of all, Junie really liked and trusted him. I suppose his good looks helped as well.

Entering his office he was smart and as usual was very gracious in his ways. He initially gained our confidence when he wouldn't take the money and operate when we first arrived. He was a good doctor and very perceptive. As we walked into his office he knew why we were there and would already know the course of action to be taken.

"Doctor, you know why we are here, we have now done all the home treatment, what now?" He looked me straight in the eye: "Mr. Briggs, I am sorry, I must be blunt, your wife should not be here with us now." I felt sick. "She is alive because of you and your boys' love and strength. I can't believe how well she looks in the circumstances, she is a credit to you all. Our hospital staff talk about you all, the shaking of the hands, the questions, many people would have given up by now. The root of the problem is that her liver is really bad and virtually non-functioning."

"We will always love her, doctor, and she has been unbelievable how she just keeps on fighting. I suppose it's not so unbelievable, she just simply wants to live. Have we got a next move, and what about the Donald Factor treatment?"

He replied: "Yes, we had great success with Donald, but no two cases are the same. Once again you need some luck, as the operation is a bit tricky. You basically unwind the umbilical cord and go directly into the liver. You then fit a catheter, which allows you to treat the liver directly, with the Laetrile and 5FU, which is an intravenous chemotherapy. I know that you don't like chemotherapy but it's not all bad if it is used along with the Laetrile."

"Doctor, we must try to explain this to her as she will have to make the decision on what to do. What are her chances of surviving this operation?"

Doctor Contreras gave a small cough and cleared his throat. He had been in this situation many times, but never with three pairs of eyes targeting him with such intensity.

"Well, with no complications and if we can get in and out within three hours, I think Mrs. Briggs should make it. But any loss of time in complications would diminish her chances greatly."

"What can we expect if the operation goes through without any hitches?"

"Well, she will be no worse off than she is now and at the very best we can expect she will get more time. God moves into these equations at times and you never quite know, but keep your prayers going as well, it's a different kind of medicine."

"Doctor Contreras, I'll just repeat what you told me, just to get it straight in my mind. If we do nothing, the end is close by. The operation is going to do no harm to Junie if you don't have any complications. If we have complications and the operation drags on, then we would have serious problems and we could lose Junie. The best that we can expect is that she will live longer in about the same condition as she is now. Is that a fair summary of Junie's future?"

"Yes, that I'm afraid is exactly as I see it," he said as he looked directly into the eyes of the three of us separately.

"One last question doctor, would you personally do the operation, and when? Of course, that's assuming that she wants to have the operation."

"Mr. Briggs, I must stress that this is a very tricky operation and not without danger to the patient but, if it is what your family wish, then I would be very pleased to do it for you." Looking at his diary he answered: "Three days on, the morning of October 17 would be my first available time."

I smiled to myself. That date 46 years ago, was the luckiest day of my life when I married Junie, hopefully it's a lucky omen?

We all shook hands with Doctor Contreras and left, telling him that he would have Junie's decision the following day. "Boys, let's go and have a drink and a talk before we speak to Junie. She will be okay as she has got Jean and Bill to chat to."

After we explained everything about the operation to Junie, including the dangers, she had no hesitation in deciding to go ahead. It was like driving down a blind alley, she really didn't have too many choices. At this stage I was still amazed at her bravery, and her smile was there as always. Yes, she was amazing but we didn't want her to lose her hope, so we kept nudging her along.

Junie got through her operation with flying colours. When Doctor Contreras visited Junie, he said everything went like clockwork and now we should keep our fingers crossed and pray.

Junie told her story of how she was really nervous waiting outside the operating theatre. Everyone getting her ready was laughing and jolly, it seemed so out of place. Junie smiled and said that maybe it helped to take her mind off what turned out to be a three-hour operation.

I really liked that we both had beds in the same room, so we could spend time talking, and reading, and just being in each other's company. The hospital was great, everybody was in the same boat and would help each other with information, or whatever was needed. They were all positive people, as were their families or loved ones.

It was late on a Sunday evening, I was with Junie and we were reading. One of the staff nurses came in and asked me if I would help as one of the patients had a problem. They didn't have the money to pay for the blood that she desperately needed. It was dark when four of us non-patients were driven five miles into the centre of Tijuana to the blood bank where we gave blood. The blood bank simply would swap our blood for the type that the needy patient required.

Sitting there with my other three blood donors, we were a mixture of two Malaysians, an Italian who couldn't speak English plus, of course, a bloody Kiwi.

I couldn't stop myself laughing as I had my cup of tea and biscuits. I could envisage Tony Hancock in that hilarious television programme called *The Blood Donor*.

This is what the real world should be like. Where else would this type of thing happen? What a 'Bloody Mary' mix, a little bit of Kiwi, plus two nips of Malay, and a drop of Italian.

We were sitting with Junie as she was given the 'Tennis Doctor's Ozone Special', the very same as we had years ago in Germany. In fact, when we went back to California we rang Dr. Yankowski in Holzwickede to try and buy his old machine. We finished up buying one in Canada from a Czechoslovakian named Jakob. The only trouble when we were back in California (where this treatment is banned), was to get someone to take the blood out to be treated. We used to have blood days, and Tony's friend Scotty, a fireman, would do it for us. It was blood celebration day as Tony and me joined Junie for a top up.

Back in California, I got my white coat out again and started washing my hands non-stop ... I was the infamous Doctor Barry again. I think Junie secretly liked having me as her doctor as I was now the master of the needle. It was also 'pay back time' for what she had done for me and the kids over the years. But do you really have to wash your hands so often? Junie was in pain, not from the cancer but because of a bed sore at the bottom of her spine, which nobody could really do much about.

Mike Smart and his son Michael were on their way to New Zealand for the road race season and his wife Jill was a matron at an old people's home in England.

She sent me some special dressings for our bed sore problem and they proved to be great. When we heard Mike was coming to see us, on the way to New Zealand, we rang him.

"Mike, can you do us a favour and bring a parcel for us?"

"Sure," he said not knowing what he had let himself in for. The parcel was, in fact, a fully functional stair lift, complete with chair and electric motor!

Junie's friend Janet, who lived in West Byfleet, Surrey, had recently lost her husband Ken, who had used the lift each day. It was now surplus to requirements there and she had given it to June as a birthday present.

The only problem was that West Byfleet is a long way from Los Angeles. I still cannot believe that they managed to talk an airline into taking it as luggage and eventually we reassembled it at our Dana Point home.

There was more good news when my brother Wayne's wife Teresa, who was one of Junie's very best mates, wanted to come and see her. She rang me and told me she was coming for the weekend. I thought it was stupid and told Teresa it was a lot of money for just two days.

I said that as soon as Junie is fit and up and about we would come back to England. We had been battling so hard for months that I had really lost track of just how much Junie's condition had deteriorated. Thank goodness Teresa took no notice of my old twaddle.

She was a real breath of fresh air and the effect on Junie was enormous, she must have been collecting jokes for months. Then she started ripping our poor house apart, washing all the curtains, cleaning everything in sight. I felt bad, we must have been living in a tip!

When Teresa left and Junie had settled back down, it dawned on me just how much my darling had slipped backwards. It was really hard to detect as she really never complained, even when she was about to throw up trying to drink her juices.

In the end I said: "Juna, don't drink that crap if it's that bad, missing it is not going to make a big difference." Still she went on trying. She still wanted to live no matter what it took.

We were back at the hospital in the middle of November for two days for a check-up. Junie wasn't feeling at her best. We both had a laugh when Evel Knievel rang and told me that the medication Junie needed was something that his doctor told him would be a big help.

When I asked our doctor he just laughed and said what he had recommended would kill a horse. But when you are in trouble, people are so kind. Not as in Evel's suggestion, but with cards and phone calls. Many times, when someone is in a serious life and death situation, many people don't want to bother them and don't call.

One of my biggest and most pleasant surprises was when we got a special book of natural foods to beat cancer. This unbelievable act of kindness came from a speedway rider and even more of a shock … he was a bloody Aussie! I know he wouldn't want to be named, but bad luck, stand up John Titman. Thanks, we both greatly appreciated this kind gesture.

We returned home still battling away but I felt Juna had lost a bit of her zip. The Ozone was helping a little. She was having difficulty with her carrot and green spinach drinks. She was having trouble, energy-wise, so we got her a wheelchair. She didn't like that too much but it was necessary.

I would put her in the car and take her down into the Dana Point harbour. Then, in her hated wheelchair, I'd zoom around, taking in all of God's free gifts. The bracing fresh air, the glorious scenery, the miracle of the sea as it went in and out, kids riding the waves.

If it was a bit chilly, I'd wrap Juna in her Kiwi lamb's wool blanket and circulate around our three-mile circuit. It wasn't hard to recognise others with the same problems as ours. We were the lucky ones, as those car-bound were missing out.

Junie told me at least a couple of times each trip of how she never really took advantage of what we had here. I'd always get a laugh from her when I said: "Darling, God made you to look after kids and shop."

She was having trouble during the night, as she was now sleeping in our special laid-back chair. In bed the pressure on her sore made it impossible for her to get comfortable. In the chair we could get her and push her feet so we could move her to get her sore spine in the crack where the back and the seat met.

The worst thing was to stop Junie from being the 'I don't want to bother anyone Junie'. I was sleeping fitfully and if she wanted to go to the toilet she wouldn't want to wake me. Early in the morning it was still dark when I was awoken with this mighty great crash. There, lying on the floor, was Junie pinned underneath her bed, the large chair, she was unable to move. I was like a mother, when her child had an accident, instead of a cuddle, it's 'you naughty, naughty girl you shouldn't have done that'. We had a good laugh, I'd seen Junie do this with one of the boys many times.

I certainly couldn't have this happen again, as Junie was weak and couldn't help herself in this kind of situation. I came up with this devilish plan, it was plain to see at this time in life it was too late to try and change Junie, and I certainly didn't want her to hurt herself.

So the next night I strapped her in … it was foolproof, and at least I knew that my darling was safe.

She tried to pressure me with: "I'm going to tell my friends that you tie me up." I answered in a half laugh: "I'm sorry my love, you showed that you couldn't be trusted to wake me, but now you must."

At the end of November Junie's resolve was slowly leaving her. So we all shot down to Mexico for the hospital to have a look at her. The report wasn't good, and her sore back was playing up.

I think she was just starting to feel bad from everything that she had endured for the last five months, but she wouldn't really say so.

We saw the pain doctor who gave me some Fentanyl patches. He told me they were very strong but would relieve the pain if needed. It was a Friday and the hospital couldn't do anything till Monday. Junie felt that she would rather go home for the weekend and we were very happy that she wanted to do so. She was a little uncomfortable when travelling but it was a worthwhile trip. On the Saturday Junie had quite a bit of pain, so I put on the patch. Within a half an hour Junie was unable to talk coherently and was drifting in and out of consciousness. After five months of being a doctor I started to believe that I really was. Which is okay until you have a real problem, then the mind goes blank. I must have tried 15 times to get the 'pain doctor' on the phone at numbers he gave me, but to no avail.

Junie was getting worse, so I thought, 'to hell with it, this is not what I want for my little darling'. So I made the decision, I didn't know if it was good, bad or dangerous but I just took the bloody patch off. Within an hour we had our Junie back. I couldn't believe we weren't told that these patches were such a heavy deal and they were actually opium.

I lay some of Junie's ashes under the old oak tree at the cricket ground in Christchurch, NZ.

The sun sets for Junie and I lose the love of my life

51

JUNIE had now given up her fight and decided to talk to Tony to get her house in order. This was lucky for me as deep down I knew I was losing her, but my body and brain wouldn't let me take it on board.

Stupid or not, I would not admit defeat, especially to Junie. I still wasn't prepared to give her up, and still wanted to believe that she was going to make it.

Now I wish I could have accepted what was real, to tell her how much I loved her and that she was my whole life.

To thank her for our great boys and how she had brought them up by example and for the millions of things she had done to enlighten my life. Sorry that I was tough to live with at times.

Even to have five minutes with her would be all that I would need to tell her my final thoughts. Did it really matter, as she knew more about me than I did myself?

It showed when she asked Tony: "Get dad to relax and accept what is happening and not to keep fighting." I really couldn't help

Junie told Jan her boyfriend was a speedway rider. Junie is using Jan as her bike.

452 **Wembley** and *beyond*

myself, it was like a race, it was never over until you get to the finishing flag. There is always a chance, while the race is still running, and I certainly wasn't going to give up the most precious part of my life while there was even the tiniest glimmer of hope.

As ever, Junie was great and realised my quandary, she knew that discussing it with me would have driven me over the edge. My feelings and emotions had been building up for months and I was so much on edge that it would only require a pin-prick to burst the dam. Even now, in our darkest hour, she was still thinking of me.

We were supposed to be back at the hospital on Monday morning. We all knew that it was going to be a one-way trip and managed to put it off until Tuesday. On the Monday we twice went down into the harbour. Wrapped in her red tartan blanket we watched the most glorious sunset, which was really beautiful but oh so sad.

With heavy hearts we set off for Tijuana the following day and halfway there me and the boys were hungry and we stopped for a burger. We opened Junie's front door of the car and stood around her eating our burgers. Junie seemed to be on a mission, and wanted to get to the hospital sooner rather than later.

She gave us a couple of, "come on boys, let's go." Did she know or feel something that we didn't?

Back at the Oasis hospital they examined Junie and got her comfortable in bed. We then all sat around and chatted and watched television, just as though the world was normal but to me it was surreal. Junie was dozing, her head gently falling on to her chest. Everytime this happened, she would awaken with a start, it was as if she knew that if she did fall asleep it could be forever.

The Briggs family was very much a touch and cuddle one. The previous two months had been hell for me, it was as if the lifeline that bonded us had been severed. I hadn't been able to give Junie a proper cuddle for months. I don't know why, but as we watched television I climbed up on to the bed and got in between Junie and her backrest so she could just lie up against me.

It was amazing, with my arms around her, all the tension drained from her body, as she snuggled back into me. With all the tension

Easy rider! Personally I hate riding on the road as it's too dangerous.

Happiness personified.

and trauma of the last six months leaving her body, she relaxed completely.

It was the best cuddle of my life. The boys remarked later how contented she looked, and wished they had a camera. I will remember it for ever.

It was 10.30pm when one of the nurses asked Junie if she'd like to get ready for bed.

The nurse got her bed made up and asked if she had any pains or if she wanted anything to help her sleep, which she did.

We lost our angel at 11.02pm on the second of December, 2003. I had my hand on her forehead when she left us and I couldn't believe it. It was like a very strong build up of electricity in her forehead for a few minutes. The boys also felt it.

She lay there peacefully but to me it was only her body that remained, her unbelievable and amazing spirit had finally left.

Hopefully, somewhere, we will meet again. Bye for now my love.

JUNIE and Janet Laidler were friends who went to school together from when they were five-year-old girls until they were young ladies of 16, often taking their holidays together as teenagers.

I've been blessed all my life, firstly by spending most of my adulthood with Junie. After the surprise, shock and the depression of losing her, I take life as it comes these days. Now I have been blessed again by being with Janet. She knows that nobody could replace Junie, and it's the same for her that I couldn't replace her Ken. I first met Janet and her parents when Junie was on holiday in Devon with them in the 1950s before we were married.

I had a couple of days off so I drove to meet them all. I just lay around, reading and relaxing. Afterwards Junie and I laughed as Janet had asked her: "Can't you get someone a bit happier?"

Junie thought that was really funny. Janet had no idea what my life was about and thought I just sat around. In fact, I was probably knackered with all the travel and, in those days, I was hitting the ground at high speed quite a bit. So, most likely, I was just sitting around licking my wounds.

Junie and me were married in October, 1956, so it was more than

40 years before I saw Janet again and she can't believe what a happy person I really am!

Junie had met her on a few occasions at school reunions. She had also met Janet and her husband when he was ill and stayed with her for a few days. When I picked up Junie they had made a date to have a couple of days together when we were back in England the following June. Sadly, this was a date that was never to be.

One thing I remember was how house conscious Jan was and she was sure that my old English Merc would drop oil on her front drive. It has taken some doing but now Jan is enjoying life in a different way. I wonder what kind of CV Junie gave Jan on me, especially as they didn't have a clue what the future would hold for us.

When times were getting bad, Junie confided to Tony to make sure that I went to see Janet. She knew I would be hopeless trying to battle through life by myself. Both girls were different, but were the same happy types, loving their food and having the same excuse that they were 'war babies', so you mustn't waste any food. But the war finished quite a few years ago, didn't it?

Junie was Jan's school hero so we have no problem with photos of Junie being around which is lovely. Also, Jan shows love for our boys who lead her a merry dance, just like they did with their Mum. We live now between our lovely homes in California and leafy Surrey. In my office I have photographs of the two leading ladies in my life, side-by-side, along with pictures of my two sons, Gary and Tony.

I feel that there is a Lord, and that I've been blessed. Life is for living and I have always preferred to look forward rather than back.

Trying to give a little back

WE'VE all done it. Opened our mouth before engaging our brain. Put our foot in it. Agreed to something before thinking it through. Had an idea that seemed good at the time, but then ...

There were times, many of them in fact, while I was trying to raise tens of thousands of pounds for disabled former speedway riders, that I wondered what on earth I had let myself in for.

"Barry," I kept saying to myself, "you may have bitten off more than you can chew this time."

It was many months before, after a conversation with a friend of mine, Dick Marconi, who told me that every year he organises a boxing extravaganza at his Motor Museum for underprivileged kids which raises over a million dollars a year. After our chat, I remounted my bike to climb and descend the major hills behind Dick's ranch.

That day my mind wandered from my riding, and it was only my sub-conscious mind that took in the beauty of the hills and ocean as I rode the hills around the area near where I live in

Southern California. My mind was thrashing about trying to think of what kind of speedway event I could do for a good charity collection.

It was Dick who bought the rambling ranch that filmmaker Bruce Brown, of *On Any Sunday* fame, moved to when he sold his house in Dana Point to me. It was there that my son Tony and I spent so much time when he was taking the first steps towards a speedway career.

It is always a joy to ride through Dick's ranch as he has transformed it into a thing of great beauty, with an avenue of Italian cypress trees as you enter and marble statues everywhere.

However, it wasn't until the Spring of 2009 when I attended a meeting in Sheffield in aid of the Speedway Riders' Benevolent Fund and watched the fans there generously donating money for riders whose own careers have been blighted by injury, and especially those who are wheelchair-bound, that my plan began to take shape.

I sustained more injuries than I can recall during my own career, including losing a finger at the Wembley World Final in 1972, but nothing can compare with those of Alan Wilkinson, Joe Owen, Per Jonsson and so many others. It is humbling to talk to these guys and see how they cope with such a life-changing experience. And I know first-hand, as described in an earlier chapter in this book, what my younger son Tony went through after a crash at Coventry that threatened to leave him paralysed. Thankfully, Tony recovered but as I stood at Sheffield that spring afternoon, talking to those less fortunate than him, I kept thinking that I could, and should, do something to help.

Some of those who have been left disabled by their injuries were at Sheffield that afternoon, doing 'wheelies' and generally having fun. It was heart-warming to witness how well they coped with adversity. But I knew as well as anyone just how tough their lives actually were and how much they depended on those around them who have had to make their own sacrifices. That very evening I decided I was going to raise money for them ... but how was I going to make a worthwhile contribution to our fallen heroes?

I STARTED to put together a plan to ride a motorcycle, on and off road, from John O'Groats, at the top of Great Britain, right down to the south, stopping off at as many speedway venues as possible, to try and raise £120,000 to help 12 former riders.

How hard could that be? Well, for starters, much harder than I could possibly have thought!

Early doors I had a great piece of luck when Matt Ford, the Poole speedway promoter, introduced me to Nigel Leahy, who is his announcer at Wimborne Road. Matt said Nigel was a good, trustworthy bloke and he certainly is and over the course of the following weeks and months he became more and more important to me and 'The Ride', as it became known.

When I first mapped out my intended route, some of it along the old General Wade military roads, it didn't appear that tough. After all, I love riding motorcycles. It would be fun. But the more I got into it, the more frightening it all became. Riding was the easy part. But the actual expenses involved, how we would collect the money, what we would do with it (a huge percentage would be coins), co-ordinating the schedule with all the speedway meetings and so much more – it was all much more complicated than I had anticipated. It quickly became obvious that what seemed quite a simple idea at first was anything but. It was by now a daunting task.

Then up stepped Nigel. He took on board so much and not for any financial gain of his own. He liked the idea, liked me and loves speedway. I owe him a great deal, as do all those who eventually benefitted from what we achieved. Nigel and the guys who work at *Speedway Star*, the sport's weekly magazine, did a great job. I was just the monkey who rode the bike!

There are many others without whom we would never have accomplished what we set out to do. We needed a large van to transport all the bits and pieces required for a near 5,000-mile journey. My mate Bill Brown, who owns Wulfsport and lives in Cumbria, loaned me one of his. Thanks to another old mate, Andy Smith, we had the loan of two bikes from Yamaha – my son Tony was planning to come along with me for some of the ride. He couldn't commit to the whole thing, but came whenever he could and it was great to have him there.

I spent a few days at the Wulfsport base getting the van ready and one of the smartest things I did was to get Dave, their handyman, to build me a fold-down bed in the back. That was my saviour on so many occasions when I tried to get to the various tracks early so that I could have an hour's sleep before embarking on another evening of going round the stadium collecting money in buckets.

By coincidence, around the same time that we planned to start 'The Ride', the BBC's Sport Relief appeal was in full flow and I managed to do a deal with them to integrate our event with theirs. As it turned out it wasn't necessarily one of my better ideas, as we had to pay a percentage of the money we raised to Sport Relief, but they did help us get off to a high-profile start. Also, I think our association with Sport Relief did much to legitimise our own efforts in the eyes of the general public and when it came to 'balancing the books' they were more than fair with us.

Our first donation came from an unexpected source. Sir David Richards, a bigwig at both the Football Association and the Premier League, is someone I have got to know quite well in recent years and I am continually battering his ears in an effort to establish a speedway museum at Wembley Stadium. (Speedway had a long history at the 'old' Wembley but unfortunately it is pretty much ignored by the new regime, more's the pity.) Sir David managed to pull a few strings and arranged for me and Tony to officially launch our venture by doing a few laps of the stadium during the half-time interval of England's friendly international against Egypt in front of over 80,000 fans.

We got a marvellous reception … and a cheque for £1,000 from the Football Association. We were off and running. And it seemed like great fun, until we got to John O'Groats!

I became really nervous as the reality of what we were doing set in and by the time we set out from the north of Scotland the smiles had gone. My old 'race face' was back, one that most of my mates had not seen before.

Once on the road, after Bill and the boys had left, it was just Tony and I, both knowing that it would be very tough trying to keep to a schedule that often required us to be at three different tracks in three different locations on consecutive nights. I had to be smart and not think I was still 20 years old and superman. I wouldn't be able to raise any money if I had a stupid accident and ended up in hospital with a broken leg – and that was quite possible given that we started with snow and ice on the ground. That wasn't in the plan!

The rear tyres on the Yamahas were crap in the snow and the early stages were littered with many crashes, caused by the ice and snow, but eventually we arrived at our first stop, Edinburgh Speedway. It was a great success, with Neil Hewitt, one of those we were raising money for, on the parade with me and then helping with the collection.

The following day I rode the Yamaha back to our Lilleshall base in the Lake District and had plenty of time to think about what lay ahead. I decided that in view of the bad weather – it was one of the worst winters on record in the United Kingdom – I would suspend 'The Ride' for a month. It turned out to be a smart move.

When we resumed another ex-rider, Dave Younghusband, stepped up to the plate to help and became our van driver for a four-meeting stint. During our day off in Hull we did some terrific riding around the Humberside coastline. Dave had been at Hull with Ian Thomas and Brian Larner when I rode for the Vikings in 1976 and we had a smashing time together. I knew Dave could only manage a few days and the thought of losing him was a big worry. Thankfully I had another stroke of good fortune. Graeme Stapleton, a Kiwi who had ridden with me at Wimbledon in 1974, was coming from New Zealand to England for a holiday and wanted some help getting around to see some of the speedway tracks. Little did he know what he was about to let himself in for! Graeme was just brilliant, a solid rock for me to lean on and without him I'm not sure I could have managed all the riding. He put up with all my bullshit when under pressure, drove the van at all times of the night and day, carried out repairs when necessary and never complained. And, guess what? We are still mates, which tells you everything about him.

Everywhere we went people went out of their way to help and

it wasn't just the money they were giving up. More often than not it was their time – a hugely valuable commodity in what we were doing. Former referee Paul Ackroyd and his wife Gill, run the benevolent fund, doing a great job. It was Gill who helped to change the work load of the Ride for me; she introduced me to the unbelievable money counting machine. After the bikes, the money counters were the most important item in the back of the van.

When I look back I begin to realise just how lucky I was and how people rallied around when I was in trouble. One such occasion was when I was riding my bike from Hull, after a collection there, to Manchester along the M62. I was following the van, which was being driven by Leo Letts, who had been mechanic for the late Peter Craven and who is now married to his widow Brenda. I had asked Leon to make sure that I was following him at all times. The plan was for him to lead me to the Cheshire home of Peter Collins, who had agreed to put me up for the night. I was flying from Manchester to Copenhagen the next day to make a collection at the Danish Speedway Grand Prix on the Saturday night.

What could go wrong? If I'm involved, quite a lot! I have run out of fuel in a car many, many times but never on a motorbike very late at night on a motorway crossing the Pennines. It would have been okay had Leon noticed that I was no longer behind him. But he didn't! I was stranded, parked on the side of a busy motorway in the black of night and with the battery in my mobile phone on its last legs.

I figured I could make just one call. PC got the vote and despite the fact that by this time he was tucked up in bed he came out and found me, got me going again and still put me up for the night. That's speedway folk for you.

Out of the blue I was sponsored on a trip to the Danish Grand Prix by Alun Biggart, a Scottish Glasgow speedway supporter living in Copenhagen. Alun treated me like family, and the chatter of his kids was a great break and a total rest for me. Not only that, he also donated a large chunk of change to our cause. It was a lovely surprise and was just unbelievable.

THERE were many points along the way to the conclusion of the ride, at the 2009 British Speedway Grand Prix in Cardiff's magnificent Millennium Stadium, that stick in my mind.

Bill Brown from Wulfsport and his mate David Gates accompanied me when we rode from Newcastle to Workington and they knew the area very well. At one stage we stopped high on the hills looking down on Lake Coniston where Sir Donald Campbell met his Waterloo when attempting to break the world water-speed record.

When I won my second World Final at Wembley in 1958 I received the *Sunday Dispatch* trophy from Donald, which was a great thrill for me. It is sad that for many years he was criticised in the media for allowing his runs on the lake to take too long. I am sure he was just waiting for the right conditions and not, as some of the newspapers seemed to suggest, that he was scared.

The tragic thing is that he was killed because on that day he didn't wait long enough before starting his second run on Coniston. His *Bluebird* craft broke up, killing him when it hit the wash still there from his first run. This was one time he definitely should have waited. He was a hero of mine.

Another thrill during 'The Ride' was when, en route, we stumbled upon the world famous Gleneagles golf course. I love golf, watching and playing, and both Tony and I took the opportunity to have our photos taken outside the gates to the course.

And we had the finale to the ride at the Millennium Stadium. Paul Bellamy and BSI, who organised the Speedway Grand Prix series that has replaced the old style World Final, were really helpful to us and we had a great day in Cardiff leading up to the GP itself. So, we started at speedway's old home and ended at its new one. That had a nice ring to it.

We raised over £70,000 which, given the financial climate at the time, was a great achievement. Of course, I wish it had been more but we gave it our best shot. The saddest part of the whole deal, but nevertheless the most important, was handing over the cheques to those we had set out to support. Our original plan was to make the presentation to those based in the UK and who could travel at John Harrhy's golf club in the West Midlands. The snow and freezing weather meant that only three could actually make it, but the smiles on their faces said it all and I felt very humbled.

I feel very blessed that I can get up and walk whenever I want and now, in retrospect, 'The Ride' was one of my better ideas.

NZ trip as a salesman, then chasing a 'schoolboy dream'

IN March 2011, partner Jan and me embarked on a trip to New Zealand to promote the hardback version of this book, first published late in 2009, and to enjoy a holiday back in the country of my birth.

We planned to zigzag across both the North and South Islands, knocking on the doors of bookshops hoping to persuade them to stock a few copies that I would be on-hand to sign personally if necessary. I hoped that people realised that I was still in the land of living! If so that my name still meant something and that I could get myself on to a few TV and radio programmes.

We flew into Auckland from Los Angeles just a few days after the February earthquakes that shook New Zealand's second city to its core. Just a few months earlier Christchurch had been hit by a couple of major 'quakes but they had occurred a long way underground and the damage caused was nothing like that resulting from those that followed. These were much closer to the surface and struck during the middle of the day. Many buildings, including the city's iconic Cathedral, were destroyed and over 150 people lost their lives and damage across the area was substantial.

By the end of 2011 over 1,200 buildings had been or needed to be demolished, 200,000 private dwellings were in peril and needed attention and around 65,000 people had upped sticks and left to live elsewhere. Even those whose property had been left relatively unscathed had to deal with the horrors of liquefaction, described by Wikipedia as 'a phenomenon whereby a saturated soil substantially loses strength and stiffness in response to an applied stress, usually earthquake shaking or other sudden change in stress condition, causing it to behave like a liquid.' Thousands of tonnes of this appalling substance continue to blight Christchurch and beyond and it will be a long, long time before life returns to normal for the residents of this beautiful city.

Jan and I approached our travels south with some trepidation. I feared the worst and as we got to the outskirts of the city it began to dawn on me just how serious the situation was. Most of the area's hotels had been flattened; those that hadn't were either closed or had no vacancies. There were many friends we could have stayed with but they had enough to cope with and, eventually, I decided that we should drive to nearby Waikuku beach, which was virtually unchanged from 50 years ago. It was our lucky day; we managed to hire a cabin for just 50 NZ dollars a night.

It was very basic but on four successive mornings we awoke to the sun shining and glistening off the sea. It was during one of our beach walks that I told Jan that after the death of my darling Junie I had planned to come here, on my own, to seek peace and solitude while I sorted my head out, to decide how I would handle my life now that she, my right arm, had gone.

That trip never came to fruition. I got through those morbid days and I am sure that Junie would have been happy with my decision to keep moving on and eventually to spend my life with Jan, who was one of her best friends.

WE couldn't put off visiting Christchurch forever. At first the damage appeared minimal but then, suddenly, a huge pothole appeared in the road, then another and another. It just got worse and worse as we approached the city centre; a no-go area remained cordoned off to the general public. There was a fallen church steeple, walls that had crashed to the ground, piles and piles of rubble and the sight and smell of the vile liquefaction.

We felt like intruders, peering into their grief. Thousands of people had run out of their houses or offices as the earthquake struck and, weeks later, still hadn't been allowed to return. Gone was the beauty and serenity of the old Avon River, flanked by the sleepy Weeping Willows, which had once flowed peacefully through our wonderful city. It was along its banks that my fellow workers and I used to lay and feed the ducks during our lunch breaks. Now it was more like a mud-filled drain, alongside crumbling buildings, many of them shops that once provided the lifeblood of the local community.

In the no-go area of Christchurch, an engineer friend who had access told me that the silence is deafening, nothing moves, 'it's eerie, bordering on frightening' a war-torn ghost town. Roads in and out of the center city remain firmly closed and patrolled by the army, all the while, the aftershocks continue. The dreaded liquefaction remained public enemy number one. Fresh water was scarce in some places, sewage pipes were damaged beyond repair and temporary toilets lined many streets, a stark reminder of the discomfort being experienced by so many families. The horrible sludge continued to work its way into nooks and crannies and the huge craters left by the 'quakes. Even when it dried out it left behind a cement-like stain.

NEW ZEALAND is no stranger to earthquakes and, in 1931, Napier on the east coast of the North Island was totally destroyed but has since been rebuilt, much of it in an Art Deco style that is renowned throughout the world. Hopefully, a new Christchurch will rise from the rubble but when and where are questions that will remain unanswered for many years to come.

Kiwis are tough people and generally the citizens of Christchurch have coped pretty well. However, it undoubtedly affected me, even though I now live on the other side of the world.

As a kid I used to mow the cricket field at the Valley of Peace, just outside the city. Next to the pavilion was a large oak tree that had been there for over 100 years. I went there after Junie's death, nailed a small cross to the tree and scattered some of her ashes around it. That tree is now gone, another victim of the 'quake, but I am sure Junie is still there spiritually.

We left Christchurch saddened by what we had witnessed and headed to Invercargill, the most southerly town in New Zealand. The next stop is the South Pole! It was while there that another personal challenge came to mind, sparked probably by something that had happened to me there many years previously. It was in Invercargill that Burt Munro, who has his own chapter in this book, was born. On one occasion he took me to his workshop – that doubled as his bedroom! – to show me the latest modifications to his ageing Indian Scout motorcycle. Burt's name is still commemorated to this day with the annual staging of the Burt Munro Challenge week in Invercargill every November. Thousands of motorcycle fans from across New Zealand, and the world, flock to Invercargill for this festival of racing.

At the ripe old age of 76 I decided that I wanted to take part, not just in a single race but several. I loved the thought of going back to my teenage years, competing in a hill-climb, road and beach races and a long-track event. The Speedway races I will skip them, as it's just like going back to work again!

It seemed like a good idea but over the years I have seen many former top riders come out of retirement only to suffer serious injury or even death. Why do they do it?

One of the world's greatest ever all-round riders, Irishman Sammy Millar, survived a spectacular crash during a demonstration race in the Isle of Man. Luckily, he walked away shaken but unhurt. In an interview before he rode and asked why he was doing it Sammy just laughed and said it was a bit of fun with no danger. Closer to home, Australian speedway star Jackie Biggs went back home and was killed in a grass-track race. In 2011 another great speedway rider, Leigh Adams, retired, returned to Australia and took part in a desert race. He crashed and sustained multiple, life-changing injuries.

One thing about getting older is that you realise you are responsible for your own actions and, naturally, the consequences.

My responsibilities, now that my boys Gary and Tony have grown up, rest with Jan but, luckily for me, her attitude is the same as it was with Junie. She accepts that I know my own capabilities and the dangers involved and it is my decision. I fully understand and accept that it is impossible to ride a motorcycle fast without any danger. But, for me, the big picture is that life is for living, but you mustn't act like an idiot and throw it all away on just a whim or a fantasy. I weighed up all the odds and felt that I was still competent enough to participate in the various disciplines at Invercargill. I felt I still had the instincts required to ride the different bikes. A motorcycle is only a sophisticated lump of metal with no brain. The rider is its brain; it is he or she who keeps it completely under control. In my case it would be with all the instincts I had absorbed over the previous 65 years since I started riding motorbikes aged just 10. But whether that old magic would allow me to ride a motorbike faster than anyone else on a given day is something else. Another question, however, was my fitness after new hip and knee operations. I still didn't have full movement in my left knee.

The idea of me participating in the 2011 Burt Munro Challenge went down well with the organisers and I left New Zealand committed to returning later in the year.

Once back in the UK I spent as much time as possible on a motorbike, mostly around the lovely hills in Cumbria and the Lake District with my mate Bill Brown for company. After five days of tough off-road riding my feel and judgement had started to sharpen and my confidence in what lay ahead increased. However, the toughest test was still to come. I had to prove to myself that I could still ride on a long-track. If I wasn't satisfied with my performance, or felt that I was in over my head, I would pull the plug on the whole idea. Where better to find out whether I still had the 'bottle' to enter the corners at over 100 mph and not shut the throttle off than the wonderful long-track circuit in Muhldorf. I had ridden there, in the south of Germany, many times during my own career. By chance an opportunity to ride at Muhldorf had presented itself and I grabbed it with both hands and a fair amount of trepidation. During the 800-mile car journey from Surrey to Bavaria, and a very bumpy sea crossing from Dover to Calais, I had plenty of time to think about what I was letting myself in for.

On the morning of my 'comeback day' I came across a local newspaper at the breakfast table. On the front page was a photograph of a motorcyclist's helmet lying by the roadside, alongside a headline which, roughly translated, read: 76-year-old motorcyclist dies in Muhldorf crash yesterday. What an omen! I just hoped it wouldn't be repeated the next day.

Former World Long-track Champion and local hero Alois Weisbock had sourced a bike for me to ride. I arrived at the track believing that it was just a Thursday practice day and that there would only be three or four people there.

Wrong! There were between 50 and 60 riders, on all types of bikes, ready for an afternoon rev-up.

By now I was quite apprehensive and nervous. Word had got around that I was going to ride. Normally, it would have been nice to chat to so many old friends but, with an hour to go, I wasn't in a talkative mood. Far from it.

What I was about to try and do had finally set in.

Joscf Hofmeister, another German mate who is the same age as me, had driven from Kempten, about three hours away, to be there. We first met in 1952 when we were racing in South Africa as 17-year-olds. Now, that's a proper mate. Another German, Karl Maier, who won the World long-track title on numerous occasions, also turned up intending to have a ride. But he decided the track was too rough and only did a couple of laps. That didn't help my mood either.

As I changed into my leathers there seemed to be more and more people and bikes around. There was no turning back now and, finally, the time came. I was on the track.

I had already decided that if I pussy-footed around to start with, it would be more difficult to get up to maximum speed. Like their speedway cousins, long-track bikes have no brakes, they are designed to ride flat-out, and if you are in good form even into the corners.

Halfway down the first straight I thought to myself, "bloody hell this is quick" and then, "bloody hell this is madness". But, coming into the corner, my body moved a little forward and within a few seconds I was sliding through it. Whoopee, I had triumphed over my brain and after I had done it once it became much easier. I was physically worn out and my nerves were shredded – and I could only manage a couple of laps at a time. But my decision was made … I was going to the Burt Munro Challenge. As I changed out of my leathers, I began to realise exactly why I wanted to go back to Invercargill and take part. It was fun meeting old friends, motorcycle people, crowding round the barbeque, laughing, joking and drinking. In Muhldorf the social side rounded off a perfect day and I wasn't going to make the headlines in the next day's newspaper.

The following morning I drove around 400 miles to Holzwickede, a small German village, to visit an old friend who I had christened Doctor Blood. I had returned to have my blood 'tuned-up' as I call it. Many years ago, when I had been doing too much racing and travelling, mostly by road in those days, a friend told me about the procedure of having your blood re-oxygenated. The results to me are amazing, it is as though you are 110 per cent fit with an amazing amount of energy which lasts for at least 3 to 4 months. The procedure is that a small amount of your blood is taken from your body, it is then re-oxygenated and then put back. The normal course is about 5 or 6 sessions. The whole process takes less than half an hour. I filmed a short interview with the doctor for a DVD I had been compiling and asked him, "I am running in the Olympics next week, how will I do in the drugs test?"

He laughed and his answer was great and I am sure the procedure is legal. Anyhow, I felt terrific afterwards and we also had a round of golf at his club in Dortmund, which also made the detour worthwhile.

Junie and I lived in Holzwikede in 1976 when I was riding in the British League for Hull. I needed a base outside the UK and flew from Dortmund to Manchester and back again on a weekly basis. We chose Holzwikede because an old British soldier, Joseph Joy, (who I have written about earlier) was there. A great mate, a scrambler, a grass-tracker, he and his family had a laundry business, then a motorcycle shop. They treated us as their own family and he is always good for a laugh.

While I was there this time Joe asked if I would like to join him in a classic car and bike rally that was taking place about 100 miles away. Joe said I could ride a Harley-Davidson that belonged to his daughter Jenny. I baulked a little as I have never been a Harley lover but agreed to go and we had a lot of fun. I spent the first part of the rally trying to ride the Harley like a normal motorcycle but that didn't work. On the way home I started to lean the bike into corners and then let it have its own head. It certainly wasn't my idea of riding a motorcycle but it seemed to work. To be a proper Harley rider you have to give the engine a couple of big, loud blips (which sounds good) whenever stopped at traffic lights so that everyone around looks at the rider of this ball of chrome that costs zillions.

Despite spending so much time in Holzwickede I never realised that the scene of the famous 'Dam Busters' raids in the Second World War is only 25 kilometres away. I visited the Mohne dam that was supposed to have been impenetrable and it is amazing that the Barnes Wallis bouncing bomb could knock over such a magnificent structure. That took place in 1943 but tourists still flock there almost 70 years later.

BACK in England I started my preparations for the Burt Munro Challenge, when I would have to ride some unfamiliar motorcycles. I decided I would like to tackle the road races and hill-climbs on a KTM Supa-Moto but I needed someone to teach me how to ride it. Who better than Ady Smith, a great off-road all-rounder, a top enduro rider, and a star moto-crosser – he was also crowned British Super-Moto Champion on more than one occasion. Ady now runs a KTM off-road school so I booked myself a place and was really looking forward to it. We were due to start practicing on a Monday but, sadly, Ady's mum passed away the previous day and we could not find another date to suit us both. By now it was time to return to California and to start a training programme that would include more exercises and weights to try to coax a little extra bend into my troublesome left knee. And, of course, I needed to ride as much as possible and would do so for between an hour and a half and two hours every second day. It really helped my general fitness and, of course, sharpened my judgement and other riding skills.

I was lucky again when former World Speedway Champion Billy Hamill, who lives close by, offered to take me to a go-kart track at Victorville to ride his 450 Honda Supa-Moto machine. Billy is a regular Supa-Moto racer, and he was competing in a speedway meeting in Las Vegas the night before we went to Victorville. Unfortunately, he crashed there and couldn't ride to show me the ropes, which was a pity. However, his 13-year-old son Curtis filled in for his dad and was fast and very tidy on the bike.

It was a great experience for me. There was a lot going on with small tight corners on the track, the use of tyre-warmers made the rubber very sticky. To me it was difficult to judge the point when you can lose traction and finish up on your bum! But it was really only a matter of time before I got the hang of it. I put a small metal plate on the back of the sole of my left boot to allow it to slide if or when I put my foot down on the ground.

During my sixth ride I did put my foot too flat on the track at around 50mph. The bike kept going forward at the same speed but my foot stuck to the ground and gave my new knee a real wrench. Luckily, I didn't do any further damage to it but it was time to pack up. However, I had gained some invaluable knowledge that would hopefully stand me in good stead further down the line.

Another stroke of good fortune quickly came my way. Former World Motocross Champion Roger De Coster head of KTM Racing in California agreed to loan me a 570 Husaberg Supa-Moto bike, which I decided to ride in the hills around San Diego. At the end of the first day I was re-fuelling the bike at a small service station and got talking to a couple of fellow motorcyclists and they told me about Palomar Mountain, which sounded brilliant.

Early the following morning I set out in search of the perfect mountain, about 30 miles away. It was so cold that I had to slow down to 20mph and ride one-handed to prevent the fingers on my other hand from freezing-up. Mount Palomar proved to be heaven sent and is a motorcyclist's absolute dream. It is pretty steep with about seven miles of road that twists and turns and defies any set pattern. The locals call it the Palomar International Raceway. I was there on a Tuesday and there was next to no traffic. I did seven ascents and even started to enjoy the descents as well, going a little faster each time. On my last run I felt I was just about spot on and was proud that only once did I go over the line that divides the road ... and then by only a foot.

When I got back to the hotel where Jan and I were staying she couldn't believe how I just kept going on and on about the day I had just had. In fact, I think it is the best day I have ever had on a motorcycle, so thanks to Roger and the guys at the service station for helping me to find Mount Palomar.

AFTER a few more days in the dirt on the mountains north of LA, this time back on my Yamaha, I was ready to pack and leave for New Zealand. I wanted to do some riding there before tackling the Burt Munro Challenge so arranged to take part in the Kaipara 200km adventure ride, starting at the Waimauku village centre, which is 25 kilometres outside of Auckland.

I had no excuses as I rode a loaned Yamaha 250 WR, which is the same as my bike back home in Dana Point. After fitting a special pillion seat, which I had designed to save the strain on my legs, I was ready to go.

The ride was organised by Pete McPhee, a good friend of mine who is the boss man at *KiwiRider* magazine. We were joined by a couple of my speedway mates, Robin Adlington and Mike Fullerton, plus Shane Hornblow my Body Talk guru mate (a system where the Body Talk treatment encourages the body to repair itself).

The weather at the start was great and we had some smooth, gravel roads followed by some sections of deep sand. It was wet and slippery through the forest and at times it was really tough going, so much so that all my riding mates managed to fall off somewhere along the line. Three of the lads taking part had even brought their girlfriends along to ride as passengers and a couple of times we had to squeeze past as they lay in a heap in the middle of the track. The weather turned sour after lunch and we had a miserable hour in wet conditions but in true Kiwi tradition we had a terrific barbeque after we had finished. I felt great and all the hard work was paying off.

NOW was the time to determine which bikes I would use in the five separate events I had entered in the Burt Munro Challenge. For the long-track I had a GM lay-down loaned to me by Brendon Manu from Palmerston North. I had a choice of two KTMs for the road race and hill climb and had a chance of a day's riding at the Ruapuna track to help me make up my mind.

The bikes belonged to Trevor Chapman, who used to race speedway, but has moved on to Supa-Moto racing. The day after our practice he was competing in the final round of the Supa-Moto's championship at the same track. My day with Trevor was very special, almost as good as riding up and down Palomar Mountain. He was very patient as I got to grips with the KTMs and at the conclusion of our session I was pleased with the progress I had made. It was all very different for me. It took a while to get used to other guys zooming past on the big, fast road-racing bikes. Trevor could see that I was nervous out with blokes I had never seen surrounding me at great speed. I was back in a situation where my life was in someone else's hands. On the other side of the coin, I was a novice, at times out-braking myself so they had to trust me as well. The bikes were bloody fast, my 500 was hitting 200kmph at the end of the straight. The following day Trevor waltzed away with the two Supa-Moto titles. It must have been the training I gave him!

For the speedway event I decided to do something a little different and ride an ice-bike rather than a conventional speedway bike. I have ridden an ice-bike, with spiked tyres, on many speedway tracks and also at Daytona in the USA. Robin Adlington had one at his home on which Bruce Cribb used to give demonstrations while in New Zealand. Cribby didn't want his engine used so thankfully Warwick Aldridge, from Christchurch, fitted one of his and got the bike ready to go.

The local lads were marvelous helping to get my licences sorted and my bikes (and books!) down to Invercargill from all over New Zealand. Unfortunately, the weather the week before the event was diabolical and at times wasn't much better when it started. Before the racing started a life-sized bronze statue of Burt, and his beloved Indian motorcycle, was unveiled in Queens Park with his son and daughter in attendance. Wednesday was long-track day and my first appearance. There had been torrential rain the day before which left the track deep and grippy. In practice it was really patchy, slick one moment, heavy the next, and it was difficult to get a smooth ride.

This was exactly what I didn't need. It involved too much physical effort, which was the one department I was lacking. I made quite a few changes to the bike but decided I would only do a few demonstration laps later in the day. To hang on is one thing but to race is quite another and I didn't feel up to that physical challenge. My decision turned out to be a godsend for Larry Ross. His bike seized in practice and Brendon generously decided to loan him "our" bike, on which Larry raced to victory.

I was told to be ready to go out for my laps after what should have been a short grading break but it went on for much longer than anticipated and I noticed that they had heavily watered the first bend twice. I thought about waiting but Larry was due out a couple of races later on our bike, and there was a few changes needed doing on the bike's set-up. I was thinking of waiting till after a couple of racers took place to get rid of the water. It was decision time, and to make matters worse Mother-Nature decided to poke her nose in, and I badly needed to go for a wee!

With everything coming to a head I thought 'TO HELL WITH IT, LETS GET IT DONE,' I had done it hundreds of times before, so this was no biggy. I decided to do two laps, my first lap was fast. But on the start of the second lap I went about a foot inside my tyre marks laid down on my first lap. Then half way round the corner I experienced something that I have never known on a long-track before. Suddenly, without any warning, the front wheel was gone. I must have hit a wet patch with no dirt on it. It caught me completely by surprise. Even with a minimum of warning you can normally bail-out on your back, which allows you to fold in your arms and become like a ball. But I was caught out and landed on all fours.

Every time I hit the ground I twisted and turned and was thrashed into the dirt. I thought it was never going to stop. Viewing a video of the crash later I could see that I must have cart-wheeled for about 80 yards at around 90mph. But I was lucky. I was more hurt by being caught out than by my injuries, although at the time I didn't appreciate what I had done to myself. Later, as I was handing out the prizes to over fifty happy winners, I could have screamed when shaking hands but gritted my teeth and offered a weak smile and a "well done".

I was relieved to get away from the track and back to the home of Frank and Tracy Brookland, where Jan and I were staying. By now the pain was really kicking in, as was the realisation that I had inflicted some serious damage to my body. When I awoke early the next morning, the day of the hill-climb, I felt very second-hand. I could barely stand on my left ankle, there was definitely something wrong there. I thought about going to the local hospital, but if they discovered something broken there would be no more riding. It was my choice, I was going to take part in the hill-climb.

Which is exactly what I did. Trevor Chapman was a hero getting me on and off the KTM and he lent me a smaller left boot so that I could change gear with my bad foot. There were a couple of bad corners on the run, one of them blind, 200 yards over the crest of a hill. I did two runs but never got close to going over the blind brow at anywhere near top speed. There were also some very strong gusts of wind and I was pretty unstable anyway with only one good leg. It would have been embarrassing to have been blown over by the wind.

I was having a great time, I was warm sitting in Dave McKenzie's van with a cuppa in my hand things didn't seem so bad. I even started to think about the road race practice at Teretonga the next day. I felt I could improve my time on the hill-climb by a couple of seconds but it started to drizzle with rain and I was in no mood to fall on my bum again.

On Friday my ankle was no better and this time I decided that I should go to hospital. They were very busy – I wasn't the only motorcycling casualty – and had to wait for five hours. Finally, I was ushered into a small cubicle and was shocked when the curtains parted and in walked my lady doctor who looked no older than 14!

"Barry," she said, "I saw the picture of your crash on the front page of our newspaper. Where have you been for two days?"

I didn't dare tell her that I had ridden in the hill-climb the previous day. She would have known I was a complete idiot. Right now, she wasn't sure. X-rays revealed that I had broken my ankle, which was put in plaster, and I was told that I needed an operation.

At least I was mobile again, albeit on crutches, but the weather remained horrendous. They had to cancel the beach races. The wind was so strong the tide wouldn't go out. And there was no beach!

On Saturday the weather was much better and so was I. It was the day of the speedway event when I had planned to race the ice-bike, which has over 300 two-inch sharply pointed spikes protruding from each wheel. It looks lethal and fast … and is. As so many people had done me favours to get the bike ready and to Invercargill I felt that I had to ride it. But there was no record time as I couldn't put my left foot on the ground as I normally would. However, it was still pretty fast and I broke my plaster in half.

Back in Christchurch a few days later, me and Larry Ross made a special plaster cast for my ankle that I could walk on. In fact, it was so good that I decided to give the ice-bike another run at Moore Park in our earthquake-ravaged city. I had only done a lap and felt that something didn't feel right so I stopped. It was the right decision. I had a flat rear tyre, which on an ice-bike can be lethal!

DID I do the right thing in tackling the Burt Munro Challenge? To me it was a 100 per cent yes. Despite the crash it was an outstanding success for me personally. It would be impossible to personally thank everyone that helped me over my enforced longer New Zealand stay, due to my broken ankle. But without Val

Andrews, Colin Tucker, Helen and Joe Hicks, Tracy and Frank Brookland, and of course my old mate Staps (Graeme Stapleton) I would have finished in the New Zealand bankruptcy court!

Over the proceeding four months before the Burt Munro I had visited and met old friends, plus I had got myself together physically and mentally and awoken my motorcycling instincts to ride fast and safely.

But, as the Americans say, "Shit happens".

During my trips to ride in the Kendal Classic in the Lake District I got to know and like a former scrambles champion 65-years-young named Norman Barrow, and in last year 2010 Classic he still rode like the wind. Over the years he had had three new hips. He just loved riding his motorbike, as I do. In November 2011, I was doing what I like doing best and finished up doing cart-wheels at 90mph, sustaining a broken ankle.

Norman a few weeks later was doing what he liked doing, and tragically, he flipped over the handlebars while doing a mere 10 mph and was killed. No, he was not on his scrambler but on his mountain bike. They say that speed kills. If so, I must be the lucky one.

Acknowledgements

... a real test of who your mates are

THERE are many people who have joined me to help make this book possible.

First my mate, good old Phil Rising. We have been buddies for a long time and he probably came into the fray thinking it would be easy. He has his life pretty well sorted now and needed my book and me like a hole in the head.

Sometimes he got really tough – I started calling him the 'angry editor' – and was immovable but I chipped away and got some things past him. But, no matter how hard I tried, he refused to budge on a fantastic story involving Bernie Ecclestone and Don King. One day ... perhaps! Amazingly, we are still great mates ... unless he has changed his introduction without telling me!

I had no such trouble with Phil's mate Frosty (Richard Frost). He just deleted some of my salty Kiwi language.

I began the Liberian passages many years ago with the help of Bruce Brown's son Dana, who provided many ideas on content, how to lay it out and what research was required.

Martin Rogers senior wrote my original *Briggo* autobiography in 1972, but it was his son Martin junior, a journalist who worked for the *Daily Mirror* in the UK before taking a top job with Yahoo in California, who really got the ball rolling. He got me to understand what you can and cannot write in a book and we also had a few heated conversations at times.

There is my son Gary, who I would telephone at 5am (his time) in the morning to find out how to spell a particular word that I couldn't find in a dictionary … my basic Kiwi spelling was sometimes so far out that it was impossible to find.

My other son Tony for staying out of the way … by the time we argued and discussed it the book would have taken a further 10 years to write.

And thanks, especially, to my partner Jan. She never complained as I tried to sneak out of bed at 4am to get some thoughts and words onto my computer, though I rarely succeeded.

David Kent, a top man and publisher, answered all sorts of questions. It helped that he is an enduro rider and that we have in Dave Kennett (Edward's dad) a mutual friend. Also from the same publishers, editor Barbara Daniel, who provided a shoulder to cry on … at least until she agreed with Phil about my Don King tale.

Everyone at *Speedway Star* – editor Clarkie, Scunny, Dave, Chrissy, Mark, Mick and Richard – were always there when I needed them, especially when coming up with all sorts of ideas for the cover.

Tony Mac and Susie of Backtrack magazine helped a great deal by making available all the research and interviews they did with me and Tony offered some sound publishing advice, too.

Thanks to photographers Michael O'Patrick, Alfonso Weedon, Ken Carpenter and Scot John Somerville for their use of many photos and to any other happy snappers who gave me photos after I had tried to smile for them.

Also, Dick Marconi for the idea for my charity bike ride, to PC (Peter Collins) for all the World Championship information and to Phil Cooper, who came to my rescue when my computer crashed.

We have survived and got here. Thanks.

Tony's gone and joined the army ...

Tony and best mate Terry (Betts) discuss if there's a few miles left in my Merc

I've always been a cross dresser!

Sammy Miller, legendary trials rider, states in his book the most important part is to look after your equipment ... with a jock-strap

Speaking to two of my heroes, five times Moto-Cross World Champion Roger DeCoster plus my great mate Moto-Cross European Champion Dave Bickers

Bruce Brown of On Any Sunday *fame acts as Tony's valet*

With Kenny Roberts, who I think is the world's greatest all-round motorcyclist and World Champion Kel Carruthers

Sneaking around the outside of America's number one Mert Lawill and Dick (Buggsy) Mann in the stifling heat at Chicago's Santa Fe Speedway

A very young Leigh Adams with my first ever dirt deflector ... ugly isn't it

A great shot which managed to capture me and the bike together. I did have a few partings from my machine and could have done with an ice skate on my backside

486 **Wembley** and *beyond*